ICELANDIC HERITAGE IN NORTH AMERICA

ICELANDIC HERITAGE in NORTH AMERICA

EDITED BY
BIRNA ARNBJÖRNSDÓTTIR,
HÖSKULDUR THRÁINSSON,
and ÚLFAR BRAGASON

UNIVERSITY OF MANITOBA PRESS

Icelandic Heritage in North America

27 26 25 24 23 1 2 3 4 5

University of Manitoba Press
Winnipeg, Manitoba, Canada
Treaty 1 Territory
uofmpress.ca

Cataloguing data available from Library and Archives Canada
ISBN 978-1-77284-021-6 (PAPER)
ISBN 978-1-77284-023-0 (PDF)
ISBN 978-1-77284-022-3 (EPUB)
ISBN 978-1-77284-021-6 (BOUND)

Cover and interior design by Sarah Wood

Printed in Canada

The University of Manitoba Press acknowledges the financial support for its publication program provided by the Government of Canada through the Canada Book Fund, the Canada Council for the Arts, the Manitoba Department of Sport, Culture, and Heritage, the Manitoba Arts Council, and the Manitoba Book Publishing Tax Credit.

Funded by the Government of Canada | Canada

Contents

Foreword

GUÐNI TH. JÓHANNESSON, PRESIDENT OF ICELAND, AND ELIZA REID, FIRST LADY OF ICELAND

IT IS WITH great pleasure that we welcome this publication on Western Icelandic language and culture. In both Iceland and North America, we have found that people are interested in the story of Western Icelanders (as they are called in Iceland), their heritage, and the future of that heritage. And so it was gratifying to see *Sigurtunga* (Victorious language), the Icelandic version of this book, come out in 2018. That edition presents a collection of informative essays, most of which are now available in this English edition. This new edition has also been expanded with an article by scholars who live and work in North America. In this way the publication provides yet another example of the strong bonds that connect Iceland and North America, the promised land where so many immigrated in their time and the old homeland that so many of their descendants hold dear.

The preface to *Sigurtunga* notes that when Icelanders who went west are memorialized by influential voices, they are remembered fondly, often at formal events, lauded for their devotion to family ties and their affection for Iceland. By the same token we have often enjoyed the hospitality and kindness of Western Icelanders, in particular at the centennial of the Icelandic National League of North America held in Winnipeg in the spring of 2019.

And those Icelanders who have attended the Icelandic Festival of Manitoba have described how it is beyond comparison, irrefutable proof of the fondness Western Icelanders have for the "old country."

We cannot overlook how many people decided in their lifetime to strike out and find their fortune in a new place, a new world. All told, there were about 16,000 people. Of course, this is a small figure compared with the masses then settled in the United States and Canada or the multitudes who were still pouring in from elsewhere in Europe and beyond. Nonetheless, this was a fifth of the Icelandic nation, and the story in Canada has been that Icelanders were the largest group of immigrants proportional to the population of their homeland. Not that it matters in the scope of history, and perhaps it says more about our zeal in Iceland for per-capita statistics—they have proven useful over the years when we need to stand out as a small nation in a big world.

It gives us great pride, the story of our countrymen and -women who sailed out into the unknown and, likewise, the story of their descendants. But it is hardly the purpose of scholarly research to stoke our national pride and emotional connections, as comforting and necessary as they may be in the hustle and bustle of modern life where globalization drives us all to fit the same mould, enjoy the same entertainment, and even speak the same language. The introduction to the present volume also points out that scholarly research obeys a different set of principles and is based on another premise entirely. It is, or should be, free of the entanglements of exaltation and ceremony. Those who sailed west, who left behind family and friends, were never seen again in most cases. Naturally people continued to write, but the letters were often marked by loss and a yearning for home. This story is, then, also one of sadness.

There was no future in Iceland. The bitter truth continues to lay bare the burdens inflicted on the masses by those in power in Iceland. The underpinnings of society were buckling under the booming population. Havoc wreaked by nature also took its toll: years of hardship and sea ice, volcanic eruptions, and other calamities. And when young people saw the chance to escape the wretched fate of toiling their lives away in strife, they were compelled to make a move. A brighter future seemed to await in other surroundings.

They may have yet found the same adversity there: poverty, hunger, and disease. Despite it all, those who emigrated west often longed for their home country in this new world of boundless prairies, usually without a mountain or waterfall in sight until the Rockies. Neither can we forget that the locals in the new world sometimes considered Icelanders lazy, that they would never amount to much.

Numerous Icelandic immigrants to North America chose to live outside Icelandic settlements, adopting new names and languages, cutting all ties with the land and nation they felt had failed them. For every story of homesickness for Iceland and sincere love for the lost country, there are also accounts of bitter feelings towards the former homeland. In Iceland history has yet to decide whether these emigrants will be rebuked as deserters or praised for emancipating themselves, or if there is at least some understanding for those who wanted to leave. But these viewpoints reverse course and change shape over the years.

New avenues of research open, new interpretations emerge, and new sources of information are still surfacing. For these reasons, collections like this are so important, every bit as much as lusty toasts at formal events. The First Lady and I celebrate the release of this book and congratulate everyone involved in the project on a brilliant and skilfully crafted publication.

Introduction

BIRNA ARNBJÖRNSDÓTTIR, HÖSKULDUR THRÁINSSON,
AND ÚLFAR BRAGASON

THE ROOTS OF NORTH AMERICAN ICELANDIC

Emigrations from Iceland began late in the immigration history of North America. The first Icelandic emigrants settled in Utah in the 1850s, but organized emigration from Iceland to North America began in the 1870s and ceased in 1914. Approximately 15,000, or 20 percent of the Icelandic population, are documented as having moved to North America during this period (Kristinsson 1983).

While some of the early Icelandic immigrants to North America settled in the Midwestern United States, such as Wisconsin, Minnesota, North Dakota, and Nebraska (see the chapters by Alda Möller and Úlfar Bragason, this volume), the largest group initially found their home in Manitoba, Canada. The impetus was the Canadian government's offer of land and financial support to newcomers. Organizers of the Icelandic immigration made use of this offer and chose to settle on a parcel of land in the Interlake region in Manitoba (between Lake Winnipeg and Lake Manitoba), which they named "New Iceland" (Eyford 2016, 22–44). Many place names in the area still bear witness to their Icelandic origins (Gerrard 1979), and New Iceland remains the hub of Icelandic heritage culture in North America. Immigration from Iceland continued until the beginning of the First World War in 1914, when it ceased almost entirely. Descendants of the Icelandic emigrants later dispersed over much of Canada and parts of the United States, as shown in Figure 0.1. North American Icelandic language and culture continued to thrive in these enclaves, developing their own characteristics that reflected the new geographic and social context (see, for example, Ásta Svavarsdóttir's chapter, this volume; Arnbjörnsdóttir 2006).

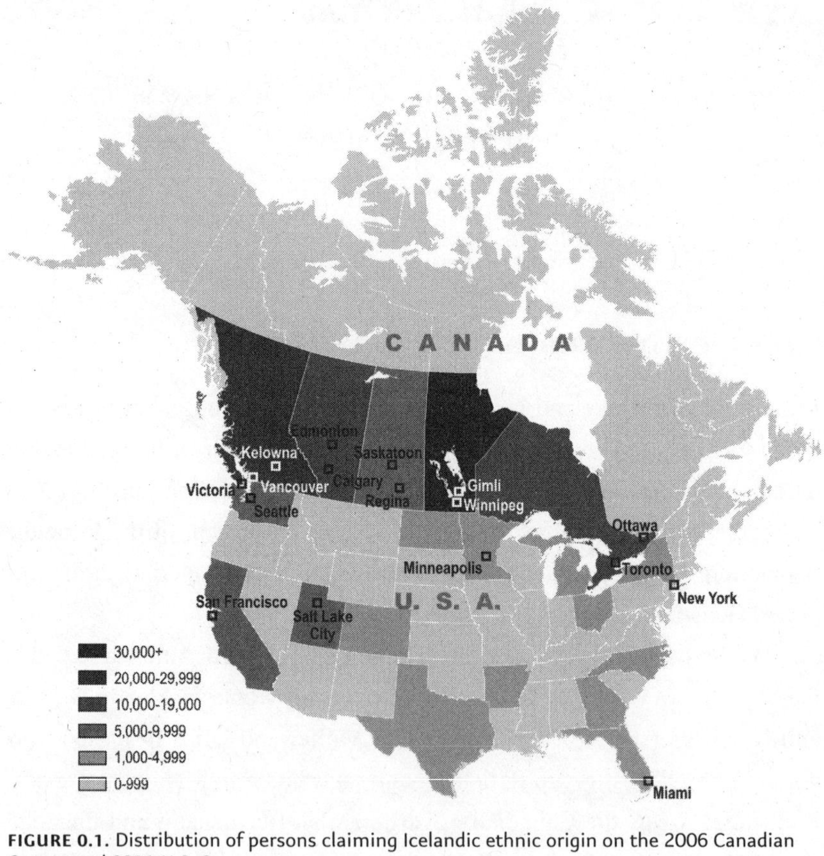

FIGURE 0.1. Distribution of persons claiming Icelandic ethnic origin on the 2006 Canadian Census and 2011 U.S. Census.

The goal of this volume is to describe the Icelandic linguistic and cultural heritage in North America and make this description accessible to English speakers. While some of the chapters were elicited specifically for the book and have not been published elsewhere, other chapters report findings of the project North American Icelandic: Heritage Language, Linguistic Change and Cultural Identity (henceforth the Heritage Language Project), a three-year (2013 to 2015) Icelandic Research Fund–supported project whose purpose was to study the nature of North American Icelandic (NAI). The project exmined NAI as a "heritage language" within the context of the development and maintenance of the cultural identity of NAI speakers. Data for the project were partly collected in Iceland (letters from the emigrants, diaries, interviews, narratives, recordings) but mainly during three field trips to North America in 2013 and 2014 to Icelandic-language enclaves in Canada and the United States. The project teams visited communities that were believed to have speakers of North American Icelandic with the purpose of gaining insight into the status of the language and the cultural identity of Canadians and Americans of Icelandic descent. The following areas were visited.

In Canada:

> Winnipeg, Gimli, Riverton, Arborg, Lundar, Brandon, and Portage la Prairie in Manitoba; Regina, Wynyard, and Foam Lake in Saskatchewan; Edmonton in Alberta; Vancouver and Nanaimo (Vancouver Island) in British Columbia.

In the U.S.:

> Point Roberts, Blaine, and Seattle in Washington; Fargo and Mountain in North Dakota.

Contact persons in each community were instrumental in identifying and inviting volunteers of Icelandic descent to participate in the study, and this proved crucial to its success. The volunteers were enthusiastic and interested in sharing their language, culture, and views with the researchers. Furthermore, and contrary to previously reported heritage language studies (Benmamoun, Montrul, and Polinsky 2013), many of our informants spoke Icelandic to the extent that they were able to express their views and provide responses to the many and varied linguistic challenges laid before them. The team conducted interviews and tests in Icelandic involving 126 participants (fifty-two men and seventy-four women) and a further 101 participants who were interviewed in

FIGURE 0.2. Heritage Language Project researchers in Manitoba in May 2013: Matthew Whelpton, Birna Arnbjörnsdóttir, Kristín M. Jóhannsdóttir, and Höskuldur Thráinsson. (Courtesy of Höskuldur Thráinsson)

FIGURE 0.3. Heritage Language Project researchers in Alberta, Washington, and British Columbia in May 2014: Kristín M. Jóhannsdóttir, Sigríður Mjöll Björnsdóttir, and Úlfar Bragason. (Courtesy of Kristín M. Jóhannsdóttir)

English. The average age of the participants was seventy-seven years, with ages ranging from twenty-six to ninety-eight years old.

The Heritage Language Project was a cross-disciplinary research project that emphasized the connection between the development of Icelandic as a heritage language and its geographical, social, and cultural context. Findings of the Heritage Language Project have been described in various papers, particularly in the volume *Sigurtunga: Vesturíslenskt mál og menning* (2018), published in Icelandic by the University of Iceland Press. Some of the chapters from that book appear also in this volume but have been revised, some substantially, for an English-speaking audience.

The editors of this volume believe that the findings of the project would also be of interest, and more accessible in English, to the hundreds of participants in the study and to the growing number of Canadian and American descendants of the early Icelandic immigrants who are curious about their cultural heritage. This volume contains chapters with a cultural focus and chapters that illustrate the language. North American Icelandic is the central core and essence of the

FIGURE 0.4. Heritage Language Project researchers in North Dakota, Saskatchewan, and Manitoba in August 2014: Höskuldur Thráinsson, Sigríður Magnúsdóttir, Daisy Neijmann, and Matthew Whelpton. (Courtesy of Höskuldur Thráinsson)

culture, and critical to an understanding of the Icelandic heritage in North America. In the first part of the book the significance of the language and culture is discussed with reference to the literature and the cultural functions of the Icelandic language in the Icelandic immigrant communities, and in the second part their manifestations are illustrated. Efforts have been made to make the language chapters accessible to non-linguists. We hope that the findings of the Heritage Language Project will inform the international discussion on heritage linguistics and contribute to a better understanding of heritage languages and cultures in the context of the opportunities and challenges that meet the courageous people who emigrate to a distant land in search of a better life.

Inevitably, the Heritage Language Project builds on the results of several previous and ongoing research projects on the Icelandic heritage in North America. The findings of many of these are available only in Icelandic. Although a comprehensive review of previous research will not be presented here, it is necessary to provide the reader with the background and context of the book's content and acknowledge the contributions of previous scholars (for further details, see Bragason 2018; Arnbjörnsdóttir and Thráinsson 2018). Therefore, a general description of the history of the Icelandic immigrant experience is presented with an effort to extract the basic themes that seem to characterize the Icelandic inheritance in North America today. This is followed by an overview of previous research on North American Icelandic history, literature, culture, and language that is accessible to readers of English.

THE ICELANDIC-LANGUAGE ENCLAVES IN NORTH AMERICA

As the name of the initial Icelandic settlement in North America, New Iceland, suggests, and by all accounts, some of the early immigrants thought of themselves as Icelanders who would live together in a community separated from other ethnic groups. Icelandic would remain their main conduit of education, communication, and governance. New Iceland was also a land reserve created by the Canadian government as part of its colonization policy (see the discussions by Thor 2002; Eyford 2016; see also Arnbjörnsdóttir 2006).

One of the more salient characteristics of the Icelandic heritage in North America is the importance placed on literacy in Icelandic and English. There is a prevailing view among the Icelandic heritage groups that many of the immigrant families brought Icelandic books with them rather than tools. Whether that view is real or imagined, many informants recounted the importance of literacy and education in their families. The emphasis on the written word has undoubtedly contributed to the maintenance of Icelandic among the immigrants.

Almost upon the Icelanders' arrival in New Iceland, instruction for the children was organized by the immigrants. Although some of the first teachers were Icelandic, the main emphasis from the outset was on reading, writing, and speaking English (Arngrímsson 1997, 270–71). At the same time, the immigrants sent a request to local education authorities to join the Canadian school system, thus laying the foundation for the bilingualism and biculturalism that seemed to prevail among many people of the early generations of Icelandic Canadians and Icelandic Americans (Arnbjörnsdóttir 2006). The idea of dual-language proficiency was supported in the writings of prominent members of the community. One proponent was the educator Jón Bjarnason, who founded an Icelandic Academy in Winnipeg that operated until 1940 (Ruth 1964). Another one was the poet Stephan G. Stephansson. At a meeting in Markerville,

Alberta, in March 1919, he argued forcefully for bilingualism. He maintained that teaching Icelandic to children would not interfere with their English. He claimed, "People who only know one home, who have only read one book and only know one language will be narrow-minded" (Hreinsson 2003, 307).

Formal schooling was in English (Arnbjörnsdóttir 2006, 35–51). However, itinerant teachers continued to teach Icelandic in the enclaves, and Icelandic was taught officially in various ways from 1885 up until today (Arnbjörnsdóttir 2006, 38–40; Ruth 1964). This practice encouraged an active bilingualism during the early decades of settlement. When the editors of the present volume were collecting data on NAI for the Heritage Language Project, many of the subjects told a similar story: "We spoke Icelandic at home when I was a kid, partly because my grandparents' English wasn't perfect. But in school everybody spoke English, so English soon became the default language at home." Despite this view there is some indication that in the early years, Icelandic literacy practices continued in immigrant homes and many of the early immigrant children learned how to read Icelandic at home prior to entering formal schooling (Arnbjörnsdóttir 2006). The fact that Icelandic immigrants in many cases came in family groups and that literacy training continued in the home must surely have extended the life of Icelandic in North America. Church services and Sunday school were conducted in Icelandic for many years in the North Dakota enclaves (Arnbjörnsdóttir 2006, 40), and visiting pastors from Iceland served in a few congregations as late as the 1960s. Some of the subjects interviewed for the Heritage Language Project were confirmed into the Lutheran Church in Icelandic. Bilingualism seems to have prevailed, as the manifold literary activities in the Icelandic communities attest to, and the home language continued to be Icelandic up until the third and fourth generations (Arnbjörnsdóttir 2006; see Laura Moquin and Kirsten Wolf, this volume).

General literacy among the immigrants (see Ásta Svavarsdóttir, this volume) supported prolific publishing activities in the Icelandic heritage community, which included a number of newsletters, journals, and books in Icelandic. As early as 1877 an Icelandic printing press (Prentfjelag Nýja Íslands) was established, which published the Icelandic newspaper *Framfari* (1877 to 1880). Several other short-lived periodicals were published in Icelandic by the immigrants from early on (Jónsson 2009, 163–64). Journals for Icelandic-speaking children were available until 1940 (Kristjánsdóttir 2014), and the women's journal *Freyja* was circulated from 1898 to 1910 (for a list of the journals, see Arngrímsson 1998, 201). In addition, numerous handwritten manuscripts of different types circulated among the Icelandic speakers (see Katelin Parsons, this volume). The oldest printed newspaper (a weekly), *Heimskringla,* was founded in 1886 and its rival, *Lögberg,* was first published in 1888. In the beginning these two newspapers were written exclusively in Icelandic, sometimes by well-known editors from Iceland temporarily residing in Canada. Gradually, English became more prominent in these newspapers and they subsequently merged into *Lögberg-Heimskringla* in 1959. *Lögberg-Heimskringla* was a dual-language publication for many years. It is still published but now exclusively in English (Arnbjörnsdóttir 2006, 38–42). *Lögberg-Heimskringla* remains the oldest continuously published heritage community newspaper in North America.[1]

In addition to printing periodicals and newspapers, traditional Icelandic literary practices prospered among Icelandic immigrants in North America. They published general immigrant histories, chronicles of the settlement of the different Icelandic enclaves, family histories and biographies, genealogies, and annals, as well as novels and books of poetry and drama. Peter Salus (1971) tallied the number of publications in Icelandic from 1900 to 1961 and identified forty-one volumes of poetry, twenty-two novels or collections of stories, thirty-five volumes of histories and biographies, and ten dramas. The chapters by Guðrún Björk Guðsteinsdóttir, Dagný Kristjánsdóttir, and Birna Bjarnadóttir in this volume discuss different aspects of NAI literary endeavours. The history of the Icelandic amateur dramatical societies that staged plays in Icelandic up until the 1950s is just beginning to appear (Þorbergsson 2020).

The Icelandic immigrants in North America also founded various cultural, political, and religious organizations (see the chapter by Vilhelm Vilhelmsson, this volume; see also Wolf 2001; Thor 2002, 110–29; Jónsson 2005, 5–9; Þorbergsson 2020). These organizations often provided forums for debates about issues affecting the community. One of the issues that was discussed in some of these societies, and in the Icelandic newspapers, was the question of acculturation versus separation. The language obviously played a major role in this context, as indicated by the early ideas about a separate Icelandic "colony" or *nýlenda*. One of the Icelandic societies that was active in the beginning of the twentieth century was Íslenzka stúdentafélagið (The Icelandic Students' Society). In 1906 the society organized a debate about *afnám* 'abolishment' versus *viðhald* 'preservation' of the Icelandic language among the Icelandic immigrants. This was a formal debate with two proponents for each position. At the end of the meeting, a panel of three judges concluded that the proponents of abolishment had won the debate (see *Lögberg*, 22 November 1906, 5). But nonetheless, disputes continued in the newspapers and elsewhere.

Another dispute was fostered by an early controversy about religious affiliations. The dispute eventually divided the reserve of New Iceland, and a group of people relocated to Pembina County in Dakota Territory in the United States (Thor 2002). No doubt the social and religious debates conducted in Icelandic served to enhance the longevity of NAI. The immigrants and their descendants continued to actively use Icelandic for longer than the two generations it commonly takes for migrants to transition to a new language (Fishman 1972).

The onset of the First World War halted the influx of Icelandic immigrants to North America, and after that there was very little renewal of inhabitants to the Icelandic enclaves. The war also pushed Icelandic immigrants, like other immigrants in North America, towards integration and a display of allegiance to their adopted countries. This was accompanied by a general push for monolingualism in the U.S. after the war (see Úlfar Bragason, this volume; Spolsky 2004, 93–96; Sontag 2007, 163–66). A considerable number of Canadians and Americans of Icelandic descent fought in the "war to end all wars" (*Minningarrit íslenzkra hermanna 1914–1918*). Úlfar Bragason (this volume) discusses the conceivable cultural dissonance between love of country and a culturally bred pacifism among servicepeople of Icelandic origin.

But there were also forces at work in the opposite direction among the Icelandic community in North America during the postwar years. Þjóðræknisfélag Íslendinga í Vesturheimi (Icelandic National League of North America, INLNA or INL) was established in 1919, partly to "work for the preservation of the Icelandic language and literature in America" (Ruth 1964, 47; see also Arnbjörnsdóttir 2006, 39). The preservation issue was debated at various meetings in the INL, especially in the 1930s, and eventually it was concluded that "Icelandic culture could be passed on to future generations through the use of the English language to express Icelandic ideas" (Ruth 1964, 47; see Laura Moquin and Kirsten Wolf, this volume). In recent years, the INL has grown exponentially and is still very active, and so is its sister organization in Iceland, Þjóðræknisfélag Íslendinga, established in 1939. According to its website the purpose of the INL is "to promote the Icelandic heritage, culture and traditions that our families brought to this continent through cooperation among North American Icelandic cultural groups and by maintaining ties with the people of Iceland."[2]

The phenomenal success of the Winnipeg Falcons hockey team around 1920 may have served to instill pride in all things Icelandic in Canada. The ethnic Icelandic underdog team went on to win the first Olympic Gold Medal in Ice Hockey in 1920. Almost 100 years later, in 2019, Parks Canada designated the Olympic victory of the Falcons as a "National Historical Event."[3] The effect on the Icelandic community in North America may have cemented the external presence of Icelandic immigrants (see Eyford 2006). The triumphs of the Falcons can only have supported the efforts of the newly established Icelandic National League.

Icelandic was taught at Wesley College in Winnipeg from 1901 to 1927 (see Ruth 1964; see also Bedford 1975), but the Icelandic immigrants in Manitoba began discussing the possibility of promoting Icelandic language and culture by endowing a University Chair of Icelandic Studies as early as 1905. In 1936 the Icelandic Collection was founded at the University of Manitoba (Arnbjörnsdóttir 2006, 38). The website for the collection states that through various stages, the collection has now developed into "the largest collection of Icelandic materials in Canada and the second largest in North America. This area studies collection serves as a primary research tool for the study of Icelandic language, literature, history and culture, while enabling the Icelandic community to preserve, reinforce and cultivate its cultural identity in the North American cultural mosaic."[4]

In 1951 an Icelandic Chair and a Department of Icelandic were established at the University of Manitoba (Arnbjörnsdóttir 2006, 38–39). Cooperation between the Department of Icelandic and the University of Iceland continues to be fortified with student and scholar exchanges and biannual partnership conferences. In 2020 the Stephan G. Stephansson Chair was founded at the University of Iceland to strengthen collaboration between the University of Iceland and the University of Manitoba in research and instruction. The chair is supported by the Icelandic government and the Vigdís Finnbogadóttir Institute, with important support from Canadians and Americans of Icelandic descent. The University of Victoria hosts Icelandic exchange professors through the Beck Foundation. These successful collaborations have met with an enthusiastic response on both sides of the Atlantic.

To some extent the Second World War had a similar effect on immigrants in North America as the previous world war had. Several descendants of the Icelandic immigrants fought in that war also (see *Veterans of Icelandic Descent, World War II, 1939–1945*). It is likely that having family members serving in the wars made the immigrants feel more like Americans or Canadians (see Úlfar Bragason, this volume). After the Second World War, there was even less contact between Iceland and "Western Icelanders" (as they are called in Iceland) for a considerable period (see Ólafur Arnar Sveinsson, this volume). This is in line with general findings about the effect of the war on the assimilation of immigrants in North America. This also supports notions that second-generation immigrants focus on "belonging," while third and fourth generations from emigration become more curious about their ethnic background (see Laura Moquin and Kirsten Wolf, this volume).

In 1974 more frequent and regular travel began between Winnipeg and Iceland with Icelandic Canadians and Icelandic Americans seeking their roots in Iceland, while Icelanders satisfied their interest and curiosity about their cousins in "Vesturheimur" (the Western world). Regular exchanges take place among young people and students through organized programs such as the Snorri Programs, established by the Snorri Foundation in Iceland in partnership with the Icelandic National League of Iceland, among others.[5] Participants in these programs are required to take the course Icelandic Online,[6] which is available free of charge and used by over 80,000 learners worldwide, including those who learn Icelandic as a heritage language. The genealogical database Icelandic Roots, based in Fargo, North Dakota,[7] and the Icelandic Emigration Center (Vesturfarasetrið) in Hofsós, Iceland,[8] have contributed to and benefited from this heightened interest in cultivating the Icelandic-Canadian and -American cultural heritage. On the Canadian side the New Iceland Heritage Museum in Gimli[9] has played an important role in this connection.

RESEARCH ON ICELANDIC CULTURAL HERITAGE IN NORTH AMERICA

Icelandic immigration to North America, the development of the various settlements, and the social and cultural life of the immigrants have been the topic of various research projects, studies, and publications. Andrea McIntosh (2004), Laurie Bertram (2010), and Ryan Eyford (2010) discuss different aspects of the history and culture in their dissertations and subsequent books, in which, for example, Bertram describes the expressions of Icelandic-Canadian identity through clothing and food, and Eyford re-examines the settlement history of the Icelandic immigrants in the context of Canadian settlement history in general. As part of the Heritage Language Project, Daisy Neijmann interviewed descendants of the Icelandic immigrants, exploring the communicative and symbolic functions of NAI and its role in the cultural self-image of the participants (Neijmann 2018). Laura Moquin and Kirsten Wolf (this volume) discuss a similar topic, namely the evolution of identity in Icelandic heritage communities.

Bertram (2010) and Eyford (2010) both shed light on the underresearched contact between the Icelandic immigrants and Indigenous peoples already living in the Interlake region in Manitoba (see also Bertram 2020; Eyford 2016). Short, general descriptions of immigrant histories are given by Elva Simundsson (1981) and Birna Arnbjörnsdóttir (2006), and more extensive accounts by Wilhelm Kristjanson (1965), Nelson Gerrard (1985), Guðjón Arngrímsson (2000), and Jonas Thor (2002). Accounts of the religious controversies that played a major role in the life and activities of many of the immigrants are described by George Houser (1990), Jonas Thor (2002), and Fred Woods (2005). More informal accounts of the life of the early immigrants can be found in the collection *My Parents: Memoirs of New World Icelanders,* edited by Birna Bjarnadóttir and Finnbogi Guðmundsson (2007). Many of the works by the writers listed above focus on the development of the different settlements in Canada, especially in Manitoba, and the life of the immigrants there. But as discussed in the chapters by Alda Möller and Úlfar Bragason in this volume, the experiences of those who settled in the United States may have followed a different trajectory.

Acculturation of the Icelandic immigrants is an important topic explored in Vilhelm Vilhelmsson's chapter in this volume. The topic is further examined by Ólafur Arnar Sveinsson (this volume), who discusses the emigration from Iceland, including the views of Icelanders towards emigrants and the development of the concept *Vestur-Íslendingur* 'Western Icelander', the term that has been used in Icelandic to this day about the descendants of the Icelandic immigrants in North America. He examines the acculturation from a theoretical perspective and from the point of view of the immigrants themselves.

In the early years of settlement, the Icelandic immigrants and their descendants in North America penned literature in Icelandic (Neijmann 2006; Guðsteinsdóttir 2006). Some of these writers and poets became well-known, both in North America and in Iceland, especially Stephan G. Stephansson (Hreinsson 2012). Later, descendants of the immigrants wrote literature in English as described most extensively by Neijmann (1995, 1997a, 1997b, 1999, 1999–2000, 2006) and Wolf (1991, 1992, 1994, 1996a—see also her edited volumes *Western Icelandic Short Stories*, 1992b, and *Writings by Western Icelandic Women,* 1996b).

Folklore and oral narratives formed an important part of the cultural environment of the Icelandic immigrants in North America. Magnús Einarsson published a selection of folklore narratives and related poems, in Icelandic and with English translations (*Icelandic-Canadian Oral Narratives,* 1991, and *Icelandic-Canadian Memory Lore,* 1992). Laurie Bertram discusses the notion of *hjátrú* 'superstition/folk belief' in her recent book, *Viking Immigrants* (2020). She describes how Icelandic stories about apparitions and *huldufólk* 'hidden people' found new contexts among North American Icelandic immigrants, albeit with the same effect. *Hjátrú* is also the topic of some of the interviews and narratives reported in Gísli Sigurðsson's chapter in this volume. His chapter is drawn from an extensive corpus of data from interviews conducted by Hallfreður Örn Eiríksson and Olga María Franzdóttir in 1972–73 (*Sögur úr Vesturheimi* 2012).

The research presented in this volume has been conducted mainly by Icelandic scholars and the findings should be read as such. In a sense the perspective is that of an outsider looking in. The outsider-versus-insider perspective is an age-old debate in sociolinguistic research and especially in ethnographic research (Geertz 1973), and there is no resolution that favours one or the other. Research by insiders in the NAI community is available in English and has been referenced here, including the important works by Gerrard (1985), Bertram (2010, 2020), and Eyford (2006, 2010, 2016), and others. We look forward to future studies by these and other Canadian and American scholars that will strengthen the knowledge base and inform the discussion on the Icelandic heritage in North America.

NORTH AMERICAN ICELANDIC

Those who study Icelandic as a heritage language are in a privileged position. One consequence of general literacy in the community is that the language is better documented than most heritage languages, and linguists have had access to informants who are conversant in the language. As described above, the immigrants wrote in Icelandic from early on and continued to do so for decades. In the beginning their language was obviously indistinguishable from the language spoken at the time in Iceland. But the social environment and the role and function of NAI in the society were very different from the Icelandic in Iceland (Arnbjörnsdóttir 2006), and this has obviously had an effect on its development, as described by Ásta Svavarsdóttir in this volume. Haraldur Bessason maintained that NAI was the only variety of Icelandic that existed outside Iceland (1984) and the only variety of Icelandic that could be called a separate dialect (1980, 7).

To some extent the development of Icelandic can be traced in the publications in NAI but also in private diaries and letters written by the immigrants and their descendants to recipients in Iceland. Some of these have been collected and edited and published in Iceland. Böðvar Guðmundsson based his important novel *Where the Winds Dwell* (2000) partly on material from such letters. Chapters by Alda Möller and Úlfar Bragason in this volume are based on extensive correspondence between immigrants in Nebraska and relatives in Iceland.

Another important source of information about NAI, as it was spoken before frequent exchanges with Iceland began in 1974, is found in the narratives published in *Sögur úr Vesturheimi*, the volume of interviews conducted by Eiríksson and Franzdóttir. The speakers involved were typically second- or third-generation immigrants, yet their language is remarkably similar to Icelandic as it is spoken in Iceland—or was spoken in the early twentieth century—except for loan words depicting a way of life in North America (see Gísli Sigurðsson, this volume).

The first "scholarly" effort to describe NAI was published in 1903, when the famous Arctic explorer and ethnologist Vilhjálmur Stefánsson (Pálsson 2005) wrote an article on English loan words in the language of the immigrants. In the 1930s the Icelandic scholar Stefán Einarsson wrote two articles (1933 and 1937) pointing out possible research topics in NAI. The phonological properties of the language are the main topic of Stephen Clausing's dissertation and book (1981, 1986), with special emphasis on the possible influence of English and a comparison with American German. Haraldur Bessason discussed Icelandic names in North America, English loan words in NAI, and other aspects of the language (1958, 1967, 1971). The most comprehensive study of NAI to date is Birna Arnbjörnsdóttir's book on the social history of the language (2006), partly based on a doctoral thesis on the phonology of NAI vowels that developed in a different direction in the North American social context from that in Iceland (1990). A more recent paper by Kristín M. Jóhannsdóttir (2006) contains a brief sketch of the status of NAI around 2000.

A more extensive description, the results of previous research on NAI, can be found in the overview by Birna Arnbjörnsdóttir and Höskuldur Thráinsson (2018).

LINGUISTIC RESEARCH IN THE HERITAGE LANGUAGE PROJECT

The linguistic research in the Heritage Language Project is based on different types of data:

- existing material (personal letters, diaries, interviews, narratives)
- additional letters copied and transcribed by research assistants in the project

- semi-formal interviews conducted in the three field trips
- spontaneous speech samples, partly elicited with the help of material like the story *Frog, Where Are You?* (Mayer 1969)
- data elicited by using a variety of tests targeting particular aspects of the language.

In the following sections, we will describe some of the linguistic results that have emerged from the Heritage Language Project. This overview is thematically organized (for a more detailed description see Arnbjörnsdóttir and Thráinsson 2018).

Phonology and Phonetics

The main method used to systematically study pronunciation was a picture-naming task. One of the goals was to see to what extent the various regional dialects in Iceland had been preserved in NAI. Since many of the immigrants came from northeastern Iceland, we expected that some of the northeastern dialectal features might have been preserved to some extent (see Arnbjörnsdóttir 2006).[10] The features include here for the benefit of future linguistic studies. The features include:

1. **a.** aspirated stops after long vowels: *api* [a:**p**ʰɪ] 'monkey', *fata* [fa:**t**ʰa] 'bucket', *aka* [a:**k**ʰa] 'drive' (the majority of Modern Icelandic speakers have unaspirated stops in this environment, for example, [a:pɪ])

   b. voiced sonorants before /p,t,k/: *hempa* [hε**m**pʰa] 'coat', *svunta* [svʏ**n**tʰa] 'apron', *stúlka* [stu**l**kʰa] 'girl' (most speakers of Modern Icelandic have voiceless /l,m,n/ in this environment, for example, [hεm̥pa])

   c. stop-pronunciation of *ngl*-sequences: *englar* [eiŋ**k**lar] 'angels' (this is rare in Modern Icelandic—most speakers would say [eiŋlar]).

As Katrín María Víðisdóttir has shown (2016), these northeastern features are only partially preserved in NAI. While aspirated stops after long vowels are well preserved in NAI, and stop-pronunciation of *ngl*-sequences is sporadically found, voiced /l,m,n/ before /p,t,k/ seem to be surprisingly rare. Aspirated stops are not foreign to English, and neither is the stop-pronunciation of *ngl*-sequences, but voiceless sonorants do not occur in English—hence the fact that voiceless /l,m,n/ are common (and the voiced counterparts rare) before /p,t,k/ in NAI is surprising. It suggests that the devoicing involved is a "natural phenomenon" in Icelandic and this is supported by the fact that voiced sonorants in this environment are actually disappearing in northeastern Icelandic.

As part of the Heritage Language Project team, Nicole Dehé's objective was to study intonation and stress in NAI and compare the results with Icelandic in Iceland and with Canadian English—for example, in *yes/no* questions (polar questions). She found that NAI did not differ markedly from Icelandic in this respect. When her subjects switched over to English during the test session, it was sometimes possible to detect Icelandic influence in their intonation (Dehé 2018).

Inflection and Auxiliary Constructions

Two tests were used to study the development of inflection or case markings in NAI. The first one is the classic *wug*-type plural test (see Berko 1958) where the subjects are asked to give the plural form of both actual and nonsense nouns. The pictures were presented to the participants in Icelandic, leaving it to them to come up with the plural form: *Hér er einn bolti* 'Here is one ball' and *Hér eru tveir* __ 'Here are two ___', et cetera. Because of the form of the numerals *einn* (m.) versus *ein* (f.) 'one', *tveir* (m.) versus *tvær* (f.) 'two', the participants were expected to be able to tell the gender of the nouns and hence be able to form the plural. Interestingly, it turned out that the heritage speakers typically had a good command of the plural of familiar nouns like *bolti* 'ball', but most of them did not seem to have mastered the plural formation rules that would make it possible for them to form the plural of unknown words. In this respect their performance was very different from that of adult speakers of Icelandic and more like that of children acquiring the language (see Thráinsson, Nowenstein, and Magnúsdóttir 2021).

The other morphology test was designed to investigate the formation and use of simple present and past tense of verbs versus the use of auxiliary constructions like the so-called progressive aspect; cf. the examples in (2):

2. a. Hann saumar / er að sauma.
he sews (pres.) / is to sew (inf.)
'He sews/is sewing'.

b. Hann saumaði / var að sauma í gær.
he sewed (past.) / was to sew (inf.) yesterday
'He sewed/was sewing yesterday'.

The main results of this investigation are reported on in the chapter by Kristín M. Jóhannsdóttir (this volume). She shows that heritage speakers tend to use the progressive construction much more frequently than do speakers of Icelandic in Iceland. Differences were also found between these groups when comparing their narrations of the story *Frog, Where Are You?* (Mayer 1969). This may be because the progressive construction is morphologically simpler than the present and past tense inflection of verbs (in the progressive aspect it is only the auxiliary verb *vera* 'be' that needs to be inflected).

Syntax

We elicited information on the syntactic properties of NAI in various ways, concentrating on the issues described below.

Word Order

Certain aspects of word order were of particular interest to us as these constructions had appeared in earlier data sets (Arnbjörnsdóttir 2006). We designed special tests to elicit judgments about relative positions of finite verbs and adverbs in constructions like the following:

3. a. Kristín **talar stundum** / **stundum talar** íslensku.
Kristin speaks sometimes / sometimes speaks Icelandic
'Kristín sometimes speaks Icelandic'

b. Næst **ætlar hún** / **hún ætlar** að læra ítölsku.
next intends she / she intends to learn Italian
'Next she intends to learn Italian'.

What is at stake here is the so-called verb-second (V2) phenomenon. The finite verb in Icelandic typically comes in second position in the sentence, as it does in the first alternative in (3a, 3b). In English, on the other hand, the verb would come in third position in sentences of this sort, as can be seen from the idiomatic translations. As shown by Birna Arnbjörnsdóttir, Höskuldur Thráinsson, and Iris Edda Nowenstein (2018), speakers of NAI tend to use the English (verb-third) order in constructions like these, especially when a non-subject occurs in the initial position of the sentence as in (3b). The test data were confirmed by spontaneous speech data, mainly elicited by using the well-known *Frog* story (Mayer 1969). But there is considerable inter-speaker and intra-speaker variation here.

Another word order phenomenon investigated in our project has to do with the relative position of adverbs and objects in examples like the following:

4. a. Ég las **ekki bókina** / **bókina ekki**.
I read not the book / the book not
'I didn't read the book'.

b. Ég las **ekki hana** / **hana ekki**.
I read not her / her not
'I didn't read it'.

In examples like (4a) the object *bókina* can be "shifted" around the negation (and other adverbs, such as *aldrei* 'never'), as shown in the second alternative. This phenomenon is called "object shift" in the linguistic literature. It is basically optional when the object is a noun (or a full noun phrase) as in (4a). If the object is a pronoun, then it *has* to shift around the negation (or similar adverbs) unless it is heavily stressed. This phenomenon does not have an exact parallel in English.[11] But Jóhannes Gísli Jónsson (2018) found a number of examples in the collection of narratives *Sögur úr Vesturheimi* where a pronoun follows the negation:

5. a. Mér líkaði **ekki** **það**.
me liked not it
'I didn't like it'.

b. ég...skildi **ekki þetta.**
I understood not this
'I didn't understand this'.

Having listened to the relevant recordings of the narratives, Jóhannes Gísli concludes that the unshifted pronouns typically carry some stress, although they are not heavily stressed. In Icelandic in Iceland these pronouns would probably be unstressed in examples of this sort. Jóhannes Gísli maintains that this is the reason why pronominal objects shift less readily in NAI than in Icelandic.

Object shift in NAI was also investigated in our project in a multiple-choice test that involved various syntactic constructions. Here, the speakers were asked to choose between the following alternatives, among others (see Arnbjörnsdóttir and Thráinsson 2018, 243–44):

6. a. Þau drukku **bjórinn** ekki / ekki bjórinn
they drank the beer not / not the beer
'They didn't drink the beer'.

b. Hann notar **hana** aldrei / aldrei hana
he uses her never / never her
'He never uses it'.

Approximately half the speakers left the object noun unshifted in sentences like (6a), and very few chose to leave a pronominal object unshifted, as in the latter alternative in (6b). This shows that the heritage speakers have a similar feel for the "shiftability" of nouns and pronouns as do speakers of Icelandic in Iceland.

Pronouns and Reflexives

As is well-known among linguists, Icelandic has so-called long-distance reflexives. A representative example is given in (7):

7. Hann heldur að þú elskir **sig.**
he thinks that you love (subjunct.) REFL
'He thinks that you love him'.

Here, the reflexive pronoun *sig* in the embedded subjunctive clause refers back to the pronoun *hann* in the main clause. A corresponding sentence in English would be **He thinks that you love himself*, which is completely ungrammatical. For many speakers of Icelandic, long-distance reflexives are possible only in subjunctive clauses. Since the indicative is often used in embedded clauses in NAI where the subjunctive would be expected (Birna Arnbjörnsdóttir 2006, 105), one might think that long-distance reflexives would also be vulnerable. Michael Putnam and Birna Arnbjörnsdóttir (2015) have argued that this is actually the case.[12]

Subject Case Marking

Verbs that take non-nominative subjects do not show any subject agreement and hence they are often called "impersonal verbs" in the linguistic literature. Recent research has shown that the case marking of these subjects is unstable in Icelandic, but the development can go in two different directions (Eythórsson and Thráinsson 2017, and references cited therein):

8. a.	hana langar	>	**henni** langar	Dative substitution
	her (acc.) wants	>	her (dat.) wants	
	'she wants'			
b.	bátinn rak	>	**báturinn** rak	Nominative substitution
	the boat (acc.) drifted	>	the boat (nom.) drifted	
c.	leiknum lauk	>	**leikurinn** lauk	Nominative substitution
	game (dat.) finished	>	game (nom.) finished	

Dative substitution is quite common in Icelandic (sometimes referred to as "dative sickness") and so is the substitution of nominative for accusative in examples like (7b). Substitution of nominative for dative is (still) rare, however. But Birna Arnbjörnsdóttir has shown (2006, 89ff.) that both dative substitution and nominative substitution are quite common in NAI, including the substitution of nominative for dative of experiencer subjects, as in example (9) from NAI, which does not really occur in Icelandic in Iceland:

9. **Ég** var alltaf illa við fisk.
I (nom.) was always badly with fish
'I always hated fish'.

The Icelandic counterpart of (9) would necessarily have a dative subject: *Mér var* . . . lit. "me (dat.) was . . . ."

Case marking of subjects was studied in the Heritage Language Project. In a test targeting various syntactic phenomena, the speakers were presented with sentences on a computer screen. The sentences were read aloud to them and then they had to choose between different variants. One of the examples was the following:

10. □ Mennirnir
□ Mennina vantar peninga.
□ Mönnunum
□ Mannanna
□ the men (nom./acc./dat./gen.) need money.

Here, the choice would indicate which subject case the speakers would prefer. The results showed considerable intra-speaker variation. Salbjörg Óskarsdóttir also searched for selected potentially "impersonal" verbs in the narratives in *Sögur úr Vesturheimi* and in unpublished interviews that Gísli Sigurðsson conducted with speakers of NAI in 1982 (Sigurðsson 1984; Óskarsdóttir and Thráinsson 2017). She found extensive evidence for both "substitutions" (dative and nominative), but one of her main results was the extensive inter- and intra-speaker variation observed: Several speakers would use different subject cases with a given verb in the same interview. In her study of personal letters written by a single speaker over seventy years, a longitudinal corpus of about 82,000 words, Sigríður Mjöll Björnsdóttir (2018) also found evidence for similar fluctuation in subject case marking in the later letters.

Object Case Marking and Agreement

Case marking of verbal and prepositional objects is only partially predictable and hence difficult to acquire. As Birna Arnbjörnsdóttir reports (2006, 99–103), unexpected object case marking frequently occurs in spontaneous speech of Icelandic heritage speakers. In the series of letters that Sigríður Mjöll

Björnsdóttir analyzed, the letters reveal the development of the language spoken by a single individual over several decades. The language of the first letters is virtually indistinguishable from the Icelandic spoken in Iceland (IceIce) at the time, but in later letters Sigríður finds evidence for systematic overgeneralization errors: for example, extensive use of dative case marking of objects. Gender agreement is also affected in the later letters, where neuter gender seems to be used as a default where gender agreement is expected. But there is significant variation in the letters throughout, with target-consistent forms co-existing with non-target-consistent forms. This is also true of the case marking of prepositional objects and similar results have been reported for these by Dehé and Kupisch (2021).

Understanding Syntactically Complex Sentences

Research on the linguistics of heritage languages usually concentrates on language production rather than comprehension. The vocabulary of heritage languages is often different from that of the corresponding "home languages," and this obviously affects mutual understanding by speakers of heritage languages and home languages. We wanted to know, however, to what extent the structure of sentences influenced their interpretability for speakers of NAI. This was done by using a special test that is described in the chapter by Sigríður Magnúsdóttir, Iris Edda Nowenstein, and Höskuldur Thráinsson in this volume. The main result is that the non-canonical order of arguments (that is, nouns referring to agents and patients of actions) makes sentences difficult to interpret for heritage speakers, partly because they can only rarely make use of the interpretation cues provided by case marking. This is not surprising in the light of the results about case marking outlined above.

Lexical Semantics

Selected aspects of the lexical semantics of NAI were studied formally in the Heritage Language Project. These studies were related to the international project Evolution of Semantic Systems (EoSS; see, for example, Majid, Jordan, and Dunn 2015). Þórhalla Guðmundsdótir Beck and Matthew Whelpton report on a part of this subproject in a paper comparing the colour naming in NAI, Icelandic, British English, and North American English (2018). Although the division of the colour spectrum is similar in the four languages, there are certain differences in the naming of the colours. In some cases, NAI is similar to Icelandic in Iceland in this respect, for example, with respect to word formation such as extensive compounding. In other instances, NAI uses English loan words, partly because the colour term in question did not exist in Icelandic at the time of the emigration to North America. Another outgrowth of this subproject is described in the chapter by Matthew Whelpton in this volume, where he compares the naming of body parts, containers, and spatial relations, in addition to colours, in the same four languages with some additional information about Icelandic sign language. He concludes that the cultural influence of North American English on NAI is obvious in some of these categories, except that NAI is very close to Icelandic in the prepositional marking of spatial relations like *under, above, behind*, et cetera, where the influence of the shared grammatical systems of the "two Icelandics" shines through.

CONCLUDING REMARKS

The chapters in this volume give a representative illustration of the interaction between history, culture, and language in the Icelandic-language enclaves in North America and their development to the present day, but they obviously do not tell the whole story. Further information can be found in the numerous references in this introduction as well as the references in the individual chapters of this volume. There is also a wealth of material for future research, including data collected, transcribed, and partially analyzed statistically in the Heritage Language Project. Much of this data is now being made public, and the editors of this volume hope that it will spur further research. In the last chapter of this book, Birna Arnbjörnsdóttir briefly discusses the important contributions that the study of NAI as a heritage language makes to our knowledge and understanding of heritage languages and language in general, a viewpoint that has been largely absent from studies of NAI until recently.

NOTES

1 See https://www.lh-inc.ca/.

2 See https://inlofna.org/what-we-do.

3 See https://www.pc.gc.ca/apps/dfhd/page_nhs_eng.aspx?id=15752.

4 See https://libguides.lib.umanitoba.ca/c.php?g=723161.

5 See http://www.snorri.is/.

6 See https://icelandiconline.com/.

7 See https://www.icelandicroots.com/.

8 See http://hofsos.is/en/the-icelandic-emigration-center/.

9 See https://nihm.ca/.

10 See, in particular, her discussion of vowel mergers and flámæli in Chapters 6 and 7.

11 The so-called particle shift in English is somewhat similar. The sentences *I looked the address up*, *I looked up the address*, and *I looked it up* are fine, but if the object is an unstressed pronoun, it has to shift around the particle. Thus **I looked up it* is not acceptable. Note that * refers to an unacceptable construction in English.

12 An extensive survey of the relationship between subjunctive and long-distance reflexives in the Icelandic spoken in Iceland (IceIce) indicates that it is not as robust as often assumed (Thráinsson and Strahan 2015).

REFERENCES

Arnbjörnsdóttir, Birna. 1990. "The Linguistic and Social Context of Apparent Vowel Mergers in North American Icelandic." PhD diss., University of Texas.

———. 2006. *North American Icelandic: The Life of a Language*. Winnipeg: University of Manitoba Press.

Arnbjörnsdóttir, Birna, and Höskuldur Thráinsson. 2018. "Hvað einkennir vesturíslensku? Yfirlit um fyrri rit og rannsóknir" [What is North American Icelandic like? An overview of previous research]. In *Sigurtunga: Vesturíslenskt mál og menning,* edited by Birna Arnbjörnsdóttir, Höskuldur Thráinsson, and Úlfar Bragason, 211–55. Reykjavík: Háskólaútgáfan.

Arnbjörnsdóttir, Birna, Höskuldur Thráinsson, and Iris Edda Nowenstein. 2018. "V2 and V3 Orders in North-American Icelandic." *Journal of Language Contact* 11 (3): 379–412.

Arngrímsson, Guðjón. 1997. *Nýja Ísland. Örlagasaga vesturfaranna í máli og myndum* [New Iceland. An illustrated account of the Icelandic emigration to North America]. Reykjavík: Mál og menning.

———. 1998. *Annað Ísland. Gullöld Vestur-Íslendinga í máli og myndum* [Another Iceland. An illustrated account of the golden age of western Icelanders]. Reykjavík: Mál og menning.

———. 2000. *Nýja Ísland. Saga of the Journey to the New World.* Translated by Robert Christie. Winnipeg: Turnstone Press.

Bedford, Allan Gerald. 1975. *The University of Winnipeg: A History of the Founding Colleges*. Toronto: University of Toronto Press.

Benmamoun, Elabbas, Silvina Montrul, and Maria Polinsky. 2013. "Heritage Languages and Their Speakers: Opportunities and Challenges for Linguistics." *Theoretical Linguistics* 39: 129–81.

Berko, Jean. 1958. "The Child's Learning of English Morphology." *Word* 14 (2–3): 150–77.

Bertram, Laurie K. 2010. "New Icelandic Ethnoscapes: Material, Visual and Oral Terrains of Cultural Expression in Icelandic-Canadian History, 1875–Present." PhD diss., University of Toronto.

———. 2020. *The Viking Immigrants: Icelandic North Americans.* Toronto: University of Toronto Press.

Bessason, Haraldur. 1958. "Um íslenzk mannanöfn í Vesturheimi" [On Icelandic names in North America]. *Tímarit Þjóðræknisfélags Íslendinga í Vesturheimi* 39: 57–65.

———. 1967. "A Few Specimens of North American-Icelandic." *Scandinavian Studies* 39 (2): 115–46.

———. 1971. "Isländskan i Nordamerika." *Sprog i Norden*: 57–77.

———. 1980. "Um íslenska tungu í Vesturheimi" [On Icelandic in North America]. *Lögberg-Heimskringla*, 21 March, 7.

———. 1984. "Íslenska er lífseigari en nokkurt annað þjóðarbrotsmál í Kanada." [Icelandic is more resilient than any other heritage language in Canada]. Interview in *Morgunblaðið*, 12 February, 64–65.

Bjarnadóttir, Birna, and Finnbogi Guðmundsson, eds. 2007. *My Parents: Memoirs of New World Icelanders*. [Translations by Katelin Parsons, Davíð Gíslason, and Árný Hjaltadóttir of selected chapters of the book *Foreldrar mínir*, edited by Finnbogi Guðmundsson, 1956.] Winnipeg: University of Manitoba Press.

Björnsdóttir, Sigríður Mjöll. 2018. "'Hún er svo montin af að vera íslenskt.' Málbreytingar í sendibréfum Vestur-Íslendings" [She is so proud of being Icelandic. Language change in the letters of a North American Icelander]. In *Sigurtunga: Vesturíslenskt mál og menning*, edited by Birna Arnbjörnsdóttir, Höskuldur Thráinsson, and Úlfar Bragason, 341–59. Reykjavík: Háskólaútgáfan.

Bragason, Úlfar. 2018. "Menning og saga. Yfirlit um fyrri rit og rannsóknir" [Culture and history. An overview of previous research]. In *Sigurtunga: Vesturíslenskt mál og menning*, edited by Birna Arnbjörnsdóttir, Höskuldur Thráinsson, and Úlfar Bragason, 21–34. Reykjavík: Háskólaútgáfan.

Clausing, Stephen. 1981. "English Influence on the American German Dialects with a Comparison to American Icelandic." PhD. diss., University of Wisconsin.

———. 1986. *English Influence on American German and American Icelandic*. Bern: Peter Lang.

Dehé, Nicole. 2018. "The Intonation of Polar Questions in North American ('Heritage') Icelandic." *Journal of Germanic Linguistics* 30 (3): 213–59.

Dehé, Nicole, and Tanja Kupisch. 2021. "Prepositional phrases and Case in North American (Heritage) Icelandic." *Nordic Journal of Linguistics*: 1–27. doi:10.1017/S033258652100018.

Einarsson, Magnús, ed. 1991. *Icelandic-Canadian Oral Narratives*. Selected by Magnús Einarsson. Mercury Series Paper. Canadian Centre for Folk Culture Studies 63. Hull, QC: Canadian Museum of Civilization.

———, ed. 1992. *Icelandic-Canadian Memory Lore*. Selected by Magnús Einarsson. Mercury Series Paper. Canadian Centre for Folk Culture Studies 64. Hull, QC: Canadian Museum of Civilization.

Einarsson, Stefán. 1933. "Hvað geta Vestur-íslendingar gert fyrir íslenzka tungu?" [What can Western Icelanders do for the Icelandic language]. *Tímarit Þjóðræknisfélags Íslendinga* 15 (1): 9–17.

———. 1937. "Nokkur sýnishorn af vestur-íslenzku og rannsóknum um hana" [Examples of Western Icelandic and related research]. *Lögberg—Fimmtíu Ára Minningarblað. Lögberg*, 22 December, 18–19 and 22–23.

Eyford, Ryan C. 2006. "From Prairie Goolies to Canadian Cyclones: The Transformation of the 1920 Winnipeg Falcons." *Sport History Review* 37 (1): 5–18.

———. 2010. "An Experiment in Immigrant Colonization: Canada and the Icelandic Reserve 1875–1897." PhD diss., University of Manitoba.

———. 2016. *White Settler Reserve: New Iceland and the Colonization of the Canadian West*. Vancouver: University of British Columbia Press.

Eythórsson, Thórhallur, and Höskuldur Thráinsson. 2017. "Variation in Oblique Subject Constructions in Insular Scandinavian." In *Syntactic Variation in Insular Scandinavian*, edited by Höskuldur Thráinsson, Caroline Heycock, Hjalmar P. Petersen, and Zakaris Svabo Hansen, 53–90. Amsterdam: John Benjamins Publishing.

Fishman, Joshua. 1972. *The Sociology of Language*. Rowley, MA: Newbury House.

Geertz, Clifford. 1973. *The Interpretation of Culture*. New York: Basic Books.

Gerrard, Nelson. 1979. "Pioneers and Place Names of New Iceland." *Icelandic Canadian* (Winter 1978–Spring 1979). http://sagapublications.com/articles.html.

———. 1985. *Icelandic River Saga*. Arborg, MB: Saga Publications.

Guðmundsdóttir Beck, Þórhalla, and Matthew Whelpton. 2018. "Það besta úr báðum heimum. Um litaheiti í vesturíslensku" [The best of both worlds. On colour naming in NAI]. In *Sigurtunga: Vesturíslenskt mál og menning*, edited by Birna Arnbjörnsdóttir, Höskuldur Thráinsson, and Úlfar Bragason, 375–400. Reykjavík: Háskólaútgáfan.

Guðmundsson, Böðvar. 2000. *Where the Winds Dwell*. Translated by Keneva Kunz. Winnipeg: Turnstone Press.

Guðsteinsdóttir, Guðrún Björk. 2006. "Home and Exile in Early Icelandic-Canadian Poetry." In *Home and Exile: Selected Papers from the 4th International Tartu Conference on Canadian Studies*, edited by Eva Rein og Krista Vogelberg, 71–81. Tartu: Baltic Center for North-American Studies and Estonian Association for Canadian Studies, University of Tartu.

Houser, George J. 1990. *Pioneer Icelandic Pastor: The Life of Reverend Paul Thorlaksson*. Winnipeg: Manitoba Historical Society.

Hreinsson, Viðar. 2003. *Andvökuskáld. Ævisaga Stephans G. Stephanssonar*. Vol. 2. Reykjavík: Bjartur.

———. 2012. *Wakeful Nights. Stephan G. Stephansson—Icelandic-Canadian Poet*. Calgary: Benson Ranches.

Jóhannsdóttir, Kristín M. 2006. "The Status of Icelandic in Canada." *Icelandic Canadian* 60 (2): 63–68.

Jónsson, Bergsteinn. 2005. *Báran rís og hnígur: Dauðastríð íslenskrar tungu meðal afkomenda íslenskra landnema í Norður-Dakota eins og það birtist í gerðabókum Þjóðræknisdeildarinnar Bárunnar 1938–1977* [Evidence for the deterioration of Icelandic in the minutes of the national league chapter Báran]. Reykjavík: Sagnfræðistofnun Háskóla Íslands and Háskólaútgáfan.

———. 2009. *Til Vesturheims: Um vesturferðir, Vesturheim og Vestur-Íslendinga* [On the emigration of Icelanders to North America]. Reykjavík: Skrudda.

Jónsson, Jóhannes Gísli. 2018. "'Þú skilur ekki þetta.' Andlagsstökk í vesturíslensku" [You understand not this. Object shift in NAI]. In *Sigurtunga: Vesturíslenskt mál og menning*, edited by Birna Arnbjörnsdóttir, Höskuldur Thráinsson, and Úlfar Bragason, 361–74. Reykjavík: Háskólaútgáfan.

Kristinsson, Júníus H. 1983. *Vesturfaraskrá 1870–1914*. Reykjavík: Sagnfræðistofnun Háskóla Íslands.

Kristjánsdóttir, Dagný. 2014. "'Við hérna í vestrinu'. Um bernsku og barnaefni í íslenskum barnablöðum í Vesturheimi" [We in the West. On childhood and material for children in Icelandic children's journals in America]. *Ritið* 1: 103–19.

Kristjanson, Wilhelm. 1965. *The Icelandic People in Manitoba: A Manitoba Saga*. Winnipeg: Wallingford Press.

McIntosh, Andrea. 2004. "In Plain Sight: The Development of Western Icelandic Ethnicity and Class Division 1910–1920." PhD diss., University of Manitoba.

Majid, Asifa, Fiona Jordan, and Michael Dunn. 2015. "Semantic Systems in Closely Related Languages." *Language Sciences* 49: 1–18.

Mayer, Mercer. 1969. *Frog, Where Are You?* New York: Dial Press.

Minningarrit íslenzkra hermanna 1914–1918 [In memory of Icelandic soldiers 1914–1918]. Edited by Rögnvaldur Pétursson. Winnipeg: Félagið Jón Sigurðsson, 1923.

Neijmann, Daisy L. 1995. "Laura Goodman Salverson, Guttormur J. Guttormsson, and the Dual World of Second-generation Canadian Authors." *Scandinavian-Canadian Studies* 8: 19–36.

———. 1997a. "Community and Identity in Icelandic-Canadian Literature." *Scandinavian-Canadian Studies* 10: 53–75.

———. 1997b. *The Icelandic Voice in Canadian Letters: The Contribution of Icelandic-Canadian Writers to Canadian Literature.* Ottawa: Carleton University Press.

———. 1999. "Fighting with Blunt Swords: Laura Goodman Salverson and the Canadian Literary Canon." *Essays on Canadian Writing* 67: 138–73.

———. 1999–2000. "Damned with Faint Praise: The Reception of Laura Goodman Salverson's Works by the Icelandic-Canadian Community." *Scandinavian-Canadian Studies* 12: 40–62.

———. 2006. "Icelandic-Canadian Literature." In *A History of Icelandic Literature*, edited by Daisy L. Neijmann, 608–42. Lincoln: University of Nebraska Press.

———. 2018. "Mál til samskipta eða tengsla. Gildi íslenskunnar í Vesturheimi" [Communicative and symbolic functions of North American Icelandic]. In *Sigurtunga: Vesturíslenskt mál og menning*, edited by Birna Arnbjörnsdóttir, Höskuldur Thráinsson, and Úlfar Bragason, 279–302. Reykjavík: Háskólaútgáfan.

Óskarsdóttir, Salbjörg, and Höskuldur Thráinsson. 2017. "Hann þótti gott í staupinu. Um breytingar á aukafallsfrumlögum í vesturíslensku" [He liked a drink. On changes in the case marking of oblique subjects in NAI]. In *Tilbrigði í íslenskri setningagerð III* [Variation in Icelandic syntax], edited by Höskuldur Thráinsson, Ásgrímur Angantýsson, and Einar Freyr Sigurðsson, 101–24. Reykjavík: Málvísindastofnun Háskóla Íslands.

Pálsson, Gísli. 2005. *Travelling Passions: The Hidden Life of Vilhjálmur Stefánsson.* Translated from Icelandic by Keneva Kunz. Hanover, NH: Dartmouth.

Putnam, Michael T., and Birna Arnbjörnsdóttir. 2015. "Minimizing (Interface) Domains: The Loss of Long-Distance Binding in North American Icelandic." In *Moribund Germanic Heritage Languages in North America: Theoretical Perspectives and Empirical Findings*, edited by B. Richard Page and Michael T. Putnam, 203–23. Leiden: Brill.

Ruth, Roy H. 1964. *Educational Echoes: A History of Education of the Icelandic Canadians in Manitoba.* Winnipeg: Columbia Printers.

Salus, Peter H. 1971. "Icelandic in Canada: A Survey of Immigration and Language Loyalty." In *Linguistic Diversity in Canadian* Society, edited by Regna Darnell, 231–43. Edmonton: Linguistic Research.

Sigurðsson, Gísli. 1984. "Viðtöl við Vestur-Íslendinga, ásamt orðasafni úr vesturíslensku" [Interviews with North American Icelanders, together with a word list]. Manuscript. Reykjavík: Stofnun Árna Magnússonar.

Sigurtunga: Vesturíslenskt mál og menning [Victorious language. North American Icelandic language and culture]. 2018. Edited by Birna Arnbjörnsdóttir, Úlfar Bragason, and Höskuldur Thráinsson. Reykjavík: Háskólaútgáfan.

Simundsson, Elva. 1981. *Icelandic Settlers in America*. Illustrations by Nelson Gerrard. Winnipeg: Queenston House Publishing.

Sögur úr Vesturheimi [Stories from North America]. 2012. Interviews with descendants of Icelandic immigrants in North America, conducted by Hallfreður Örn Eiríksson and Olga María Franzdóttir 1972–1973. Edited by Gísli Sigurðsson. Reykjavík: Stofnun Árna Magnússonar í íslenskum fræðum. [The interviews largely consist of folk tales and they are accessible at http://www.arnastofnun.is/sogururvesturheimi.]

Sontag, Susan. 2007. *At the Same Time: Essays and Speeches*. Edited by Paolo Dilonardo and Anne Jump. London: Hamish Hamilton.

Spolsky, Bernard. 2004. *Language Policy*. Cambridge: Cambridge University Press.

Stefánsson, Vilhjálmur. 1903. "English Loan-Nouns Used in the Colony of North Dakota." *Dialect Notes* 2: 354–62.

Thor, Jonas. 2002. *Icelanders in North America: The First Settlers.* Winnipeg: University of Manitoba Press.

Thráinsson, Höskuldur, Iris Edda Nowenstein, and Sigríður Magnúsdóttir. 2021. "Hvað gerist þegar ein *darga* fjölgar sér í Vesturheimi? Um fleirtölu nafnorða í vesturíslensku" [What happens when one *darga* multiplies in North America? On the plural formation of nouns in NAI]. In *Sálubót. Afmælisrit til heiðurs Jörgen L. Pind*, edited by Árni Kristjánsson, Heiða María Sigurðardóttir, and Kristján Árnason, 123–50. Reykjavík: Háskólaútgáfan.

Thráinsson, Höskuldur, and Tania Strahan. 2015. "Fornöfn." In *Tilbrigði í íslenskri setningagerð III* [Variation in Icelandic syntax], edited by Höskuldur Thráinsson, Ásgrímur Angantýsson, and Einar Freyr Sigurðsson, 155–76. Reykjavík: Málvísindastofnun Háskóla Íslands.

Veterans of Icelandic Descent, World War II, 1939–1945. 1990–1993. A sequel to *Minningarrit íslenskra hermanna 1914–1918.* Winnipeg: Jon Sigurdsson Chapter IODE.

Víðisdóttir, Katrín María. 2016. "Hér og þar. Afdrif norðlenskra framburðareinkenna heima fyrir og vestanhafs" [Here and there. The development of northern dialect traits in Iceland and in North America]. Master's thesis, University of Iceland.

Wolf, Kirsten. 1991. "Heroic Past, Heroic Present. Western Icelandic Literature." *Scandinavian Studies* 63: 432–52.

———. 1992a. "Icelandic-Canadian Literature: Problems in Generic Classification." *Scandinavian Studies* 64: 439–53.

———, ed. 1992b. *Western Icelandic Short Stories*. Translated by Kirsten Wolf and Árný Hjaltadóttir. Winnipeg: University of Manitoba Press.

———. 1994. "Western Icelandic Women Writers: Their Contribution to the Literary Canon." *Scandinavian Studies* 66: 154–203.

———. 1996a. "The Pioneer Woman in Icelandic-Canadian Women's Literature." *Scandinavica* 35: 187–211.

———, ed. and transl. 1996b. *Writings by Western Icelandic Women.* Winnipeg: University of Manitoba Press.

———. 2001. "Emigration and Mythmaking: The Case of Icelanders in Canada." *Canadian Ethnic Studies* 33: 1–15.

Woods, Fred E. 2005. *Fire and Ice: The Story of Icelandic Latter-Day Saints at Home and Abroad.* Provo, UT: Religious Studies Center, Brigham Young University.

Þorbergsson, Magnús Þór. 2020. "'Ég brenni flest leikrit mín': Um leikskáldið Jóhann Magnús Bjarnason" [I burn most of my dramas. On the playwright Jóhann Magnús Bjarnason]. *Skírnir* 194: 294–320.

CHAPTER 1

Moving a Language between Continents: Icelandic Language Communities 1870–1914

ÁSTA SVAVARSDÓTTIR

THE ICELANDIC HERITAGE language in North America is rooted in the linguistic background of the immigrants, that is, in the linguistic and sociolinguistic situation of late nineteenth-century Iceland, which was in many respects very different from the modern Icelandic language community. These facts must be taken into account when one is examining the language use of today's Icelandic-speaking descendants of the emigrants to North America. Any differences in language varieties could be traced to at least three scenarios of language change: that a particular language feature has changed in North American Icelandic but not in Iceland, that a change has taken place in Iceland that has not reached the immigrant communities, or that a feature in both language varieties has changed but not in the same way. The Icelandic language in North America has long been retreating as a living, naturally acquired language and followed a different development path from Icelandic in Iceland. Nevertheless, as exemplified in this book, there are third- or fourth-generation descendants of Icelandic emigrants who acquired Icelandic in their childhood home and still speak it to some extent, even if Icelandic-speaking interlocutors in their community have become ever fewer.

The main focus of this chapter is on the linguistic and sociolinguistic background of the emigrants from Iceland and the external and internal changes affecting their language during the emigration period from 1870 to 1914. Later development is considered only briefly.

NINETEENTH-CENTURY ICELAND: THE SOCIOLINGUISTIC BACKGROUND OF THE EMIGRANTS

Politically, the nineteenth century in Iceland was characterized by increased nationalism and demands for independence from Denmark. The first milestone in the Icelanders' struggle for independence was reached when they got their own constitution in 1874. Emigration to North America had recently started at that time and would continue until the outbreak of the First World War in 1914, shortly before Iceland gained sovereignty in 1918. The emigration period was therefore concurrent with the most important period of the campaign for independence in Iceland, and this contributed to negative attitudes among some Icelanders towards emigration.

As was common for languages of nations seeking independence from other states (Barbour 2000; Joseph 2004, 92–94), the Icelandic language became an important national symbol in the nineteenth century and one of the main arguments for the Icelanders' claim to independence. The language of Iceland's medieval texts—cherished as essential national heritage—became a key model for the language standard emerging in the nineteenth and early twentieth centuries. Standardization efforts were characterized by language purism (Thomas 1991, 12), which was directed both at words and linguistic features of (allegedly) foreign origin, especially Danish, and at language variants traceable to post-medieval language changes.

Even if Iceland had been part of the Danish kingdom for centuries, Icelandic was the dominant language within the country, and there is no history of efforts to suppress it by the authorities in Denmark. For centuries direct contact with the Danish language was mostly confined to a small group of officials, but in the nineteenth century direct language contact became more widespread. Contributing factors include increased mobility between Iceland and Denmark and the gradual modernization of Icelandic society, with expanding trade enterprises and new technologies and skills introduced mainly by educated Danish professionals and craftspersons who settled in Iceland or by Icelanders who had studied or apprenticed in Denmark. It is generally accepted that the linguistic influence of Danish on Icelandic was extensive at that time (Ottósson 1990; Hauksdóttir 2011; Svavarsdóttir 2017, 2021), although contact with other countries (for example, Norway and Great Britain) was growing as well.

Ongoing language contact affected all discourse on language and language use in the nineteenth century, and the dominant language attitudes and attempts at language standardization were partly a response to the Danish influence. Language standardization efforts, seeking to establish norms for the correct or desirable use of language (Milroy 2012, 576), were primarily directed at the written language, with less concern for variation in speech.

In the early nineteenth century, the Icelandic language had very little institutional support. Even if it had been obligatory to teach children to read since the eighteenth century, with writing and arithmetic added in 1880, instruction was the responsibility of parents or guardians and usually took place at home. Elementary schools were few and far between until the last decades of the nineteenth century, and even then schools were mostly confined to towns and villages.

By the late nineteenth century, reading skills had become general and most people could write as well (Halldórsdóttir 2003a, 249–53). The old Latin school, enlarged and moved to Reykjavík in 1846, for a time had been the only secondary school in the country, but the number and variety of schools at the secondary level gradually increased in the last quarter of the century. Reading societies and other community-level associations also contributed to folk education (Jónsson 2003; Halldórsdóttir 2003b). It is unclear if, how, and to what extent the emerging language standard actually reached the general public before general and compulsory school attendance was introduced in 1907. However, with increased publication of books, newspapers, and periodicals, many of them widely distributed (Guttormsson 2003, 55, 65), people had access to more diverse texts than before. Newspapers were an important forum for discussions about language and language use, and they served as a showcase for the growing standardization of the written language, even if the orthography was not fully standardized until the 1920s (Jónsson 1959, 110–16). It is, however, difficult to demonstrate their effect on the language attitudes of the general public or their importance as a direct model for language use.

In short, the social background of the Icelandic emigrants to North America had been shaped by nationalism and the struggle for independence, gradual modernization of society, increasing contact with other countries, a growing number of schools and other domestic institutions, wider circulation of publications that gave the general public access to more varied reading material, and growing social activity in many fields. There was thus considerable progress and activity, even if Icelandic society still was conservative in many ways.

Significant population growth in Iceland during the nineteenth century—from 47,000 to almost 78,000—placed pressure on traditional rural Icelandic farming society. This limited the possibilities for young people to acquire a farm, become independent, establish a family, and make a living, and led to considerable migration, especially after 1870. This spurred both increased urbanization within Iceland and emigration to North America. Iceland was, nevertheless, primarily a rural society throughout the nineteenth century: in 1880 almost 90 percent of the population lived in rural areas, and the proportion was still over 75 percent at the turn of the century ("Sögulegar hagtölur" 2017). Foreign contact affected urban centres more than rural areas, and changes were more extensive and more rapid in towns and villages than in the countryside, but there were nonetheless progressive changes in rural areas, including the agricultural school in Ólafsdalur, founded in 1880 by Torfi Bjarnason, who had studied agricultural methods and technology in Scotland and later also in the United States (Ólafsson 1924, 7–9; see also Alda Möller, this volume). Foreign influence and new ideas also spread around the country with books, newspapers, and periodicals.

NINETEENTH-CENTURY ICELANDIC: THE LANGUAGE OF THE EMIGRANTS

There exists no diachronic linguistic overview of Icelandic in the nineteenth century, but primary texts show considerable language variation, not only in informal private writings but also in formal published texts. By *variation*, we refer to the manifestation of two (or more) forms that have the same linguistic function and can appear in the same context. These include variant orthographical forms, such as *gegna*, *gégna,* and *gjegna*, all occurring for the verb *gegna* 'respond, obey' in nineteenth-century texts, or variant word forms, for example, the noun *ritgerð* or *ritgjörð* 'essay, thesis' (cf. ROH, Ritmálssafn Orðabókar Háskólans [Written Language Archive]).

There is, of course, no direct attestation of nineteenth-century pronunciation, only indirect sources. The spelling in private letters, especially letters written by people without formal education and little writing practice, often seems close to speech and may tend to reflect the writers' pronunciation. It is, however, important to be cautious when drawing conclusions from their spelling, as research has shown that even if private letters may resemble the colloquial language of their writers, they can also include formulaic expressions as well as formal and archaic language features, originating, for instance, in old letters and texts used in the teaching of reading and writing (Elspaß 2012, 46; Rastrick 2003). The handwriting can also be difficult to interpret, as the differentiation of certain symbols is not always clear. The difference between a handwritten *i* and *e* can be minimal, for example, causing a problem when investigating so-called *flámæli*, a variant pronunciation deriving from the close vowels /i/ and /u/ being (partly) merged with the mid-vowels /e/ and /ö/. This variation was attested in early twentieth-century speech and must have been present in the speech of some nineteenth-century Icelanders as well, supported by the presence of *flámæli* in North American Icelandic (Arnbjörnsdóttir 1987; 2006, 113ff.), though the frequency and distribution of variants are difficult to detect in writing for the above-mentioned reason. Investigations from the 1930s and onwards have shown that there was considerable dialectal variation in pronunciation in the mid-twentieth century and that this variation gradually diminished over the course of the century (see an overview in Árnason 2005, 365ff.). Such dialectal variation was presumably at least as extensive in the late nineteenth century, even if the actual extent of variation and the distribution of variants remain unknown.

The inflectional system has been relatively stable throughout the centuries despite changes in individual forms or paradigms leading to a variation between old and new variants. In some cases educated and influential language enthusiasts in the eighteenth and nineteenth centuries were conducive to variation by promoting old and retreating inflectional forms instead of newer forms that had become widespread and even dominant. An instance of this is variation in the first-person plural of middle voice verbs between the old ending *-umst*, now the standardized form, and the newer ending *-ustum*, yielding variant forms like *við hittumst* or *hittustum* 'we met (each other)' and *við þykjumst* or *þykjustum* 'we pretend' (Ottósson 1990–91, 117–23; Bernharðsson 2018, 154). Variations in the inflection of masculine nouns ending in *-ir*, such as *læknir* 'doctor' and *vísir* 'clock hand, sprout', is another example. Originally, the final *-r* was the nominative singular ending and did not appear in other inflectional forms, but it was later reinterpreted as a part of the stem and retained throughout the paradigm, yielding variation (for example, the accusative case forms *lækni* or *læknir*, the genitive *læknis* or *læknirs*, and plural nominative *læknar* or *læknirar*). A third example is variation in the highly irregular forms of many pronouns, for instance between forms with rounded and unrounded vowels in interrogative *hver* 'who' (*hvör*, *hvor*, *hvur*, or *hver*) and the indefinite pronouns *einhver* 'somebody' (*einhvör*, *einhvur*, or *einhver*) and *enginn* 'nobody' (*öngvan* or *engan* in accusative) (Bernharðsson 2018, 150–54). Inflectional variation of these types was common throughout the nineteenth and early twentieth centuries but has mostly vanished due to standardization.

Changes in word order and syntactic structure also led to variation. An example of syntactic variation appears in gender agreement with plural nouns like *foreldrar* 'parents' and *krakkar* 'kids', where there is a mismatch between the grammatical gender of the words (here, masculine) and the biological gender of the referents (mixed gender, yielding neuter plural), as shown in the following example from a nineteenth-century personal letter where variation occurs within the same utterance:

> **Krakkarnir** (m.pl.) voru **frískir** (m.pl.) og **kát** (n.pl.), **þau** (n.pl.) . . .
> 'The kids were healthy and cheerful, they . . .'

The first adjective agrees with the grammatical masculine of the preceding noun, while the second adjective and the personal pronoun conform to the natural gender of the referents, that is, boys and girls. In private writings, including letters from emigrants, there was a tendency for the meaning of such nouns, rather than their grammatical gender, to decide the gender of following co-referential adjectives and pronouns (Þórhallsdóttir 2015, 172–74), though grammatical gender agreement was the standard and presumably more common in published texts.

There were many changes to the Icelandic vocabulary in the nineteenth century, especially in the latter part of the century, due to social changes, technological innovations, and the introduction of new language domains and topics in Icelandic. Purism encouraged the formation of Icelandic neologisms and discouraged the use of borrowed words, especially from Danish. Even old borrowings were affected by purism, such as words of Low German origin with prefixes like *be-/bí-* and *an-*, for example, *befala* (v.) 'order, consign' and *anstöndugur* (adj.) 'appropriate'. Such words may never have been frequently used in Icelandic except in official documents, and in the nineteenth century their use was clearly retreating due to standardization efforts (Óskarsson 2015; Svavarsdóttir 2017, 55–60).

The total number of imported words in Icelandic newspapers and periodicals did increase towards the turn of the century (Svavarsdóttir 2017, 61–71), mostly borrowed from or via Danish and nativized to some extent, and words of foreign origin increasingly appeared in private letters as well, especially by educated and urban writers (Svavarsdóttir 2021, 56–62). Under the influence of purism, synonym pairs of a neologism and a lexical borrowing were frequent. These included the nouns *eintak* and *exemplar* 'copy', *smjörlíki* and *margarín* 'margarine', and *vindlingur* and *sígaretta* 'cigarette', all attested in texts from the nineteenth and early twentieth centuries. Over time one of these words often won out and the other fell out of use or shifted in meaning. Nineteenth-century Icelandic texts thus contain many words rarely used today, such as the borrowed nouns *elixír* 'elixir' and *mansétta* 'cuff'.

Another type of lexical variation, perhaps regional, occurs when words can have different inflection, such as nouns with variant gender, for example, *skúr* 'rain shower', which can be either feminine or masculine, and *sykur* 'sugar', which is either masculine or neuter.

Due to orthographic, morphological, syntactic, and lexical variation in nineteenth-century Icelandic, it may be expected that the language and language use of the Icelandic emigrants to North America was not uniform. Furthermore, some words, word forms, and variants that were relatively frequent in the late nineteenth century have since receded or disappeared in Iceland, especially in the standard written language, while others have gained ground and new lexical items have been introduced.

THE EMIGRATION PERIOD: AN OLD LANGUAGE IN NEW SURROUNDINGS

Individuals had various reasons for emigrating, but the main causes are considered to be economic. The Canadian government and, to a lesser extent, American authorities actively promoted emigration in Iceland, offering cheap land and support. This was an obvious enticement for the rural poor and the landless, and regular sea transport and favourably priced fares in the last decades of the nineteenth century made it easier for individuals to make the move (Kjartansson 1977; Kjartansson and Heiðarsson 2003, 137–43).

Many emigrants dreamt of an Icelandic colony in North America, where the Icelanders could live by themselves, control their own affairs, and maintain their customs, culture, and language, and this dream of a New Iceland echoed the struggle for independence in Iceland (Thor 2002). Apart from ideology there were practical reasons for newcomers with a shared language and ethnic background to form communities. Sociolinguist James Milroy observed that "ethnic groups use the close-knit network as a means of protecting their economic and social interests while their community develops the resources to integrate more fully. . . . These close-knit communities are functional for their members in that they offer security and mutual support" (Milroy 1992, 212–13).

Icelandic settlements of varying sizes formed in the western part of Canada and the United States. Of these, the New Iceland settlement in Manitoba, where Icelandic immigrants were a majority, and the Icelandic community in Winnipeg gradually became the main centres of Icelandic cultural and linguistic heritage in North America (Arnbjörnsdóttir 2006, 31–32). In the early years of New Iceland, Icelandic—both written and spoken—was commonly used in public as well as private life, whereas immigrants in Winnipeg and in the smaller rural settlements had more contact with speakers of other languages, especially English. By the turn of the century, Winnipeg had become a hub for Icelandic-language publishing activities, representing an important contribution to the maintenance of Icelandic language and identity. Religious services were held in Icelandic, and various other social activities in Icelandic communities also facilitated use of Icelandic outside of the home (see, for example, Heiðarsson 2003; see also Vilhelm Vilhelmsson, this volume). Mobility was another factor in language use, as there was regular contact and migration between Icelandic settlements in North America as well as movement between Iceland and North America throughout the emigration period, with a steady influx of new immigrants and smaller numbers of migrants moving back to Iceland after a temporary residence (Kjartansson and Heiðarsson 2003, 100). Friends and family maintained extensive private correspondence across the distances separating them. In consequence there was considerable direct contact between Icelandic language communities in Iceland and North America, in addition to indirect contact through books and newspapers.

The first attested use of the noun *vestur-íslenska* 'Western Icelandic' for the language of Icelandic settlers in North America and their descendants appeared in an article from 1901 (Pjetursson 1901). The author had served as a minister in Winnipeg for several years before relocating to Copenhagen and thus knew the Icelandic community in North America from personal experience. The article is an interesting account of the *Vestur-Íslendingar* 'Western Icelanders' and their nationality and language at the turn of the century (see also Ólafur Arnar Sveinsson, this volume).

According to Hafsteinn Pjetursson, the Icelandic population in North America fell into three categories. First were those who had so recently arrived that they had not gained citizenship (obtainable after living for three years in Canada or the United States) and not lost "any of their Icelandic nationality" (Pjetursson 1901, 46–47; translation by the author). The second category consisted of those born in Iceland but holding Canadian or American citizenship. The third group comprised persons who were born in North America of Icelandic descent and "are not Icelanders but Americans by birth, upbringing, education, customs, and nationality" (Pjetursson 1901, 48).

At the time of his writing, the second group was the largest. The article characterizes their language use as follows: “English is their language for matters concerning governance and legislation, public schooling, and all legal commerce. Their daily language is a mixture of Icelandic and English, but their written language is Western Icelandic [that is, *vestur-íslenska*]” (Pjetursson 1901, 47).

The comment about the spoken language being a mixture of Icelandic and English indicates that English had already left its mark on spoken North American Icelandic, at least in Winnipeg, though nothing is said about the nature or extent of the interference. Interestingly, the term *vestur-íslenska* is taken to refer only to the written language. The author states that some of those who were born and raised in North America could speak and even read basic Icelandic, but they could not write it (Pjetursson 1901, 48).

In 1903 Vilhjálmur Stefánsson published an article on lexical borrowings used by Icelandic immigrants in his home community in North Dakota. He presented a list of nearly 500 nouns from English and their gender(s) when they were used in Icelandic context; the gender of some nouns varied. Although the author retained English spellings for the loan words, he noted that the pronunciation varied widely between speakers, from being close to the usual English pronunciation to being “so modified as to make the word scarcely recognizable” (Stefánsson 1903, 355). However, the article does not clarify whether this observation extended equally to all borrowings from English or whether the degree of adaptation differed from word to word. The author makes the interesting suggestion that variation in pronunciation could be a consequence of dialectal differences between immigrants from different regions of Iceland, though he neither explains this further nor gives examples.

Vilhjálmur Stefánsson’s list includes a number of loan words used in Iceland in the nineteenth century. These nouns, which likely entered the Icelandic vocabulary from or via Danish, include *albúm* ‘album’, *auktion* (*áksjón*) ‘auction’, *cigar* (*sígar*) ‘cigar’, *doktor* ‘doctor’, and *gítar* ‘guitar’ (cf. ROH; Magnússon 1989). Speakers may therefore have known them already in Iceland, which could explain a pronunciation different from what might be expected for direct borrowings from English. Linguistic purism was, however, present in Icelandic communities in North America, and Vilhjálmur

Stefánsson (1903, 355) states that some Icelandic immigrants were so opposed to English borrowings that they avoided borrowings such as *mower* in favour of Icelandic terms such as *sláttuvél*, first attested in Iceland in 1859 (cf. ROH).

Even if English borrowings soon entered the speech of Icelandic immigrants, the language evidently thrived in newly established Icelandic communities throughout the emigration period. Icelandic immigrants lacked words for many concepts in their native language relating to their new surroundings: the landscape, nature, climate, and various farming practices and other skills were unfamiliar to them. Adapting to their new environment involved adapting their language to new conditions. Nevertheless, written sources indicate that the language use of Icelandic immigrants in North America and their contemporaries in Iceland did not fundamentally differ during the emigration period. Differences primarily appear in the vocabulary, mainly words referring to North American phenomena or recent innovations non-existent in Iceland at the time of the emigrants' departure. The word *loggahús* 'log house' is, for example, attested in a letter from 1875 (Ólafsson 2001, 106). A diary entry from 1884 lists tree species in New Iceland and species of fish in Lake Winnipeg, their names ranging from familiar Icelandic words (for example, *eik* 'oak' and *styrja* 'sturgeon') to neologisms and loan translations modelled on English equivalents (for example, *gullauga* 'goldeye', *sólfiskur* 'sunfish', and *kattfiskur* 'catfish'), to direct lexical borrowings such as *poplar* 'poplar' and *willo* 'willow' (Ólafsson 2001, 114).

The language in immigrants' private letters bears surprisingly few indications that their writers had lived and worked in North America for years or even decades.[1] English borrowings are rare, and those that do occur usually refer to something in the writers' North American reality unknown in Iceland: for example, *corn* and *alfalfa* in a letter written by Aðalbjartur Bjarnason (b. 1864), a farmer in Nebraska (see Alda Möller, this volume), towards the end of the emigration period in 1913 (see Figure 1.1); and *treinið* 'the train' in a letter from Ásgeir Tr. Friðgeirsson (b. 1860), a saddler and carpenter in Manitoba and later California, written in 1910. A letter from 1899, written by Sigfús Jónasson Bergmann (b. 1836), a farmer and bookbinder in North Dakota, contains no English borrowings except the word *cent* and symbols like $ and C.

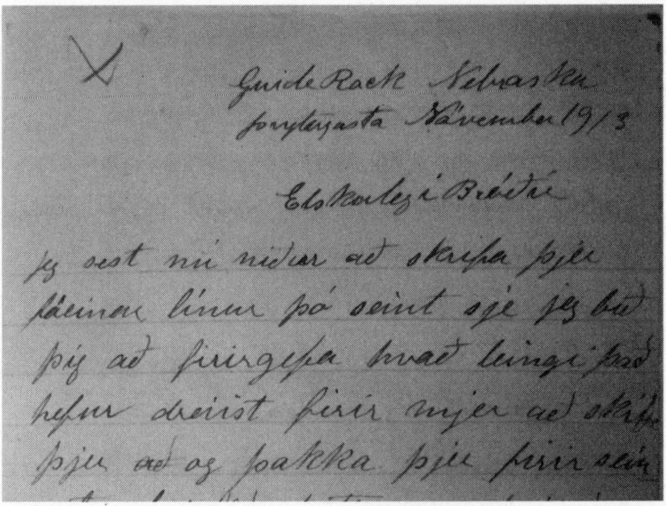

Guide Rock Nebraska
Nóvember 1913

Elskulegi Bróðir

Jeg sest nú niður að skrifa þjer fáeinar línur þó seint sje jeg bið þig að firirgefa hvað leingi það hefur dregist firir mjer að skrifa þjer og þakka þjer firir sein

FIGURE 1.1. The opening lines of a private letter from farmer Aðalbjartur Bjarnason in Nebraska to his brother in Iceland, written in 1913: "Dear Brother. I will now sit down to write you a few lines, even though they are late; I apologize for how long it has taken me to write you and thank you." (Icelandic National Library collection, Lbs. 3078 4to)

All three letter writers had come to North America as adults, but the length of time spent away from Iceland (in Aðalbjartur Bjarnason's case, nearly his entire adult life) did not have a significant impact on their written Icelandic, which remained virtually indistinguishable from that of individuals of a similar age still living in Iceland. Most private letters that are easily accessible for research were written to family or friends in Iceland, and as such their writers may have consciously avoided words or language that they realized were unfamiliar to the recipients. However, the same tendencies can be observed in Icelandic-language immigrant newspapers published in North America, where the language use is very similar to comparable newspapers in Iceland despite being mainly targeted at subscribers in North America. Their North American origin is recognizable from the topics covered and the occasional English borrowings not used in Iceland, as well as English names of persons and businesses, while the Icelandic papers contain recent neologisms and Danish borrowings. Figures 1.2 and 1.3 show examples of advertisements from two of the main Icelandic newspapers in February 1914, at the end of the emigration period. The translations that retain English words and borrowings in the original text are in bold (excluding proper nouns).

FIGURE 1.2. From *Heimskringla*, 5 February 1914. "**Violin** teaching. The undersigned offers instruction for boys and girls in playing the violin. I have studied violin for many years with excellent teachers, with the main aim of being able to teach it myself. I can be met at 589 Alverstone St. from 11 to 1 and 5 to 7 o'clock on weekdays. Theodor Arnason."

FIGURE 1.3. From *Lögberg*, 26 February 1914. "The King George Tailoring Co. The best tailors and fur vendors. Colour, clean, and iron, mend and alter clothes. [The] best fabrics. Latest fashions. Come and take a look at our new fabrics. 866 Sherbrooke St. **Telephone** G. 2220 Winnipeg. **Coupon**. King George Tailoring Co. takes this **Coupon** valid as a $5.00 payment towards the cost of an outfit, the whole month of February."

Apart from proper names there are surprisingly few words of English origin in these advertisements—only *violin* in the first one, where the corresponding Icelandic word *fiðla* is also used, and *coupon* and *fón* 'telephone' in the second—and they are remarkably similar to advertisements appearing in Iceland at the same time.

Even if Icelandic had a relatively strong position in the language community in North America at the end of the emigration period, not all individuals maintained their native language to the same extent. People's situations differed greatly, as did their attitudes to the Icelandic language and community, and it also mattered where they lived. Those living in or near the largest and most dense Icelandic settlements had better opportunities to speak Icelandic than those who lived far from other Icelandic speakers (Arnbjörnsdóttir 2006, 30–32). Jón Halldórsson, an Icelandic farmer in Nebraska, an area with few Icelandic immigrants, wrote about the poor fluency of his grown children in Icelandic in a letter dating from 1910, confirmed by their Icelandic-speaking mother writing them in English at about the same time (Bragason 2015; see also Úlfar Bragason, this volume). The support of a relatively strong Icelandic language community was paramount for the language to be passed on to the next generation.

POST-EMIGRATION DEVELOPMENT OF THE ICELANDIC LANGUAGE COMMUNITIES

After the emigration period the Icelandic language communities in Iceland and North America started to drift apart. Direct contact between them decreased, and new speakers who had acquired the language in Iceland only infrequently joined the language community in North America. As the numbers of first-generation immigrants shrank, ties with friends and family in Iceland weakened, and as time went by the majority of Western Icelanders were no longer individuals born in Iceland. These new generations had been raised in North America and saw themselves primarily as Canadians or Americans, even if they cherished their Icelandic roots.

Over the course of the twentieth century, the status of the Icelandic language changed on both sides of the Atlantic. In Iceland its position was strengthened as the national language of a sovereign state, with increasing institutional support from growing systems of administration and education and the establishment of various cultural institutions. This, in turn, advanced the standardization of the language by disseminating an awareness of "desirable" language use among the general public, and even if language planning efforts were primarily directed at the written language, the uniformity of the spoken language gradually increased as well. As Icelandic society became more complex, the usage domains of the language multiplied, and the language had to be adapted to fulfill all necessary functions of a modern national language.

On the other hand, the status of Icelandic in North America weakened as the speakers became fewer and their daily life was increasingly intertwined with that of their English-speaking fellow citizens. Social activity and publication in Icelandic decreased, and the domain of the language consequently narrowed as the use of Icelandic became increasingly limited to the private sphere. Relatively dense settlements—where Icelandic could be used among relatives, friends, neighbours, and even colleagues—provided better conditions to maintain the language and pass it on to the next generation than areas where people of Icelandic descent were few. Even in the larger communities, however, the necessary language input for the full acquisition of Icelandic diminished as time went by, and Icelandic-speaking community members were generally bilingual from an early age and presumably used more English than Icelandic in their daily life. Consequently, there are now very few North American speakers left who acquired Icelandic in their childhood community, and most young and middle-aged people of Icelandic descent either do not speak the language at all or have learned it as a second language later in life, motivated by their Icelandic roots. Nevertheless, their linguistic heritage is revealed in Icelandic borrowings in their English, related primarily to family ties, home life, and cultural heritage, such as *amma* 'grandmother' and *afi* 'grandfather' and phrases like *góða nótt* 'good night', and for many of them Icelandic still has a symbolic value (Neijmann 2018).

‖ CONCLUSIONS

Judging from contemporary texts, language use in Icelandic communities in North America during the emigration period (1870 to 1914) does not appear to have been markedly different from that in Iceland at the same time. Lexical borrowings from English and neologisms (usually loan translations) referring to phenomena in the immigrants' new surroundings did appear early, but they are not a salient feature of immigrants' writing, whether in newspapers in Icelandic or in personal writings such as private letters and diaries.

There are indications of lexical borrowings having been more frequent in speech, although this conclusion relies on indirect evidence such as word lists and metalinguistic comments that cannot be verified in the absence of direct sources on the spoken language during the period. It might be expected that language changes in general, whether influenced by English or internal language development, would first have appeared in colloquial speech in the Icelandic language community in North America and next in informal writing. Personal correspondence between immigrants, not available for this chapter, would therefore be of great interest and would likely represent the best source for further investigation.

NOTES

1 The letters analyzed belong to a larger corpus of nineteenth- and early twentieth-century private letters from the project Language Change and Linguistic Variation in 19th-Century Icelandic and the Emergence of a National Standard (LCLV19), which received initial project funding from the Icelandic Research Fund 2012–2014 (grant no. 120646021).

REFERENCES

Árnason, Kristján. 2005. *Hljóð. Handbók um hljóðfræði og hljóðkerfisfræði*. Íslensk tunga I. Reykjavík: Almenna bókafélagið.

Arnbjörnsdóttir, Birna. 1987. "Flámæli í vesturíslensku." *Íslenskt mál og almenn málfræði* 9: 21–40.

———. 2006. *North American Icelandic: The Life of a Language*. Winnipeg: University of Manitoba Press.

Barbour, Stephen. 2000. "Nationalism, Language, Europe." In *Language and Nationalism in Europe*, edited by Stephen Barbour and Cathie Carmichael, 1–17. Oxford: Oxford University Press.

Bernharðsson, Haraldur. 2018. "Spreading the Standard: The Nineteenth-Century Standardization of Icelandic and the First Icelandic Novel." *Journal of Historical Sociolinguistics* 4 (2): 149–76.

Bragason, Úlfar. 2015. "Þrennt að muna." In *Ástumál*, 78–79. Reykjavík: Menningar- og minningarsjóður Mette Magnusson.

Elspaß, Stephan. 2012. "Between Linguistic Creativity and Formulaic Restriction: Cross-Linguistic Perspectives on Nineteenth-Century Lower Class Writers' Private Letters." In *Letter Writing in Late Modern Europe*, edited by Marina Dossena and Gabriella Del Lungo Camiciotti, 45–64. Amsterdam: John Benjamins Publishing.

Guttormsson, Loftur. 2003. "Framleiðsla og dreifing ritaðs máls." In *Alþýðumenning á Íslandi 1830–1930*, edited by Ingi Sigurðsson and Loftur Guttormsson, 37–65. Reykjavík: Sagnfræðistofnun Háskóla Íslands and Háskólaútgáfan.

Halldórsdóttir, Erla Hulda. 2003a. "Af bréfaskriftum kvenna á 19. öld." In *Alþýðumenning á Íslandi 1830–1930*, edited by Ingi Sigurðsson and Loftur Guttormsson, 247–67. Reykjavík: Sagnfræðistofnun Háskóla Íslands and Háskólaútgáfan.

———. 2003b. "Fræðslu- og menntaviðleitni kvenfélaga 1870–1930." In *Alþýðumenning á Íslandi 1830–1930*, edited by Ingi Sigurðsson and Loftur Guttormsson, 269–90. Reykjavík: Sagnfræðistofnun Háskóla Íslands and Háskólaútgáfan.

Hauksdóttir, Auður. 2011. "Danske minder i Island. Om mødet mellem dansk og islandsk kultur." *Danske studier—tidsskrift for dansk sprog, studier og folkeminder*: 5–49.

Heiðarsson, Steinþór. 2003. "Í sláturpotti umheimsins. Brot úr baráttu fyrir varðveislu íslensks þjóðernis í Vesturheimi." In *Þjóðerni í þúsund ár?*, edited by Jón Yngvi Jóhannsson, Kolbeinn Óttarsson Proppé, and Sverrir Jakobsson, 105–17. Reykjavík: Háskólaútgáfan.

Jónsson, Jón. 2003. "Lestrarfélög fyrir almenning." In *Alþýðumenning á Íslandi 1830–1930*, edited by Ingi Sigurðsson and Loftur Guttormsson, 171–93. Reykjavík: Sagnfræðistofnun Háskóla Íslands and Háskólaútgáfan.

Jónsson, Jón Aðalsteinn. 1959. "Ágrip af sögu íslenzkrar stafsetningar." *Íslenzk tunga* 1: 71–119.

Joseph, John E. 2004. *Language and Identity: National, Ethnic, Religious*. Basingstoke/New York: Palgrave Macmillan.

Kjartansson, Helgi Skúli. 1977. "The Onset of Emigration from Iceland." In *Nordic Population Mobility: Comparative Studies of Selected Parishes in the Nordic Countries 1850–1900*, edited by Bo Kronborg, Thomas Nilsson, and Andres A. Svalestuen, 87–93. Oslo: Universitetsforlaget.

Kjartansson, Helgi Skúli, and Steinþór Heiðarsson. 2003. *Framtíð handan hafs. Vesturfarir frá Íslandi 1870–1914*. Reykjavík: Sagnfræðistofnun Háskóla Íslands and Háskólaútgáfan.

Magnússon, Ásgeir Blöndal. 1989. *Íslensk orðsifjabók*. Reykjavík: Orðabók Háskólans.

Milroy, James. 1992. *Linguistic Variation and Change: On the Historical Sociolinguistics of English*. Oxford: Blackwell.

———. 2012. "Sociolinguistics and Ideologies in Language History." In *The Handbook of Historical Sociolinguistics*, edited by Juan M. Hernández-Campoy and J. Camilo Conde-Silvestre, 571–84. Oxford: Wiley-Blackwell.

Neijmann, Daisy. 2018. "Mál til samskipta eða tengsla?" In *Sigurtunga: Vesturíslenskt mál og menning*, edited by Birna Arnbjörnsdóttir, Höskuldur Thráinsson, and Úlfar Bragason, 279–302. Reykjavík: Háskólaútgáfan.

Ólafsson. Davíð. 2001. "Í frásögur færandi. Vesturheimsferðir í persónulegum heimildum." In *Burt—og meira en bæjarleið: Dagbækur og persónuleg skrif Vesturheimsfara á síðari hluta 19. aldar*, edited by Davíð Ólafsson and Sigurður Gylfi Magnússon, 71–128. Reykjavík: Háskólaútgáfan.

Ólafsson, Grímúlfur. 1924. "Torfi Bjarnason skólastjóri og bóndi í Ólafsdal." *Andvari* 49: 5–27.

Óskarsson, Veturliði G. 2015. "Loan Words with the Prefix *be-* in Modern Icelandic: An Example of Halted Borrowing." *Orð og tunga* 17: 1–26.

Ottósson, Kjartan G. 1990. *Íslensk málhreinsun. Sögulegt yfirlit.* Reykjavík: Íslensk málnefnd.

———. 1990–91. "Breytingar á persónubeygingu miðmyndar: Málkerfisbreytingar í félagslegu samhengi." *Íslenskt mál og almenn málfræði* 12–13: 105–25.

Pjetursson, Hafsteinn. 1901. "Frá Vesturheimi." *Árný* 1: 33–48.

Rastrick, Ólafur. 2003. "Lestrarkennsla og ritþjálfun í barnaskólum og alþýðlegum framhaldsskólum 1880–1920." In *Alþýðumenning á Íslandi 1830–1930*, edited by Ingi Sigurðsson and Loftur Guttormsson, 93–113. Reykjavík: Sagnfræðistofnun Háskóla Íslands and Háskólaútgáfan.

ROH. Ritmálssafn Orðabókar Háskólans [The Written Language Archive]. The Árni Magnússon Institute for Icelandic Studies. Accessed 30 January 2021. https://ritmalssafn.arnastofnun.is.

"Sögulegar hagtölur" [Historical statistics for Iceland]. 2017. Statistics Iceland. Accessed 30 January 2021. https://sogulegar.hagstofa.is/.

Stefánsson, Vilhjálmur. 1903. "English Loan-Nouns Used in the Icelandic Colony of North Dakota." *Dialect Notes* 2: 354–62.

Svavarsdóttir, Ásta. 2017. "'Annaðhvort með dönskum hala eða höfði, enn að öðru leiti íslenskt': Um tengsl íslensku og dönsku á 19. öld og áhrif þeirra." *Orð og tunga* 19: 41–76.

———. 2021. "Málþróun og samfélagsbreytingar á síðari hluta 19. aldar: Málnotkun í fjölskyldubréfum." *Orð og tunga* 23: 35–68.

Thomas, George. 1991. *Linguistic Purism*. London: Longman.

Thor, Jonas. 2002. *Icelanders in North America: The First Settlers.* Winnipeg: University of Manitoba Press.

Þórhallsdóttir, Guðrún. 2015. "Notkun málfræðilegra kynja í íslensku og færeysku." In *Frændafundur* 8, edited by Turið Sigurðardóttir and María Garðarsdóttir, 159–81. Tórshavn: Fróðskapur.

CHAPTER 2

Icelanders and America: What is it to be *Vestur-Íslendingur*?

ÓLAFUR ARNAR SVEINSSON

IN SEPTEMBER 1889 the weekly newspaper *Lögberg* published a letter to the editor from the Reverend Jón Bjarnason, the leading Icelandic Lutheran minister in North America.[1] In his letter, which was written in Edinburgh, Scotland, Bjarnason described his tour from North America to Europe, one of the topics being his comparison of Quebec with the western region of Canada and the United States. He asked: "Wouldn't Manitoba be better off with Dakota than Quebec, which is strongly Catholic?" (Bjarnason 1889, 3).[2] Rev. Bjarnason considered the boundary between western Canada and the United States as one of the hindrances that would keep Icelandic migrants apart. "What God has joined together, let not man put asunder," Rev. Bjarnason said, adding that "we, *Vestur-Íslendingar*, should at least say: 'Shame on them!'" (1889, 3).[3]

Rev. Bjarnason's letter is in many ways symbolic. The transnational expression that appears in the beginning of the letter, as he claimed to look over the ocean from Edinburgh, "both to the East and the West: home to Iceland and home to Winnipeg,"[4] underlines the link between the two places at the height of migration from Iceland to Canada (Bjarnason 1889, 3). The piece also includes somewhat of a paradox, in that Rev. Bjarnason emphasizes that *Vestur-Íslendingar* should criticize that people were divided, while at the same time using the concept *Vestur-Íslendingar* exactly in that manner. At the same time it seems that Rev. Bjarnason was addressing the separation of Icelandic immigrants in North America: they had been spread over the continent but were pulled apart where the *takmarkalínan* 'line of separation', the 49th parallel, kept some of them on the southern side of the border while others were on the northern side. This emphasis was common during the 1880s: as will be further addressed below, Icelandic migrants frequently discussed how they were spread all over the continent, which resulted in no central space that could be called "Icelandic," although Winnipeg certainly developed to become one such hub with time. The most remarkable thing with the Reverend Bjarnason's article is, however, the concept that he put forth to argue for the unity of Icelandic Lutherans in Dakota and Manitoba, while at the same time arguing to separate them from the Catholic inhabitants of Quebec: the concept of *Vestur-Íslendingar*. Bjarnason's article is likely the first time this term was used in print. The timing was no coincidence, given the cultural debates that had already endured for some time concerning Icelandic migrants to North America. Using the concept was an obvious response to those debates, which soon became engrained in the meaning of being Icelandic in America.

In this chapter the concept of *Vestur-Íslendingar* is analyzed in the public debates and historiography from the 1880s and onwards. The concept holds a particular status as part of the broader history of Iceland. A common perspective today regarding *Vestur-Íslendingar* is that despite "thousands of kilometres, more than a whole century and many generations," they still carry "within themselves genuine love for Iceland,"[5] as Iceland's Prime Minister Sigmundur Davíð Gunnlaugsson said in his address on the country's National Day, 17 June 2013 (Gunnlaugsson 2013). A discourse of this kind has deep roots within the historiography of Icelandic migrants to North America, but it emphasizes the notion that if one is identified as a *Vestur-Íslendingur*, one is considered as a part of a long and unbroken chain, which for decades has maintained graceful and unchanged connections to the old country. Scholarship and contemporaneous sources, however, reveal that the concept of *Vestur-Íslendingar* has had many different meanings depending on the circumstances and concept of its use.

According to the theories of scholars Stuart Hall (1996) and Zygmunt Bauman (2004), cultural identity—such as being *Vestur-Íslendingur*—is neither natural nor essential. It brings about a certain kind of standing or strategy. Considering these theories, we analyze the idea of *Vestur-Íslendingar* as a tag or a label. Such a tag can either be used by the subject to describe their own cultural characteristics or it can be applied by someone else to interpret behaviour as manifested in Icelandic emigrants or their descendants. In this understanding, the concept of *Vestur-Íslendingar* does not only speak to a historical past: it is first and foremost a concept of culture and politics that is applied to the past and the present.

A CONCEPT OF DEBATES AND ARGUMENTS

From the beginning of the Icelandic mass migration to North America in the 1870s, the migration was hotly debated. Many people in Iceland considered this movement of people to be negative and undesirable for the welfare of the Icelandic nation. Some periodicals published articles treating the migration as *vesturfaraæsingur*, an agitation or frenzy for going West, and the word *vesturheimska* 'stupidity of going West' was also used to belittle the migration and those who departed (*Norðlingur,* 7 April 1876, 194; *Ísafold,* 5 August 1878, 75). In fact, an unnamed author claimed in his 1874 article that North America had for "a long time been an asylum for all kinds of riff-raff from Europe and beyond" (Húnvetningur 1874, 54).[6] The author, furthermore, by entangling thoughts on nationalism and Christianity, maintained that petty thieves and betrayal would be persistent in America and that those who would migrate would have to face major changes to their nationality and ethics (Húnvetningur 1874, 54).

In the minds of those who could not bear the thought of migrating, moving to America meant betraying their nationality and religion. In other words migrating meant rejecting dedication, leaving the group of which one had been a part. Icelandic society, namely the farming community, was also thought to face difficulties because of the migration. At the Icelandic Parliament—the Althing—fears were raised that people would not only run away from their debts and *öðrum óbættum sökum* 'other unresolved matters' but also that farmers would lose a valuable workforce as more and more people would emigrate (*Alþingistíðindi* 1893, B, cols. 1003, 1868). Debates of this kind show how considerations of industrialization and migration were entangled, as can also be seen in a letter written by Eiríkur Magnússon, a librarian in Cambridge, England, on 13 June 1874: "It is obvious that mechanical forces will have to aid us, instead of our lazy workers, who now trail off to America" (Lbs 150 NF, 13 Eiríkur Magnússon).[7]

Icelandic migrants who were rebuked with criticism of this kind responded by arguing that Iceland had been uninhabitable for a long time, mostly because of hardships and pandemics. In April 1878 the New Iceland–based periodical *Framfari* published one of the best-known critiques by the Icelandic migrants of their old country, the poem "Kveðja Ameríkufara til Íslands" (An American emigrant's farewell to Iceland). The poem opens with the words "I love you little or not at all, / you Icelandic stench of sulphur" (*Framfari,* 5 April 1878, 70).[8] Back in Iceland these kinds of texts were branded as slander that highlighted how "the discord amongst Icelandic men abroad was everywhere known,"[9] as reported in *Fréttir frá Íslandi,* which above all would prove their loss of Icelandic language and nationality (Steingrímsson 1888, 48).[10]

Around the same time Icelandic migrants' appearance and behaviour in North America were met with reproval, which also questioned their position as immigrants. After misfortunes in New Iceland, Canada, some people believed the Icelanders were simply a burden on Canadian society. Some sources show that they were at times described as a group of silly and simple-minded individuals, who would, however, have the prospect of climbing higher in the social hierarchy in North America. One example is Mary FitzGibbon's account of her travels around Manitoba and the Canadian northwest, published in 1880. After describing the clothing of Mennonites, whom she praised as "all thrifty and energetic" as well as "excellent settlers," this was her portrayal of the Icelanders: "The dress of the Icelander is somewhat similar, but they are more lethargic-looking. They have bright 'milk and roses' complexions, great opaque blue eyes, and a heavy gait that gives them an appearance of stupidity, which is not a true index of their character; they learn English rapidly, and are teachable servants, neat, clean, and careful, but have not constitutional strength to endure hard work, and when separated from their friends become lonely and dispirited" (FitzGibbon 1880, 57–58).

FitzGibbon also added that because of a smallpox epidemic that had broken out in the New Iceland area during the winter of 1876–77, the Icelandic migrants had only been "an expense to the Canadian government" (1880, 58). Some public officials in Canada were of the same opinion, demonstrating how identities of Icelandic immigrants were described as being all over the societal spectrum, from being ideal migrants to settle the prairies to encompassing a frail and weak group of people. Those who took the latter position expressed the idea that Icelanders had for centuries been isolated in the middle of the North Atlantic, far away from all nations of culture and prosperity, and therefore lost all their mental and physical strength (Eyford 2016, 40, 115, 189–190; see also Vilhelmsson 2018).

It was in this context—allegations in Iceland of leaving the home country during a critical moment, and insinuations in North America of being a burden on society—that the importance of cultural value and justification for the migration became a matter of significance for the Icelandic migrants. Writings in periodicals in the late 1880s shed light on the fact that their engagement was not simply their own initiative or a response to these aforementioned characterizations but also their reaction to public debates that had already taken place within the continent. This is evident when articles are scrutinized regarding the importance of the medieval figure of Leifur Eiríksson supposedly discovering the American continent. On that subject, the book by Marie A. Brown from 1887, *The Icelandic Discoverers of America; or, Honour to Whom Honour Is Due*, was influential, and Icelanders in America started collecting signatures for a proposal that recognized Leifur Eiríksson not only as the discoverer of the continent but also as a bearer of Icelandic nationality (Brown 1887; *Heimskringla,* 31 May 1888, 2; *Heimskringla,* 1 March 1888, 2).

It can be argued that during the years of 1888 and 1889, Icelandic migrants had started to use Icelandic nationalism to defend their cause regarding Leifur Eiríksson's nationality. Nonetheless, the Icelanders had now become active participants in the identity politics in North America. On that stage, Nordic people were often described as noble carriers of freedom, whereas Christopher Columbus was identified as a greedy bigot (Brown 1887, 34). The book

Icelandic Discoverers of America was only one of many that emphasized elevating the North as an ideology opposed to the South (Pálsdóttir 2006, 70–71). One of the most common themes within this discourse in an Icelandic context was the idea of settlement or *landnám*, which is closely related to the idea of discovery. In their historiography Icelandic migrants and their descendants emphasized that this notion of settlement was in their blood, even a part of their destiny. Early historical accounts from the first half of the twentieth century narrated almost every household man as a *landnámsmaður* 'a man of settlement'. In the late nineteenth century, the migration was justified with the means of courage, as appeared in *Heimskringla* on 27 December 1888, 2: "It requires absolutely as much bravery nowadays to leave all that is yours and migrate westwards to America as it did in the past to go from Norway those rather few miles over to Iceland."[11] Within this aura the necessity for Icelanders in North America to compose their own Book of Settlement was brought to migrants' attention, citing the medieval text of *Landnámabók* (Magnússon 1889, 3).

The late 1880s were without a doubt a critical point in the discourse regarding Icelanders in North America and in Iceland. Debates over whether the Icelandic emigrants were still a part of the Icelandic nation hardened as the number of emigrants increased. One of the most well-known flashpoints was the small book *Um Vesturheimsferðir* (On the emigration to the West) by the poet Benedikt Gröndal, which illuminated negative views towards those who had migrated there (Gröndal 1888).[12]

It was thus after extended debates about the worth and characteristics of Icelandic migrants in North America that the concept of *Vestur-Íslendingar* came about. It emerged during a period when uncertainty surrounded the status and desirability of Icelandic migrants in America. The uncertainty was also at play in Iceland. The concept was supposed to act as a connection amongst Icelanders in America, either as a specific group or as an extension of the Icelandic nation, while simultaneously it was utilized as a tool of separation from other cultural groups, namely Catholics. Therefore, *Vestur-Íslendingar* sprung out of both the tension concerning Icelandic nationality and debates relating to North American identity politics.

A SYMBOL TO SEPARATE AND UNIFY

The early historiography of Icelandic migrants in North America includes more concepts than just *Vestur-Íslendingar* that have the purpose of pinpointing a given cultural group in a certain location. These are words such as *Winnipeg-Íslendingar* 'Winnipeg-Icelanders' and *Ný-Íslendingar* 'New-Icelanders', pointing to two locations in Manitoba. Other names were given to the group of Icelanders in North America in several periodicals and newspapers in Iceland during the migration period, such as *Ameríku-Íslendingar* 'American-Icelanders', *Kanada-Íslendingar* 'Canada-Icelanders', and *Bandaríkja-Íslendingar* 'U.S.-Icelanders', but none of those gained the same foothold as part of the discourse on Icelanders in North America.

During the early years of the migration period, often framed around the years of 1870 to 1914, the migrants themselves commonly used terms such as *landar* 'fellow countrymen' in correspondence. After the debates of the late 1880s, however, and with the attestation of *Vestur-Íslendingar* on paper, more and more texts came out in which authors would compare the two separated groups: Icelanders in North America, and Icelanders in Iceland. The comparison often discussed economic affairs. Initially, debates about emigration centred on the question of whether people were financially better off by migrating than by staying in Iceland.

As stated before, the migration had been a hot topic since the beginning of the mass emigration. However, after a decade or two of continuous emigration, writings focused on topics other than financial matters. An extensive number of articles appeared in newspapers where authors tried to make a distinction between the two groups' characteristics and culture. Many of these articles named Icelanders who still lived in Iceland as *Austur-Íslendingar* or Icelanders of the East. One could look at these writings as an ongoing dialogue. The author and playwright Jóhann Magnús Bjarnason said, for example, in an article in April 1894 simply titled "Vestur-Íslendingar": "It is as if some coldness had materialized between them, so that sometimes it appears that the national connection, which is supposed to connect the two in the future, has already been disrupted" (Bjarnason 1894, 2).[13] Jóhann Magnús furthermore stated that *Vestur-Íslendingar* were unlike their brethren in a way that they were more liberal, happy, courageous, determined, and more practical than *Austur-Íslendingar*, "and not as hesitant and overall pessimistic" (Bjarnason 1894, 4).[14]

With this approach Bjarnason's article falls into line with earlier-mentioned criticism towards Iceland, which stated that the country was uninhabitable and that, by living there, people would turn into weaklings and milksops. The idea of *Vestur-Íslendingur* was already developing into what the renowned author Halldór Kiljan Laxness said later about the Icelandic-Canadian poet Stephan G. Stephansson, after Stephansson's death in 1927: "Stephan G. is the image of the strongest and the most noble in the character of the *Vestur-Íslendingur*, who has come here with the intention of overcoming difficulties and resistance, to do or die" (Laxness 1927, 4).[15]

The historiography on Icelandic migrants was for a long time clouded with this emphasis, especially the influential work *Saga Íslendinga í Vesturheimi* (The history of Icelanders in America) by Þorsteinn Þ. Þorsteinsson. The first volume narrates a history of hardship in Iceland from the settlement to the time of migration in the 1870s, with the migrants having no option but to leave the country (Þorsteinsson 1940). *Saga Íslendinga í Vesturheimi*—and other historical accounts about the Icelandic migrants at that time—followed historiographical trends that were common in the first half of the twentieth century in the portrayal of most European migrants in America. Many common images and tropes that appear in historical publications on *Vestur-Íslendingar* were also used in books about other nationalities. These figurative and metaphorical uses of words, narrative, and storytelling were substantial for what was credited as the pioneer spirit, which above all else depicted the migrants as groups of people ushering in civilization. Most settlements had accounts of the birth of the "first white child," the building of a school or church, and the leaders of the given community, whereby certain individuals were given the role of Moses leading the group out of the wilderness (Jackson 1919, 6; Jackson Walters 1926; Þorsteinsson 1935, 84). A common theme of the narration of the many challenges that the pioneers faced was the writers' emphasis that during the hardest times the emigrants always thought warmly of the old country (Þorsteinsson 1940, 253).

As the years passed the concept of *Vestur-Íslendingar* encompassed increasing contention as to whether or how the Icelandic migrants were separated from the Icelandic nation. On one hand was the idea that *Vestur-Íslendingar* were an extension of the Icelandic nation: *Vestur-* and *Austur-Íslendingar* would have to work closely on matters for the betterment of the whole nation. Such subjects included reforms to church affairs in Iceland and the founding of an Icelandic educational institution in North America at the end of the nineteenth century (*Lögberg,* 12 March 1890, 4; Pjetursson 1891, 117–19). On the other hand, there was the impression that *Vestur-Íslendingar* had started to form their own distinct characteristics as a group, and that they were furthermore developing into something bigger than Icelanders.

FIGURE 2.1. Icelandic immigrants at a picnic in River Park, Winnipeg, 1905. (Nelson Gerrard/ Eyrarbakki Icelandic Heritage Centre Photo Archive)

At a celebration of Icelanders in America in 1891, the Reverend Friðrik J. Bergmann considered this matter by saying: "We are named something more than we were before. But one who is named something more, also must become something more. We *Vestur-Íslendingar* must remember that we are something more than just Icelanders. Our name compels us to be something more than our brethren across the ocean" (1891, 3).[16] The immigration agent Baldwin L. Baldwinson was of the same opinion in a speech in August 1894: "It seems to me that *Vestur-Íslendingar* are growing; it appears to me that our young females are more or less bigger than their mothers, which most certainly has transpired, for they have better amenities than their mothers had in Iceland" (Baldwinson 1894, 2).[17]

At the beginning of the twentieth century, public discussions in Iceland about *Vestur-Íslendingar* were more often performed by individuals who had first-hand experience from North America and had dwelled for a few years on the continent and were eager to give "reliable" news of the group. Several lectures were held over the next years and decades on the subject, and a number of books were published. The depictions of *Vestur-Íslendingar* in those books and lectures were ambivalent: either *Vestur-Íslendingar* were filled with deep, genuine love for Iceland or they weren't Icelanders by nature. Those in the latter category spoke distorted Icelandic, and in terms of their ethics and ideology, they had been transformed into North Americans. Once again, the term *Vestur-Íslendingar* not only referred to Icelandic origin but also caried with it the image of North America. Among the oldest and most notable of these publications were writings by the minister and poet Matthías Jochumsson and by Valtýr Guðmundsson, the historian, editor, and later politician. Both had travelled to North America for another purpose than "to evaluate" *Vestur-Íslendingar*, but both encouraged that some sort of relationship between the community and Iceland be maintained (Jochumsson 1893, 52; Guðmundsson 1897, 61).

In 1895 the writer Einar Hjörleifsson Kvaran (see Guðrún Björk Guðsteinsdóttir, this volume) gave a lecture, which probably was amongst the first of its kind in Iceland, in which he gave his account of *Vestur-Íslendingar* as a group. Einar faced the question that many Icelanders were anxious to have answered: Had the situation for the Icelandic migrants become better or worse by moving to America? Kvaran himself had lived in Winnipeg for a few years. He had been the editor of *Heimskringla*, and in his printed version of the presentation he avoided comparing Icelanders, whether they were in Iceland or North America. He did, however, state that *Vestur-Íslendingar* had experienced some progress and new thought by moving to the West. They were, as he said, "confident, better-looking men for the most part, in all their outer appearance,"[18] which would not have happened had they stayed in Iceland. Kvaran also considered them more liberal, whilst at the same time responsible and more sociable than before. *Vestur-Íslendingar* had also obtained some education and they were, in his opinion, avid readers. Kvaran's conclusion was in stark contrast with debates amongst *Vestur-Íslendingar* themselves during the 1880s: he stated that they were not spread all over the continent and that their society would not be dissolved at all. On the contrary *Vestur-Íslendingar* were quite solid and a proper society, where the church "is one of the strongest guards for their nationality" (Kvaran 1895, 8, 24, 27).[19] In a lecture given by Páll Bergsson in 1908, one can find similar themes; Bergsson states that *Vestur-Íslendingar* had achieved respect in North America and their own ideology had completely changed. They wouldn't look at themselves anymore as godforsaken losers, and, Bergsson continued, "They know the [Icelandic] language, most of them think warmly about their motherland, and they've learned to work in one of the most progressive countries when it comes to vocational matters" (Bergsson 1908, 18, 21).[20]

An opposite view was taken in the book *Vestan um haf* (1916) by Rev. Magnús Jónsson, who later became a professor in theology at the University of Iceland. The Reverend Jónsson claimed it to be a wrong usage of a word to call the Icelandic migrants *Vestur-Íslendingar*. In his opinion, their desire for change had caused them to alter their appearance and behaviour, for example with their names. Some of the changes should not be considered negative, however, because in some places Icelandic names were being kept in use. His positive remarks were that *Vestur-Íslendingar* would be quite generous and gain quite a lot from being hard workers. Overall, however, Rev. Jónsson believed that they would emulate North Americans far too often, and he also claimed they made bad coffee (Jónsson 1916, 28–41). Jónsson was unequivocal in his final remarks: he thought it would be impossible to believe that Icelanders had any future as Icelanders, should they continue to live in North America. Such a belief would be "as much of a wonder as to think that a small clear river would keep its clarity all the way from the mountains and into the ocean, after it had already gotten into a big muddle of glacial water" (Jónsson 1916, 110).[21] As reflected in his words, images of Icelanders and North America were often narrated according to loaded ideas of Icelandic nationality as being pure and unspoiled, in contrast to which North America was suggested to be a mucky and unpleasant puddle.

BETWEEN TWO WORLDS

The usage of the concept *Vestur-Íslendingar* was often influenced by an understanding of the image of *America* in Iceland. Therefore, accounts changed according to the ever-fluid image of North America. It was not always viewed as the continent of freedom and prosperity but increasingly as the home of capitalism and mass industrialization as the twentieth century began. The writer Jóhannes Birkiland followed this line with his book *Ameríka í ljósi sannleikans* (America in light of the truth): "Some of the people who have moved to America have been garbage, futile men and mischief-makers of the Icelandic nation. It is therefore clear that for good and noble men, torture and termination awaits in America" (Birkiland 1928, 22).[22] One could argue that these views were a return to the claims in the 1880s, during which period those who emigrated to North America were met with antagonism. The reason was, however, completely different from that expressed by the author who went by the pseudonym Húnvetningur about fifty years prior, namely, the lack of consistency and uniformity in religion and nationality. According to Birkiland most "leading Vestur- 'Íslendingar'... [were] capitalistic, submissive, cheap, and boastful snobs, numbskulls, and people of arrogance" (Birkiland 1928, 22).[23] *Vestur-Íslendingar* would, in other words, be beyond saving, since America was considered contaminated and they had already joined undesirable forces by migrating there.

During the years of the Second World War, similar ideas appeared in newspapers, shedding light on the growing tension between the East and the West in world politics. *Mjölnir*, the periodical of the Socialist Association of Siglufjörður, a small fishing village in the north of Iceland, reported that Sigfús Halldórs frá Höfnum, an Icelander who had lived in North America for a long time, was now giving lectures on the Icelandic National Radio about North American society. The editors of *Mjölnir* sarcastically called Sigfús Halldórs "neutral" but claimed that Icelanders who had lived for too long in America were a certain kind of "figures" or types of persons. The periodical even claimed that several comic stories were circulating of these people (*Mjölnir* [12 April 1940], 3).

These ideas did not, however, gain much ground and were not commonly expressed. With the founding in 1919 of Þjóðræknisfélag Íslendinga í Vesturheimi, the predecessor of today's Icelandic National League (INL), as well as the planned trip by hundreds of *Vestur-Íslendingar* to Iceland's parliamentary festival of 1930, the image of their "flawless love" for the old country became a dominant one. Þjóðræknisfélag Íslendinga í Vesturheimi first and foremost emphasized national unity amongst its members, while at the same time it hid any class difference and disputes amongst *Vestur-Íslendingar* (McIntosh 2004, 376–89). In its first years the association's journal published one article after another with the recurring motif that Icelandic migrants had managed to protect all the best values of Icelandic culture and promulgated them in America (Pétursson 1919–1926; Beck 1926; Matthíasson 1921). As the association grew, it became one of the leading contacts for cultural connections between Iceland and North America. Furthermore, what had been considered negative in the eyes of *Vestur-Íslendingar* in the early era of migration was now considered positive: the Icelandic migrants were spread over the continent (Sigurðsson 1929, 190–92). Such a wide geographical distribution would promote even further the stature of *Vestur-Íslendingar* as active participants in the society of the West.

The parliamentary celebrations in Iceland in 1930 can be seen as a moment of reconciliation of sorts, where the quarrels of the emigration era were for the most part put to rest, as can be seen in official speeches on that occasion (Jónsson 1943, 248–52). Subsequently the usages of the term *Vestur-Íslendingar* became more simplified and gained a stronger foothold in Iceland.

Over the next few decades, cultural ideas in Iceland as regards to *Vestur-Íslendingar* became somewhat normalized, with interference by the Icelandic authorities. In 1943 discussions started at the Icelandic parliament to support the two Icelandic newspapers in North America, *Lögberg* and *Heimskringla* (*Alþingistíðindi* 1942–1943, C, 3346–52), and they were later supported annually. The Icelandic authorities also established committees whose purpose was to start or maintain cultural relationships with Icelandic communities in North America (ÞÍ. Forsætisráðuneyti Íslands, B–275, 2). It was during the postwar period that using the term *Vestur-Íslendingar* in Iceland became normalized, and the concept was largely removed from the squabbles and differences of opinions from which it initially originated.

In North America the development was quite different from in Iceland, although there was also some kind of unofficial usage of the term there. The idea of being *Icelandic* in North America was based on a different knowledge, as the Icelandic language was less and less used as an everyday language by the community. The understanding of a homeland changed: Canada and the U.S. had taken the role for most people of a homeland, and being *Icelandic* now shifted to the thought of heritage in North American society. In Canada, for example, the term *Vestur-Íslendingar* has been taken over by the term *Icelandic Canadian*. There are certainly active cultural relations between the Icelandic community in North America and Iceland, but the understanding of terminology has changed rapidly and is not based as much (at least from the perspective of North American identities) on Icelandic nationality.

FINAL REMARKS

The idea of being *Vestur-Íslendingur* has changed from being an ignominy for one who leaves their motherland, and therefore their nationality and customs, to an idea of someone being an outside guardian of the old country, bearing unconditional love towards it. These two contrasting ideas have for a long time been marked by images of the purity of Icelandic nationality and the immorality of North America. The line between the two is often thin or even porous: a shift from positive to negative narration can easily occur based on thoughts of Iceland being inhabitable while America is the land of freedom and prosperity. Between these poles are the shifting evaluations of the *Vestur-Íslendingur*, who is either a pioneer and a hard-working individual or a strange figure with no roots who exaggerates everything and tells big-fish stories of his experiences and America.

The 1983 Icelandic film *Nýtt líf* (A new life) includes a scene at a dance in the Westman Islands that encompasses this shift in many ways. One of the movie's protagonists, Þór, starts talking to a few of the locals from the Islands, who mistake the new arrival for an American. The locals are initially unhappy with his presence and tell him that if he's "some devil from the base"[24]—meaning the controversial U.S. Air Base at Keflavík in Iceland—then he'll be beaten up. Þór reacts and says—in broken Icelandic—that he is a *Vestur-Íslendingur*. The mood changes immediately and the locals become very interested and happy to hear that Þór—who tells them that his name is John Reagan—has come to Iceland to "work in a fish factory and drink [the Icelandic schnapps] *brennivín* with his grandmother."[25] From there on the scene shows the status of the *Vestur-Íslendingur* as both being a part of the group, chugging alcohol and throwing in a few Icelandic words that all cheer the locals, and appearing as an out-of-this-world figure coming from the big land of America. The locals are amazed when "John" tells them that he is closely related to President Reagan.

The scene in which Þór assumes the role of John Reagan is of no great importance for the narrative of the movie, but it sheds light on how the cultural term of *Vestur-Íslendingar* could operate about 100 years after its first appearance in public debate. At the same time the scene shows an interesting comparison with American soldiers in Iceland. Unlike (most) American soldiers in Iceland, the *Vestur-Íslendingur* can use words and ideas that connect people via the historical past of the grandmother. The scene also indicates how *Vestur-Íslendingar* has been used in satire and irony in Iceland.

The title of this article asks the question, "What is it to be a *Vestur-Íslendingur*?" Cultural identities such as *Vestur-Íslendingar* are never carved into stone; on the contrary they are a fragile matter. They are commonly applied when uncertainty surrounds the subject or when necessity arises for someone to be identified as *Vestur-Íslendingur*, and still more when one feels a need to separate themselves from a given group. The question should perhaps be: "When is one a *Vestur-Íslendingur*?" As a concept the word *Vestur-Íslendingur* has certainly developed from an idea that underlines struggles and disagreement to a tag for people and groups, either to separate or unify. It may appear to us as a part of a long and unbroken chain, but sources suggest a long-standing debate regarding its meaning. Although there is not much debate about it in modern society, all discussions regarding the meaning of being Icelandic in North America can potentially lead to uncertainty, and therefore feud and animosity.

To answer the above question, one must first address another question: "In what context does one act as a *Vestur-Íslendingur*?" At the end of the nineteenth century and during the first half of the twentieth century, the idea was surrounded by images of Icelandic nationality and the image of America. These matters were not ones people agreed upon, but from the mid-twentieth century one could say that the term has been disconnected from the debates from which it initially sprung, while it has simultaneously functioned with a new meaning as a key for people to unlock understanding of cultural relations.

NOTES

1 In this chapter the concept of Vestur-Íslendingar (sing. Vestur-Íslendingur) will be consistently written in Icelandic, because this chapter argues that in its direct translation—into Western Icelanders—the meaning of the concept is lost, and neither would a translation fully convey how the concept has been utilized.

2 "Skyldi Manitoba ekki eiga betur saman við Dakota en hið rammkoþólska [*sic*] Quebec?"

3 "Það sem guð hefur samtengt, á maðurinn ekki að skilja að… og við Vestur-Íslendingar að minnsta kosti ættum að segja: Hafi þeir skömm fyrir!"

4 "Bæði í austur og vestur: heim til Íslands og heim til Winnipeg."

5 "Þótt þúsundir kílómetra, meira en heil öld og margar kynslóðir skilji þá frá ættjörðinni… [bera] Vestur-Íslendingar . . . í brjósti fölskvalausa ást til Íslands."

6 "lengi verið athvarf alls óþjóðalýðs frá Norðurálfu og annarstaðar að." The author was identified by the pseudonym Húnvetningur (a person in or from Húnavatnssýsla in northwest Iceland), but Úlfar Bragason has shown that the writer was actually Sigurður Gunnarsson (1812–1878), a Lutheran minister at Hallormsstaður in East Iceland, and a member of Iceland's parliament. See Úlfar Bragason (2017, 70–72).

7 "Það er dagsanna, að mechanisk öfl verða að koma oss til liðs, í stað hinna lötu vinnumanna vorra, er slæpast nú brottu til Ameríku."

8 "Ég elska þig lítið eða alls ekki neitt / þú íslenzka brennisteins-'pæla.'"

9 "Ósamlyndi meðal íslenskra manna [er] alstaðar erlendis orðlagt."

10 The author was Rev. Bjarni Sveinsson, a priest in his mid-sixties, living at Stafafell in southeast Iceland, who never once stood upon North American soil. See Lbs. 3984 4to, Rannveig Briem.

11 "Það útheimtir öldungis eins mikinn kjark nú að yfirgefa alla sína og flytja vestur til Ameríku, eins og forðum að flytja úr Noregi svo tiltölulega fáar mílur til Íslands."

12 The debates after the publications have been covered extensively by many sources. See, for example, Bragason (2017, 87).

13 "Það er eins og ofurlítill kali hafi átt sjer stað með köflum, milli þeirra, svo stundum hefur virzt sem þjóðernis-sambandið, er átt hefði að tengja þá saman um ókomnar aldir, væri þá og þegar slitið."

14 "Og ekki eins hikandi og upplitsdaufir yfir höfuð."

15 "Þannig er Stephan G. ímynd hins sterkasta og göfugasta í fari Vestur-Íslendingsins sem hingað er kominn með þeim ásetningi að sigra erfiðleika og andspyrnu, duga eða drepast."

16 "Vjer heitum meira en vjer hjetum áður. En sá, sem heitir meira, verður líka að vera eitthvað meira. Við Vestur-Íslendingar verðum að muna eptir því, að vera eitthvað meira en eintómir Íslendingar. Nafnið skyldar oss til að vera eitthvað meira en bræður vorir fyrir handan hafið."

17 "Mér sýnist ekki betur en að Vestur-Íslendingar séu að stækka; mér sýnist vort unga kvenfólk vera upp og ofan stærra en mæður þeirra, sem kemur sjálfsagt til af því, að þær hafa hér betri aðbúð, heldur en mæður þeirra höfðu á Íslandi."

18 "Mannborlegri, myndarlegri menn yfirleitt í allri sinni ytri framkomu."

19 "Einn öflugasti vörðurinn fyrir þjóðerni þeirra."

20 "Þeir kunna málið, bera flestir hlýjar tilfinningar í brjósti til fósturjarðarinnar, og hafa lært að vinna í því landi, sem einna lengst er á veg komið í öllu verklegu."

21 "Jafnmikil firn eins og að hugsa sjer, að lítill, tær bergvatnslækur hjeldi sjer alla leið ofan af fjöllum og út í sjó, eftir að hann er runninn út í stóra jökulvatns móðu."

22 "Sumt af því fólki, sem hefir flutt búferlum til Ameríku, hefir verið rusl, úrhrak og illþýði íslenzku þjóðarinnar. Það er því augljóst, að góðra og göfugra manna bíður kvöl og tortíming í Ameríku."

23 "Leiðandi Vestur-'Íslendingar'... auðvaldssinnaðir, þrællundaðir, nískir, og hégómagjarnir uppskafningar, angurgapar og stórbokkar."

24 "Einhver djöfull af vellinum."

25 "Að vinna í frystihúsi og drekka brennivín með ömmu sinni."

REFERENCES

Primary Sources

Lbs = Landsbókasafn Íslands [National and university library of Iceland].

Lbs 150 NF. Letter Collection of Torfi Bjarnason in Ólafsdalur.

Lbs 3984 4to. Letter Collection of Torfhildur Hólm.

ÞÍ. = Þjóðskjalasafn Íslands [National archives of Iceland].

Forsætisráðuneytið [Records of the Prime Minister's Office]. 1989–037. B–275, 2. Vestur-íslensk nefnd [Western-Icelandic committee].

Gunnlaugsson, Sigmundur Davíð. 2013. Prime Minister's Address at Austurvöllur on 17 June 2013. Accessed 31 August 2016. http://www.forsaetisraduneyti.is/radherra/raedur-greinar-sdg/nr/7625.

Nýtt líf [A new life]. 1983. A film directed by Þráinn Bertelsson. Reykjavík.

Secondary Sources

Alþingistíðindi [Records of the Icelandic parliament]. 1893–1943.

Baldwinson, Baldwin L. 1894. "Íslendingar í Vesturheimi" [Icelanders in America]. *Heimskringla*, 4 August, 2–3.

Bauman, Zygmunt. 2004. *Identity: Conversations with Benedetto Vecchi*. Cambridge: Polity Press.

Beck, Richard. 1926. "Hlutdeild Íslands í heimsbókmenntunum" [Iceland's contribution to world literature]. *Tímarit Þjóðræknisfélags Íslendinga* 8: 61–69.

Bergmann, Friðrik J. 1891. "Minni Vestur-Íslendinga" [A toast to the Western-Icelanders]. *Lögberg*, 1 July, 3.

Bergsson, Páll. 1908. *Ísland og Ameríka. Fyrirlestur fluttur í Reykjavík 5. febrúar 1908* [Iceland and America. A lecture given in Reykjavík 5 February 1908]. Reykjavík.

Birkiland, Jóhannes. 1928. *Ameríka í ljósi sannleikans* [America in the light of the truth]. 2nd ed. Reykjavík: n.p.

Bjarnason, Jóhann Magnús. 1894. "Vestur-Íslendingar." *Landneminn* 28: 2–4.

Bjarnason, Jón. 1889. "Ferðabrjef til ritstjóra Lögbergs" [A travel letter to *Lögberg*'s editor]. *Lögberg*, 4 September, 3.

Bragason, Úlfar. 2017. *Frelsi, menning, framför: Um bréf og greinar Jóns Halldórssonar* [Freedom, culture, progress: On letters and articles by Jón Halldórsson]. Reykjavík: Háskólaútgáfan.

Brown, Marie A. 1887. *The Icelandic Discoverers of America; Or, Honour to Whom Honour Is Due*. London: Marie A. Brown.

Eyford, Ryan. 2016. *White Settler Reserve: New Iceland and the Colonization of the Canadian West*. Vancouver: University of British Columbia Press.

FitzGibbon, Mary. 1880. *A Trip to Manitoba; Or, Roughing It on the Line*. Toronto: Rose-Belford Publishing Company.

Gröndal, Benedikt. 1888. *Um Vesturheimsferðir* [On the emigration to the West]. Reykjavík: Ísafoldarprentsmiðja.

Guðmundsson, Valtýr. 1897. "Frá Vesturheimi" [From America]. *Eimreiðin* 3 (1): 53–74.

Hall, Stuart. 1996. "Introduction. Who Needs 'Identity'?" In *Questions of Cultural Identity*, 1–17. London: Sage Publications.

Húnvetningur. 1874. "Um Ameriku ferðir" [Regarding migration to America]. *Norðanfari*, 5 May, 54.

Jackson, Þorleifur Jóakimsson. 1919. *Brot af landnámssögu Nýja Íslands* [A part of the settlement history of New Iceland]. Winnipeg: Prentsmiðja Columbia Press.

Jackson Walters, Thorstina. 1926. *Saga Íslendinga í Norður-Dakota* [The history of Icelanders in North Dakota]. Winnipeg: City Printing and Publishing.

Jochumsson, Matthías. 1893. *Chicago-för mín 1893* [My trip to Chicago in 1893]. Akureyri: Prentsmiðja Björns Jónssonar.

Jónsson, Magnús. 1916. *Vestan um haf. Smávegis um Ameríku og landa vestra* [From the West. A little bit about America and Icelanders there]. Reykjavík: Prentsmiðjan Rún.

———. 1943. *Alþingishátíðin 1930* [The Icelandic parliamentary celebrations in 1930]. Reykjavík: Leiftur.

Kvaran, Einar H. 1895. "Vestur-Íslendingar. Fyrirlestur fluttur í Reykjavík 2. nóvember 1895" [Vestur-Íslendingar. A lecture given in Reykjavík 2 November 1895]. Reykjavík: Bókaverzlun Sigfúsar Eymundssonar.

Laxness, Halldór Kiljan. 1927. "Landneminn mikli" [The great settler]. *Lögberg*, 8 September, 4–5.

McIntosh, Andrea. 2004. "In Plain Sight. The Development of Western Icelandic Ethnicity and Class Division 1910–1920." PhD diss., University of Manitoba.

Magnússon, Guðlaugur. 1889. "Um sögu Íslendinga í Vesturheimi" [On the history of Icelanders in America]. *Lögberg,* 27 February, 3.

Matthíasson, Steingrímur. 1921. "Viðhald þjóðernis Íslendinga í Vesturheimi" [Maintaining Icelandic nationality in America]. *Tímarit Þjóðræknisfélags Íslendinga* 3: 83–87.

Pálsdóttir, Sigrún. 2006. "*Northern Antiquities* og dularfulli ritstjórinn Blackwell" [Northern antiquities and the mysterious editor Blackwell]. *Saga* 44 (1): 65–80.

Pétursson, Rögnvaldur. 1919–1926. "Þjóðræknissamtök meðal Íslendinga í Vesturheimi" [Patriotic organizations among Icelanders in America]. *Tímarit Þjóðræknisfélags Íslendinga* 1–4, 6, and 8.

Pjetursson, Hafsteinn. 1891. "Kirkjan á Íslandi" [The church in Iceland]. *Aldamót* 1: 117–44.

Sigurðsson, Jónas A. 1929. "Vestur-Íslendingar." *Tímarit Þjóðræknisfélags Íslendinga* 11: 186–98.

Steingrímsson, Jón. 1888. *Fréttir frá Íslandi.* Reykjavík: Prentsmiðja Einars Þórðarsonar.

Vilhelmsson, Vilhelm. 2018. "Þjóðerni, hagsmunir og hugsjónir í verkalýðshreyfingu Íslendinga í Winnipeg 1890–1900" [Nationality, interests, and ideologies in the Icelandic labour movement in Winnipeg 1890–1900]. In *Sigurtunga: Vesturíslenskt mál og menning*, edited by Birna Arnbjörnsdóttir, Höskuldur Thráinsson, and Úlfar Bragason, 87–103. Reykjavík: Háskólaútgáfan.

Þorsteinsson, Þorsteinn Þ. 1935. *Vestmenn. Útvarpserindi um landnám Íslendinga í Vesturheimi* [Men of the West. A radio presentation about the Icelandic settlements in America]. Reykjavík.

———. 1940. *Saga Íslendinga í Vesturheimi* [The history of Icelanders in America]. Vol. 1. Reykjavík: Þjóðræknisfélag Íslendinga í Vesturheimi.

CHAPTER 3

Acculturation on Their Own Terms: The Social Networks of Political Radicals among Icelandic Immigrants in Canada in the Early Twentieth Century

VILHELM VILHELMSSON

AN OBSCURE BOOK of poetry in Icelandic published in Winnipeg in 1905 by Sigfús B. Benedictsson includes three back-to-back poems, which all discuss Canada as seen through his immigrant eyes. The first, "Minni Canada" (A toast to Canada), praises Canada as a sanctuary for migrants, a land of freedom where diverse nations gather to become one. The second, "Canada," and third, "Canada eins og sumir sjá það" (Canada as some see it), however, describe it as a land of displacement, discrimination, and exploitation, tricking poor migrant labourers into its bosom only to line the pockets of the country's elite and leaving immigrants "out to dry," marginalized, powerless, and penniless in their adopted home (Benedictsson 1905, 87–90).

Sigfús, husband of the well-known feminist pioneer Margrét J. Benedictsson (Sangster 2018, 86–89), had emigrated from Iceland to Canada in 1888 when he was twenty-three years old. As an outspoken atheist, anarchist, and feminist, he was infamous in the Icelandic immigrant community in Manitoba around the turn of the twentieth century for his radical views and contentious discourse and for being constantly at odds with his Icelandic peers (Vilhelmsson 2013).

Yet, his aforementioned poems are emblematic for the views of a small but vocal group within the Icelandic community in the early 1900s that subscribed to a variety of radical ideologies such as feminism, socialism, anarchism, freethought, atheism, and Unitarianism, and actively promoted such ideas within the community.[1] Through periodicals such as *Freyja*, *Baldur*, and *Dagskrá II,* and debating societies such as Menningarfélagið (The culture society) and Hagyrðingafélagið (The verse poetry society), radicals created for themselves a space where they could simultaneously criticize their adopted home and its social and cultural flaws and negotiate their acculturation to Canadian society in their own language and on their own terms. This led to conflicts within the Icelandic immigrant community, whose leadership had for decades promoted what historian Laurie K. Bertram describes as "an image of the community as able and willing to assimilate" to Canadian society in an uncritical manner, actively encouraging the adoption of the English language and espousing the ideas, culture, and values of British liberalism, both of which the Anglo-Canadian elite strongly emphasized as desirable traits for immigrants (Bertram 2019, 43; Korneski 2007).

By the first decade of the twentieth century, Icelanders were indeed commonly praised by the Anglo-Canadian elite as model immigrants. In 1901 the Manitoba provincial government introduced a literacy test that was intended to deny the franchise to recent immigrants of "foreign" origin. Historians Royden Loewen and Gerald Friesen indicate that exempt from this rule were those who could read selected chapters from the Manitoba Act in "English, French, German, Icelandic or any Scandinavian language" (Loewen and Friesen 2009, 49). The addition of the Icelandic language to this list is a strong indication that by then Icelanders had already achieved the status of "desirable" immigrants, something that had previously been cast in doubt by some Anglo-Canadians following the difficult experience of the formative years of the Icelandic settlement in the 1870s and 1880s (Eyford 2016; Bertram 2018). By the early 1900s prominent journalists such as George Chipman, however, described Icelanders as having "taken the foremost place among the adopted people" of Canada (Chipman 1909, 412) and praised their "phenomenal" success in adopting Canadian customs and the English language (Scott 1914, 532). Although still deemed "foreigners," the Icelanders were described in the *Manitoba Free Press* in 1912 as an "illustration par excellence of how a people of ambition and industry can master difficulties, triumph over prejudice, and attain their desired place in the commercial, the political, the intellectual and the social life of a hustling and growing city in a strange land" (*Manitoba Free Press,* 16 November 1912, 1).

Viewed from within the Icelandic ethnic community itself, however, the process of acculturation was contentious and divisive in the early decades of the twentieth century, and recent historical studies have described it as "problematic" (see, for example, Bertram 2019, 110). Indeed, the related issues of ethnic identity and patriotic allegiance were central, though sometimes only implicitly, to many of the well-documented divisions and debates on religion, politics, education, and other affairs that characterized the Icelandic community in North America in the late nineteenth and early twentieth centuries (McIntosh 2004; Heiðarsson 1999; Matthiasson 1979). The radicals discussed in this article, many of whom were active participants in such debates, were in many regards at odds with their ethnic compatriots while also not fully integrated into Anglo-Canadian society. As a result they created their own associations and networks that encapsulated both their political world view and their ethnic identity. As historians Gerald Friesen and Royden Loewen have emphasized, associations such as religious organizations and secular clubs provided "the very tools by which the immigrant gained entry into the wider community" and allowed them to integrate into their adopted society while retaining their own sense of identity (Loewen and Friesen 2009, 14). However, as historian Per Nordahl has argued, social networks were often a matter of contention within immigrant communities, with smaller groups forming their own autonomous "havens" operating to the side of other more mainstream networks, reflecting the heterogeneous nature of immigrant groups. These havens were in turn interlinked, connecting different social and ethnic groups and thereby serving as mediators of ideas, knowledge, and experiences (Nordahl 1994).

This chapter presents three types of networks that radicals among Icelanders in Manitoba either developed or participated in around the turn of the twentieth century, which became vehicles for acculturation through radical social and political criticism and debate. These networks were periodicals that focused on radical issues or became platforms for discussions about them, cultural associations that functioned as open spaces for discussion and dissemination of critical and subversive ideas, and the participation in Anglo-Canadian-dominated reform politics that correlated with the ideas most prominent within this group. This type of associational life helped the radicals within the Icelandic community to navigate the complexities of North American society and culture in a turbulent era and find their place within it.

JOURNALS

In the period from 1898 to 1911, Icelanders in Manitoba published at least six newspapers and journals that can be termed "radical" publications.[2] Sigfús and Margrét Benedictsson bought a used printing press in 1898 and began publishing the feminist journal *Freyja* (1898 to 1911), first in Selkirk, Manitoba, and later in Winnipeg, Manitoba. It was apparently the only women's suffrage magazine published in Canada in this period (Crippen 2016). Sigfús became a prolific printer, publishing three serial publications in the next decade—the newspapers *Selkirkingur* (1900 to 1901) and *Tuttugasta öldin* (1909 to 1911), and the yearly *Maple Leaf Almanac* (1900 to 1905)—as well as some books and pamphlets in addition to the monthly *Freyja*. A group of men connected to the Icelandic socialist club in Winnipeg (Jafnaðarmannafélag Íslendinga í Winnipeg) published the journal *Dagskrá II* (1901 to 1903) and some pamphlets, and in Gimli, Manitoba, the weekly magazine *Baldur* (1903 to 1910) became a forum for the discussion and dissemination of radical ideas.

Most of these publications printed mission statements describing them as politically independent publications. "*Baldur* will not be a political paper," the editors declared on the front page of the first issue but rather would encourage readers to "think independently" (*Baldur* [12 January 1903]: 1), while the biweekly newspaper *Tuttugasta öldin* declared that it had no specific agenda but would address issues that "aim for human improvement and culture" (*Tuttugasta öldin,* 26 March 1909, 2).[3] Yet, they quickly became vehicles for discussion on radical politics and proliferation of radical ideas, reflecting the primary interests of the editors and publishers. The first several volumes of *Freyja* focused extensively on women's rights, not least on criticism of marriage as an institution and the restrictive Canadian divorce legislation, as well as printing many articles and shorter pieces on freethought, labour struggles, political trials and censorship, temperance, and child and animal welfare. *Baldur* and *Dagskrá II*, in turn, criticized the economic logic and social impact of unbridled capitalism and the control that financial trusts had over politics and society, promoting instead a socialism based on Christian moral values and egalitarianism (Vilhelmsson 2011). The editors of *Baldur* in particular lamented how capitalism led, in their minds, to an increasing urbanization and the subsequent human disassociation from nature and the moral restraint that they believed rural life imposed. *Dagskrá II* and *Baldur* also agitated strongly for democratic reform, advocating for "direct legislation" through referendums and for social reform issues such as temperance (see, for example, *Baldur* [22 and 29 August 1906]: 2–3; *Dagskrá II* [8 May 1902]: 1). Sigfús, on the other hand, published anarchist tracts, articles critical of religion and mainstream politics, opinion pieces on social and moral reform, and scathingly sarcastic and occasionally vitriolic contributions to current issues within the Icelandic community in all his publications (Vilhelmsson 2011, 53–61).

With the exception of *Freyja*, these publications have rarely been scrutinized by scholars.[4] When they are analyzed together, as opposed to individually and separately, it becomes immediately apparent, however, that they represent a network of radically minded Icelanders in conversation about shared ideals, concerns, and issues. Recurring themes include criticism of capitalism on moral grounds (that is, that excessive accumulation of wealth and an economy based on competition are considered morally wrong and the main causes of various social problems that would be solved by adopting socialism in some form), and the championing of political and social equality and the elimination of gender- or class-based privilege. Issues such as suffrage and marriage-law reform, direct democracy, and cooperative economics, and a focus on general moral reform issues such as animal welfare, pacifism, and temperance are prominent in all of them (Vilhelmsson 2012). These periodicals also share a mutual discontent with the uncritical attitude adopted by the Icelandic community leadership in Manitoba towards North American society and its many injustices. The editors of *Baldur*, for example, dedicated a special column, called "Hrukkur" (Creases), to critical articles about North American society since "other editors"—referring to the major Icelandic newspapers in Canada, *Lögberg* and *Heimskringla*—refrained from such topics in their publications (*Baldur* [1 June 1903]: 2).

Although most of the issues that occupied the pages of these papers corresponded with many of the major concerns of radicals and reformers in Canada at the time (McKay 2008; Dewalt 1985), the approach adopted by these Icelandic immigrants, and the causes and networks they aligned with, situate at least some of them in the more radical camp of social politics at the turn of the twentieth century. Thus, the Benedictssons were not only suffragists and women's rights advocates but also proponents of free love and sexual liberation, anarchism, and social revolution (Vilhelmsson 2011). Tracing the origin of translated works in their publications reveals their connection to an extensive underground network distributing radical material of various sorts. Table 3.1 lists the original place of publication of all non-fiction writing that appeared in translation in the publications of Sigfús and Margrét Benedictsson. Out of the nineteen named journals and magazines, nearly one-third (six in total) were anarchist and free-love publications that circulated primarily through underground channels and relied on subscriptions and donations for survival, as most bookshops and newsstands refused to carry them to avoid trouble with the authorities (Passet 2003).

In particular, Sigfús and Margrét were connected to the journal *Lucifer, the Light-Bearer*, an anarchist free-love paper published out of Kansas by Moses Harman and his daughter Lillian. In addition to translating material from *Lucifer* for their own publications, the Benedictssons also distributed copies of the journal among Icelanders and wrote several letters to the editors offering support when Moses was incarcerated for his writings, voicing their support for their cause. Sigfús was also a distributor of the anarchist firebrand Emma Goldman's journal *Mother Earth* for a short while and regularly advertised anarchist and free-love literature for sale (Vilhelmsson 2011; Eyford 2007; Passet 2003).

The journal *Baldur*, based in Gimli, was part of a similar network associated with the American socialist magazine *Appeal to Reason*, the most widely read socialist magazine in North America in the early 1900s. The

PUBLICATION NAME	TOTAL NO. OF TRANSLATIONS
Discontent	1
Fair Play	1
Foundation Principles	1
Frank Leslie's Magazine	3
Free Society	2
Free Thought Magazine	2
Jus Suffragii	1
Ladies' Home Journal	1
Liberal Review	7
Lucifer, the Light-Bearer	14
Mother Earth	1
Our Dumb Animals	4
Review of Reviews	18
Scientific American	6
The Outlook	2
The Voice	2
The Woman's Journal	5
Woman's Home Companion	1
Women's Standard	2
Other	45
Unknown	63

TABLE 3.1. Origin of translated material in publications by the Benedictssons.

NOTE: This table lists only non-fiction translations (thus excluding poetry, short stories, jokes, and other such material) that were published in *Freyja*, *Selkirkingur*, *Tuttugasta öldin*, *Maple Leaf Almanac*, and *Freyr*. The "other" category includes a variety of publications such as the *Manitoba Free Press* and the *Winnipeg Tribune*, as well as newspapers from other major cities in North America.

editors of *Baldur* not only printed translated material from *Appeal* but also distributed the paper through their own distribution network, sometimes giving copies for free to subscribers of *Baldur*. The editors rallied to the *Appeal*'s support when the Canadian postal authorities gave in to pressure from the United States and banned the distribution of *Appeal* through the mail in 1906 following its publication of a revolutionary call to arms written by Eugene Debs, the American socialist leader and presidential candidate. A pre-printed protest letter was published in *Baldur* that readers could cut out, sign, and send to the authorities (*Baldur* [6 April 1906]: 4). The editors also collected signatures for a protest letter and published repeated reports on the affair (Vilhelmsson 2012, 45–46). Networking of this sort was the basis of the success of the *Appeal*, which had a circulation of 760,000 subscribers in 1912, and was a carefully constructed strategy that turned its readership into a formidable force in American social life. The Canadian postal authorities, for example, reversed their ruling and allowed the continued mailing of the magazine following the torrent of protests they received (Streitmatter 2001, 110–11).

Of more immediate importance than networking with subversive English-language political periodicals, however, were the associational bonds between radicals within the Icelandic community itself that these publications fostered. When one reads *Freyja*, *Baldur*, *Dagskrá II*, and the various papers of Sigfús Benedictsson, it quickly becomes apparent how these journals and magazines served as a forum for debate of radical ideas and current affairs from a critical standpoint, to connect with each other, and to form support networks based not only on shared ethnicity but also on similar beliefs and world views. The editors of these six publications wrote for each other's papers, distributed them within their networks, and referred to each other's works, using the pages of their journals as forums for debate and so on. Radically minded Icelanders from communities ranging from Minnesota to British Columbia also corresponded regularly with the editors, who in turn published their writings in their periodicals, from poetry to short stories, essays, and news articles. While the editors often fiercely debated amongst themselves on the pages of their respective publications, they also used them as forums of support when others within their disparate group came under public criticism within the broader Icelandic community for their published writings (Vilhelmsson 2011, 71–72). In that sense the journals functioned as a "haven on print," an informal association of people who shared both an ethnic identity and a philosophical outlook and ideological passions. Although most Icelanders had settled in Manitoba, they were still spread out over a vast geographic area, and journals such as *Freyja* and *Baldur* became a channel for similarly thinking individuals of Icelandic ethnicity to connect with each other and create support networks through print publications, which scholars have long recognized as important facilitators of immigrant acculturation and identity development (Hickerson and Gustafson 2016; Zecker 2013; Blau et al. 1998; Hoerder 1987; Danielsen 1985; Zubrzycki 1958).

CULTURAL ASSOCIATIONS

For those radicals who lived in Winnipeg, physical meetings in suitable settings were common as well, and they formed their own associations that facilitated radical politics in the broadest sense of that term. There was only one attempt to form an association solely based on radical politics, the short-lived Jafnaðarmannafélag Íslendinga í Winnipeg (the Icelandic socialist club in Winnipeg). The club was founded in June 1901 by a group of men, including William Anderson (Guðmundur Björnsson), Stephan Thorson, Fred Swanson (Friðrik Sveinsson), and Sigurður Júlíus Jóhannesson, all of whom were also involved with the publication of *Dagskrá II*. The stated purpose of the club was to introduce Icelanders to socialism. It held occasional open meetings and published two collections of translated articles in addition to debating the merits of socialism with the editors of *Lögberg*, which openly supported the Liberal Party and was one of two major newspapers published in Icelandic in Winnipeg. *Lögberg*'s editors had written editorials associating the Icelandic socialist club with anarchism, which, in the political climate in North America after the assassination of U.S. President William McKinley in September 1901, was akin to labelling them "terrorists" (Fine 1955; Vilhelmsson 2011, 25–26). According to one community historian and personal acquaintance of the aforementioned men, the club had few members and was short-lived (Þorsteinsson [1935] 1994, 230). It can be assumed that it was simply not viable to run an association based on a single political creed for the small group of ideologically diverse radicals among the Icelanders in the city.

Instead, the radicals found refuge in organizations that were not overtly political but were nonetheless modelled in such a way that they could serve as havens for radical ideas and activities. One such was the Unitarian church founded by a group of Icelanders in Winnipeg in 1891. In fact, several radicals were founding members and took an active part in its work, including Sigfús and Margrét Benedictsson, Einar Ólafsson (the long-term editor of *Baldur*), William Anderson, and Fred Swanson (*Fimtíu ára afmæli* 1941, 19; Gudmundsson 1984, 97–102). Indeed, Unitarianism could itself be considered a radical ideology, as it goes against many of the main tenets of mainstream Christianity, rejecting supernatural elements such as the virgin birth and seeking rather to interpret the Bible as a collection of fables that forms a basis for human morality and social life (Wilbur 1925; Gudmundsson 1984; Dewalt 1985, 18–21). This is reflected in the writings of radical Icelanders in Winnipeg, who commonly described the Unitarian church as a rebellious association formed with the explicit intention of subverting the moral authority of Lutheranism, which these writers associated with conservative authoritarianism and cultural backwardness, seeing Unitarianism as a way of promoting popular education, women's emancipation, and social enlightenment within the community (Pétursson 1908; Sólmundsson 1904; Benedictsson 1930). Some of them even described the Unitarian church as a "revolutionary organization" and interpreted Unitarian teachings as an anti-capitalist and anti-authoritarian doctrine (*Baldur* [10 June 1907]: 2). The Icelandic community elite, predominantly Lutheran in this era, responded with outrage to the Unitarian presence amongst Icelanders and actively organized to counter their influence within the community but to no avail (Vilhelmsson 2011, 66; McIntosh 2004, 249–53).

Closely related to the Unitarian church, a group of Icelanders formed Menningarfélagið, or the Cultural Society, in 1906. This association was formally neutral and independent politically, its declared purpose being to "strengthen liberty and enhance broadmindedness," but sources about its activities indicate that it was first and foremost an avenue for discussion on politics and philosophy with a penchant for radical issues. It held lectures and discussion meetings on a regular basis, and topics included "Icelandic socialism," "Exposition of morality," "Pantheism," and "The economics of Henry George," an immensely popular reformist economist in the late nineteenth century ("Félagsmálin" 1908, 239–40). Along with the regular names of Icelandic radicals such as Fred Swanson and Sigurður Júlíus Jóhannesson, speakers included native English speakers from local radical organizations such as the Socialist Party of Canada, a revolutionary socialist party on the political fringes (McCormack 1977). Reports of the meetings were sometimes printed in the Icelandic press in Winnipeg and described heated discussions where radicals such as Sigfús Benedictsson and various other members of the Icelandic community debated about various topics ranging from the merits of revolutionary violence to the nature of journalism (*Tuttugasta öldin,* 14 May 1909, 2; *Lögberg,* 2 March 1911, 3).

Another cultural association that served as a haven for Icelandic radicals in Manitoba was Hagyrðingafélagið, or the Verse Poetry Society, formed in the home of Margrét and Sigfús in Winnipeg sometime around 1903; meetings were usually held in their living room (Jónsson 2007, 89–93). It was not a radical association in any formal sense. Its purpose was to study "modern literature" and to enable its members to practise writing verse poetry in Icelandic "as pure, correct, and undiluted" as possible (*Dagskrá II* [20 January 1903]: 1; *Heimskringla,* 24 August 1905, 2). The membership, however, was limited to the handful of people who were involved in the radical publications and the Unitarian social circuit discussed above, and it was later described by one of them as merely an excuse to meet and talk about current affairs (Guttormsson 1966). Others described the Poetry Society as a direct response to the intolerance and opposition to new ideas that they associated with the conservative leadership of the Icelandic cultural community in Winnipeg, and declared their group free, independent, and egalitarian (*Heimskringla,* 24 August 1905, 2). Their poetry was regularly printed in the periodicals that they themselves published. The mere existence of the organization provoked the ire of more conservative Icelanders in Winnipeg, who wrote letters to the Icelandic newspapers decrying the "spiritual anarchism" of the association, which should immediately be dissolved in order to defend civil dignity and common propriety (*Heimskringla,* 2 June 1904, 3). The society in turn ridiculed the conservative religious leaders of the Icelandic ethnic enclave by declaring three of the most prominent clergymen honorary members of Hagyrðingafélagið and then publicly rebuking them for not attending its meetings (Þorsteinsson [1935] 1994, 232–33).

PARTICIPATION IN REFORM POLITICS

In addition to creating their own associations, or havens, to fulfill their multi-faceted socio-cultural needs as both immigrants of Icelandic origin and political radicals at odds with Icelandic leaders and the structure of their host society, many of the persons discussed in this chapter participated in reform politics or joined political networks outside the confines of the Icelandic ethnic group. As early as 1890 a large group of Icelanders was involved in the labour movement in Winnipeg, forming the Icelandic Labour Union at the urging of members of the English-speaking labour movement, which was at that time in its infancy. They became increasingly more involved in the movement, first through specifically Icelandic unions but later through joining the ranks of English-speaking unions, including participating in the first female union in Winnipeg, local 35 of the United Garment Workers of America, formed in 1899 in the midst of a seamstress strike. Some prominent members of the Icelandic Labour Union were also involved with the radical associations discussed above, such as Stephan Thorson, Fred Swanson, and William Anderson. These Icelandic labour organizers actively worked towards the increased acculturation of Icelanders into Canadian society on critical terms, organizing voter registration and promoting socialist or at least labour-friendly candidates and arguing for further involvement of Icelanders in grassroots politics for reform (Vilhelmsson 2022).

FIGURE 3.1. Plaque commemorating the Printers' Strike of 1872, an important milestone in the Canadian labour movement. (*https://www.readtheplaque.com/plaque/the-printers-strike-of-1872*)

It has already been noted how Sigfús and Margrét Benedictsson were connected to a network of anarchists and free-love advocates across North America, corresponding with them, distributing their literature in Winnipeg, and promoting their causes in their own publications, and the same goes for *Baldur* and their connection to *Appeal to Reason*. Margrét also formed the First Icelandic Woman Suffrage Association of America in 1908, an organization that then joined the Canadian Suffrage Association and the International Woman Suffrage Alliance. The association organized petition drives and public meetings and advocated for the cause of women's suffrage within the Icelandic immigrant community, which generally supported the cause. Her collaboration with Anglo-Canadian suffragists in Manitoba was nonetheless minimal, which most scholars have attributed to differences in ideology and social status rather than ethnic barriers (Johnson 1994; Kinnear 1986; Holenski 1980). Margrét has long been acknowledged as a pioneer of the suffrage movement, with the *Manitoba Free Press* describing her in 1916 as "the mother of the organized suffrage movement in Manitoba and the west" (*Manitoba Free Press,* 28 July 1916, 5), although by the time women got the vote in Manitoba in 1916, she had already given up her political activism, following an acrimonious divorce and due to her failing eyesight, and moved to Seattle.[5]

Several Icelanders, most of whom were active in the network of radicals discussed in this chapter, were also involved in the formation of a short-lived political party in Manitoba named the Political Reform Union (PRU) in 1901. It was a coalition of various reform organizations, including Arthur Puttee and the Winnipeg Labour Party, several agrarian political organizations, the temperance movement, and others. It was led by former Winnipeg mayor for the Conservative Party, A.J. Andrews, and disgraced former MP for the Liberal Party, R.L. Richardson, both of whom had fallen out of favour within their respective parties (Hall 1985, 29; Eyler 1972, 9). Its platform was a mishmash of reform issues such as direct legislation (putting all legislation up for public referendum), the nationalization of public services, temperance, moral reform, and fighting political corruption, or "machine" politics, all of which were high on the agenda for most of the Icelandic radicals (*The Voice,* 2 August 1901, 1; *Dagskrá II* [10 September 1902]: 2; *Dagskrá II* [23 February 1903]: 1). Active members from the Icelandic community included Einar Ólafsson and J.P. Sólmundsson, both of whom were socialists and editors of

Baldur; Sigurður Júlíus Jóhannesson, the editor of *Dagskrá II*; and Stephan Thorson and Fred Swanson, both of whom were involved in the socialist club, the Icelandic Labour Union, and the Unitarian church. Einar Ólafsson and Stephan Thorson were particularly active and served on the governing board of the PRU along with several other Icelanders. Their participation in PRU became the subject of significant debate in the Icelandic press, particularly in *Lögberg*, which was closely connected to the Liberal Party and commonly took the side of the political status quo and laissez-faire economics in public debate. The debate became heated, and A.J. Andrews himself got involved, publishing an open letter to Magnús Pálsson, the editor of *Lögberg*, where Andrews challenged Pálsson to a public debate about the platform and policies of the PRU (*Lögberg,* 11 September 1902, 1; *Dagskrá II* [20 September 1902]: 3). The debate never happened, and the PRU never achieved any electoral success and faded to obscurity a few years later as it failed to make any impact on the political landscape of Manitoba.

The participation of Icelandic radicals in political movements was in line with their frequently stated view that Icelanders in Manitoba should become more active in Canadian political life on a grassroots level. While the Icelandic community leadership had advocated from early on for active participation in Canadian political life (Kristjansson 1965, 288–96), it remained common for them to encourage Icelanders to form a "political front" and vote as a unified mass (Matthiasson 1979, 197). Indeed, contemporary political observers sometimes noted the influence of "the Icelandic vote" on local elections (Trachtenberg 1998, 5, 10; Dewalt 1985, 63). The radicals criticized this approach, often agitating instead on behalf of independent candidates such as Arthur Puttee and thus provoking the ire of some of their readership (*Heimskringla,* 3 November 1904, 3). They argued that Icelanders should concern themselves with social matters and make their voices heard as citizens rather than merely as immigrants, not voting, as *Dagskrá II* reported, "only, as they have been asked to, for the party of Sigtryggur [Jónasson, i.e., the Liberal Party] or Baldvin's party [Baldwin L. Baldwinsson, MP for the Conservative Party]" (*Dagskrá II* [30 November 1901]: 1).[6] Instead, they should explore and analyze the complex hierarchies and entrenched inequalities of North

American society and draw their own conclusions (*Tuttugasta öldin,* 1 July 1910, 4; *Baldur* [14 October 1908]: 2; Vilhelmsson 2011, 72–74).

CONCLUDING REMARKS

As historians Christiane Harzig, Dirk Hoerder, and Donna Gabaccia have argued, participation in local politics is an important step in the process of immigrant acculturation and signifies that the group in question has already become quite integrated in their adopted home (Harzig, Hoerder, and Gabaccia 2009, 102–8). The activities of the radicals discussed in this chapter indicate the degree to which Icelandic immigrants were already acculturated to Canadian society by the turn of the twentieth century. The fact that their activism was mostly in the Icelandic language and within the Icelandic community, despite the fierce opposition their ideas and activities met within it, is a reminder that these were first-generation immigrants whose integration in broader society remained fragile and dependent on support networks and a strong sense of community. Being Icelandic remained an important part of the identity of the radicals discussed in this chapter, while at the same time they acknowledged that they had become citizens in a multicultural society and needed to enhance their understanding of it in order to become fully integrated. In that sense one can interpret their ideas and activities as tools to navigate and internalize the grassroots culture and politics of North American society and in turn to mediate it to their own fellow citizens. In fact, they regularly described the purpose of their activism as such.[7] Rather than uncritically assimilating to the liberal values and political culture of the Anglo-Canadian elite, as the leadership of the Icelandic community had so strongly encouraged, they argued instead that integrating into Canadian society meant being critical of the "creases" in the social structure and political life of their adopted country. The criticism and radical stance evident in the publications and the various reform activities detailed and discussed in this chapter were thus a form of acculturation to Canadian society through grassroots participation in efforts to change it.

NOTES

1 The concept of "radicalism," as used here, is borrowed from the work of Egyptian-American historian Ilham Khuri-Makdisi, who has analyzed the melting pot of ideas among political activists globally around the turn of the twentieth century, where nationalists, socialists, anarchists, feminists, and cultural modernists intermingled both socially and ideologically. In her view, "the vagueness of the term itself captures the lack of orthodoxy and rigid boundaries that was a key characteristic of the fin de siècle, whether intellectually, culturally, or socially" (Khuri-Makdisi 2010, 3). The concept is commonly used in similar terms in North American historiography (see, for example, Kaye 1995).

2 The papers *Voröld* (1918 to 1921), *Freyr* (1924 to 1925), and *Dagrenning* (1935 to 1943) can also be characterized as radical publications by Icelanders in Canada, but they are outside the temporal scope of this study and were rarely consulted. For an incomplete list and bibliographical information, see Keneva Kunz (1987).

3 All translations from Icelandic to English are mine unless otherwise noted.

4 There are a handful of studies on Margrét Benedictsson and *Freyja*. See, for example, Crippen (2006); Wolf (2001); Johnson (1994); Kinnear (1986); Holenski (1980).

5 Historians of the women's movement in Canada generally acknowledge her role in the suffrage movement even though her radical views and flirtations with anarchism and free love are seldom mentioned, with the notable exception of the recent work of Joan Sangster (Sangster 2018, 86–89; Kinnear 1998, 31–32, 143–44; Bacchi 1983, 27–28; Cleverdon 1974, 49). See also Carter (2020).

6 Sigtryggur Jónasson and Baldwin L. Baldwinsson were candidates for the Liberals and the Conservatives in the 1896 provincial elections and regularly in the following years. Both were very influential within the Icelandic community in Manitoba for a long time (Kristjansson 1965, 294–95).

7 See, for example, Margrét Benedictsson's letter to the editors of *Lucifer, the Light-Bearer*, where she describes herself as "a foreigner who has grasped your . . . teachings and is trying to teach the same to her country people through a small monthly magazine" (*Lucifer, the Light-Bearer* [15 March 1906]: 483).

REFERENCES

Bacchi, Carol L. 1983. *Liberation Deferred? The Ideas of the English-Canadian Suffragists 1877–1918*. Toronto: University of Toronto Press.

Benedictsson, Sigfús B. 1905. *Ljóðmæli*. Winnipeg: Freyja Printing and Publishing Company.

———. 1930. *Opið bréf til séra Rögnvalds Péturssonar og Heimfararljóð, dularfull fyrirbrigði og fleira*. Winnipeg: Maple Leaf Press.

Bertram, Laurie K. 2018. "'Eskimo' Immigrants and Colonial Soldiers: Icelandic Immigrants and the North-West Resistance, 1885." *Canadian Historical Review* 99: 63–97.

———. 2019. *The Viking Immigrants: Icelandic North Americans*. Toronto: University of Toronto Press.

Blau, Judith, Mim Thomas, Beverly Newhouse, and Andrew Kavee. 1998. "Ethnic Buffer Institutions. The Immigrant Press: New York City, 1820–1984." *Historical Social Research* 23 (3): 20–37.

Carter, Sarah. 2020. *Ours by Every Law of Right and Justice: Women and the Vote in the Prairie Provinces.* Vancouver: University of British Columbia Press.

Chipman, George. 1909. "Winnipeg: The Melting Pot." *Canadian Magazine* 33: 409–16.

Cleverdon, Catherine L. 1974. *The Woman Suffrage Movement in Canada.* 2nd. ed. Toronto: University of Toronto Press.

Crippen, Carolyn. 2006. "Three Manitoba Pioneer Women: A Legacy of Servant-Leadership." *Manitoba History* 53: 11–21.

———. 2016. "Margret Benedictsson." In *The Canadian Encyclopedia*. Historica Canada. https://www.thecanadianencyclopedia.ca/en/article/margret-benedictsson.

Danielsen, Jens Bjerre. 1985. "Ethnic Identity, Nationalism and Scandinavianism in the Scandinavian Immigrant Socialist Press in the U.S." In *The Press of Labor Migrants in Europe and North America 1880s to 1930s*, edited by Christiane Harzig and Dirk Hoerder, 181–205. Bremen: Universität Bremen.

Dewalt, Bryan T. 1985. "Arthur W. Puttee: Labourism and Working-Class Politics in Winnipeg 1894–1918." Master's thesis, University of Manitoba.

Eyford, Ryan. 2007. "Lucifer Comes to New Iceland: Margret Benedictsson's Radical Critique of Marriage and the Family." Unpublished paper presented at the Canadian Historical Association Annual Meeting, Saskatoon, 30 May 2007.

———. 2016. *White Settler Reserve: New Iceland and the Colonization of the Canadian West*. Vancouver: University of British Columbia Press.

Eyler, Philip. 1972. "Public Ownership and Politics in Manitoba, 1900–1915." Master's thesis, University of Manitoba.

"Félagsmálin." 1908. *Heimir* 4 (10): 239–40.

Fine, Sidney. 1955. "Anarchism and the Assassination of McKinley." *American Historical Review* 60 (4): 777–99.

Fimtíu ára afmæli frjálstrúarsafnaðarins í Winnipeg, 1891–1941. 1941. Winnipeg: Stjórnarnefnd Fyrsta Sambandssafnaðar í Winnipeg.

Gudmundsson, V. Emil. 1984. *The Icelandic Unitarian Connection. Beginnings of Icelandic Unitarianism in North America 1885–1900*. Winnipeg: Wheatfield Press.

Guttormsson, Guttormur J. 1966. "Sigurður Júl. Jóhannesson og íslenzka hagyrðingafélagið í Winnipeg" [Sigurður Júl. Jóhannesson and the Icelandic Verse Poetry Society in Winnipeg]. *Eimreiðin* 72 (2): 152–60.

Hall, David J. 1985. *Clifford Sifton.* Vol. 2: *A Lonely Eminence 1901–1929.* Vancouver: University of British Columbia Press.

Harzig, Christiane, Dirk Hoerder, and Donna Gabaccia. 2009. *What Is Migration History?* Cambridge: Polity Press.

Heiðarsson, Steinþór. 1999. "Íslands ástmegir og þrælar: Drættir úr sjálfsmynd Vestur-Íslendinga" [Aspects of Icelandic-Canadian identity]. *Saga* 37 (1): 17–61.

Hickerson, Andrea, and Kristin L. Gustafson. 2016. "Revisiting the Immigrant Press." *Journalism* 17 (8): 943–60.

Hoerder, Dirk. 1987. "An Internationally Mobile Working Class and Its Press in North America: A Survey." In *The Immigrant Labor Press in North America, 1840s–1970s. An Annotated Bibliography.* Vol. 1: *Migrants from Northern Europe*, edited by Dirk Hoerder, 1–47. New York: Greenwood Press.

Holenski, Evelyne R. 1980. "Margret Jónsdóttir Benedictsson: Created Equal—Our Fair Share." Master's thesis, University of Manitoba.

Johnson, Sigrid. 1994. "Margret Benedictsson, *Freyja* and the Struggle for Women's Equality." *Icelandic Canadian* 52 (3): 117–27.

Jónsson, Björn. 2007. *Fyrsti vestur-íslenski feministinn. Þættir úr baráttusögu Margrétar J. Benedictsson* [The first Icelandic-Canadian feminist: The story of Margrét J. Benedictsson]. Reykjavík: Bókaútgáfan Hólar.

Kaye, Harvey J. 1995. "Radicals and the Making of American Democracy: Toward a New Narrative of American History." *History Teacher* 28 (2): 217–25.

Khuri-Makdisi, Ilham. 2010. *The Eastern Mediterranean and the Making of Global Radicalism, 1860–1914.* Berkeley: University of California Press.

Kinnear, Mary. 1986. "The Icelandic Connection: *Freyja* and the Manitoba Woman Suffrage Movement." *Canadian Woman Studies* 7 (4): 25–28.

———. 1998. *A Female Economy: Women's Work in a Prairie Province, 1870–1970.* Montreal: McGill-Queen's University Press.

Korneski, Kurt. 2007. "Britishness, Canadianness, Class, and Race: Winnipeg and the British World, 1880s–1910s." *Journal of Canadian Studies* 41: 161–84.

Kristjansson, Wilhelm. 1965. *The Icelandic People in Manitoba: A Manitoba Saga.* Winnipeg: Wallington Press.

Kunz, Keneva. 1987. "Icelanders." In *The Immigrant Labor Press in North America, 1840s–1970s. An Annotated Bibliography.* Vol. 1: *Migrants from Northern Europe*, edited by Dirk Hoerder, 259–67. New York: Greenwood Press.

Loewen, Royden, and Gerald Friesen. 2009. *Immigrants in Prairie Cities: Ethnic Diversity in Twentieth-Century Canada.* Toronto: University of Toronto Press.

McCormack, A. Ross. 1977. *Reformers, Rebels and Revolutionaries: The Western Canadian Radical Movement, 1899–1919.* Toronto: University of Toronto Press.

McIntosh, Andrea L. 2004. "In Plain Sight: The Development of Western Icelandic Ethnicity and Class Division 1910–1920." PhD diss., University of Manitoba.

McKay, Ian. 2008. *Reasoning Otherwise: Leftists and the People's Enlightenment in Canada 1890–1920*. Toronto: Between the Lines.

Matthiasson, John, S. 1979. "The Icelandic Canadians: The Paradox of an Assimilated Ethnic Group." In *Two Nations, Many Cultures: Ethnic Groups in Canada*, edited by Jean Leonard Elliott, 195–205. Scarborough: Prentice-Hall of Canada.

Nordahl, Per. 1994. *Weaving the Ethnic Fabric: Social Networks Among Swedish-American Radicals in Chicago 1890–1940*. Umeå: Umeå University.

Passet, Joanne E. 2003. *Sex Radicals and the Quest for Women's Equality*. Chicago: University of Illinois Press.

Pétursson, Rögnvaldur. 1908. "Conformity." *Heimir* 5 (5): 97–114.

Sangster, Joan. 2018. *One Hundred Years of Struggle: The History of Women and the Vote in Canada*. Vancouver: University of British Columbia Press.

Scott, William Duncan. 1914. "Immigration and Population." In *Canada and Its Provinces: A History of the Canadian People and Their Institutions by One Hundred Associates*. Vol. 7, edited by Adam Shortt and Arthur G. Doughty, 517–90. Toronto: Glasgow Brook.

Sólmundsson, Jóhann P. 1904. "Tilgangur hins únitaríska kyrkjufjelags Vestur-Íslendinga." *Ný dagsbrún* 1 (1): 17–38.

Streitmatter, Rodger. 2001. *Voices of Revolution: The Dissident Press in America*. New York: Columbia University Press.

Trachtenberg, Henry. 1998. "Ethnic Politics on the Urban Frontier: 'Fighting Joe' Martin and the Jews of Winnipeg, 1893–96." *Manitoba History* 35: 2–14.

Vilhelmsson, Vilhelm. 2011. "'Allt skal frjálst, allt skal jafnt': Um hugmyndaheim og félagsskap róttæklinga meðal Íslendinga í Vesturheimi, 1890–1911" [All shall be free, all shall be equal: The ideas and social networks of radicals among Icelanders in America, 1890–1911]. Master's thesis, University of Iceland.

———. 2012. "'Ánægja með það sem er—ið gamla, er andlegur dauði': Af hugmyndum og félagsskap íslenskra róttæklinga í Manitoba við upphaf 20. aldar" [Ideology and social networks of radical Icelandic immigrants in Manitoba in the early twentieth century]. *Saga* 50 (2): 34–69.

———. 2013. "'Það gefur enginn mér kredit': Sigfús B. Benedictsson og vestur-íslensk sagnaritun" [Nobody gives me any credit: Sigfús B. Benedictsson and the historiography of Icelandic immigration in Canada]. In *Söguþing 2012: Ráðstefnurit*, 1–10. Reykjavík: Sagnfræðistofnun Háskóla Íslands. http://hdl.handle.net/1946/15931.

———. 2022. "Proving Their Worth: Icelanders and the Winnipeg Labour Movement, 1890–1900." In *Exploring Canada: Exploits and Encounters*, edited by Gerd Bjørhovde and Janne Korkka, 237–256. Bern: Peter Lang.

Wilbur, Earl Morse. 1925. *Our Unitarian Heritage: An Introduction to the History of the Unitarian Movement*. Boston: Beacon Press.

Wolf, Kirsten. 2001. "Til varnar mannúð og jafnrétti: Margrét J. Benedictsson og *Freyja*" [In defence of humanitarianism and equality: Margrét J. Benedictsson and *Freyja*]. *Skírnir* 175: 119–39.

Zecker, Robert M. 2013. *Race and America's Immigrant Press: How the Slovaks Were Taught to Think Like White People*. New York: Bloomsbury.

Zubrzycki, Jerzy. 1958. "The Role of the Foreign-Language Press in Migrant Integration." *Population Studies* 12 (1): 73–82.

Þorsteinsson, Þorsteinn Þ. (1935) 1994. *Vestmenn. Útvarpserindi um landnám Íslendinga í Vesturheimi* [Westerners: Lectures on the settlement of Icelanders in North America]. Reykjavík: n.p.

CHAPTER 4

The Barnason Brothers in Nebraska: Two Pioneer Farmers

ALDA MÖLLER

THE SUBJECTS OF this chapter are two Icelandic brothers, Larus and Albert Barnason (Lárus and Aðalbjartur Bjarnason), who emigrated to the United States in the 1870s, worked as farmhands, and rented land for years until they were able to buy their own land on the Great Plains of Nebraska. They lived far from Icelandic settlements and seldom met their countrymen but wrote to their elder brother in Iceland, who preserved their letters in his vast collection. The brothers wrote mostly about their farming activities but also described their private life, sorrows, and happiness. Little else is known about them, although their names were sometimes mentioned by other Icelandic settlers in Nebraska and Toronto, Ontario.

The recipient of the letters was their brother Torfi Bjarnason, who travelled with Larus to America in the summer of 1873, intending to survey the land for a future Icelandic colony. Torfi's letters home that summer reveal his sharp observations of the richness and possibilities of the land but also his thoughts on the limitations of an Icelandic colony. He returned home that autumn, but Albert emigrated in 1878. Torfi was a friend and role model for his brothers, and his journey in 1873 also provided insight into Nebraskan life and agriculture, which provided a common ground for their letters.

The purpose of delving into these old letters is to study the life of the two brothers, how they fared in daily life and whether their life-changing choice led to fulfillment or a degree of regret. There are, however, also gaps in the letters, which are tentatively interpreted. The study is therefore related to the idea of microhistory. Most of the unpublished references are from the private letter collection of Torfi Bjarnason in the National Library of Iceland (*Lbs 150 NF*). The letters are referenced by date and the writer's initials, TB for letters from Torfi Bjarnason, LB for letters from Larus Barnason, and AB for letters from Albert Barnason.[1]

FIGURE 4.1. Albert Barnason. (Courtesy of the family)

FIGURE 4.2. Larus Barnason. (Courtesy of the family)

BACKGROUND AND PREPARATIONS

Torfi Bjarnason (1838–1915) was a farmer's son from Bessatunga in Dalasýsla in West Iceland. Already as a young man he showed great interest in agricultural development in Iceland and became a well-known advocate for progress in agriculture and commerce. He established and headed the Agricultural School in Ólafsdalur (1880 to 1907). His life story and the history of the school have been widely chronicled (see, in particular, Júlíusson 1986).

In the spring of 1873, Torfi was at a crossroads in his life; he was a family man, but his dreams of a progressive teaching farm in Iceland had been thwarted due to lack of interest and funding in the stagnant agricultural society.

FIGURE 4.3. Torfi Bjarnason. (Courtesy of the family)

Reports of a better life in America, such as in the newspaper *Norðanfari* (Halldórsson 1873), may have been a decisive factor, but Torfi had also been in contact with the Allan Brothers shipping company for a year, clearly considering emigration and establishing a small colony (GL 2.6.1872; GL 26.6.1872; GL 26.3.1873). A draft of a letter by Torfi to a friend just before departure shows that he intended to explore areas in New Brunswick and America because they were not so far away and might therefore have some similarities with Iceland (TB 6.5.1873). Travelling with Torfi was his younger brother Larus.

NO BARREN EARTH OR BOGS

A long letter from Torfi to his wife describes his first few weeks in America (TB 15.6.–19.6.1873). On arrival in Milwaukee, he found the Icelanders downhearted due to unemployment, but the brothers continued westwards to Lincoln, Nebraska, and from there they travelled by train and on horseback looking for available land. They explored the area owned by the Northern Pacific Railroad Company and finally arrived in Columbus, north of Lincoln, where Torfi found the land truly suitable and described it as a dream for an Icelandic farmer: "It is quite beautiful here, rolling grassy plains and not a single hummock in sight, not one rock in the way and no barren earth, no damp patches or bogs and only a few ditches so that you can drive a wagon on the land for miles and miles like on a prepared road."[2]

The land, however, was being claimed rapidly, and there was no large area left for a settlement near the railway tracks. He wrote that it would be unwise for Icelanders to ramble deep into the wilderness, far from inhabited land and human civilization. Furthermore, Icelanders did not speak English and had no knowledge of American agriculture; they would need to learn from more established farmers. He also wrote about the weather and forestry and agricultural societies, and observed that the expansion of cities would make markets for agricultural produce stronger in the future.

In August Torfi received a letter from the Northern Pacific Railroad Company in Saint Paul, Minnesota, in response to his enquiry for land. The reply includes the following:

> We have a large amount of vacant land within our grant, and a few miles away from tracks there is yet to be had some of the most fertile of the Govt lands but they are being rapidly taken, particularly the Prairee. In the timber there is yet good claims within a few miles of the stations. For a small colony I think you could find a desirable track of country between Perham Station and the Red River, a trip through our land grant will be advisable should you determine upon raising a colony. I shall be glad to see you at our office here, and give you such information and assistance as I may be able to do to further your plans. (James B. Power 11.8.1873)

There is no indication that Torfi followed up on this, but it shows that he had expressed interest in forming a colony beyond Nebraska.

At the end of September, Torfi met with Icelanders in Milwaukee on his way home, as reported by Jón Halldórsson many years later (Halldórsson 1913, 150–56). It is likely that Torfi's family concerns and lack of resources prompted the decision but also that he judged settlement to be outside his reach. It seems, however, that he had a positive view of emigration to America, borne out by the fact that twenty-three of his students (almost one in every six) emigrated, as did his youngest brother a few years later (Júlíusson 1986, 212–15).

LARUS BARNASON

Observations of a Newcomer

Lárus Bjarnason (1849–1918) was eleven years younger than his brother Torfi. The letter collection of Torfi Bjarnason includes nineteen letters from him written in Nebraska from 1874 to 1880, as well as several sent prior to the brothers' departure. Lárus adopted the name Larus Barnason.

Larus was a farmhand in Kollafjarðarnes in Strandasýsla when the journey to America was being planned by Torfi. The decision to join him seems to have been rather casual, as he informed his employer just a few weeks earlier that he might be leaving, much to her irritation (LB 10.2.1873). There was probably not much holding him back in Iceland, and earlier letters show that he relied on his brother for help and guidance (LB 1869; LB 12.3.1869).

Larus was initially employed by a German farmer near Firth.[3] In his first letter in early 1874, he writes mostly about the weather and farming conditions (LB 18.1.1874). There is almost no snow; livestock is kept outside in the bright, cool, and calm weather; and he observes that cattle farming is certainly easier than in Iceland. He milks cows and tries to understand the pricing of produce, and he is learning English from the farmer. In his next letter, Larus writes partly in English and is already convinced that "going to America is the best decision I have made and will ever make for myself" (LB 20.3.1874).[4]

A little later the weather had changed for the worse, and people had told him that this was the hardest winter since white men arrived in Nebraska—frosty every night and heavy snowfalls. He had recently heard that Icelanders in Milwaukee wanted to explore Nebraska and Minnesota for land, and they had asked Larus about food prices. He felt that his countrymen were impatient and vacillating, since they wanted to run away from difficulties so soon after their arrival (LB 26.4.1874). Larus appreciates praise for his hard work and has had time to read during the winter. Reading has been useful. He feels that his spirit has lifted, and notices that he is not as distrustful as he used to be. In his opinion America is "the best land to learn everything on Earth."[5]

In the summer of 1874 Larus temporarily left his employer due to harsh words and disagreement on wages; he states that he dislikes the Germans and prefers to work for Americans (LB 7.6.1874; LB 12.7.1874). A little later he writes about locust swarms eating up all the corn and leading to large-scale migration of desperate people from western Nebraska (LB 29.8.1874). In the autumn farmers nearby have been badly affected by poor harvest and high costs, and Larus says he prefers to be a farm labourer earning eighteen dollars a month rather than a farmer in Nebraska (LB 7.10.1874). His main work is threshing, for which he is sought after, and he greatly appreciates his independence. He also says that he has no worries and can talk well enough and stand up to everyone. Furthermore, he can "carry out any task that has to be tackled on a farm here in America."[6] Larus also goes to inspect the plot in Saltillo that Torfi ploughed the summer before, but it had been laid to waste by weeds, hailstorms, and heavy rain; he tells Torfi that this piece of land is not worth returning to (LB 29.11.1874).

Larus on the Alaskan Adventure

In 1874 and early 1875, Larus writes further about Icelanders in Milwaukee wanting to find a new Icelandic settlement, and he is clearly not impressed by their plans. In June he comments on the arrival of Sigfús Magnússon and Jón Halldórsson in Firth on their behalf (LB 7.6.1874). A little later he writes derisively about the quest led by Jón Ólafsson to provide land for Icelanders in Alaska and the journey of three Icelanders who went to explore the territory (LB 29.11.1874):[7]

> I've heard that if these messengers liked it and thought it cold enough!!! they were going to split up in the sheep-gathering. Jón was to go back to Iceland and fetch all the sheep that could be gathered and pushed to Alaska, but Ólafur was to gather the unruly sheep that are already in the United States and Canada—I'm afraid I'll hide in the hollows of Nebraska and will not be found in the first round-up. Páll is to live in Alaska, meanwhile, to make sure nobody comes to steal Alaska from them and to help Ólafur and Jón drive the flock finally into Alaska!!![8]

Larus is clearly amused by these events and uses the analogy of sheep gathering in Iceland. He writes further on the subject (LB 18.1.1875; LB 29.1.1875; LB 21.3.1875) and reports that the U.S. government has been asked for free travel for Icelanders north to Niflheimar, the frosty wasteland of Norse mythology. This description by Larus tallies with an account by Jón Halldórsson about the plans for movement to Nebraska in 1874 and the exploration of a settlement in Alaska (Halldórsson 1913, 150–56), although it is rather more balanced in Jón Halldórsson's treatment![9]

News of locust plagues kept people away from Nebraska. Only Jón Halldórsson and his family stayed in Nebraska and formed the small nucleus of Icelanders south of Lincoln, but they moved from the area in 1884 to Long Pine in Brown County (Halldórsson 2005, 109).[10]

Daily Toil and Melancholy

Over the next few years, letters from Larus dwell mostly on the weather, farming conditions, and the harvest. Locusts spread like wildfire over the fields, and he comments that their destructive power is like the raging sheep-scab disease in Iceland (LB 5.6.1875). Droughts and flooding rain alternate, and his only company is Jón Halldórsson and his family (LB 12.10.1875). Despite all this, Larus feels that life would be better for Torfi in America (LB 6.5.1876). He intends to farm wheat and oats but fears that the grasshoppers will eat everything that starts to grow. He dreams of a good harvest and the possibility of using the money to visit Torfi, but, then again, he knows this is foolishness because he will be better off in America (LB 28.1.1877). Conditions, however, improve and he writes a long letter about his own farming and the harvest (LB 10.1.1878). He rents land from the railway company; he has bought two horses, a plough, harrow, and harnesses; and he has harvested 109 bushels of wheat, which sold for eighty cents a bushel; 113 bushels of flax at one dollar per bushel; and 550 bushels of corn, which he has not sold yet, due to low prices. From another plot he had also harvested 115 bushels of wheat and 200 bushels of oats. He sells and buys horses and cattle and feels he is doing quite well in his wheeling and dealing in livestock and produce. He answers his brother's call for news of Icelanders, reads the Lundi newspaper *Framfari*, and compares conditions for farming in Manitoba and Nebraska.

For a while, Larus reports, he is the caretaker of the property of House Representative T.R. Burling in Firth, but the same letter also reveals that Larus is burdened by sadness (LB 17.3.1879). He is bored by idleness and would like to go home and see friends from his younger days, but there is an "invisible hindrance" to this. He is physically well but feels quite useless to himself and others and often "wishes he was dead instead of living this carefree and simple Nebraska life."[11] But soon, he believes, he is bound to be feeling much more lively, and when the winter is over melancholy will have left him.

In the last preserved letter from Larus (LB 22.4.1880), he sends summer greetings to Torfi and his old friends, he is well, and says he is well liked for his work. He has bought eighty acres (32.3 hectares) of good farmland just four miles (about six kilometres) west of Firth and says that much has changed since Torfi was there. Small cottages have been replaced by handsome houses, beautiful fruit orchards, and large barns.

Lancaster County Historical Records

Historical records of Lancaster County in Nebraska include a snippet on Larus Bjarnason as an early resident in the area (Barnason 1888). The biography reads:

> We find on the streets of our great cities people from all nations, but perhaps the most seldom met are those born in the far-off northern island of Iceland. . . . In this brief sketch . . . we give a record of the life of a native of Iceland, a gentleman who is to-day an influential and enterprising farmer of Buda Precinct, residing on section 36, . . . he was a pioneer of the precinct in which he now owns a good farm, and is a well-to-do and respected citizen.
>
> [Larus's arrival in Nebraska with Torfi is then mentioned and that his brother returned to Iceland.]
>
> Larus preferred to remain here, and for the following eight years was engaged at work among the farmers in the ordinary labor of a farm hand, in the meantime making his home with Hon. T.R. Burling, of Firth. Larus had labored diligently, had been economical, and in the year 1884 was enabled to settle upon his present farm. Here he owns eighty acres of good land, which has been developed by his own labor. . . . Mr. Barnason is an enterprising and public-spirited citizen, and considering the limited advantages which he has enjoyed has wielded considerable influence toward the improvement and betterment

> of the precinct, and the years of his greater usefulness are yet to be enjoyed, for . . . Mr. Barnason is yet a young man.

The Silent Years

Benedikt Hálfdanarson and Albert Barnason became the main contacts for news of Larus after 1880. In 1884 Larus married an American woman, and they had a daughter named Mary, born in 1885 (AB 29.7.1884; AB 2.3.1890). Albert says that Larus is in debt due to his large investments but he has a fine house, a large barn, and many outbuildings, and overall his farm is among the best (AB 25.8.1901). Albert, however, feels that Larus is still too temperamental and cites examples that he is not a very good farmer (AB 24.1.1905). The brothers meet only once a year, although for many years they live very close to each other, and Larus never takes the initiative to visit. Benedikt also comments that Larus is no longer able to talk Icelandic with Albert (BH 27.05.1911). In 1913 Larus has had to lease his land as he is worn out by work and by having to nurse his wife in her ill health (BH 3.4.13; AB 30.11.1913).

Letters from Benedikt to Torfi Bjarnason indicate that Torfi was concerned about Larus when he stopped writing. Later Benedikt comments that Larus no longer thinks about his relatives or anything in Iceland, and that there are people who behave like this when they become prosperous in America. He says farmers are notably lazy writers, saying that they do not have time to write, and all their thoughts are focused on their farms (BH 19.01.1903; BH 12.12.1906).

Larus's letters stopped just seven years after arrival in America. There was probably no single reason for this but most likely, judging from his friends' comments, work on the farm took all his energy and gradually his old life became foreign to him, especially after he married and had his own family. It also seems that he was prone to melancholy, caused by his being far from old friends. His way of coping may have been to abandon thoughts of his old life. Albert's comments indicate that Larus was not a social man and already in his first year preferred to stay away from his countrymen.

Although Larus may have missed his friends and family for some time, there is no mention of missing his old life or feeling guilty about leaving Iceland, and he never mentions the beauty of his homeland. Larus is not peculiar in this regard. It is well-known that early settlers had few regrets leaving hardship in Iceland and that early periodicals such as *Framfari* deemed the country uninhabitable (Heiðarsson 1999). Larus may have considered himself an immigrant shortly after arrival, but he quickly assumed the self-image of an American citizen determined to succeed. For success he had to be tough on himself, but his temperament and somewhat gruff manner meant that he alienated himself from his friends and contemporaries.

Larus died in 1918 and was buried in Cortland Cemetery, Nebraska (Larus Barnason headstone n.d).[12]

ALBERT BARNASON

A Young Man with Some Regrets

Aðalbjartur Bjarnason (1860–1944) was twenty-two years younger than his brother Torfi and was brought up by Torfi and his wife, Guðlaug Zakaríasdóttir, after their mother's passing. The letter collection of Torfi Bjarnason includes twenty letters from Aðalbjartur written in Canada and the U.S. from 1878 to 1915. He adopted the name Albert Barnason. Several remarks in Albert's letters indicate that Torfi encouraged him to emigrate, which he did when he was eighteen years of age in 1878. He was accompanied by Benedikt Hálfdanarson and Sigríður Gísladóttir, who was his first cousin (Kristinsson 1983; Guðmundsson 2001, 326).

Albert describes the voyage from Glasgow to Quebec in a letter to Torfi (AB 1.8.1878). He was among 200 Icelanders on-board the ship and felt that the crew treated passengers like animals and that the food rations were spoilt and meagre. The three of them did not follow the others to Manitoba but remained in Toronto. Albert soon found employment with an elderly pastor and his wife in Davenport (Toronto). He was paid only a small wage and there was no chance of attending school to improve his English as he had been promised; he suspected that his employer wanted him present for running errands (AB 9.2.1879; AB 4.5.1879). He felt that "America as a country is a good school and diverse enough to make a man of every person who wants to progress."[13] His next letter starts in English with general news and his dream of moving into the country: "I do not like the Sity [*sic*] so well as I would like the Country, I know" (AB 2.3.1880). He grows roses and vegetables, cuts grass with a machine twice a week, waters the garden with a hose every evening, tends to a horse and a cow, and drives the old couple around.

Albert writes that he is ashamed for not using his time and opportunities better when he was growing up with his elder brother and feels that his poor position is the result of his negligence (AB 29.5.1880). He has had a few temporary jobs, but the pay is always low, and he still cannot afford the journey to Nebraska (AB 6.4.1881). Later that year, however, he found work at harvest time with Jón Halldórsson and was also able to attend school during the winter. Farmhands are in great demand during corn harvesting, and he is pleased with his wages of twenty dollars a month (AB 14.10.1883). Nearly a year later he has started his own farming in a small way; he has bought himself a "team of horses, wagon and harnesses and rented eighty acres of land with a house and fairly good barns." He grows mostly corn but also some oats and exchanges work with neighbouring farmers (AB 29.7.1884).[14] In this letter from 1884 he also writes about the recent rescue mission of Arctic explorers and the U.S. presidential election, in which the Republican candidate is "a tea-totaller promoting women's rights," while the Democrat "is a 'beerbelly' from New York named Cleveland who promises free aquavit and free trade with other nations."[15]

This letter, written six years after his arrival in America, shows Albert's adaptation to new life and integration into the farming community, but he also seems to regret that his old life and family are fading in his mind: "You know that I am not much of a writer and when I try to write something, it is as if my mind does not stretch beyond the desk I'm sitting at, although once in a while my minds drifts to you, so full of energy and tireless desire to get necessary things done."[16]

Farming and Family Life

A few years pass and the next preserved letter from Albert is also written near Firth (AB 2.3.1890). He writes about farming conditions in Nebraska but also of great market price instability. All land has been taken and has increased greatly in price; smallholders have given up and the rich have taken over their land. The cities have expanded and Lincoln has grown to a large city of 60,000 inhabitants. Albert works for other farmers and also on his own rented land, but his farming has not been successful due to the high cost of living as a bachelor and having to pay for boarding, which eats up all his income. He also tells of his engagement to an Icelandic girl, who arrived in America two years earlier; she is from a good family and has many virtues, and he wouldn't like to let her go for a carload of American girls.[17] He explains this further: "I would never marry if I had only English women to choose from, I feel it would be somehow unnatural to live your life with someone who had no idea of our fair homeland."[18]

This sentiment is also echoed when he writes, "When I have become rich, I'll return home to you, dear brother. I have always wanted to go home and will always do as long as I live. Every man in his full senses must miss his homeland all his life" (AB 2.3.1890).[19] Letters continue to be infrequent, and Albert's next letter is dated seven years later. In the meantime his friend Benedikt writes to Torfi that Albert is going through difficult times and many things have gone against his wishes and aspirations (BH 8.10.1892).

Finally, Albert writes an upbeat letter from Firth (AB 3.1.1897). He is no longer a bachelor and has married an American woman named America H. Graff and they have a son. He is full of praise for his wife's virtues and knows her family well. He still rents eighty acres (32.3 hectares) of farmland and pays a third of the harvest as rent. He also rents an extra twenty acres (8.1 hectares) of grassland and forty acres (16.2 hectares) for cereals. His livestock includes three horses, four cows, three heifers, twenty pigs, and plenty of poultry. He also owns all the machinery needed, such as ploughs and a self-binding harvester. He grows mostly corn and oats, but severe drought and low market prices cause great difficulties. Many farmers have gone bankrupt, but he has been careful and not borrowed money.

In 1901 Albert is still a renter in Firth and writes at length about the harvest and market prices. He grows corn, oats, and wheat, and keeps pigs, cattle, and poultry, but the summer is very hot and too dry (AB 14.1.1901; AB 25.8.1901). A year later conditions are much better, the cereal harvest is excellent, and apples and other fruits are plentiful in the garden. The price of farmland, however, increases steadily, and landowners extend their farms and become wealthy, while renters do not prosper. The saying goes that "enything [*sic*] is good enough for a renter." In due course, however, hard-working men are able to buy land (AB 22.9.1902).

Progressive Thoughts

In 1905 Albert has become a landowner and bought eighty acres (32.3 hectares) of farmland, including a family house, outbuildings, and a large orchard for $3,800, but fortunately he is not greatly in debt. He has an overview of the drought problems of Nebraska, and follows the news that irrigation systems are being developed near the mountains in the desert of western Nebraska. He feels this will soon be among the most beautiful countrysides in the world. Furthermore, the government sells farming land in the West to smallholders for the cost of the irrigation system only. Albert is clearly looking at the possibility of moving in order to expand his farm (AB 24.1.1905).

Albert is a contented man, and in the same letter he thanks his brother for sending him to America because "the United States are in my view the best place in the world for a man to live and raise his children because of personal freedom, good administration, a fine country, good public health, and the good moral conduct of the people."[20]

Letters from Firth become more frequent as Albert describes the cultivation of alfalfa, because Torfi had asked for information on this feed crop (AB 4.6.1905; AB 2.12.1905; AB 24.3.1906). Alfalfa is grown extensively in Nebraska as feed for cattle in winter, and Albert describes its properties of "collecting nitrogen from the air and leaving it in the soil for other plants to utilize, and hence both clover and alfalfa are agents for life on Earth."[21] Successful cultivation of alfalfa in Iceland would therefore be better than a gold mine. He sends Torfi cuttings from a newspaper and a scientific report on alfalfa cultivation, and enthusiastically plans how to send seeds and bacterial culture from a research institute in Nebraska. First shipments are generous—nine half-pound (0.22 kilogram) envelopes due to weight limits for posted letters. Albert also describes in detail how to prepare the soil and sow the seeds (AB 24.1.1905).

Albert is now on equal footing with his brother as regards crop-growing expertise. He has left his regrets of time badly spent and learnt to appreciate his own knowledge. The Nebraskan farmer guides the Icelandic headmaster on the properties and treatment of the feed crop, and at long last he is able to assist his brother and repay him to some extent for guidance in his early years.

Prosperity

In the spring of 1908, Albert and his family moved west to Guide Rock in Webster County in Nebraska, having sold the farm in Firth and purchased 160 acres (64.7 hectares) of land at a much lower price.[22] He is doing very well, his debts will soon be fully paid, and his house and outbuildings are well built. He has four healthy children named Perry, Lucy, Joseph, and Larus. All around him there is progress; schools and churches are built, every household has a "telephon," many own "horseless carriages," and railway lines lead everywhere (AB 15.5.1910). In his time in Nebraska farmland prices have increased from twenty dollars up to 150 dollars an acre, and it has become much more difficult to acquire land. He sometimes longs to visit Iceland but thinks it is impossible because his family would not possibly enjoy it and he would not enjoy it without his family.

In Albert's last letter (AB 22.1.1915), written the year of Torfi's death, he describes the development of the countryside nearby and conditions for agriculture in Nebraska. The last few years have not been very favourable and all land is taken. Smallholders are the mainstay of agriculture, and farm labourers are difficult to find. Land is very expensive and those without land roam from farm to farm. He reckons that it is better for emigrants from Iceland to settle in Canada. He himself is doing so well because he has always been honest and careful with money.

Albert Barnason died in 1944 and was buried in Guide Rock Cemetery (Albert Barnason headstone n.d.).[23]

CLOSING REMARKS

An overview of the correspondence from Larus and Albert shows that the two brothers had very different temperaments and views on their circumstances, but their letters also show great similarities. In the early years they ask about relatives and friends, but gradually description of their own life in farming becomes the central theme, with details of weather conditions, harvest, prices, and property clearly being their main concern and interest. For both brothers it took years of incessant labour and setbacks to become independent farmers and their own masters. The Lancaster County records indicate that Larus owned his own farm eleven years after settling in America and was well regarded as a pioneer farmer, while Albert rented land for many years and had finally become a smallholder nearly twenty-five years after arriving in Nebraska.

Larus never showed regrets about leaving his homeland and greatly appreciated his independence and reward for his hard work in Nebraska. His own words and those of his closest friends indicate that he was quite anti-social, while the Lancaster County biographical sketch describes him as a public-spirited citizen with considerable influence on the improvement of the area. The inference must be that his life was dominated by an extreme workload until he was eventually worn out in his mid-sixties.

Albert was a thoughtful and observant man by all accounts. He missed his homeland and family for many years and regretted spending his youth unwisely, but gradually got his footing and became a happy family man and a successful farmer. A letter written just six years after he arrived in North America shows that he was concerned that his mind was closing in and his thoughts of Iceland were fading. His letters through a period of thirty-seven years show, however, that he had little trouble expressing himself in Icelandic, despite American family life and geographical isolation from other Icelanders. His writing in Icelandic remained fluent, although he used some local terms for his work and new technology. Albert's description of the best qualities of American life must also have reflected his own values. He said he found the United States to be the best place in the world for a man to live and raise his children because of personal freedom, good administration, a fine country, good public health, and the good moral conduct of the people.

NOTES

1 There are over 11,000 letters in the collection, which spans sixty years. Correspondents include twenty-three emigrants. The most prolific writer from America was Benedikt Hálfdanarson (Hall) who wrote thirty-four letters from 1878 to 1913. The collection provided research material in a course, "Icelandic in the Nineteenth Century," at the University of Iceland. This led to the author's interest in the letters from Nebraska.

2 "Hjer er ljómandi fagurt öldóttar grassljettur sem ekki sjest ein einasta þúfa á, ekki einn steinn og ekki nokkur blettur graslaus, engin flái eða mýri og lítið af skurðum eða skorningum og má keyra í vagni um alt margar þingmannaleiðir, eins og tilbúnum vegi."

3 The name Frank Wittstruck appears in other letters from Larus.

4 "Ég er orðinn sannfærður um það að það er það þarfasta verk sem ég hef og mun gjöra að fara til Ameríku uppá mína síðu."

5 "Þettað er það besta land til að læra alla skapaða hluti."

6 "Gjört hvurt verk sem firir kjemur á bóndabæ hjer í Amiríku."

7 The group consisted of Jón Ólafsson, Ólafur Ólafsson, and Páll Björnsson.

8 "Nú ef þessum sendi mönnum litist vel á sig og þætti nógu kalt !!! þá hef jeg heirt að þeir ötluðu að skjipta sjer í Smalamenskuni og skjildi Jón fara heim til Íslands og sæka alt sem regstrar fært er og reka til Alaska en Ólafur skjildi koma til baka og smala saman þessum irrum sem þar eru í Banda ríkjenum og Canada. Jeg er hálf hræddur um að jeg skjótist hjá honum í lægðonum í Nebraska og komi ekki firir í fistu leit. Páll átti að búa í Alaska á meðan bæði til að sjá um að aungvir kjæmu til að stela Alaska og so til að hjálpa Ólafi og Jóni að reka in safnið þigar þeir koma úr gyngonum !!!"

Larus's spelling is in many ways particular to him. He often writes *y* where *au* is the norm. Examples are *dyður, kypa, kypið, hyst, yngvir, gyngonum, vitlys, umhiggulysa,* for *dauður, kaupa, kaupið, haust, aungvir, gaungunum, vitlaus umhyggjulausa.*

9 The full account of the quest for Alaska has been published by Hjörtur Pálsson (1975).

10 Long Pine in Brown County, Nebraska, is about 400 kilometres northwest from Firth in Lancaster County.

11 "Hvorki mjer nje öðrum til gagns og þessvegna vildi jeg opt og tíðum heldur vera dyður en að lifa þessu umhiggulysa og einfalda Neb. Lífi."

12 Two letters from Larus (referenced here as LB 18.1.1875 and LB 17.3.1879) were published in *Bréf Vestur-Íslendinga*, edited by Böðvar Guðmundsson (2001).

13 "Ameríka er góður skóli og nógu margbreitt til að gera hvurn einn að manni, þ.e.a.s þann sem vill verða það."

14 "hestatím, vagn og búninga og rentaði 80 ekrur af landi með húsi á og fremur góðum útihúsum."

15 "bindindismaður og uppheldur kvennarjettinum" [en fyrir demókrata] "er bjórbelgur að nafni Cleveland sem lofar fríu ákavíti og frjálsum viðskiptum við aðrar þjóðir."

16 "Þú veist að mjer er ekki lagið að skrifa og þegar ég mindast við að skrifa eitthvað þá er eins og hugur minn nái ekki lengra en útifir borðið sem jeg sit við, þó hann einstöku sinnum kvarli heim til þín þar sem þú ert fullur af andans fjöri og óþreitandi laungun til að koma nitsömum hlutum í verk."

17 Albert writes that she is the niece of Jón Halldórsson, but there are no other records of this relationship.

18 "Jeg mundi alldrei giptast ef jeg ætti að velja úr enska kvennfólkinu mjer hefur fundist það einhvern vegin ónáttúrlegt að eiga að lifa alla sína æfi saman við einhvern sem ekki hefði neina hugmind um fósturlandið fríða."

19 "Þegar ég er orðin ríkur þá kjem jeg heim að finna þig elsku bróðir mig hefur opt langað heim og langar víst alltjend heim eins lengi og jeg lifi og jeg bíst við að það sakni hver einn heilvita maður fósturlands síns meira eða minna alla æfi sína."

20 "Bandaríkin eru að jeg held það besta pláss í heimi firir mann að lifa og ala upp börn sín þar sem frjálsleika, góða stjórn, gott ríki, góða heilsu og gott siðferði snertir."

21 "Safnar nitrogen úr loftinu og skjilur það eftir í jörðinni firir aðrar jurtir að lifa á og þannig eru clover og alfalfa agentar firir þettað jarðarlíf."

22 Guide Rock is about 190 kilometres west-southwest of Firth.

23 Seven letters from Albert (referenced here as AB 9.2.1879; AB 2.3.1880; AB 29.5.1880; AB 29.7.1884; AB 3.1.1897; AB 15.5.1910; and AB 22.1.1915) were published in *Bréf Vestur-Íslendinga*, edited by Böðvar Guðmundsson (2001).

REFERENCES

Published References

Guðmundsson, Böðvar, ed. 2001. *Bréf Vestur-Íslendinga I.* Reykjavík: Mál og menning.

Halldórsson, Jón. 1873. *Norðanfari* 12 (Jan. 31): 5–6.

———. 1913. "Tildrög til íslenskrar nýlendustofnunar í Nebraska" [Background to the Icelandic settlement in Nebraska]. *Almanak 1895–1914.* Published by Ólafur S. Thorgeirsson, 20th year 1914: 150–56. Winnipeg.

———. 2005. *Atriði ævi minnar: Bréf og greinar*. Edited by Úlfar Bragason. Reykjavík: Reykjavík University Press.

Heiðarsson, Steinþór. 1999. "Íslands ástmegir og þrælar. Drættir úr sjálfsmynd Vestur-Íslendinga." *Saga* 37: 17–61.

Júlíusson, Játvarður J. 1986. *Saga Torfa Bjarnasonar og Ólafsdalsskóla.* Reykjavík: Búnaðarfélag Íslands.

Kristinsson, Júníus H. 1983. *Vesturfaraskrá 1870–1914. Record of Emigrants from Iceland to America 1870–1914*. Reykjavík: Sagnfræðistofnun Háskóla Íslands.

Pálsson, Hjörtur. 1975. *Alaskaför Jóns Ólafssonar 1874*. Edited by Þórhallur Vilmundarson. Studia historica 4. Reykjavík: Bókaútgáfa Menningarsjóðs.

Manuscripts – Unpublished References

Lbs 150 NF "Torfi Bjarnason: Skjala- og handritasafn, Sendibréf til Torfa Bjarnasonar" [Torfi Bjarnason: Manuscript Collection, Letters to Torfi Bjarnason]. National Library of Iceland.

(Box 1) "Bréf frá Aðalbjarti Bjarnasyni" [Letters from Albert Barnason]. AB 1.8.1878, AB 9.2.1879, AB 4.5.1879, AB 2.3.1880, AB 29.5.1880, AB 6.4.1881, AB 14.10.1883, AB 29.7.1884, AB 2.3.1890, AB 3.1.1897, AB 14.1.1901, AB 25.8.1901, AB 22.9.1902, AB 24.1.1905, AB 4.6.1905, AB 2.12.1905, AB 24.3.1906, AB 15.5.1910, AB 30.11.1913, AB 22.1.1915.

(Box 6) "Bréf frá Benedikt Hálfdanarsyni" [Letters from Benedikt Hall]. BH 8.10.1892, BH 19.01.1903, BH 12.12.1906, BH 27.05.1911, BH 3.4.1913.

(Box 20) "Bréf frá Guðmundi Lambertsen" [Letters from G. Lambertsen]. GL 2.6.1872, GL 26.6.1872, GL 26.3.1873.

(Box 36) "Bréf frá Lárusi Bjarnasyni" [Letters from Larus Barnason]. LB 1869; LB 12.3.1869, LB 10.2.1873, LB 18.1.1874, LB 20.3.1874, LB 26.4.1874, LB 7.6.1874, LB 12.7.1874, LB 29.8.1874, LB 7.10.1874, LB 29.11.1874, LB 18.1.1875, LB 29.1.1875, LB 21.3.1875, LB 5.6.1875, LB 12.10.1875, LB 6.5.1876, LB 28.1.1877, LB 10.1.1878, LB 17.3.1879, LB 22.4.1880.

(Box 39) "Bréf frá James B. Power" [Letter from James B. Power]. JP 11.8.1873.

(Box 56) "Bréf frá Torfa Bjarnasyni til Guðlaugar Zakaríasdóttur" [Letters from Torfi Bjarnason to Gudlaug Zakariasdottir]. TB 5.5.1873, TB 15.6–19.6.1873.

(Box 56) "Bréf Torfa" [Letter from Torfi]. TB 6.5.1873.

Online References

Albert Barnason headstone. n.d. Accessed 28 January 2021. https://www.findagrave.com/memorial/55315117/albert-barnason.

Larus Barnason. 1888. Portrait and Biographical Album of Lancaster County, Nebraska, 1888. NEGenWeb Project, pp. 304–305. Date of original publication: David Gochenour, private communication. Accessed 24 January 2021. http://www.usgennet.org/usa/ne/topic/resources/OLLibrary/pbal/pages/balc0062.htm.

Larus Barnason headstone. n.d. Accessed 28 January 2021. https://www.findagrave.com/memorial/52487331/larus-barnason.

CHAPTER 5

Ralph E. Halldorson and the Great War

ÚLFAR BRAGASON

ACCORDING TO *Minningarrit íslenzkra hermanna 1914–1918*, a publication commemorating Icelanders who did military service in the First World War, published in 1923 by the Jon Sigurdsson Chapter IODE in Winnipeg, 1,245 Canadians and Americans of Icelandic descent ("Western Icelanders") had enlisted in the military forces of those countries: 989 for Canada and 256 for the U.S.[1] In addition over 100 Icelandic names appeared in military records but without any further information on the men in question. The *Minningarrit* goes on to say: "So far as can be ascertained, one hundred and forty-four died in the war, while eleven hundred and one survived. Of those who died, 94 were killed in action, 2 died in accidents, two [are] missing in action, 19 died of wounds, and 27 (including one nurse) died of diseases. 207 were wounded in action but survived. 10 were captured by the enemy" (Jónsson 1923, 44; see also Bjarnason 2015, 236).

One of those who died of disease was Hrólfur Jónsson, or Ralph E. Halldorson, who was born at Long Pine, Nebraska, on 15 January 1888. His parents were Jón Halldórsson (1838–1919) from Stóruvellir in Bárðardalur, in North Iceland, and his wife, Þórvör Sveinsdóttir (1849–1912) of Garður in Aðaldalur, also in the North. Jón was one of the first Icelandic emigrants to the New World, leaving Iceland in 1872. Þórvör emigrated in 1873. They married in 1875 and lived in Nebraska for the rest of their married life. They had five children who lived to adulthood. All were named after family members, except Hrólfur, the youngest son (Halldórsson 2005).

FIGURE 5.1. Ralph E. Halldorson in Camp Dix, New Jersey, August 1918. (Courtesy of the family)

Many of Jón Halldórsson's letters to relatives and friends have survived, and a selection was published in the book *Atriði ævi minnar* (Details of my life) in 2005. The idea behind the publication was to tell Jón's life story, which he had intended to write himself. In the letters Jón refers, for instance, to the war and U.S. participation in it, his sons being drafted into military service, and the German enemy. Among the descendants of Jón Halldórsson, many letters from Hrólfur Jónsson have been preserved, including letters written after he was drafted. The last of those letters are discussed here: letters received by the family before Hrólfur departed for France to take part in the war, letters from after he arrived there, and letters written to him by his brother Tómas or Thomas (Tom) E. Halldorson (1878–1970) and sent to him in the field, which were returned after Hrólfur's death. Hrólfur was an example of the acculturation of a child of immigrants. Although immigrants in the Midwestern United States were shaped by a vision of two worlds—their heritage from the home country and the culture of their New World—their children could share that world view only to a limited extent (Gulliksen 2004, 19). This was manifested *inter alia* in the fact that Hrólfur started to call himself Ralph E. Halldorson.

FIGURE 5.2. Sophia and Tom. (Courtesy of the family)

LETTERS AND LANGUAGE

Among Ralph's letters that survive together with the correspondence and photographs of Sofía or Sophia Halldorson (1882–1973) are twenty-three from the summer of 1918. The first was written on 25 July, probably in Syracuse, New York State, when Ralph was preparing for his military service, and the last out on the Atlantic Ocean in early September. A postcard he sent to Sofía on 11 September, telling her that he had arrived in France, also survives. Tom's letters were written in September and October 1918; all were sent from Chicago, except one from St. Paul, Minnesota, where he was attending a conference of photographers. The correspondence was accompanied by a letter dated 18 September, from Sergeant Street, the head of the ward at the field hospital where Ralph died, informing Jón Halldórsson of his son's death, and another letter from Mr. E.H. Cashmore to Tom, dated 2 February 1919, in which he gives an account of Ralph's illness and death. A letter dated 24 February 1919 survives from Captain D.M. Salter of Ralph's infantry, who writes about his interactions with Ralph in the last weeks of his life. In addition a telegram survives from the U.S. Army, dated 8 October 1918, informing Jón Halldórsson of Ralph's death from pneumonia; also a letter from Sveinn or S. Harry Halldorson (1877–1938) to Páll or Paul J. Halldorson (1883–1964), dated 12 October in Bassett, Nebraska, in which he reacts to the news of the death of their brother Ralph.

All but one of Jón Halldórsson's extant letters are in Icelandic, but his sons' letters are all in English. This may of course have been necessary for reasons of censorship, but all indications are that Jón and Þórvör's children had abandoned speaking Icelandic, let alone writing it, at an early age.

In a letter to his friend in Iceland Benedikt Jónsson of Auðnir (1846–1939), written in Lincoln, Nebraska, on 20 January 1910, Jón Halldórsson writes:

> There was a lot of talk about journeys to Greenland in 1845 back home, and then about going to Brazil in 1865, but that was nothing to the talk of travel to Iceland that is going on now in this family, and now all the volumes are dug out (at the library) that have anything to say about the country—true or false—for the kids know only a little, poor Icelandic. They more-or-less stopped speaking it after they started at school, and after Sveinn brought an American wife into the family it ceased entirely. When they were young, they thought that Icelandic stopped them pronouncing English correctly. That was in many ways foolish, but we couldn't persuade them, and that was that. And now they regret it after all, having got more education. Now they are trying to speak Icelandic now and then, but it is so awfully garbled that it might bring one to tears. If they continue as they have begun, perhaps they'll be no worse that the town-dwellers back home?[2] (Halldórsson 2005, 147)

Jón's description of his children's limited command of Icelandic is confirmed by four extant letters written by his wife, Þórvör, to their children in 1908–09. They are all in English.

It has often been maintained that Western Icelanders continued to use their mother tongue for longer than other Nordic minorities in the New World (see Haugen 1969, 289–92). This has been attributed to their strong national identity. But the statistics apply only to Canada, where people of Icelandic origin were sufficiently numerous to be specifically identified in the figures. The situation of Western Icelanders in the United States was somewhat different from those in Canada—at least for those who chose to settle elsewhere than in the Icelandic settlements in North Dakota and Minnesota.

In her book *North American Icelandic: The Life of a Language*, Birna Arnbjörnsdóttir pinpoints three main factors in the decline and disappearance of Icelandic: "the close and intense contact with English; the narrowing functional range of Icelandic; and the disintegration of formerly tight-knit social networks" (Arnbjörnsdóttir 2006, 34). Jón Halldórsson wrote an article about the Icelandic settlement in Nebraska for the 1914 *Almanak,* published in Winnipeg in 1913 by Ólafur S. Thorgeirsson; Jón was one of the settlement's founders. He writes that, while the number of Icelanders in Nebraska has never been high, most of them are located near to Jón's family, as these are friends and relatives of the family (Halldórsson 2005, 162–66). Jón himself had set off in search of freedom, progress, and education in the New World, and had no intention of living in some closed-off Icelandic "colony" (see Bragason 2017, 153–71). Thereby, English became the principal language of interaction outside the home, with the exception of the few Icelandic friends and relatives living nearby. Icelandic became the language of the home. Þórvör and Jón read extensively, including newspapers in Icelandic, and they corresponded with relatives living in the Icelandic communities in North America and back home in Iceland. With their passion for ensuring that their children received a good education, they must surely have taught them to read Icelandic. While their schooling was in English, it is unlikely that the children made a conscious decision to switch languages until they reached high school. It was not until after the First World War that U.S. authorities started to make any real progress in the monolingual ideology that has been pursued ever since (Spolsky 2004, 93–96). But the Halldórsson children surely wanted to get on in U.S. society; and as their parents spoke English, they might have seen no reason to maintain their Icelandic, when they had limited contact with Icelanders.

THE UNITED STATES AND THE GREAT WAR

The United States declared war on Germany on 6 April 1917, after Germany had announced on 1 February that all passenger and freight vessels sailing the oceans without their permission would be liable to be sunk. President Woodrow Wilson deemed Germany to have declared war on the world at large. The United States was far from prepared for conflict at that stage, but rapid preparations were made and conscription was introduced for all healthy males aged eighteen to forty-five. Initially the draft was confined to those aged twenty-one to thirty-one, then was followed by the other age groups (Peterson 1923, 35–37; see also Howard 2002, 91–95).

Jón Halldórsson wrote in a letter to his relative Thór Stefánsson in Winnipeg, dated in Chicago, 28 April 1918:

> I hardly know whether I should mention our future. My youngest son, Ralph, received his call-up papers last year, but his draft number was so high that it hasn't come up yet, but he has been examined and deemed fit to serve.
>
> He has often found it hard to have this hanging over him, and he would long have been in the volunteer corps by this time, had he not promised his employers to work for them until the U.S. needs him. And they have promised to take him back, in the same position, if he comes back. He runs a photographic studio for them in a town in N.Y. state, and has 30 dollars a week.
>
> Páll, who has run the workshop here and is over the age of conscription (twenty-four),[3] is determined to go, but he wants to get into the air service, and take photographs from flying-

> boats, but there are so many ahead of him seeking that position that he hasn't been admitted yet (surprising as that may seem).
>
> This uncertainty turns everything upside-down. Tómas, who has been travelling in advertising and sales, has taken over the workshop, but there is no-one to take his place. Sofía works in the workshop as much as she can along with the housework, and then there are two men working there, who the boys have hired. (Halldórsson 2005, 190)

At that time the siblings Thomas, Paul (Páll), and Sophia ran a photography business in Chicago, while Ralph worked as a photographer in Rochester and Syracuse, New York State.

There was much debate among Western Icelanders about participation in the war, and opinions were divided. The Reverend Björn B. Jónsson took the view that all those who were born in the New World or were naturalized citizens must heed the call to military service but added that "the vast majority of the Icelanders who during the war years entered military service did so voluntarily, without and before being strictly obliged to do so by law." Björn considered what had motivated these men to volunteer. He explained that the vast majority of them were young men, who were motivated by 1) ambition for themselves and their country, 2) desire to defend the oppressed, and 3) loyalty to the Allied cause but also 4) desire for adventure (Jónsson 1923, 42–44). Lawyer George Peterson also points out that the men had fought "side-by-side with doughty Frenchmen, and no less with doughty and steadfast Britons, for the freedom of mankind, that democracy might flourish in the world" (Peterson 1923, 37). Here, he brings out the ideals the United States were seen as representing: freedom and democracy. Jón Halldórsson, however, says that Ralph wanted to get it over with, while Paul saw the opportunity for aerial photography of the conflict.

Many Germans had settled in Nebraska; Jón Halldórsson found them overbearing and did not like them much, although he mixed with them. Jón's brother-in-law, the husband of his sister Halldóra, was one such Nebraskan of German descent. Jón mentioned in a letter to Benedikt Jónsson of Auðnir, dated 17 August 1884, at Long Pine, Nebraska, that one of the main reasons for his moving with his family from Lancaster County, just south of the state capital of Lincoln, to settle in Brown County, in northern Nebraska, was that they had been surrounded "by Boches who have been enriched by time and their land, and in whom their wealth has stirred up their German chauvinism, so it was unpleasant for small farmers to be in among them" (Halldórsson 2005, 111). The war had had an impact on Jón's children's production of photographic flash lamps, as the flash powder and fuse material had been imported from Germany. They had to give up producing such lamps (Halldórsson 2005, 185). The war had also put an end to Jón's children's plans to travel to Iceland and visit their relatives in the North. Their father wrote that the visit would be delayed by the war (Halldórsson 2005, 185), but it was never made.

THE NAME HRÓLFUR

In an essay about Icelanders' naming customs in the first half of the nineteenth century, Ólöf Garðarsdóttir concluded that as a rule the elder children were named after members of the parents' families, while the younger siblings were less likely to have such names. Parents often chose unconventional names for these children (Garðarsdóttir 1999; see also Björnsson 1996, 140–44). Jón and Þórvör clearly followed this convention. Their eldest son, Sveinn, was named after his maternal grandfather; the next was named Tómas after his paternal great-grandfather; the third, Páll, after his maternal uncle; and the daughter, Sofía, received the name of her maternal grandmother. It is also consistent with Icelandic naming customs that Hrólfur, the youngest son who lived to adulthood, was not named after a relative. The question is: How did the parents come to pick that name?

The name *Hrólfur* was known from early times: a contraction of Hróð-ólfr/-úlfr, it also existed in Scandinavia, Germany, and English-speaking countries in the form *Rolf*. Hrólfur is a name that occurs in the Icelandic sagas: most famously Hrólfr *kraki* and Göngu-Hrólfr in their respective eponymous sagas (Kvaran and Jónsson 1991, 313). Jón Halldórsson is known to have had an interest in Göngu-Hrólfr (Halldórsson 2005, 73). Jón's interest in Göngu-Hrólfr was probably a function of this Hrólfr being conflated with his namesake, Hrólfr, son of Rögnvaldr Eysteinsson, Earl of Møre in Norway

(Ragnvald Mørejarl). That Hrólfr is said to have gone to Normandy, where he became an earl—known as Rollo in English and Rollon in French. He was said to have brought from Norway to France the concept of democracy, which in due course took root and flourished in the United States (Øverland 2000, 152–60). This interpretation of the roots of democracy—like the story that Leifr Eiríksson the Lucky had discovered the New World—was cited by Nordic immigrants in the United States to justify their presence and claim equal status with the population of British origin (Øverland 2000, 63; see also Bragason 2017, 96–99). Hence, for Jón, the name *Hrólfur* must have had implications of freedom and democracy.

But there were still other factors. Jón's words were quoted above about his children's (lack of) Icelandic skills, and mention was made of the fact that Þórvör's letters to her children, written after the couple moved to Lincoln in 1907, are all in English. By that time all the children had anglicized their names, and Hrólfur now went by the name Ralph E. Halldorson (not Rolf). This could reflect a long-standing confusion between the two names *Rolf* and *Ralph*; the latter was also a far more common name in the United States (babynamespedia.com).

A different Rolf/Ralph, however, was probably no less significant to Jón and his family than Göngu-Hrólfr: the renowned American poet and philosopher Ralph Waldo Emerson (1803–1882). Hrólfur wrote his name as Ralph E. Halldórson, in which the E. stood for Emerson. Emerson was well-known to Icelanders in North America. For instance, he gave a lecture, "The Fortune of the Republic" on 30 March 1878, and shortly afterwards part of it was published in Icelandic translation in *Framfari* (The progressivist), the periodical of Icelanders in New Iceland, Manitoba. If Jón and Þórvör were not familiar with Emerson before—which is unlikely—they would have read the passages from the lecture in *Framfari,* to which they were subscribers. Emerson's speech included the following:

> Ours is the country of poor men. Here is practical democracy; here is the human race poured out over the continent to do itself justice; all mankind in its shirt-sleeves; not grimacing like poor rich men in cities, pretending to be rich, but unmistakably

> taking off its coat to hard work, when labor is sure to pay. . . . The new times need a new man, the complemental man, whom plainly this country must furnish. . . . I hope America will come to have its pride in being a nation of servants, and not of the served. . . . Whilst every man can say I serve,—to the whole extent of my being I apply my faculty to the service of mankind in my especial place,—he therein sees and shows a reason for his being in the world, and is not a moth or incumbrance in it. (Emerson 1904, 526–42)

Emerson's words must have been music to the ears of Jón and Þórvör, who had emigrated to America in search of democracy and freedom. Hence, most indications are that Jón and Þórvör's choice of the name *Hrólfur* for their son was made after careful consideration—and was in fact bound up with the ideas they had adopted by moving to the New World.

Their children, whom Jón called the "only riches" he had, chose to become American (Halldórsson 2005, 147). Ralph E. Halldorson was called up to fight on the side of freedom in the war against the German Kaiser Wilhelm II—who had the same name as one of Göngu-Hrólfr's antagonists. Ralph was sent to Normandy, where Hrólfr or Rollo, son of Earl Rögnvaldr of Møre, had sown the seeds of democracy. Such parallels were also in the minds of other Icelanders: George Peterson writes, in an article about the U.S. role in the First World War: "That fair and valiant company was transported by [U.S. General John Joseph] Pershing out of the West, and joined forces with the English and French who, combat-wearied and undermanned, fought in unequal and horrifying battle against the Germans—just as the Great Masked Man came to the aid of Hrólfr and Stefnir in their struggle against Grímr *ægir* and Earl Eiríkr" (Peterson 1923, 37). But Ralph's mind was more probably on Emerson's ideas of the American, the New Man, as his change of name indicates.

BAND OF BROTHERS

Ralph attended school in Long Pine, then graduated from high school in Lincoln after his parents gave up their farm and moved there. He studied at the University of Nebraska from 1908 to 1912, then worked in photography and production of photographic goods, with his siblings or as an employee of other studios—lastly for Morall-Hoole Studios in Rochester and Syracuse, New York State, until he was conscripted at the end of July 1918. Ralph was sent to Camp Dix, New Jersey, for training, and then embarked for France with his unit at the end of August or early September. He fell ill aboard the troop ship on the way to Brest, where he was admitted to hospital on 14 September and died on the 18th.

Ralph wrote to his family in Chicago from Syracuse on 25 July 1918, as he was making ready to leave for the war. He writes that he has said his farewells to his colleagues that day and that they have given him small gifts. He also tells them about a farewell dinner held for the men who were leaving. He writes about his finances, and who will take responsibility for the Morall-Hoole Studios in Syracuse in his absence. Finally, he says: "It will take over ten hours to get to Dix and I suppose it will be a rather dreary ride, but I am sort of looking forward to the trip, and am anxious to see how I will look in the new uniform. As soon as I have an opportunity of getting photographed, I will send you a portrait of a real American soldier." In a letter dated 27 August 1918 at Camp Dix—the last before he embarked—he refers to these photographs of himself, which he had either enclosed with this letter or sent previously: "As soon as you have developed those prints, please send me a set of them. I am very anxious about them. I am sorry that I didn't have my trench helmet at the time."

It emerges in the letter that restrictions applied to military personnel's correspondence, but he urges his family not to give up writing to him, all the same. He also mentions that he had been thinking of using the death of his paternal aunt, Halldóra, as a reason to make a visit home: "I thought some of trying to get a furlough home when I heard that Aunt Dora died. That would have given me a pretty good cause to come home, but I wasn't exactly financially fixed. Besides, the stay would have been very short. And

I am not especially fond of saying goodbyes. Under the circumstances, I think it is the best for all of us as it is. The real enjoyment will be coming home after the war." Halldóra had died on 15 August, so if Ralph had applied for furlough due to her death, he would not have gone to France with his comrades. He goes on: "All the boys here seem especially happy tonight after learning definitely that we are moving. I, personally, am very glad, too. And I hope I will be able to do my share when I get over there." His only concern is that his father and sister may not have enough to live on if the older brothers are also conscripted. He promises to send them some money if possible.

While the passenger liner *Leviathan*, which transported many U.S. troops to France—up to 14,000 on each passage—lay in harbour in Hoboken, New Jersey, Ralph wrote two letters to his family, probably on 30 and 31 August; he appears to have posted them in France. Both have been heavily censored, and large parts of the letters are blacked out. Ralph complains about the poor food and the crowded facilities on-board. In the latter letter he writes about sailing out of port:

> We marched upstairs in good order, so I think we could get out easily if the ship sank. Just when we got upstairs the ship started from the dock + we staid on deck for nearly 2 hours. The band played some good pieces among which was "Good-bye Broadway, Hello France" and the "Marseilles." I was certainly glad to get away from dock. Of course, I rather hate to see the good old U.S.A. slip away, but I hope it will not be very long until I come back again. If I ever get back it will be the last time I'll ever be in the army.

The last letter from Ralph that reached the family was written at sea, just before the troop ship arrived at Brest in France. He expresses the wish that he will soon be home, as he does not much like the company on-board. He is longing to hear from the family and promises to send half his pay home to support them. But he says he is ready for battle, having recovered from the sea journey and illness. He ends his letter with the words: "Above all, don't worry about me. It's the Huns who should worry." Sofía received a postcard from Ralph dated 11 September, telling her that he has arrived in France.

Thomas Halldorson responded to his brother's entreaty to keep on writing, even if they did not hear from Ralph. After Ralph's death Thomas's five letters were returned. In the first letter, dated 3 September in Chicago, Tom writes about the family's worries about Ralph, and the film he had sent, which Tom was developing. He enclosed some contact prints with the letter, commenting: "Really now the one at rifle salute is the best and it is simply fine, and we will probably have a 11 x 7 made up from it as the negatives are strong enough to stand the enlarging." He continues: "It is certainly too bad that you could not avail yourself of chance to come home when Auntie died. It would have been fine to have seen you before leaving U.S.A. but I really feel like you do about good byes and I am figuring on how to get out of such a thing if I go, for there is usually a bunch gathers right across from our office whenever a contingent leaves Ravenswood and it is a sad looking sight usually." At the end of the letter Tom says he expects that he and Paul will soon be conscripted—and that Paul is trying to enlist as soon as possible.

The last of the letters is written on 2 October in Chicago. The family are waiting anxiously to hear from Ralph. Tom mentions that the Spanish Flu is "all over town," but the family are all well. He ends with the words:

> Nothing more now but I will again report that the last letter read from you was when you were on board a troopship. Where you are this minute, Id give a lot to know. Really, I can't see why the soldiers' mail is not carried through quicker. There must be a reason.
>
> With love from all here at home to you over there. I hope you are getting along fine. Write, even tho[ugh] a card at all opportunities.

The letter was posted by Tom in Chicago on 3 October; the family, then, had not yet received notification of his death.

DEATH NOTICE

Jón Halldórsson and his children appear to have received notification of Ralph's death by telegram from the military authorities in Washington, DC, dated 8 October. Jón also received a letter from Sergeant Street, the head of the ward at the field hospital where he died, dated 18 September, the day of Ralph's death. He writes: "Your boy was brought into my ward about September 12 with pneumonia and although he put up a determined fight for life, that most virulent of all diseases (over here) took the last spark of life, but left a smiling form lying peacefully upon the bed." He also writes that Ralph received the best nursing care, and that he was ministered to by a pastor before he died. Jón received another letter, from nurse Marie C. Frost (not preserved but referred to in the obituary), informing him that, following a military funeral, Ralph had been buried in Kerfauntstrasse Cemetery, where many valiant American boys repose. The nurse writes that upon the casket, which was draped in the U.S. flag, a small evergreen branch from a tree near the grave was laid by members of the YWCA. The grave, she writes, was marked with a cross and a flag. She enclosed the evergreen branch with the letter, with the words that Ralph had declared himself ready to sacrifice his life for freedom and democracy, although he never reached the battlefield (Halldórsson 2005, 195).

S. Harry Halldorson's letter to his brother Paul, written after he had received news of Ralph's death, throws light on how Jón and his children took the news. Harry writes:

> I received Tom's Telegram with the sadest news that I have ever got, also your letter with the Particulars as much as you know + possibly as much as we will probably ever know about his last days. It seems awful to think that none of us could have been with him during his last days. And it seems awful to think that life so young + with the Bri[gh]test Prospects should have, through most likely exposure, been sacrified.
>
> . . .
>
> I am thankful that his hands were not stained with Blood even though we might feel like going into the fight + doing our Bit.

The family probably felt that they had not received enough information about Ralph's death, as a letter from Tom to the military authorities is extant, in which he requests answers. He also asks for Ralph's typewriter to be returned to the family; one of the last photographs of Ralph shows him with the typewriter. Perhaps it was because Ralph seemed rather discontented in his last letters received by the family that they sought more information. Captain D.M. Salter writes about the troop transport across the Atlantic, and reports that his men disembarked in Brest on 8 September. He remarks that the weather was particularly bad, and that raw recruits such as Ralph had suffered from the cold. Ralph had been taken to hospital before the unit went to the Front. The captain goes on to say that he had not been able to get to know most of the men under his command during that short time, but that he remembers Ralph clearly: "He certainly was a willing, capable, clean cut young fellow, who after completing a hard day spent some time in writing on his typewriter, while others found little time for anything in that line and interested themselves with shows, games, etc." During those times Ralph was typing out his letters home, and that explains why the family was so keen to have the typewriter returned to them.

MEMORY

Sigfús Magnússon in Duluth, Minnesota, wrote in memory of Ralph in the Winnipeg newspapers, in a gesture of friendship to Jón Halldórsson. The obituary, written on 3 January 1919, was published in *Heimskringla* on 29 January and appeared in near-identical form in *Lögberg* on 30 January. The obituary was based to a large extent upon letters and information that Jón's family had clearly sent to Sigfús. He writes, summing up the development of a son of immigrants:

> Photography was Ralph's greatest passion, and he believed that with good photographs it was possible to show all the qualities (true interpretation) of men, women and children. His greatest desire was thus to continue his experiments in that direction on his return. And there was another thing which

> characterised this young man, and that was his talent for verse; this first emerged when he was studying at the University in Lincoln, where some of his work was published in a student paper. At the university Ralph was also a member of a dramatic society, and plays written by him were performed there—and perhaps they still are today. The plays demonstrated that Ralph had sufficient talent to become a playwright—but he lacked practice, and they were also written in his free time, alongside his studies. But that is a common fate for young men who must give priority to the necessities of life, so that desires and talents go to waste. (Halldórsson 2005, 194)

Sigfús concludes the obituary by tracing the descent of Jón and Þórvör and referring to their surviving four children.

Ralph E. Halldorson is mentioned in *Minningarrit íslenzkra hermanna 1914–1918*. The chapter appears to be largely based upon Sigfús's obituary, although there are some differences. In the *Minningarrit* Rev. Björn B. Jónsson writes about the significance for Western Icelanders of their participation in the war: "It is certain that the participation of Western Icelanders in the war had huge consequences for themselves. They will no longer be deemed *foreigners* in this country. They paid a high price for that domiciliary right. . . . The horrors of the war, the wounds and the tears, have purchased for us sincere *patriotism* here in this country" (Jónsson 1923, 45).

Jón Halldórsson's sons were probably thinking similar thoughts as they waited to be called up to the war, although they may not have fully realized the gravity of the situation. Jón Halldórsson died only a little more than a year after his youngest son, on 23 September 1919, at the age of eighty-two. During that autumn Tom was starting to wonder when the government would bring Ralph's body home, as he says in a letter to his brother, S. Harry, about the settlement of their father's estate. Newspapers in Lincoln, Nebraska, reported on Ralph's funeral on 10 January 1922. Nearly fifty years had passed since his father had stepped ashore in New York. Ralph was buried next to his parents in the Wyuka churchyard in Lincoln. Next to his name on the gravestone is a military star, a reminder of the sacrifice paid for the freedom and democracy they had sought in North America—a part of the only riches they had: their family. But the star is also testimony that their children had not only changed their language from Icelandic to English, they had also assimilated American culture and values. They were free-born Americans, just as Emerson had described.

NOTES

1 I wish to thank Carolyn Hinds for copies of letters in the keeping of her family that are cited here, and for photographs that accompany this chapter. Her assistance has been invaluable. Thanks are also due to Anna H. Yates for translating this chapter.

2 Residents of towns and villages were reputed to speak a debased form of Icelandic, heavily influenced by Danish.

3 Jón means thirty-four. Paul was born in 1883, and therefore he was not in the age group conscripted first.

REFERENCES

Unpublished Sources

Sophia Halldorson. Collection of letters and photographs. In the keeping of Carolyn Hinds.

Published Sources

Arnbjörnsdóttir, Birna. 2006. *North American Icelandic: The Life of a Language.* Winnipeg: University of Manitoba Press.

Bjarnason, Gunnar Þór. 2015. *Þegar siðmenningin fór fjandans til: Íslendingar og stríðið mikla 1914–1918.* Reykjavík: Mál og menning.

Björnsson, Árni. 1996. *Merkisdagar á mannsævinni.* Reykjavík: Mál og menning.

Bragason, Úlfar. 2017. *Frelsi, menning, framför: Um bréf og greinar Jóns Halldórssonar* [Freedom, culture, progress: On letters and articles by Jón Halldórsson]. Reykjavík: Háskólaútgáfan.

Emerson, Ralph Waldo. 1878. "Skáldið Emerson um Ameríku." *Framfari* 1 (32), 24 July.

———. 1904. "The Fortune of the Republic." In *The Complete Works.* Vol. 11: *Miscellanies,* 509–44. Boston: Houghton Mifflin.

Garðarsdóttir, Ólöf. 1999. "Naming Practices and the Importance of Kinship Networks in Early Nineteenth-Century Iceland." *History of the Family* 4: 297–314.

Gulliksen, Oyvind T. 2004. *Twofold Identities: Norwegian-American Contributions to Midwestern Literature*. New York: Peter Lang.

Halldórsson, Jón. 2005. *Atriði ævi minnar: bréf og greinar.* Edited by Úlfar Bragason. Reykjavík: Háskólaútgáfan.

Haugen, Einar. 1969. *The Norwegian Language in America: A Study in Bilingual Behavior.* Bloomington: Indiana University Press.

Howard, Michael. 2002. *The First World War*. Oxford: Oxford University Press.

Jónsson, Björn B. 1923. "Vestur-Íslendingar í stríðinu" [North American Icelanders in the war]. In *Minningarrit íslenzkra hermanna 1914–1918*, 41–46. Winnipeg: Félagið Jón Sigurðsson.

Kvaran, Guðrún, and Sigurður Jónsson frá Arnarvatni. 1991. *Nöfn Íslendinga*. Reykjavík: Heimskringla.

Minningarrit íslenzkra hermanna 1914–1918. Edited by Rögnvaldur Pétursson. Winnipeg: Félagið Jón Sigurðsson.

Øverland, Orm. 2000. *Immigrant Minds. American Identities: Making the United States Home 1870–1930.* Urbana: University of Illinois Press.

Peterson, George. 1923. "Hluttaka Bandaríkjanna." In *Minningarrit íslenzkra hermanna 1914–1918*, 35–40. Winnipeg: Félagið Jón Sigurðsson.

Spolsky, Bernard. 2004. *Language Policy*. Cambridge: Cambridge University Press.

CHAPTER 6

Icelandic Immigrants, Modernity, and Winnipeg in Einar Hjörleifsson Kvaran's "Hopes"

GUÐRÚN BJÖRK GUÐSTEINSDÓTTIR

WRITER EINAR HJÖRLEIFSSON Kvaran (1859–1938) lived for ten dramatic years in Winnipeg, where he was a central community force from 1885 to 1895. He participated in launching some of the institutions that remain the underpinnings of Icelandic identity, like the newspapers *Heimskringla* in 1886, *Lögberg* in 1887, and the Icelandic festival of Íslendingadagurinn in 1890. In addition to working as editor, journalist, translator, and reviewer, Einar would commemorate special occasions with poetry, give public lectures, train people in reading out loud and acting, and participate in immigration management, as well as scout for new potential settlements and engage in politics, to name a few of his activities. According to Skuli Johnson, "the young Icelandic colony in Winnipeg was enthralled by Einar and as events show, nothing appeared capable of achievement without his assistance" (Johnson 1948a, 48). He had already established himself as an important writer of poetry, drama, and fiction during his student days in Iceland and Denmark, before emigrating to Canada (Guðsteinsdóttir 2018, 139–40).

As Skuli Johnson points out, "The crowning achievement of Einar in these years is his short story *Vonir*. It was written in 1888, read by the author on one or two occasions . . . and later published in Iceland, 1890. . . . It was almost at once translated into German . . . and into Danish" (Johnson 1948b, 49). The story was engendered by Einar's involvement in a major clash in 1888 between some of the leading writers in Iceland on the issue of emigration to Canada, which could at least in part to be attributed to him. "Vonir" (Hopes) is a highly experimental creative response, reflecting upon his impressions of the complex cross-currents motivating migration and characterizing the experience of immigration to the Prairies.

FIGURE 6.1. Einar Hjörleifsson Kvaran.

EINAR HJÖRLEIFSSON, THE STORM-CENTRE

When Einar returned to Iceland to work as assistant editor of the largest newspaper, *Ísafold*, he had an intimate understanding of the immigrant's pain and disappointments, as well as hopes and joys. In 1887 his one-year-old son died, and soon thereafter his Danish wife died in childbirth, but their infant son lived for nine months in poor health (Guðmundsson 1997, 52–53). But Einar found love again in the Icelandic community of Winnipeg and started a family again. He and his wife returned twice to Canada for extended visits, and they might very well have preferred to stay in Winnipeg. However, as Skuli Johnson demonstrates in ample detail in his remembrance of Einar, despite frantic and varied activities to scrape together a living, he was "a gentleman of meagre means" during his Winnipeg years (Johnson 1948a and 1948b).

In Iceland Einar was the first writer who managed to support himself and his family by the pen alone (Höskuldsson 1996, 83). He was an influential and prolific writer of all genres but mostly of narrative fiction and drama. His works were widely translated and well received. He was considered for the Nobel Prize in 1923, but another writer was consulted, a professor of Icelandic literature at the University of Iceland, and he adamantly refused to support the nomination ("Kvaran" 1997, B5). Einar turned increasingly towards ethical and spiritual concerns, and Úlfar Bragason notes that he himself attributed to his Canadian years the human empathy and ethical maturity for which he became known (Bragason 2009, 241).

Because he spoke—and wrote—his mind, Einar's friends would at times become enemies, and yet he would retain their respect, or reclaim their friendship when differences were settled, in Winnipeg as well as in Reykjavík. Einar's colleague in politics remembered him as complicated and controversial, "the embodiment of gentle beauty," who would undoubtedly have preferred "lovely and indolent Lotusland" but, "paradoxically, he was fated to be a fighter for diverse causes and to spend his days as the storm-centre of contending factions" (Jónas Jónsson from Hrifla, quoted in Johnson 1948a, 7).

EMIGRATION OR RELOCATION?

Immigration to North America peaked in 1887, when around 2,000 people left during the summer (Kristinsson 1983, xxii, Table 3; Steingrímsson 1888, 45). The emigrant numbers were being driven up by the combined effect of the annual drop in transportation fares between 1884 and 1887 and increased dissatisfaction with social conditions in Iceland (Kjartansson 1980, 59, 71). But most immediate was the threat of famine in the northern parts of Iceland, where land-bound ice and inclement weather wreaked havoc, with severe loss of livestock and people, and health was generally poor. By united effort and distribution of loans, livestock, feed, and other necessities to the stricken parts of the country, disaster was avoided. Rumours of starvation fatalities in 1887 were untrue, however, according to Jón Steingrímsson's annual report on Iceland (1887, 31–44).

To the chagrin of the editor of *Ísafold*, there were, nonetheless, consistent reports abroad of deaths by starvation and heavy emphasis that the only viable solution was assisted emigration from Iceland to Canada. According to the London paper *Christian Life*, all Icelanders were so desperate to get away from their icy wasteland that women would sell their engagement rings for the fare (Jónsson 1887a, 137). The *Manitoba Daily Free Press* reported that the Reverend Jón Bjarnason was urgently calling for immediate financial assistance from the government to transport at least 6,000 Icelanders for free to Canada before the onset of winter, to avoid further deaths from famine (1887b, 169–71).[1]

An explosive reaction came in a little booklet by Benedikt Gröndal in March 1888 with a colourful, and variously contradictory, diatribe on emigration to Canada. It was distributed to all subscribers of *Ísafold* and made available at the paper's office in Reykjavík. Benedikt objects to the complicity of Icelandic papers in the one-sided discourse of immigration agents who sing the praises of the blissful existence awaiting all and sundry in North America, never mentioning the darker aspects, which he will expose for a more balanced view. He has nothing good to say about Icelandic emigrants or the Icelandic settlements in Canada. Included is his widely quoted but never credited accusation that the emigrants had betrayed Iceland's battle for independence by leaving the country. He claimed that no educated people had emigrated, except a few troublemakers who would do nothing constructive in Iceland, anyway, so good riddance to them. He is livid that Icelandic journalists did not correct and reprimand Rev. Jón Bjarnason in their reports of his claims that assisted relocation of thousands of Icelanders would save them from certain death from hunger. He compares the immigration agents with human traffickers and loudly objects to the consistently disparaging and demeaning depiction of Iceland in *Heimskringla*, pointedly ignoring the newly established *Lögberg* (Gröndal 1888b).

Massive upheaval ensued in the papers. Benedikt was a versatile writer, artist, and natural scientist who had returned to Iceland after roughly twenty years in Europe, mostly in Copenhagen; his satires and his memoirs were immensely popular, but he was in general at odds with his contemporaries (Pétursson 1978, 33, 37). Significantly, Benedikt's publications included textbooks on geography, so he was likely to be taken seriously. Frímann B. Anderson responded with outrage in *Heimskringla*, as did Einar in *Lögberg*, but they were tame in comparison to poet and journalist Jón Ólafsson, for whom some of Gröndal's pointed slurs were intended. He was a freedom fighter who had fled to the U.S. from 1873 to 1875 to avoid fines and imprisonment for libel, as well as acts in defiance of publication laws and Danish officials;

earlier, he had fled to Norway for the same offences (Gudsteins 2006, 73). In both instances he returned to Iceland.

Jón Ólafsson published a booklet effusively denouncing Benedikt as a senile, good-for-nothing drunkard, among other things. His title in English translation indicates his line of argument: "One single word of sanity about emigration to the West: Editor Björn Jónsson answered and addressed regarding the lying-nonsense, slander, and delusionary drivel distributed in and with *Ísafold*. Benedikt Gröndal undressed, disciplined, and pilloried" (1888). Jón Ólafsson was eventually sentenced and heavily fined for libel, but Einar and the *Lögberg* publishers collected enough money in the Icelandic community to cover the fine and bring him over to Winnipeg in 1890 (Guðmundsson 1997, 77).

The reverberations continued for months. The Reverend Jón Bjarnason pronounced that Iceland was a geographical and spiritual desert (Bjarnason 1888), elaborating on the imagery introduced in his sermon at the millennial celebration of Iceland's settlement in Milwaukee in 1874 (Bjarnason 1874). Among reactions in the Icelandic papers was Jón Ólafsson's attempt to mollify and gently chastise Bjarnason, his old friend and roommate, saying that he ought not to destroy people's faith in themselves and their hope for the future. Bjarnason responded that the only correction he needed to make was that it was the Icelanders who had turned their own land into an uninhabitable desert, not nature. Benedikt published another pamphlet on emigration, specifically citing news reports in *Heimskringla* to demonstrate that America was a vastly overrated continent of murder, mayhem, and natural and human disasters. But he also nodded in Rev. Bjarnason's direction, noting that harsh judgment could indeed be a sign of care, concern, and good intentions (Gröndal 1888a).

Peace was eventually established, and the editor of *Ísafold* soon resumed his customary neutral attitude towards migration, later defending emigration when Benedikt and returning migrants spoke out against it (Jónsson 1890a, 237–38; 1890b, 229). But the annual number of emigrants dropped from 2,000 in 1888 to around 1,100 in 1889, and sometimes even below 100 in the following years, although the cost of travel continued to go down. This drop may have numerous explanations, like improved climate and social conditions, but the interrogation of the emigration discourse that Benedikt launched may also have made a difference. Helgi Skúli Kjartansson and Steinþór Hreiðarsson believe that 16,408 people, or slightly less than 20 percent of the total population of roughly 70,000 to 87,000 people, emigrated to North America between 1870 and 1914 (Kjartansson and Hreiðarsson 2003, 102–4).

EINAR AND "THE MODERN BREAKTHROUGH"

Generational and ideological differences, poetics, and egos combined as a driving force behind the clash on emigration. Einar and Jón embraced modernity and liberal values, which they saw as being pursued in North America, and defined Benedikt as a passé establishment representative. Einar obviously raised Benedikt's hackles when an Icelandic paper reported on his Winnipeg lecture on "Icelandic literature since 1850," where he disdainfully dismissed the handful of writers who were regarded as foremost in Icelandic letters, describing Benedikt Gröndal as "a poet in name only" (Ásmundarson 1886, 22). Benedikt retaliated in a book review by describing the U.S. as the only civilized country in the Americas; "the rest is worse than savage," he said. Einar took the bait and forcibly objected in *Lögberg* that Benedikt "should be mentally pilloried and exposed to public ridicule" for his "deliberate" and "nonsensical lies" (Hjörleifsson 1888, 2). Jón Ólafsson aligned himself with Einar when he borrowed these phrases in his own lengthy title in response to Benedikt's invective.

Einar had first become acquainted with realist theories through Jón's translations in his paper *Skuld* of chapters from Danish critic Georg Brandes's books on nineteenth-century trends in literature and modernity. Realism became Einar's Gospel and Brandes his main prophet. "Everything old was nothing. Everything had become new," Einar recalled (Guðmunsson 1997, 31). Both Jón and Einar lived and wrote by the precept expressed by Brandes as "the modern breakthrough": "The only literature that is alive today is one that provokes debate" (quoted in Wilkinson 2017, 696–97). Brandes's main emphasis was on throwing off the harness of tradition as well as religious and social institutions and claiming freedom of thought through free inquiry—engaging in vibrant, radical debate on social reality (Wilkinson 2017, 697). In

Copenhagen Einar participated in bringing out the literary journal *Verðandi* (1882), which is seen as a landmark in Icelandic literature, being the first publication dedicated exclusively to realist writing.

Although ever ready to speak his mind and stand by his opinion, be it on immigration, politics, or poetics, Einar "found newspaper controversies uncongenial," according to Skuli Johnson, and the quarrels with Benedikt in the papers obviously left him shaken (Johnson 1948a, 52). He later recalled how he had fallen asleep on a hot day in June and "dreamt the main substance of the story ["Hopes"], especially the occurrence at the Immigration Hall. I suddenly awoke restless with desire to proceed to write this down and I began on the same day. I had other tasks to which to attend, but I nevertheless finished it on the third day. I marvelled at this speed, especially because the story was utterly dissimilar to everything I had attempted to write before" (Johnson 1948b, 49; translated by Johnson). Einar felt for the first time that he had discovered his own powers as a writer of stories and was as happy as a child (Hjörleifsson 1909, 48).

However, during this time Einar also began to doubt things he had previously been unshakeably certain of, including his faith in the cold, scientific distance of naturalism (Hjörleifsson 1909, 46). As Matthías Sæmundsson observes, the realist emphasis on social reform gained prevalence in Einar's writing (Sæmundsson 1996, 773). Einar became a spokesman for balance in his newspaper articles, himself preaching and practising a balanced approach to cultural engagement: full participation in Canadian life, politics, and education but without sacrificing Icelandic identity and culture. In fact, he favoured the felicitous approach prevailing in Icelandic-Canadian writing, according to Daisy Neijmann: "the ambition to be both the best Icelanders and the best Canadians" (Neijmann 1997, 79). The power of "Hopes" arises from a finely tuned balance between critical observation and empathy for human vulnerability, as well as playful demonstration of the relativity of truth—how dependent reality is on context.

MODERN ENCOUNTERS

Winnipeg provides an important context for "Hopes." The city grew by leaps and bounds, with a population of 225 in 1870, 6,500 in 1880, and 27,000 in 1890 (Ólafsson 1891, 3). The biggest jump in population in the nineteenth century followed the completion of the Canadian Pacific Railway in 1885 from coast to coast with Winnipeg as its hub. The railways made the city the main centre for transportation of people and goods in all directions and, according to historian Alan Artibise, "brought the city a period of growth and prosperity unequalled in Canadian urban development" (Artibise 2019).

The 1880s were a time of high drama and rapid changes in the Icelandic community as Winnipeg became its centre. According to Frímann Anderson's immigration report, Winnipeg had 1,800 Icelandic inhabitants in 1888, a number Einar thought was undoubtedly too low (Hjörleifsson 1889b, 2). Fortunes were made and lost during the boom years, and the Icelandic Investment Company was established with high hopes. By the summer of 1882, however, the bubble had burst and a depression followed. But the boom had secured the Winnipeg Icelanders' social and economic basis, according to Wilhelm Kristjanson. He reported they had "graduated from Shanty Town to Point Douglas, and to the East End, including Jemima, Ross, and McWilliam (Pacific Avenue) streets, towards Nena Street and the prairie beyond" (Kristjansson 1965, 151–53, 165–70, 212–13).

There is hardly any action to speak of in "Hopes," other than a train ride into Winnipeg and the fateful meeting of two central characters, as Gestur Pálsson points out in an appreciative review (Pálsson 1890, 2). In the story, Einar combines two narratives. One is the experimental, modern narrative of Icelandic immigrants in 1887, new arrivals and established Winnipeggers. The other is a more traditional narrative of a young woman's seduction of a naïve young man for her own ends and his painful realization of how he has been duped.

GO, GO! GO, AGAINST THE WIND . . .

In Einar's narrative we share the experience of Icelandic immigrants to prairie Canada in 1887. First we follow new arrivals travelling on the train on the last leg from Iceland to Winnipeg, and then we follow the more settled immigrants who come to greet them. Einar appeals to all the senses as he leads the reader to participate in impressions ranging through a wide array of emotions and shifting the angles from which we view events and people, thereby complicating the simple dualism of Canada, which Einar characterized as "the land that the officials back home described as hell, and the immigration agents described as paradise!" (Hjörleifsson 1908, 3; my translation).[2] We share the experience of the immigrants by listening to their thoughts and speech, as well as viewing them from the outside, and even smelling and touching the environment of their geographic and cultural transition. The character depiction in the story of the new and established immigrants is unusual because Einar consistently describes groups as if they were a single entity, of a uniform character, but shows them from numerous different angles, so that they appear to be different people.

Einar's initial emphasis is on the Icelandic newcomers' encounter with modernity—speed, rapid changes—using the train as a central symbol of the modern transition from rural to urban life. As cultural studies scholar Marian Aguiar points out, the "railway's ability to reconstruct space and time through movement made it a primary space for the constitution of new identities. The train was an agent of deterritorialization, for it transferred its occupants into a new collectivity out of their original local context" (Aguiar 2008, 73). The train goes like lightning across the burning hot prairie on a summer day, slowing and blowing its whistle past the miserable shacks of Shanty Town, past the ruins of the Dominion Government Immigration Agency that burned down in spring 1887, and coming to a loud halt at the CPR station, where Winnipeg Icelanders wait. Eventually, the two groups join in the temporary Immigration Hall, which historian Robert Vineberg describes as being "at the corner of King Street and the CPR tracks, just west of the station" (Vineberg 2011, 15).

FIGURE 6.2. Canada welcoming immigrants. (*Canadian Illustrated News*, 14 August 1880)

The story opens dramatically on a mood of breathless thrill and impatience and youthful exuberance: "Go, go! Go, against the wind, heavy with sun, burning hot, breathing on the immigrant if he sticks his head out the window of the railway car. . . . Go, to the wonderland, the promised land, the land where friends and countrymen impatiently wait for you, eager to welcome you, hug you, kiss you; the country where wealth and happiness and fortune and freedom and respect await you, and run to hug you upon arrival. . . . Go, go!" (3). This bold, brave, and excited mood of the collective consciousness captures the spirit of *útþrá*, which Daisy Neijmann identifies as one of the prevailing identity myths of Icelandic-Canadian literature; author Walter Lindal explains it as "a yearning to reach beyond" (Neijmann 1997, 77; Lindal 1967, 100). Einar elaborates further on the yearning of *útþrá*: "And out everyone wants to get, out from captivity . . . out to life, toil and trouble, or debauchery and dissipation, to battle and conquer, or to enjoy life" (4–5).

The same group appears quite different from this description when seen from the outside. We get a quick overview of them on the train as they sit or lean, exhausted in a crowded coach, children laughing, women crying, men snoring, and the stench of sweating bodies and smelly food containers adding sounds and scents to the scene. But we also share their first glimpses of Winnipeg as the train rumbles through Shanty Town, roasting in the sun, people gasping for a breath of air. And we see the different inhabitants in a glimpse as they freeze in their tracks and stare after the train with its loudly screaming whistle.

As the train arrives at the CPR station, we have yet another impression of the group as it is scrutinized by fashionably dressed Winnipeg maids, with their parasols and kid gloves. Einar deftly turns the successive glimpses of the

Shanty Town people, all staring, into a delightful depiction of the maids' acute embarrassment. They feel that everyone is staring—not after the screeching train coming to station, but at the nearby Immigration Hall because the horribly pokey "Icelandic immigrants are here" (25). The immigrants look "outlandish. Not like people from another continent, but from a different planet," wearing dark, "unspeakable," heavy scarves, pants, skirts and other utterly inappropriate garments in the scorching heat, the women looking even more alien than the men (25).

But we also have deeply sympathetic impressions of the exhausted travellers. The most pathetic scenes are of men staggering in the heat as they carry not only heavy clothing and baggage but sick women and children to the Immigration Hall, where a doctor spoons out medicine.

The final scene of the immigrant groups is, however, in glorious fulfillment of the initial anticipation of being welcomed with open arms, kisses, and hugs. Einar shows the old and new immigrants, refined and alien, joining into a single mass confusion in the Immigration Hall: "And now they all mix. Pale-blue mousseline dresses and pale-yellow linen dresses rub against black and russet bodices; jackets of black cloth and homespun and pastel-coloured, dirty pyjama tops against white and shining vests and thick golden chains. The Icelandic silk tassel hangs next to a straight-brimmed, feathered straw-hat, and the spokes of the feather-light, sparkling white parasols are caught in the warm, woolen *lopi* scarves" (28). The noise turns into a numbing din with words and snatches of phrases in English and Icelandic breaking through, some in greeting, others in reference to the land-bound ice that surrounded the country and drove people to despair—and to emigrate.

Brandes, the prophet of realist writing in Scandinavia, who had swept budding Icelandic writers like Einar Hjörleifsson and Gestur Pálsson into the whirl of realist trends ranging from naturalism to impressionism, applauded Einar's story when it came out in Danish translation. He was particularly enthusiastic about the effect of the final scene of the older and new immigrant groups uniting in a swirling mass union, regardless of all surface differences (Erlingsson 1901, 9). What is especially unusual and effective in Einar's narrative is how he teases out the contradictions and complexities of inner experience in various ironic counterpoints to external realities. The final irony is that at the end of the story, we must assume that the future of the exhausted, sick, and alien-looking migrants is predicted in the self-confident modernity of the Icelandic Winnipeggers who came to greet them. They will be among the well-dressed crowd that comes to welcome the next batch of immigrants.

A RING WITH A GLASS BUTTON OR SPARKLING GEMS?

In counterpoint to the happy ending of the story of the immigrant groups, Einar shows us the more traditional story, which does not end as happily. When everyone rushes from one window of the train to another at the other end, excitedly asking when they will reach Winnipeg (although knowing it full well), one person cannot be reached by any means, despite numerous attempts: Ólafur. He is frozen in a stasis of recollection and anticipation of his reunion with his sweetheart, Helga. Unlike all the others, Ólafur has no interest in, or even awareness of, his new surroundings; he neither hears nor sees anything. He has not come to Canada because of *útþrá*—the desire to reach beyond—but because he yearns for his fantasy of Helga, faithfully awaiting his arrival.

Ólafur's recollections reveal that he and Helga worked at the same farm when they were eighteen, two years earlier. He was as clumsy, awkward, and ungainly tall as she was short and plump, pretty, quick, witty, and charming. Her most endearing and distinctive habit was to throw back her head and laugh if she was lost for words or unwilling to answer. With persistence she gradually won him over with kisses and threats, after having ridiculed him painfully in front of others. She leaves with all the money he has in the world and wearing his two-penny ring with a glass button and his initials scratched illegibly inside, promising him eternal faithfulness.

The Immigration Hall is the turning point in this story, as it is in the group narrative. A certain Nellie catches Ólafur's eye, reminding him somewhat of Helga when he frantically looks for her. Nellie is, however, exquisitely beautiful, and speaks English only, and when she removes her delicate glove and lifts her hand to her lips, there are big gems sparkling in the ring on her hand.

When Nellie throws back her head and laughs, however, Ólafur knows that she is Helga and calls out her name, and she heads out the door in a hurry. When Ólafur finally catches up with Helga/Nellie, grabbing her arm, she notices an Anglo-Canadian friend watching them, smirking. Crying with anger at the humiliation, she threatens to call the police and have Ólafur locked up if he does not leave her alone. She is outraged that he could shame her so terribly after all the pity and kindness that she showed him back in Iceland.

As Ólafur wanders in a daze out of town and on to the prairie in desperation, he starts realizing that all his elaborate fantasies about Helga will be fulfilled by someone else. He had envisioned her prettily waiting at the door, with a feast ready, when he would come home at the end of the day to the riches and comforts of their splendid home. As Ólafur hears church bells in the distance, he throws himself upon the prairie and cries in loud sobs. This ending ought to be pathetic and awful, but the narration is so poetic and empathetic that Ólafur's disillusion becomes emblematic for the powerful pain of all lost dreams and hopes and castles in the air.

Ólafur falls into the embrace of the infinite prairie, which will be his eternally peaceful, eternally true, sweetheart: As it says in the story, "For she makes men richer, while many a sweetheart makes them poorer; for she never turns her back on a man, for she is ever-young and ever-strong, and never dies away from a man, but on the contrary, takes a man into her arms, when the man himself is dead, and embraces him to eternity; the prairie, immeasurable, infinite, which is full of peace, and reminds one of the rest eternal" (Hjörleifsson 1908, 47; quoted in Johnson 1948b, 51; translated by Johnson). This ending, with its eternal peace and deathlike stasis, is in ironic counterpoint to the kinesis of the opening with its energy, speed, and restless daring but parallels the scene with Ólafur on the train, dead to the world around him. Nonetheless, as Matthías Sæmundsson points out, Einar's final paradoxical description of Ólafur's bonding with the prairie is both evocative and mysterious (Sæmundsson 1978, 35).

Whereas the united immigrant groups depict the balance and humanity that Einar was learning to embrace, Helga and Ólafur break away from the welcoming confusion. Helga represents the Icelanders who were ashamed of their ethnicity and preferred to assimilate so completely to Anglo-Canadian identity that they seemed like "drops in the ocean," an image that Einar made famous in a lecture turned into a *Lögberg* article (Hjörleifsson 1889a; Johnson 1948b, 23). As Skuli Johnson says, Einar insisted that "Icelanders need not have any minority complex" but should consider themselves equals to local Anglo-Canadians, whose main concerns were "politics, business and formal religion" but who had "no interest in science, poetry and the fine arts, there are no books of merit, no drama of quality" (Johnson 1948b, 23). Ólafur is Helga's extreme opposite. He is the immigrant who never wanted to leave home and naïvely believes that everything in his new world can stay the same as at home, except that he will gain wealth and comfort without effort. Johnson notes that Einar would visit the rural Icelandic settlements on his lecture tours, but stresses that he was a "cultured European with no real liking for frontier life," explaining the ambivalent connotations that he assigns to the prairie in his story (Johnson 1948b, 51).

"Vonir" was well received when it came out. Gestur Pálsson's review in *Lögberg* was highly enthusiastic, praising how the story manages to provide varied psychological insight despite its brevity (Pálsson 1890, 2). Reputedly, however, Winnipeg maids were hurt and angered by Einar's depiction of them (Guðmundsson 1997, 75). In Iceland the reviews were positive except for one that took offence at the embarrassed attitude towards the new arrivals from Iceland and the commentary on the Icelandic national costume (Jónsson 1890c, 74; D. 1890, 78–79). In Iceland, the story is still readily available and widely anthologized, including in textbooks for elementary school, but it has yet to be published in English, aside from Skuli Johnson's first and last paragraphs and his summary of the story (1948b, 49–51).

CONCLUSION

Einar Hjörleifsson Kvaran's Winnipeg years were a trying, turbulent time in his life, but they were also the time when he found his own voice as writer. His story "Hopes" is a Winnipeg story, an integral part of the Icelandic legacy in Canada, and undoubtedly the most interesting contribution that came out of the crossfires in the Icelandic newspapers in 1888 on westward emigration from Iceland. The story that erupted from Einar's unconscious is his vivid and honest response to the anger and name-calling that Benedikt Gröndal incited. In his overview on Shanty Town, Einar acknowledges that miserable poverty may be found in Canada as well as in Iceland, and that one cannot emigrate from life's sorrows and hardship, but, above all, the immigrants' lot has improved.

The story is Einar's most original and experimental work, and it still provides a fresh look on migration and the ethnic community, capturing in a fistful of scenes and images the drama of immigration. Einar multiplies and variously inverts the viewpoints on the wide range of desires, hopes, and despair that propel migration, giving compelling impressionist insight into the complexity of the immigrant experience when Icelanders were rushed from medieval life into modernity during their passage from Iceland to Winnipeg, the Gateway to the West.

NOTES

1 *Manitoba Daily Free Press*, 8 August 1887, 2. The article cited here incorrectly names the newspaper as the *Winnipeg Daily Express*.

2 Further references to this text will appear as page numbers in parentheses. All translations of this text are mine unless indicated otherwise.

REFERENCES

Aguiar, Marian. 2008. "Making Modernity: Inside the Technological Space of the Railway." *Cultural Critique* 68: 66–85.

Artibise, Alan F.J. 2019. "Winnipeg." *The Canadian Encyclopedia*. Historica Canada. First published 11 September 2012. Last edited 13 March 2019. https://www.thecanadianencyclopedia.ca/en/article/winnipeg.

Ásmundarson, Valdimar. 1886. "Frá Íslendingum í Ameríku." *Fjallkonan*, 23 March, 22.

———. 1890. "Vonir." *Fjallkonan*, 19 March, 31.

Bjarnason, Jón. 1874. *Prédikun, er Jón Bjarnason flutti á þúsund ára þjóðhátíð Íslendinga: 2. ágúst (9. sd. e. Trin.) 1874 í Milwaukee, Wisconsin, innan Bandaríkja Vesturheims*. Copenhagen: S. Trier.

———. 1888. *Ísland að blása upp*. Reykjavík: Bókverzlun Sigfúsar Eymundssonar.

Bragason, Úlfar. 2009. "Images of North America in Writings by Three Icelandic Authors: Matthías Jochumsson, Jón Ólafsson, and Einar H. Kvaran." In *Canada: Images of a Post/National Society*, edited by Gunnilla Florby, Mark Shackleton, and Katri Suhonen, 235–44. Études canadiennes—Canadian Studies 19. Brussels: Peter Lang.

D. 1890. "Bókafregn." *Þjóðviljinn*, 30 May, 78–79.

Einarsson, Stefán. 1937. "Þættir af Einari H. Kvaran." *Eimreiðin* 43 (2): 145–60.

Erlingsson, Þorsteinn. 1901. "Tveir ritdómar eftir dr. Georg Brandes." *Bjarki*, 25 January, 9.

Gröndal, Benedikt. 1888a. *Enn um Vesturheimsferðir*. Reykjavík: Ísafoldarprentsmiðja.

———. 1888b. *Um Vesturheimsferðir*. Reykjavík: Ísafoldarprentsmiðja.

Guðmundsson, Gils. 1997. *Í nærveru sálar: Einar Hjörleifsson Kvaran*. Reykjavík: Setberg.

Gudsteins, Gudrun Björk. 2006. "Home and Exile in Early Icelandic-Canadian Poetry." In *Home and Exile*, edited by Eva Rein and Krista Vogelberg, 71–81. Cultural Studies Series 7. Tartu, Estonia: Tartu University Press.

Guðsteinsdóttir, Guðrún Björk. 2018. "Margræðar 'Vonir' Einars H. Kvarans." In *Sigurtunga: Vesturíslenskt mál og menning*, edited by Birna Arnbjörnsdóttir, Höskuldur Thráinsson, and Úlfar Bragason, 137–58. Reykjavík: Háskólaútgáfan.

Hjörleifsson [Kvaran], Einar. 1888. "Þekking á Ameríku." *Lögberg*, 1 February, 2.

———. 1889a. "Hverfum við í sjóinn?" *Lögberg*, 3–24 April and 8–22 May, 2–3.

———. 1889b. "Ný innflutningaskýrsla frá F. B. Anderson." *Lögberg*, 13 March, 2.

———. 1908. "Vonir." In *Vestan hafs og austan: Þrjár sögur*, 1–47. 2nd ed. Reykjavík: Ísafoldarprentsmiðja.

———. 1909. *Vesturför: Ferðapistlar*. Akureyri: Norðurland.

Höskuldsson, Sveinn Skorri. 1996. "Hinn langi og skæri hljómur: Um höfundarverk Einars H. Kvarans." *Andvari* 121 (1): 78–97.

Johnson, Skuli. 1948a. "Einar Hjörleifsson Kvaran in Winnipeg." *Icelandic Canadian* 7 (1): 7–10, 48–52.

———. 1948b. "Einar Hjörleifsson Kvaran in Winnipeg, Continued." *Icelandic Canadian* 7 (2): 23–26, 49–52.

Jónsson, Björn. 1887a. "Hallærissögur." *Ísafold,* 27 July, 137.

———. 1887b. "Íslendingar í Ameríku." *Ísafold,* 8 September, 169–71.

———. 1890a. "Gröndalskt frumhlaup og Vesturheimsferðamálið." *Ísafold*, 26 July, 237–38.

———. 1890b. "Hagur Íslendinga í Vesturheimi." *Ísafold*, 19 July, 229.

———. 1890c. "Vonir." *Ísafold*, 5 March, 74.

Jónsson, Þorsteinn. 1943. "Einar Hjörleifsson Kvaran." *Andvari* 68 (1): 3–26.

Kjartansson, Helgi Skúli. 1980. "Emigrant Fares and Emigration from Iceland to North America, 1874–1893." *Scandinavian Economic History Review* 28 (1): 53–71.

Kjartansson, Helgi Skúli, and Steinþór Hreiðarsson. 2003. *Framtíð handan hafs. Vesturfarir frá Íslandi 1870–1914*. Reykjavík: Háskólaútgáfan.

Kristinsson, Júníus H. 1983. *Vesturfaraskrá 1870–1914*. Reykjavík: Sagnfræðistofnun Háskóla Íslands.

Kristjanson, Wilhelm. 1990. *The Icelandic People in Manitoba*. Winnipeg: R.W. Kristjanson.

"Kvaran og bókmenntaverðlaun Nóbels." 1997. *Morgunblaðið*, 25 November, B5.

Lindal, W.J. 1967. *The Icelanders in Canada*. Ottawa: National Publishers.

Neijmann, Daisy. 1997. *The Icelandic Voice in Canadian Letters*. Ottawa: Carleton University Press.

Ólafsson, Jón. 1888. *Eitt orð af viti um Vestrfara og Vestrheimsferðir: Svar og ávarp til Bjarnar ritstjóra Jónssonar upp á allan þann ósanninda-þvætting, óhróðr og óráðs-bull, sem útbreitt er í og með "Ísafold." Benedikt Gröndal afklæddr, hirtr og settr í gapastokkinn*. Reykjavík.

———. 1891. "Dálítið um Winnipeg." *Öldin*, 14 October, 3.

Pálsson, Gestur. 1890. "Um Vonir." *Heimskringla*, 9 October, 2–3.

Sæmundsson, Matthías Viðar. 1978. "Sléttan ómælilega: Athugun á smásögu." *Mímir* 17 (1): 27–36.

———. 1996. "Sagnagerð frá þjóðhátíð til fullveldis." In *Íslensk bókmenntasaga*. Vol. 3, edited by Halldór Guðmundsson, 767–882. Reykjavík: Mál og menning.

Steingrímsson, Jón. 1888. *Fréttir frá Íslandi*. Reykjavík: Prentsmiðja Einars Þórðarsonar.

Pétursson, Valtýr. 1978. "Dýraríki Íslands—Teiknibók Gröndals." *Morgunblaðið*, 15 January, 32–33, 37.

Vineberg, Robert. 2011. "Welcoming Immigrants at the Gateway to Canada's West: Immigration Halls in Winnipeg, 1872–1975." *Manitoba History* 65: 13–22.

Wilkinson, Lynn R. 2017. "The 1872 Introduction to *Hovedstrømninger i det 19de Aarhundredes Litteratur* (*Main Currents of Nineteenth Century Literature*)." *PMLA* 132 (3): 696–98.

Þorsteinsson, Steingrímur J. 1955. "Fyrsta Akureyrarár séra Matthíasar Jochumssonar." *Skírnir* 129 (1): 35–49.

CHAPTER 7

Another Emigrant Ship Crossing the Atlantic: The Poetics of Migration in the Poetry of Undína and Stephan G. Stephansson

BIRNA BJARNADÓTTIR

THE RICH COMPLEXITY of the mass exodus from Europe to the Americas was not lost on European writers such as the German-speaking Bohemian novelist and short story writer Franz Kafka (1883–1924); and the Icelandic poet, writer, illustrator, and naturalist Benedikt Gröndal (1826–1907).[1] The same is true of yet another European writer who was equally captivated by the exodus, the Bohemian-Austrian poet and novelist Rainer Maria Rilke (1875–1926). Rilke's poem "Auswanderer-Schiff. Neapel" or "Emigrant Ship. Naples" charts the historic event, seen from a seaport in Italy.[2]

As the title of Rilke's poem indicates, the emigrant ship is the centre of gravitas, and the reader can perceive the centripetal force of the mass exodus. What the reader cannot anticipate, though, is the poem's shattering closing image. While the anticipated voyage has been in sight, with boats lifting fish, bread, and fruit into "the huge grey ship," the ship was "full of scorn" and took "coal into its womb, open like death" (Rilke 2001, 239), as if the emigrant ship has transformed into death's harbinger, with the emigrants serving as its fuel.

FIGURE 7.1. Icelanders on board the emigrant ship *Camoens*. (Photo by Sigfús Eymundsson, c. 1887)

As to be expected there is more to the saga of this single poem within the context of the rich complexity of the transatlantic historic event. If one is to agree with writer and critic Michael Hofmann, who perceives in the poem an expression of an "anonymous column of émigrés, the caravan of departing souls," the emigrants seem to have "accepted willingly or unwillingly their function as raw material loaded into a vast and rapacious economy," the sort of "technical, collective and futuristic vision to which Rilke didn't like to be exposed" (Hofmann 2021).

But what about the expressions of individual experiences of those European poets who departed with other emigrant ships from various seaports in Europe? Their chance of serving as "raw material loaded into a vast and rapacious economy" was real. In addition to meeting the demands of the rapidly evolving industrialization of North America in the latter part of the nineteenth century, the immigrants who arrived from Europe on the big wave of the mass exodus had a role to play in the processes of the economy of colonialism.[3] Drawing on the individual expressions of European poets who crossed the Atlantic, there are, however, other pressing transatlantic issues. Apart from the (already in place) subtle mechanisms of capitalism

FIGURE 7.2. Undína.

FIGURE 7.3. Stephan G. Stephansson.

in Europe,[4] an even greater mayhem of servitude awaited both Europe and North America, thanks to the First World War.

Thus, despite its shattering images, Rilke's poem on the emigrant ship can serve as a backdrop to the rich complexities of the subjects of culture and heritage in the poetry of European immigrants of North America. A case in point is the poetry of two of the leading pioneer poets among Icelandic immigrants in Canada and the U.S.: Helga Steinvör Baldvinsdóttir (1858–1941), who would write her poetry under the pseudonym Undína, and Stefán Guðmundsson (1853–1927), later known as Stephan G. Stephansson. On 4 August 1873, they emigrated from Iceland as young aspiring poets from the town of Akureyri, Iceland, with the horse transport ship SS *Queen*.

Undína and Stephan G. wrote only in Icelandic and could, therefore, be said to manifest a lifelong attachment to and engagement with the culture and heritage of their land of birth.[5] This is not to say that the Icelandic language sets these two pioneer poets free from the complexities of being and habitat in the tempestuous transatlantic region.[6] Neither does the language secure their poetry a uniform account of the subjects of culture and heritage. The evident differences of their individual aesthetics are of equal importance, not to mention the varieties of their expressions and reflections. The question arises whether there are clear signs of a transformation and/or conversion from national to heritage culture in Undína's and Stephan G.'s poetics of migration, or if universal and even extraterritorial elements in the worlds of literature, nature, and human existence obscure such a reading.

UNDÍNA, OR IS IT UNDINE?

Whereas much has been written on the life and poetry of the Icelandic-Canadian poet, farmer, essayist, pacifist, and social prophet Stephan G. Stephansson, who was a pioneer in Wisconsin and Dakota Territories until 1889, when he homesteaded in Markerville, Alberta, existing sources on the life and poetry of Helga Steinvör Baldvinsdóttir are few and far between. As was the case with Stephan G., Helga was no stranger to the flux of migration. On arrival in the new continent, she settled with her parents, Baldvin Helgason and Soffía Jósafatsdóttir, in Muskoka District, Ontario, and in 1881 she moved to Dakota Territories with her husband, Jakob Jónatansson Líndal. In 1892, following her divorce, Helga moved to Selkirk, Manitoba, where she lived with her surviving children, Stephan and Soffía (Sophia), and her father until she relocated with her children to the Pacific Coast.[7] Skúli Árni Stefánsson Freemann was her second husband, and they had a son, Walter. In 1904 Skúli suffered an accident and died. A few years later Stephan, Helga's son from her previous marriage, passed away. Helga's last dwelling place was Poulsbo, Washington, where she lived with her daughter, Soffía (Mrs. H,F. Kyle).[8] She was laid to rest in Deer Island, Oregon.[9]

During her lifetime prominent poets and critics on both sides of the Atlantic recognized her gift in the art of poetry, including the editor, poet, and translator Jón Ólafsson (1850–1916), who was instrumental in the favourable reception of Undína's poetry and her recognition as a profoundly talented poet in the transatlantic region. The Icelandic-Canadian poet, novelist, short story writer, and playwright Jóhann Magnús Bjarnason (1866–1945) was another firm believer in Undína, and the one who assisted her to prepare her collection of poems for publication.[10] However, unlike Stephan G. and other leading poets, novelists, short story writers, and playwrights of Icelandic immigrants and their descendants, including Jóhann Magnús Bjarnason, Jakobína Johnson

(1883–1977), and Guttormur J. Guttormsson (1878–1966), Helga did not live to witness the publication of her poetry in a book.[11] *Kvæði* (1952), the only book published with her poetry, still awaits translation.

While sailing away with the SS *Queen* in early August 1873, Undína composed the poem "Á burtsigling frá Íslandi 1873" (Departure from Iceland 1873), published in *Kvæði* (1952, 5–6):

> [The solid ship, it well may carry
> a pale maiden on the waves,
> from the cold, icy skerry
> out into that blue scenery.
>
> Now on a wave on the salty sea
> the clear sun sinks and stoops,
> just as the tender tear would be,
> that drops from eyes so weary.
>
> Gone are the peaks and the village dear,
> gone quickly the dale,
> gone is the spring that is crystal-clear,
> gone is the bliss far and near.
>
> Farewell, to man and woman I sigh,
> farewell, grove of blossoms;
> farewell o ground to me most nigh,
> farewell, time gone by.][12]

As noted by Kirsten Wolf (1994, 163), this poem can be referred to as the beginning of Western Icelandic women's literature, and in a review by Richard Beck (1897–1980) on *Kvæði*, which appeared in *Heimskringla* on 20 January 1953, Undína is referred to as the key poetess during the years of settlement of Icelandic immigrants. Her poem on the voyage of departure can also be viewed as one of the poems that initiated the arrival of Icelandic-Canadian and Icelandic-American literature, and, thereby, the arrival of the poetics of migration in modern literature by North America's pioneer Icelandic poets.

Contrary to Rilke's poem, where the reader encounters an abstract spectator in its speaker, who highlights the collective pull of emigration in "the anonymous column of émigrés, the caravan of departing souls" (Hoffmann 2021), the speaker's point of view in Undína's poem is personal, and the moment of emigration is seen from the perspective of an emigrant. While a gleaming yet realistic image of the "cold, icy skerry" homeland is drawn with precision, a shattering experience gradually unfolds through the emotionally charged voyage of departure. Everything known and cherished is disappearing, and only the fateful ship feels "solid," the one that is ferrying a "pale maiden on the waves," all the way "out into that blue scenery."

In this poem, which Undína composed as a teenager, some of the key features of her poetry appear. According to Kirsten Wolf (1994, 164), Undína's poetry "deals mostly with the psychological costs of emigrating: the uprooting, the losses and insecurity" and her "deep-rooted love for Iceland," which is evident from many of her poems, including her last one, "Í Lincoln Park" (In Lincoln Park). It was composed in 1937, not long before the passing of the poet, and Wolf may be right in assuming that Undína's "attachment to her native soil lasted throughout her life" (1994, 164). Here are the poem's two last verses:

> [We, Iceland's children, in the homeland born,
> and our motherland with love we bound,
> a heartache, almost, if from her we're torn
> and all the ships of hope run thus aground.
> Since youth it thus became my cross to bear
> to have to lose the books and horses fair.
>
> But Lady Luck has westwards led us,
> until at last we reached Pacific shores;
> and Time Eternal, best of all the healers,
> the ties of trust he ne'er cut, eased all sores;
> so here we are, but minds and souls do roam;
> for who remembers not first love at home?][13]

As noted by Daisy Neijmann (1999, 245), the group of Icelandic immigrants who settled in New Iceland, Manitoba, wanted to preserve their culture through isolation. Helga Steinvör lived for the most part in other regions of Canada and the U.S., but with her choice of the language, she willingly or unwillingly preserved her poetic enterprise through isolation. A poem like "Í Lincoln Park" also raises the question of a certain dimension of the psychology of emigration, which appears to apply to the human condition in general. Virginia Woolf (1882–1941) casts some light on the universal element of the psychology on display, or why the past holds human beings captive: "I can only note that the past is beautiful because one never realizes an emotion at the time. It expands later, & thus we don't have complete emotions about the present, only about the past" (1982, 5).

There are other features to speak of in Undína's individual aesthetics, and critics have noted the lyrical quality of her poetry, her indebtedness to a romantic view of nature, and her melancholic perception of human existence (Bjarnadóttir 2020).[14] Her numerous love poems—which may, in part, belong to the tradition of lament in the history of love poetry—are equally worthy of critical exploration, including the poem "Undína á hafsbotni" (Undína on the seabed), which the poet composed in 1893, not long after her divorce from her first husband. Kirsten Wolf may be right, again, in suggesting that the experience of an unhappy marriage and subsequent divorce serves as its inspiration (1994, 165). But who is the character Undína in this poem?

The poem's speaker is Undína, who resides on the seabed and laments her previous life on land with her greatly flawed human companion and their capricious love. Those familiar with the Undines in world literature may reflect upon the possibility that in addition to the biographical aspect, the poem "Undína á hafsbotni" could draw on the character of Undines. Undines are humanoid water-elementals, who are also referred to as "nymphs" in some sources, including Paracelsus's *A Book on Nymphs, Sylphs, Pygmies, and Salamanders, and on the Other Spirits* ([1941] 1996), and they can be traced through Ovid's *Metamorphoses*, Friedrich de la Motte Fouqué's *Undine* (1811),[15] and Hans Christian Andersen's *Den lille havfrue* (1837) or *The Little Mermaid*.[16] If this is the case, the pale maiden's voyage in Undína's emigrant ship poem from 1873 could be viewed as centripetal in Undína's aesthetics and poetics of migration. Furthermore, it can be said to illuminate how universal and extraterritorial elements lie at the heart of Undína's poetics of migration in the transatlantic region, right next to her lifelong attachment to her native language and soil.

As the rich subject matter indicates, also within the context of the poet's choice of pseudonym,[17] the subjects of being and place are brimming with complexities. According to the Term Bank at the Árni Magnússon Institute for Icelandic Studies, the personal name *Undína* is most likely of Danish origin, drawn from the Latin word *unda* (wave).[18] Furthermore, the word *und* in Icelandic means *wound*, and if the *wave* and the *wound* are taken into consideration within the context of the pale maiden's voyage into the ocean at the moment of her emigration, the reader cannot but wonder about the character's destiny in the transatlantic region. Simultaneously, when one confronts the universal and extraterritorial elements right next to Undína's lifelong attachment to her native language and soil, the rich complexities of the subjects of culture and heritage in her poetics of migration are evident.

Undína's striking perception of emigration, which results in an equivocal sense of being and place, can also be said to herald, in part, the poetics of better-known emigrants in the world of literature, figures like the German writer W.G. Sebald (1944–2001), but the term *extraterritoriality* is believed to illuminate his poetics.[19] Sebald is a child of another transatlantic tempest and—like the European writers Rilke, Kafka, and Gröndal—never crossed the Atlantic as an emigrant. Sebald was no stranger to emigration, though, and in his key works, the emigrant's perception seems to hold a centripetal force. This is at least the case in his book *Die Ausgewanderten. Vier lange Erzählungen* (1992) or *The Emigrants* (1996), which is made up of four long narratives, including one on German immigrants in America.

STEPHAN G. STEPHANSSON'S VOYAGE HOME, THROUGH EXILE

As noted by Viðar Hreinsson in his groundbreaking book *Wakeful Nights* (2012, 97), which provides a detailed discussion on Stephan G. Stephansson's life and work, while Stephan G. was crossing the Atlantic, he wrote notes that included descriptions of the circumstances of the Icelandic emigrants and the horses on-board the SS *Queen*. Whereas the English travellers occupied the first class, the 153 Icelanders were kept in less comfortable quarters and closer to the horses.[20] Rilke may have connected to the image that arises from these notes and seen in them a manifestation of the fateful lure of the mass exodus from Europe to the Americas. But what to make of Stephan G. Stephansson's poetics of migration?

His poetry has earned him titles like "the greatest poet of the Western world" from Harvard's Frank Stanton Cawley (1938, 99), and "Canada's Leading Poet" from Canadian scholar Watson Kirkconnell (1936, 263). It was Halldór Laxness (1902–1988) who stated that Stephan G. was one of the most powerful spirits of his times. The statement appeared in "Landneminn mikli" (The great settler), the eulogy Halldór wrote at the death of Stephan G., which appeared in the Icelandic newspaper *Heimskringla* in Winnipeg, Canada, on 7 September 1927, and later in *Af skáldum* (1972), his book of essays on poets. Halldór is, however, not very optimistic with regards to the reception of the poetry by one of modernity's most powerful spirits in the non-Icelandic part of the world: "I don't know if the outer world will ever become aware of the universes this poet has created in the minds of Icelandic readers. If we are to rely on our experience, the treasures of our language are not easily translatable" (in *Heimskringla,* 7 September 1927, 8).[21]

As the book *Two Lands, One Poet* (2019) manifests,[22] in his lifetime, Stephan G. enjoyed excellent translations of his poems by, for example, the poet and his friend Jakobína Johnson. Through the twentieth century and into the twenty-first, renowned translators of Icelandic literature such as Bernard Scudder (1954–2007) have also contributed their share to the visibility of the transatlantic treasure. Still, a poem like "Vopnahlé" (Battle-pause) from 1915, which charts the horrific killing fields of Europe during the First World War with unspeakable profundity, and has been referred to by John Ralston Saul in his foreword to *Wakeful Nights* as "the most important Canadian" anti-war poetry (2012, 13)—the poem that is written by "the greatest poet of the Western world" (Cawley 1938, 99), Canada's "leading poet" (Kirkconnell 1936, 263), and one of modernity's "most powerful spirits" (Laxness 1972, 7) —is scarcely known in the "outer world."

Should one blame the relative obscurity of the work on a cultural isolation that accompanies the usage of a language that only an infinitesimal fragment of humanity speaks?

Nevertheless, there is a great paradox at work here. Those who encounter the poetry of this pioneer poet in the transatlantic region soon realize that Stephan G. Stephansson's creative engagement with Icelandic literature and its long-standing poetic tradition transcends that of most other poets of modernity.[23] Simultaneously, the readers of his poetry perceive why Stephan G. has been referred to as Ralph Waldo Emerson's (1802–1882) disciple in the ranks of North American poets and philosophers (Bjarnadóttir 2010, 39), and, as noted by Viðar Hreinsson in *Wakeful Nights* (2012, 179), why his philosophy of life is also shaped by Henry David Thoreau (1817–1862). In other words, the young farmboy who emigrated from Iceland on the same ship as Undína in 1873, and who taught himself to travel in world literature and philosophy of man and nature, was equally engaged with the outer world as with his beloved language and land of birth.

Though Stefán Einarsson may be right in suggesting that the "homeland, though distant, never relinquished its hold on the poet" (Einarsson 1957, 342), Stephan G. seems to have worked his way through the shattering experience of emigration. The poem "Útlegðin" (Exile) from 1891 does reveal what is at stake in the inherent drama of emigration in the transatlantic region, with its unforgettable opening lines, here in a translation by writer Paul Sigurdson (1927–1991): "Somehow it has come upon me, / I've no fatherland" (Stephansson 2019, 62). The new land, the foster mother, does not hold a chance, it seems, in comparison with the mother: "Always there was something lacking, / she could not replace"; and "always there's an awkward feeling" (Stephansson 2019, 62) between the foster mother and her newly arrived son.

Again, the reader of the poem on exile may have landed in the psychology of emigration, and/or been held captive by the beauty of the past. The poetics of migration in the writing of Stephan G. does, however, move in a different direction from the one the reader perceives in Undína's. There is a voyage to speak of, it is true, but in the case of Stephan G., its centripetal force doesn't feel like the seemingly endless voyage of departure out into the ocean but more like a voyage home, through exile. In fact, Guðrún Guðsteinsdóttir maintains that

Stephan G. embraces the idea and the experience of migration (Guðsteinsdóttir 2006, 20). If this is the case, the discussed disposition sets Stephan G. apart from his fellow pioneer poet Undína in the poetics of migration.

A couple of decades after Stephan G. composed the poem "Útlegðin," he returned to Iceland for his first and only visit after his emigration. In the poem "Austurvegur" (The path east), which is inspired by the visit, his poetics of migration may have reached a kind of equilibrium with regards to the subjects of being and habitat. The ocean can be termed as a unifying element, with the notion of home on both sides of the Atlantic. The speaker in the poem acknowledges not one homeland but two, concluding: "Öll höf eru heimleið" (All waters are homeward paths). Here is the poem in Kristjana Gunnars's English translation (Stephansson 2019, 258):

> I set sail from home
> for I want to go home.
> With my native country before me
> I leave my adoptive land.
> In the calmness of shore
> I loose the cable
> and set out on your expanse,
> you, lasting blue depths.
>
> You, Ocean, are my comrade.
> Now I sit down beside you
> and we share the heaven
> and all the world's shores.
> All waters are homeward paths;
> Though the gunwales be awash
> we cross the fjords
> between our homesteads.

The question remains whether and how this voyage includes possible extraterritorial elements. Clearly, when one explores the poetry of Stephan G., there are universal literary themes to take into consideration. Even Skagafjörður, the place where he was born and raised, cannot be viewed as a secluded universe within the context of the poetic force in question (Bessason 1997). Perhaps Stefan Jonasson is right in suggesting that readers should pay attention to Stephan G. not only as a "poet in the literary sense" but also as a "social prophet and philosopher" (Jonasson 2003, 51). The spirit in question, Jonasson argues, is best captured in the title of his first collection of poetry, *Úti á víðavangi* (Out in the open air) (1894), and the reason seems to point towards yet another extraterritorial element: "Emerson wrote that 'poets are thus liberating gods' and there can be little doubt that Stephansson's influence during his lifetime, and his enduring influence since, has been as a liberating force in the life of his readers, whether in politics, religion or literature. It is still out into the open air where this poet and prophet leads us" (Jonasson 2003, 51).

If this is the case, one can perceive how a poet like Stephan G. transcends the macabre outlook of the speaker in Rilke's poem by his creative engagement with the universal forces at play in the world of emigrants, and other human beings: language, literature, philosophy, and the extraterritorial elements of both air and water.

CONCLUSION

The two aspiring poets Helga Steinvör Baldvinsdóttir and Stephan G. Stephansson emigrated from Iceland on 4 August 1873, with the horse transport ship SS *Queen*. Rilke may have connected with the living conditions of the Icelandic passengers, both people and horses, and when reflecting on these conditions, some readers of his poem "Emigrant Ship. Naples" may understand more clearly why Rilke hesitated to embrace the mass exodus from Europe to the Americas. For a gifted poet, it is, however, one thing to take on the position of an abstract spectator in a seaport in Italy and another to cross the Atlantic, willingly or unwillingly, and share the individual findings of the voyage of "the caravan of departing souls," within the context of the rich complexities of the subject of culture and heritage in the tempestuous transatlantic region.

As has been discussed, Undína and Stephan G. are great examples of European immigrant poets in North America who continue to engage with the culture and heritage of their land of birth. Their lifelong attachment to the Icelandic language doesn't secure their poetry a uniform account of the subjects of culture and heritage, though. In addition to the evident differences of their individual aesthetics, including the wide range of interests and sources of inspiration in the worlds of literature, nature, and philosophy, and in human existence, the varieties of their expressions and profound reflections offer a spectacular testimony of being and habitat, which can be said to oscillate between tragic and liberating revelations. Whereas these variations may, in part, manifest signs of a transformation and/or conversion from national to heritage culture, the poetics of migration in the poetry of Undína and Stephan G. also provide the reader with an opportunity to acknowledge equally poignant signs of both universal and extraterritorial elements.

As it is, a handful of poems by two of the leading pioneer poets among Icelandic immigrants of North America invite the reader to perceive the scope of their poetics of migration. The poetics of migration in the poetry of Stephan G. does move in a different direction from what the reader perceives in Undína's. In both cases there is certainly a voyage to speak of, but in the case of Stephan G., its centripetal force doesn't feel directed at the seemingly endless voyage of departure out into the ocean but more like a voyage home, through exile. Thus, the conclusion is in the form of an acknowledgment of both universal and extraterritorial elements in the worlds of literature, philosophy, and nature, and in human existence, right next to a lifelong engagement with the language, literature, and soil of the land of birth.[24]

Time will tell if the "outer world" will become aware of the liberating profundity of the poetry of Stephan G. Stephansson. It remains to be seen, also, if the "outer world" will have the opportunity to reflect upon Undína's art of poetry, which is reminiscent of world-known works of literature, across centuries. Her striking, and at times shattering, perception of emigration, which results in an equivocal sense of being and place, can also be said to herald, in part, the poetics of better-known emigrants in the world of literature, figures like the German writer W.G. Sebald. For now, it is safe to conclude that Undína and Stephan G. Stephansson provide us with a testament of expressions from within the lived experiences of the mass exodus from Europe to the Americas, thanks to their voyage with an emigrant ship.

NOTES

1 The oceanic novel *Der Verschollene* (1927) or *America* by Franz Kafka manifests his great interest in the subject, and Benedikt Gröndal Sveinbjarnarson expressed his highly critical views on the emigration of Icelanders in his booklet *Um Vesturheimsferðir* (On the journey west) from 1888.

2 Rilke made two attempts on both the subject and the title. The first poem was composed in 1894 (in Bohemia) and the latter, with the subtitle "Naples," appeared in 1908 in *Der neuen Gedichte anderer Teil* (New poems: The other part). See Hofmann (2021).

3 See, for example, Ryan Eyford's groundbreaking research in *White Settler Reserve* (2016), where he discusses the white settler reserve of New Iceland in Manitoba, Canada, and how Icelandic immigrants participated in the process of Canada's colonization.

4 In 1859, half a century before Rilke composed his poem, Karl Marx (1818–1883) stated the following: "I must pursue my goal through thick and thin and I must not allow bourgeois society to turn me into money-making machine." See the fragment on Karl Marx in Mason Currey's *Daily Rituals* (2013).

5 The book *Sigurtunga* (2018), edited by Birna Arnbjörnsdóttir, Höskuldur Thráinsson, and Úlfar Bragason, includes the most comprehensive research to date on the subject of Icelandic language and culture among Icelandic immigrants of North America and their desendants. See also Haraldur Bessason's research (1967) and Birna Arnbjörnsdóttir's *North American Icelandic* (2006).

6 See Birna Bjarnadóttir's discussion of the subject in connection with Guttormur J. Guttormsson's *Ten Plays/Tíu leikrit in Sigurtunga* (2018, 199–200) and in *Brick* (2015b, 64–65).

7 During their marriage Helga and Jakob suffered the unspeakable misfortune to bury three of their children, who all died at a young age.

8 In this biographical sketch, I have drawn on the findings of Snæbjörn Jónsson (1952, vii–xxvi), Kirsten Wolf (1994, 163n7), Helga Kress (2001, 136), and Jóhann Magnús Bjarnason (1941).

9 Katelin Parsons kindly provided this information.

10 See, for example, Jón Ólafsson's "Ritstjóra-spjall" (Editorial) (1893), in *Öldin*, and Jóhann Magnús Bjarnason's "Undína skáldkona" (The poetess Undína) (1941) in *Eimreiðin*. The manuscript in question was kept safe by Undína's daughter, Soffía, who, after her mother's death, sent it to Snæbjörn Jónsson.

11 In 1952, eleven years after the passing of Helga Steinvör Baldvinsdóttir, the book *Kvæði* (Poetry) was published in Reykjavík by Ísafoldarprentsmiðja. Snæbjörn Jónsson was the editor and he also wrote the introduction, which is titled "Undína."

12 Translated by Julian Mendoza.

13 Translated by Julian Mendoza.

14 In addition to the already cited sources on Undína, see also Helga Kress (2001).

15 The novella Undína was translated into Icelandic by the Icelandic poet and scholar Steingrímur Thorsteinsson (1831–1913) and first published in 1861 in Copenhagen. In 1907 it was republished in Winnipeg by Lögberg.

16 Recent examples of Undines in the transatlantic region are Anne Carson's short story at the exhibit *Tears/Dýpsta sæla og sorgin þunga* (2021), and the poem "Heimkoma" (Homecoming) by Birna Bjarnadóttir (2015a).

17 Understandably, the name Undína must have seemed foreign in the minds of English-speaking European immigrants in North America in the late nineteenth century. A film review by Peter Debruge (2020) on the 2020 German film *Undine* seems to indicate that the Undine character still feels foreign for some people in present-day North America.

18 See https://malfar.arnastofnun.is/greinar//flokkur/10.

19 For a detailed discussion on this subject, see Matthew Hart and Tania Lown-Hecht (2012).

20 The subject of horses in the life and poetry of Stephan G. is, in fact, a major one. See also Guðrún Guðsteinsdóttir (1996) and Úlfur Friðriksson (1997, 30–39).

21 My translation.

22 This bilingual edition of a selection of poems by Stephan G. features the original poems in Icelandic and existing English translations from both sides of the Atlantic, including those by writers Bernard Scudder (1954–2007), Viðar Hreinsson, Kristjana Gunnars, Finnbogi Guðmundsson, and Jakobína Johnson (1883–1977).

23 In addition to both Icelandic and Icelandic immigrant poets, this applies also to poets of other nationalities, who made themselves familiar with Icelandic literature in translation.

24 The editors of this book provided excellent feedback, for which I am very grateful. I would also like to thank Katelin Parsons for her most careful reading, and Pat Sanders for her excellent proofreading.

REFERENCES

Andersen, Hans Christian. 2014. *The Little Mermaid.* Translated by H.B. Paull. New York: Hythloday Press.

Arnbjörnsdóttir, Birna. 2006. *North American Icelandic: The Life of a Language*. Winnipeg: University of Manitoba Press.

Arnbjörnsdóttir, Birna, Höskuldur Thráinsson, and Úlfar Bragason, eds. 2019. *Sigurtunga: Vesturíslenskt mál og menning* [Western Icelandic language and culture]. Reykjavík: Háskólaútgáfan.

Bessason, Haraldur. 1967. "A Few Specimens of North American-Icelandic." *Scandinavian Studies* 39 (2): 115–46.

———. 1997. "Skagafjordur and a Step Beyond." *Canadian Ethnic Studies* 29 (3): 43–50.

Bjarnadóttir, Birna. 2010. *a book of fragments*. Winnipeg: Kind Publishing,

———. 2015a. "Heimkoma." *Stína* 15 (1): 25.

———. 2015b. "*Ten Plays* by Guttormur J. Guttormsson." *Brick Magazine* 96: 64–66.

———. 2018. "Í dularhjúpi Atlantshafsins. Örlagaþræðir manns og heims í leikritum Guttorms J. Guttormssonar" [Shrouded in a cross–Atlantic enigma: The plays of Guttormur J. Guttormsson]. In *Sigurtunga*: *Vesturíslenskt mál og menning*, edited by Birna Arnbjörnsdóttir, Höskuldur Thráinsson, and Úlfar Bragason, 189–207. Reykjavík: Háskólaútgáfan.

———. 2020. "Við erum hér en hugur okkar er heima. Um líf og skáldskap Undínu" [Here we are, but our mind dwells at home. On the life and poetry of Undína]. *Stuðlaberg* 2: 27–29.

Bjarnason, Jóhann Magnús. 1941. "Undína skáldkona" [The poetess Undína]. *Eimreiðin* 3 (July–September): 273–78.

Carson, Anne. 2021. *Tears/Dýpsta sæla og sorgin þunga*. Exhibit with other artists: Halla Birgisdóttir, Margrét Dúadóttir Landmark, and Ragnar Kjartansson. Kling & Bang Gallery, Reykjavík, 21 January–14 March.

Cawley, F. Stanton. 1938. "The Greatest Poet of the Western World: Stephan G. Stephansson." *Scandinavian Studies and Notes* 15 (4): 98–109.

Currey, Mason. 2013. *Daily Rituals: How Great Minds Make Time, Find Inspiration and Get to Work.* New York: Alfred A. Knopf.

Debruge, Peter. 2020. "Undine." *Variety*. Film review published 23 February 2020. Accessed 12 January 2021. https://variety.com/2020/film/reviews/undine-review-1203511838/.

Einarsson, Stefán. 1957. *A History of Icelandic Literature.* Baltimore: Johns Hopkins University Press.

Eyford, Ryan. 2016. *White Settler Reserve: New Iceland and the Colonization of the Canadian West*. Vancouver: University of British Columbia Press.

Fouqué, Friedrich de la Motte. 1907. *Undína*. Translated by Steingrímur Thorsteinsson. Winnipeg: Lögberg.

Friðriksson, Úlfur. 1977. *Í ríki hestsins* [In the region of the horse]. Reykjavík: Skuggsjá.

Gröndal, Benedikt. 1888. *Um Vesturheimsferðir* [On the emigration]. Reykjavík: Ísafold.

Guðsteinsdóttir, Guðrún Björk. 1996. "'Ameríku-Stephán': 'reiðfantur á ótemju' tungunnar" [Stephan, the American: Trailblaser through language]. *Skírnir* 170: 389–412.

———. 2006. "Home and Exile in Early Icelandic-Canadian Poetry." In *Home and Exile: Selected Papers from the 4th International Tartu Conference on Canadian Studies*, edited by Eva Rein and Krista Vogelberg, 71–81. Cultural Studies Series 7. Tartu, Estonia: Tartu University Press.

Hart, Matthew, and Tania Lown-Hecht. 2012. "The Extraterritorial Poetics of W.G. Sebald." *Modern Fiction Studies* (58) 2: 214–38.

Hofmann, Michael. 2021. "Slashed, Red and Dead." *London Review of Books* 43 (2). https://www.lrb.co.uk/the-paper/v43/n02/michael-hofmann/slashed-red-and-dead.

Hreinsson, Viðar. 2012. *Wakeful Nights: Stephan G. Stephansson: Icelandic-Canadian Poet*. Calgary: Benson Ranch.

Jonasson, Stefan. 2003. "Out in the Open Air: The Liberating Legacy of Stephan G. Stephansson." *Icelandic Canadian* 58 (2): 50–63.

Jónsson, Snæbjörn. 1952. "Undína." In *Undína. Kvæði* [Undína. Poems], VII–XXVI. Reykjavík: Ísafoldarprentsmiðja.

Kafka, Franz. 2004. *America (The Man Who Disappeared)*. Translated by Michael Hofmann. New York: New Directions Books.

Kirkconnell, Watson. 1936. "Canada's Leading Poet: Stephan G. Stephansson (1953–1927)." *University of Toronto Quarterly* 5 (2): 263–277.

Kress, Helga. 2001. "Undína 1858–1941." In *Stúlka. Ljóð eftir íslenskar konur* [Maiden. poems by Icelandic women], edited by Ásdís Egilsdóttir and Helga Kress, 136. Rev. ed. Reykjavík: Bókmenntafræðistofnun Háskóla Íslands.

Laxness, Halldór. 1972. *Af skáldum* [Of poets]. Reykjavík: Bókaútgáfa Menningarsjóðs.

Naso, Ovidius. 2014. *Metamorphoses*. Translated by Frank Justus Miller. Cambridge, MA: Harvard University Press.

Neijmann, Daisy. 1998. *The Icelandic Voice in Canadian Letters: The Contribution of Icelandic-Canadian Writers to Canadian Literature*. Ottawa: Carleton University Press.

———. 1999. "Icelandic-Canadian Literature and Anglophone Minority Writing in Canada." *World Literature Today* 73 (2): 245–55.

Ólafsson, Jón. 1893. "Ritstjóra-spjall" [Editorial]. *Öldin* 1 (1): 15–16.

Paracelsus [Theophrastus von Hohenheim]. [1941] 1996. *Four Treatises of Theophrastus von Hohenheim Called Paracelsus*. Translated by Henry E. Sigherist. Baltimore: Johns Hopkins University Press.

Rilke, Rainer Maria. 2001. *Rainer Maria Rilke*: *New Poems*. Rev. bilingual ed., edited and translated by Edward Snow. New York: North Point Press.

Saul, John Ralston. 2012. "Foreword." In Viðar Hreinsson, *Wakeful Nights: Stephan G. Stephansson: Icelandic Canadian Poet*, 13. Calgary: Benson Ranch.

Sebald, Winfried Georg. 1996. *The Emigrants*. Translated by Michael Hulse. New York: New Directions Books.

Stephansson, Stephan G. 2019. *Two Lands, One Poet*: *The Reflections of Stephan G. Stephansson Through Poetry*. Bilingual publication in English and Icelandic of a selection of Stephansson's poems, edited by Birna Bjarnadóttir and Mooréa Gray. Reykjavík: Hin kindin and Vigdís Finnbogadóttir Institute.

Undína. 1952. *Kvæði*. Edited by Snæbjörn Jónsson. Reykjavík: Ísafoldarprentsmiðja.

Wolf, Kirsten. 1994. "Western Icelandic Women Writers: Their Contribution to the Literary Canon." *Scandinavian Studies* 66 (2): 154–203.

Woolf, Virginia. 1982. *The Diary of Virgina Woolf.* Vol. 3: *1925–30.* Edited by Anne Olivier Bell. London: Penguin Books.

CHAPTER 8

The Young Icelander Grows Up: Nationalism and Ethnic Identity in Jóhann Magnús Bjarnason's Life and Work

DAGNÝ KRISTJÁNSDÓTTIR

MANY DIFFICULT QUESTIONS come to mind when one reflects on the career and writings of teacher and author Jóhann Magnús Bjarnason (1866–1945).[1] At the core is the issue of his position on nationality and language. His activities as an author formed such a central part of his life and identity that they can be characterized as the backbone of his existence. Bjarnason was only nine when he immigrated to Canada and spoke English as a second language. Why, then, did he not write in English in his adoptive country? Why did he instead decide to write books in the language of a tiny nation in the North Atlantic and a small, rapidly dwindling group of immigrant readers? Did he have any alternative? Could he have published his books in English instead and claimed a place in Canadian literary history?

The present chapter seeks to tease out answers to these questions, challenging the position that Bjarnason was motivated by nationalism. Although it has become common to refer to Bjarnason as a "nationalist," the concepts of *nation* and *ethnic identity* are key to untangling his life and work in his adoptive society. The argument is presented here that his Icelandic nationality quickly lost its hold on him in Canada, but he retained his

FIGURE 8.1. Jóhann Magnús Bjarnason.

Icelandic ethnic identity throughout his life, even as this identity changed and adapted to Anglo-Canadian culture over time (see Kjartansson 2018; Sveinsson 2018). Bjarnason's choice to write for an Icelandic-speaking readership is re-examined in light of the options open to Icelandic immigrant authors in Canada in the early twentieth century.

NATIONALITY AND ETHNICITY

The first immigrants shared little by way of a Canadian national identity. A national identity must be constructed in order to act as a common denominator and a consensus as to what defines "us" and excludes "them"—essential for us to make peace or war with other nations. At a bare minimum a nation consists of the people who feel they belong to it (Watts 2016, 111–12). However, one's nationality cannot be chosen on a whim: formal criteria must be fulfilled to gain citizenship. In "DissemiNation," Bhabha (1990) argues that while the concept of nation unifies, it is also recognition that the "nation" is already split; otherwise, unification would be an unnecessary exercise. "Nationality" can in this sense be considered to be the political and ideological decisions to which national citizens submit.

The immigrants who had arrived in ships' holds from Europe did not all understand English or French. They needed to learn one of these two languages, usually English, to obtain their papers and employment. Many of the immigrants sought to keep together, maintain a peaceful relationship with other immigrant groups, and find their footing in the new country. They saw themselves as Ukrainian, Swedish, Dutch, or Icelandic, and not at all as Canadians. As Hoerder said (1999, 26), "Canadian society of the century from the 1850s to the 1940s was not multicultural in the modern sense but it was many-cultured." Earning a living was the newcomers' first priority, above all other things. Once their financial standing was secure, they could send for relatives, unite extended families, and attempt to provide their children with an education and thereby a future in the new country.

The many "parallel realities" contained within the larger concept of the nation have been described as "ethnicities" or "ethnic identities." In contrast to the political concept of nationalities, these are attachments at the personal and emotional level. Edwards defines ethnic identity as "allegiance to a group—large or small, socially dominant or subordinate—with which one has ancestral links. There is no necessity for a continuation, over generations, of the same socialisation or cultural patterns, but some sense of a group boundary must persist. This can be sustained by shared objective characteristics (language, religion, etc.), or by more subjective contributions to a sense of 'groupness', or by some combination of both. Symbolic or subjective attachments must relate, at however distant a remove, to an observably real past" (Edwards 2009, 162).

Initially, individual immigrants and immigrant groups within Canada could be identified by their names, languages, clothing, and cuisine, making them recognizable minority groups. All of these markers of a collective identity gradually became optional and effectively symbolic; anyone could choose to reject or adopt symbols from another culture. Despite the difficulty inherent in pinning down the concept of ethnicity, it remains just as evident that individuals' ethnic identity is deeply important to them, and they experience disenfranchisement if their ethnic identity is criticized or downplayed—still more so if those in power attempt to strip them of their ethnic identity or forbid certain elements of its expression.

AMBIVALENCES

Some Icelanders who emigrated to North America in the late nineteenth century had mixed feelings for their home country and their nation, perceiving that neither had served them well. These dissatisfied emigrants were quick to relinquish their ethnic identity upon arrival to a new homeland, assume new names, and lose contact with the other Icelanders. A more visible group was filled with national pride and patriotism, seeking to create New Iceland in North America, and wanting to retain their language and culture and not to assimilate to a new culture to a greater degree than necessary. Why, then, did they immigrate in the first place? Such a contradiction calls for an origin myth.

Neijmann argues that Icelandic immigrants in Canada attempted to bring together two origin myths: escape from natural disaster and hardship, and a thirst for freedom—the same thirst for a better life in a new land that had once driven their ancestors to flee from Norway and settle in Iceland. This ancestral precedent was a legacy still imprinted on the genes of their descendants, and nothing was more natural than to seek to follow in their forebears' footsteps and build a new Iceland in North America. Two myths merged into one, which was used to argue that the Icelanders could fare just as well in Canada as in Iceland. The new myth was existential in the sense that it focused on what the Icelandic people "did" rather than what they "were" (Neijmann 1997a, 78).

Faced by the difficulties of their first decades in North America, many immigrants saw their Icelandic nationality as a source of strength. Their ethnic identity bolstered their self-confidence and their cultural capital, as described by Bourdieu (1992, 81). However, debate on the issue of assimilation or isolation could turn venomous. This was particularly in evidence among teachers and others concerned with childhood education in North America in the first years of the twentieth century. These conflicts emerge clearly in the children's periodicals published at this time (Kristjánsdóttir 2015).

A remarkably pervasive theme in writings on patriotism and Icelandic affairs is that if the Icelandic language is lost, then the Icelanders' ethnic identity will cease to exist with it, and they will founder and perish. Pastor N. Steingrímur Thorlaksson (1857–1943), editor of the Icelandic-Canadian children's magazines *Börnin* (The Children) and *Framtíðin* (The Future), emphasized the importance of "nationality" and cultivating one's ties to one's nation. In addition to supporting a Lutheran upbringing and Christian solidarity, Thorlaksson hoped that these magazines would encourage young readers "to remain *Icelandic* youth and to take pride in their Icelandic roots" and give them a better understanding of Iceland and the Icelandic nation—"*that nation and that country* to which we ought to be bound with unbreakable bonds" (Thorlaksson 1908, 3, emphasis in original):

> We must not vanish like a drop in the ocean. . . . Just as any man ought rightfully to shudder at the thought of being reduced to nothing, any true Icelander—to whom his own honour and the honour of his nation is dear—ought to shudder at the thought that this [nation] should face obliteration here in this country.
>
> This must never come to pass! Our motherland and all the guardian spirits who have protected her sanctuary now look to every upright Icelander to do his duty and work tirelessly to ensure that we do not end the losers in the nationalist battle in which we are currently engaged.[2]

Increasingly, however, the nationalist battle became a fight for the Icelandic language. The land and the nation were gradually sidelined and belonged to the past. Language became the "fatherland" that could be defended. The struggle revolved around children's use of the Icelandic language, and teachers were expected to form the vanguard in this war. Even so, there was no consensus in the matter, any more than for any other issue faced by the immigrants in North America. Some parents wished to integrate into the new society as rapidly as possible and believed that teaching Icelandic to their children would impede their studies in English because they would be unable to learn two languages.

One of the teachers entrusted with looking after children's interests on this language battlefield was Jóhann Magnús Bjarnason. He was born in 1866 on the farm of Meðalnes in the region of Norður-Múlasýsla in East Iceland. His family was among the many uprooted by the 1875 eruption of Askja. They immigrated to Canada that same year, fleeing the famine and hardship that followed in the immediate wake of this natural disaster. Jóhann Magnús was nine years old at the time. The family initially moved to Nova Scotia, but the soil in Markland (Mooseland) where the Icelandic settlement was located was hard and rocky. Despite the immigrants' best efforts, the settlement was completely abandoned within seven years, with most of the Icelanders travelling west to the Prairies (Gunnarsson 2000, 1). Among them were Jóhann Magnús and his family. He taught children in Icelandic settlements in North America until 1922, with several breaks due to illness.

During Bjarnason's years as a teacher for Icelandic immigrant students, he was hired by the local school boards within the Icelandic immigrant settlements. The work was far from easy. Jóhannes Páll Pálsson, a former student of Bjarnason's, described Bjarnason's lot in the Geysir district in Manitoba. According to Pálsson, there were scarcely four English-speaking Icelanders in the entire district, so it fell to Bjarnason to translate, write letters, interpret, draft agreements, and serve as an assistant to the community justice of the peace—all in addition to his regular teaching duties.

> His pay was thirty dollars a month at most. [Jóhann] Magnús and [his wife] Guðrún scrimped and saved as they could, but his wages weren't enough unless he managed to scrounge some teaching at other locations in addition to the Geysir school. He sometimes taught part of the year at Hnausa, often walking daily to and from home—seven miles. In 1895 he taught at Mikley [Hecla Island]. I worked as an errand boy at his house at the time, so I know that he would walk home from school on Fridays and back again on Sunday afternoon. That distance is forty miles, on top of which he needed to catch a ferry between the island and the mainland. (Pálsson 1945, 8)

The rural schools at which Bjarnason taught were part of the public school system. Thus, it was always one of Bjarnason's duties to teach immigrant children English, as per the curriculum, in addition to Icelandic. Even after his health prevented him from continuing his teaching work, his former pupils continued to remember him faithfully. He had been so good with his young students that many named their own children after him and would send him and Guðrún gifts out of their own small means for as long as the Bjarnasons lived.

In spite of his poor health and poverty, he wrote a book of poetry and six novels and short story collections alongside his teaching work. These books continued to be widely read in Iceland for many years after the author's death in Elfros in Saskatchewan in 1945, by which time he had lived for nearly sixty years in North America.

THE IMMIGRANT CHILD

Jóhann Magnús Bjarnason dedicated the first volume of his three-part novel *Eiríkur Hansson*, first published in the years 1902 to 1904, to the inhabitants of the "old Icelandic settlement in Nova Scotia." The protagonist, the titular Eiríkur, arrives in Nova Scotia with his grandparents as a seven-year-old boy. Hard work is Eiríkur's lot from an early age. His grandfather's health fails, and his grandmother is unable to support him on her own. Like the other children in the colony, Eiríkur attends a public school presided over by an English-speaking teacher, Cracknell, described in the book as a sadist whose pedagogy aims at beating the books into his pupils' heads. Cracknell forbids the children from speaking Icelandic, since he is unable to understand a word of the language. He disrespects their nationality in every possible way, detesting anything un-Anglo. Despite Cracknell's lack of other merits, Eiríkur reflects in retrospective that Cracknell did succeed in teaching them good English.

Eiríkur's grandfather dies, and his grandmother accepts the offer of the widow Mrs. Patrick, who wants to adopt the boy. Her desire to transform the child into an Irish boy soon emerges. She mocks his Icelandic name and rechristens him Patrick in memory of her late husband. She is obese and drunken and displays an unhealthy affection for the boy. When he runs away and is returned to her, she whips him viciously as if he were her runaway slave, heaping ethnic hatred and scorn upon him: "You didn't know, maybe, that I took you from the vile, filthy Icelanders—that I plucked you off the street and made you my son and was going to leave you all I own—that I wanted to make you, you vile little tiger-whelp, into an honest Irishman" (Bjarnason 2012b, 94). Mrs. Patrick is at once comic and grotesque, while Cracknell is outright terrifying. Either character might have come straight from a Dickens novel. They take pleasure in tormenting and humiliating children. Eiríkur Hansson escapes again from the widow and plans to flee to Halifax, where he has friends who can help him. His grandmother has died and he himself is an orphan. He has no alternative but to work to survive and to complete his journey. Along his way, prying by strangers into Eiríkur's nationality and cultural origins can transform into dangerous attention: mistrust, cruelty, or—worse—desire. An adult reader can clearly observe the young protagonist's attempts to explain away most such behaviour, adding a second layer to the narrative.

After surviving a string of hardships and working situations of varyingly harsh degrees, the boy makes it to Halifax, where he is received with open arms by trustworthy allies. Eiríkur fares well but does not escape wholly unscathed from his childhood:

> I was thirteen winters old now. I was neither tall nor strong for my age, but I knew just as well as anyone of that age what life and the world holds for you. I'd seen more of the world than most children, the Icelandic ones at least. Those thirteen years had brought me plenty of sunshine, and I'd often been happy and healthy, but they could also be cold and dark at times. Many times I'd been lonely, sad and afraid. My knowledge of the world around me and the people in it had been dearly paid for already. (Bjarnason 2012b, 13–14)

For readers in Iceland, *Eiríkur Hansson* felt like a wildly unrealistic adventure. However, in a letter dated 22 December 1902, following the publication of the novel's second volume, the immigrant and poet Stephan G. Stephansson wrote to his friend Bjarnason that "thus far, *Eiríkur Hansson* is the story of your own life, which is not to say that every event in the novel necessarily befell you exactly as related, but you would invariably have behaved and thought essentially just as he did" (Stephansson 1938–39, 115). Bjarnason did draw directly on his own experiences to some extent when writing *Eiríkur Hansson* (Bjarnason 2016a, 24). He emphasized, however, whenever he did a reading from the novel or otherwise discussed it, that Eiríkur Hansson's life was for the most part fiction and that the book was by no means an autobiography.

MIXED RECEPTION

Eiríkur Hansson received a mixed reception in Iceland and in North America but for very different reasons. In Iceland prejudice and bitterness toward migrants who had left the country infused the book's reviews. Critics in Iceland derided the "broken" Icelandic and English influences and the emotional "feminine" style, with overuse of repetition and exaggerated Dickensian characters. Critics within the immigrant community also attacked Bjarnason's use of language but on the grounds that Icelanders who had immigrated ought to display twice as good a command of the Icelandic language as their countrymen to prove, as Friðrik Bergmann said, that they had "lost nothing but gained something" by leaving their country (Bergmann 1902, 226).[3]

Literary criticism in the early 1900s could be ruthless, but Bjarnason's treatment was unusually harsh. Social activist Margrét J. Benedictsson hit the nail on the head when she observed in her Selkirk-based periodical, *Freyja*, that it was odd that the Icelanders would want to hear absolutely nothing spoken of the struggles of poor Icelandic children and youths for survival in their new country (1904–05, 95). Little wonder that Benedictsson should ask for answers as to the origins of critics' animosity.

The message from literary critics in Iceland to the immigrant writer was clear: he had no right to call himself a poet or an Icelander. Bjarnason took this criticism very personally, as can be seen in his correspondence with Stephansson (Skulason 1996, 35). In 2009 Borga Jakobson's English translation of *Eiríkur Hansson* was published under the title *The Young Icelander*, with an introduction by Birna Bjarnadóttir. It was the first time the book became available to a wider Canadian readership, over a century after its initial publication.

THE LOFTY ICELANDER

There has been a general consensus that Bjarnason was an ardent nationalist who passionately championed the excellence of Iceland and the Icelanders. Bjarnason's contemporaries declared as much in their tribute and memorial writings, and this view has been repeated again and again by later scholars (Beck 1977, xiv–xv; Bjarnarson 1970, xiii; Hafstað 2011, 15; Elíasson 2011, 21).

Closer examination reveals Bjarnason's nationalism to be far less clear-cut, particularly in light of the difference between immigrants' nationality and their ethnic identity, as discussed earlier. In Neijmann's words, "There can be no doubt that Icelandic immigrant authors were extremely self-conscious about the way in which they used and portrayed Icelandic language and culture and its preservation, and that they felt considerable pressure to prove to Iceland that the immigrants to Canada were not traitors to their culture and nationality. Obviously, this limited the way in which acculturation could be expressed in literature. At the same time, however, there is an undeniable fascination with the Canadian social and natural environment and a desire to be part of it which makes the literary involvement a decidedly dual one" (Neijmann 1997b, 67). Here, one can concur fully with Neijmann. The dual or bipartite identity of the immigrant, split between the old country and the new, draws no line between an "old" and "new" culture. Constant intercultural mediation and translation occur in the in-between zone that is the immigrant's own identity.

The reception of *Eiríkur Hansson* left Bjarnason wary of returning to similar narrative territory. His later books describe worlds equally foreign to readers in Iceland and Canada and become increasingly less reality-bound, in the spirit of British fantasy and adventure literature (Kristjánsdóttir 2015, 234–38). This is apparent in the descriptions of society and attitudes expressed in these later books. If the Icelanders in his books are unrealistically perfect, it is precisely because they are characters in a fantasy. Too good to be true.

AN ICELANDIC OR ICELANDIC-CANADIAN AUTHOR?

This chapter began by asking why Bjarnason chose to write in Icelandic from the outset. It is a question also asked by Icelandic poet Gyrðir Elíasson (2012, 25). Bjarnason's diaries and letters contain no direct answer. Neijmann suggests that it was a conscious decision or obvious choice on the part of first-generation Icelandic immigrants to write in Icelandic for their fellow countrymen both near and far but that many believed that all immigrant languages would ultimately meld together into one, with the outcome being a Canadian literary establishment open to all (Neijmann 1997b, 65–66).

Gísli Jónsson wrote in *Eimreiðin* in January 1913: "When all these similar and dissimilar, related and unrelated ethnic groups have come together in the melting pot, a new race with a new national consciousness will arise that is neither English nor French nor anything else that has come before" (Jónsson 1913, 44–45).

Jóhann Magnús and his wife, Guðrún, were sociable by nature. Their hospitality brought many guests to their tiny house, including visiting intellectuals from Iceland, who were often accompanied by Bjarnason's friends and admirers. Bjarnason also kept up with the publications of Stephan G. Stephansson and other friends and acquaintances in the Icelandic-Canadian community. Bjarnason was well aware that Icelandic-Canadian authors writing in English did not face fewer difficulties than he did when he was writing exclusively in Icelandic; their language choices did not make writing a more financially viable career.

One of Bjarnason's friends, a newcomer on the Icelandic-Canadian literary scene, was Laura Goodman Salverson (1890–1970). She wrote to Bjarnason, describing herself as a great fan who had read *Eiríkur Hansson* in childhood (Bjarnason 2016a, 153). On 20 January 1924, Bjarnason finished reading her recently published first novel, *The Viking Heart*, remarking that he had liked the story (Bjarnason 2016a, 165). When Salverson later visited Elfros in person, Bjarnason admired her ability to speak clear Icelandic, despite having spent little time among other ethnic Icelanders as an adult and writing exclusively in English (Bjarnason 2016b, 293).

One may read between the lines in Bjarnason's diaries that Icelandic authors in North America sought to improve their English and dreamed of gaining recognition, but it was an uphill battle. Salverson might have met success with her tale of an immigrant's daughter, but there were limits to publishers' patience for immigrant stories about adversity and conflicted ethnic identities. They wanted modernism, not realism. They wanted chaos narratives familiar to the literary elite. They wanted men, not women. Salverson's literary career was no bed of roses, yet she was one of the few authors of Icelandic background who garnered even a mention in Canadian literary histories of the first half of the twentieth century (Neijmann 1999). In general, there was little demand in Canadian literary circles for diversity or immigrant literature in English originating from outside British and French traditions (Lecker 2013).

TRANSLATING ICELANDIC CULTURE

Bjarnason's fantasy *Karl litli* (Little Karl) was published in Iceland in 1935. Jóhann Magnús and Guðrún were childless but had adopted a daughter, Alice Juliet Cooper (1892–1967), whose biological mother was Icelandic but who had an English father. Alice was only four months old when she joined the Bjarnason family. From his diaries it is clear that Jóhann Magnús and Guðrún loved Alice deeply and took pride in her accomplishments. After studying to become a teacher, Alice married and had two children. *Karl litli* came into being when Alice sent her son, Gordon Henry (born 12 November 1915) to visit his grandparents. According to Bjarnason, the boy had been bored, "so I told him various stories about little boys who traveled to Dreamland" (Kristjánsdóttir 2015, 238–48).

A tension exists in *Karl litli* between oral storytelling and the literary fairy tale. Gordon Henry likely understood Icelandic well, given his time spent with his grandparents when he was little. Nevertheless, for Bjarnason to open up an Icelandic storyscape for his Canadian grandson required intercultural mediation, and the punctuation of his narrative with information necessary for Icelandic-Canadian readers has a distancing effect. Conversely, Bjarnason needed to explain wordplay based on English terms (such as *April fool* and *court fool*) for his readership in Iceland.

Bjarnason wrote little in his diary about his literary activities, inspirations, thoughts, and ambitions; the difficulties and pleasures in the writing process; or the relationship between life and art. In a rare personal observation dated 23 March 1919, he writes, "I'm progressing slowly on the story of little Karl; I've just started on the fifth chapter. It's as if the fire has died and the thread has snapped. Still, I haven't given up on the story altogether" (Bjarnason 2012a, 264). In a diary entry from 20 April 1940, he remarks briefly that Alice had sent a picture of herself with Gordon Henry, who seemed to be a strapping young man, "but Guðrún and I haven't seen him since 1923" (Bjarnason 2016b, 291–92). On 14 March 1944 came the tragic news that his grandson had died in the Second World War.

The author's energy seems to gradually ebb within the space of his diaries, with entries shrinking as his health began to fail. Guðrún died on 10 August

1945, and he thanked his friends for their sympathy and support, but there was little else to write. The diary's final entry is dated 25 August. Bjarnason died less than a month after his beloved wife, on 8 September 1945.

Bjarnason's diaries provide little insight into his emotions and thoughts. In his diaries his character descriptions seem somewhat cookie-cutter: his guests are invariably neat and good-looking, intelligent, and well-read. Not a few rank "among the best-esteemed Icelanders on this side of the Atlantic." Bjarnason writes as if he were a public figure, choosing his words carefully, and there are conspicuous silences regarding his personal affairs. In this respect his self-presentation in his diary is reminiscent of a modern Facebook profile, where darker currents and deep-felt anxieties are often kept tidily from view. A more personal side of Jóhann Magnús Bjarnason emerges when he writes to his beloved friend and idol, Stephan G. Stephansson. Jóhann Magnús cried figuratively on Stephan's shoulder over the harshest review of *Eiríkur Hansson* in 1904. Stephan seemed to sense intuitively when his sensitive fellow author was at his lowest, and his letters attempt to provide some consolation.

Bjarnason's ethnic identity was a mooring for the author as he wrote his novels and carved out a future for himself in Canada. His ethnicity continued to have a strong presence throughout his life, even as it became gradually coloured by Canadian culture and thinking. As a writer and an immigrant, both his Icelandic and his Canadian identities shaped him. By contrast, Bjarnason's nationalist sentiments gradually waned and faded to nothing. This was a predictable development as Iceland became an ever more distant memory but one hastened considerably by the aggressiveness of Icelandic nationalists and by the bitterness displayed toward immigrant authors in Iceland's literary circles.

When Bjarnason wrote his books, Icelandic immigrant children in Canada were losing their connection to the language of their parents and grandparents. By publishing his books in Iceland, where his young readers lacked the background to comprehend the realism in his stories, Bjarnason was relegated to the margins of the literary histories of both nations. He deserved better.

NOTES

1 Thanks to Katelin Marit Parsons for the translation of this chapter.

2 Three issues of *Börnin* were published before it was consolidated with *Sameiningin* (Unity), the monthly periodical of the Evangelical Lutheran Synod of North America, which had been founded in 1886 and was printed in Selkirk. Níels Steingrímur Thorlaksson was its editor. N.Steingrímur Thorlaksson: "Gerum við nóg fyrir börnin okkar," *Börnin in Sameiningin*, Selkirk, 121–24.

3 On the reception of Bjarnason's early work, see Dagný Kristjánsdóttir (2015, 207–48).

REFERENCES

Beck, Richard. 1977. "Jóhann Magnús Bjarnason: Formáli." In Jóhann Magnús Bjarnason, *Gimsteinaborgin. Karl litli og ævintýri*, i–xxxi. Akureyri: Bókaútgáfan Edda.

[Benedictsson, Margrét J.]. 1904–05. "Eiríkur Hansson: Annar þáttur." *Freyja* 7 (4): 94–96.

Bergmann, Friðrik. 1902. "Eiríkur Hansson." *Aldamót* 12: 165–68.

Bhabha, Homi K. 1990. "DissemiNation: Time, Narrative and the Margins of the Modern Nation." In *Nation and Narration*, edited by Homi K. Bhabha, 291–322. London: Routledge.

Bjarnarson, Árni. 1970. "Æviágrip Jóhanns Magnúsar Bjarnasonar. Formáli að Jóhann Magnús Bjarnason." In *Vornætur á Elgsheiðum: Sögur. Ritsafn 5*, xi–xiii. Akureyri: Bókaútgáfan Edda.

Bjarnason, Jóhann Magnús. 1935. *Karl litli: saga frá Draumamörk*. Reykjavík: E.P. Briem.

———. 2012a. *Dagbók vesturfara 1902–1918*. Vol. 1. Reykjavík: Lestu.is.

———. 2012b. *Eiríkur Hansson. Skáldsaga frá Nýja Skotlandi. 1–3. Þáttur. Bernskan, Baráttan, Þráin*. Reykjavík: Lestu.is.

———. 2016a. *Dagbók vesturfara 1919–1931*. Vol. 2. Reykjavík: Lestu.is.

———. 2016b. *Dagbók vesturfara 1932–1945*. Vol. 3. Reykjavík: Lestu.is.

Bourdieu, Pierre. 1992. *Distinction: A Social Critique of the Judgement of Taste*. London: Routledge.

Edwards, John. 2009. *Language and Identity: An Introduction*. Cambridge: Cambridge University Press.

Elíasson, Gyrðir. 2011. "Jóhann Magnús Bjarnason." In Jóhann Magnús Bjarnason, *Dagbók vesturfara 1902–1918*, Vol.1, 18–31. Reykjavík: Lestu.is.

Gagnon, Erica. 2017. "Settling the West: Immigration to the Prairies from 1867 to 1914." *Canadian Museum of Immigration at Pier 21*. https://www.pier21.ca/research/immigration-history/settling-the-west-immigration-to-the-prairies-from-1867-to-1914.

Gunnarsson, Helgi. 2000. "Landnám Íslendinga í Nova Scotia á nítjándu öld." *Íslendingaþættir Dags*, 17 June, 1, 3.

Hafstað, Baldur. 2011. "Inngangur: Örstutt æviágrip metsöluhöfundar." In Jóhann Magnús Bjarnason, *Dagbók vesturfara 1902–1918*, 8–17. Reykjavík: Lestu.is.

Hoerder, Dirk. 1999. *Creating Societies: Immigrant Lives in Canada*. Montreal: McGill-Queen's University Press.

Jónsson, Gísli. 1913. "Gunnsteinn Eyjólfsson." *Eimreiðin* 19 (1): 44–50.

Kjartansson, Helgi Skúli. 2018. "Var okkar fólk eitthvað spes? Nokkur sérkenni Íslendinga sem vesturfara og Vesturheimsbúa." In *Sigurtunga: Vesturíslenskt mál og menning*, edited by Birna Arnbjörnsdóttir, Höskuldur Thráinsson, and Úlfar Bragason, 53–65. Reykjavík: Háskólaútgáfan.

Kristjánsdóttir, Dagný. 2015. *Bókabörn: Íslenskar barnabókmenntir verða til*. Reykjavík: Bókmennta- og menningarfræðastofnun Háskóla Íslands.

Lecker, Robert. 2013. *Keepers of the Code: English-Canadian Literary Anthologies and the Representation of Nation*. Toronto: University of Toronto Press.

Neijmann, Daisy L. 1997a. *The Icelandic Voice in Canadian letters: The Contribution of Icelandic-Canadian Writers to Canadian Literature*. Ottawa: Carleton University Press.

———. 1997b. "In Search of the Canadian Icelander: Writing an Icelandic-Canadian Identity into Canadian Literature." *Canadian Ethnic Studies* 29 (3): 64–74.

———. 1999. "Fighting with Blunt Swords. Laura Goodman Salverson and the Canadian Literary Canon." *Essays on Canadian Writing* 67: 138–74.

Pálsson, Jóhannes Páll. 1945. "J. Magnús Bjarnason." *Tímarit Þjóðræknisfélagsins Íslendinga* 27 1: 2–14.

Skulason, Hrund. 1966. "Úr dagbókum J. M. Bjarnason." *Tímarit Þjóðræknifélags Íslendinga* 1: 29–40.

Stephansson, Stephan G. 1938–39. *Bréf og ritgerðir. I. Bindi. Bréf frá árunum 1889–1913*. Reykjavík: Hið íslenska þjóðvinafélag.

Sveinsson, Ólafur Arnar. 2018. "Íslendingar og Ameríka: Hvað er að vera Vestur-Íslendingur?" In *Sigurtunga: Vesturíslenskt mál og menning*, edited by Birna Arnbjörnsdóttir, Höskuldur Thráinsson, and Úlfar Bragason, 35–51. Reykjavík: Háskólaútgáfan.

Thorlaksson, N. Steingrímur. 1907. "Gerum við nóg fyrir börnin okkar?" *Börnin* 4: 121–22.

———. 1908. "Nýja blaðið hneigir sig." *Framtíðin* 1 (1): 3–4.

Watts, Carl. 2016. "Nation, Ethnicity, and Canada in Laura Goodman Salverson's *The Viking Heart*." *American Review of Canadian Studies* 1: 107–21.

CHAPTER 9

Icelandic-Canadian Oral Lore: New Life in a New Land and How the Women's Tales May Shed Light on the Classification of the Edda Poems

GÍSLI SIGURÐSSON

OVER THE WINTER of 1972–73, the Icelander Hallfreður Örn Eiríksson and his Czech wife, Olga María Franzdóttir, made a journey through the Icelandic-Canadian and -American settlements in North America, collecting ethnological material in Icelandic.[1] These travels generated approximately sixty hours of recorded material, from which can be extracted twenty or so hours of actual stories and poems related by eighty-seven respondents, thirty-one of them women. The material is very varied and includes reminiscences from Iceland; accounts of the pioneer years and early life in the new settlements; stories about Indigenous people, notable characters, and famous strongmen; and tales of hunting, dreams, and supernatural phenomena. The material also includes poems and traditional folk tales.

The stories and verses collected by Hallfreður and Olga were to a large extent told in Icelandic. The language is interesting in its own right for its Icelandic-Canadian and -American dialect features and its English influences. The respondents had generally had no schooling in the language, and their Icelandic is remarkably little touched by normative pressures. They read

FIGURE 9.1. Hallfreður Örn Eiríksson and Olga María Franzdóttir at Willow Point, Manitoba, 1972. (Courtesy of the Árni Magnússon Institute for Icelandic Studies)

and write little in the language, and thus their spoken Icelandic is largely free from the influence of the culture, literacy, and language politics of official institutions. Some of the respondents, however, are conscious of using English loan words in a way they feel is excessive, and they try to purge them from their speech when they meet Icelanders from Iceland. The collection gains value from its having been made before the explosion of contact between homeland Icelanders and Canadians and Americans of Icelandic descent that followed in the wake of the 1,100th anniversary of the settlement of Iceland in 1974 and the centenary celebrations in 1975 of the establishment of the New Iceland colony on the shores of Lake Winnipeg. The culture described by the informants is disappearing; some of the informants are deceased, and with them Icelandic is little by little dying out as a spoken language in North America.

Within this wide-ranging corpus, the material collected from female informants stands apart in the sense that their contributions (excluding poetry) are restricted almost entirely to traditional folk tales and tales about dreams and the supernatural (Sigurðsson 2002).[2] The example of the women's tales can be helpful in understanding gender-based differences within the corpus of the ancient Edda poems. In the scholarship on the Edda, these differences have been explained as evidence of the different age of the poems, such as the Atli poems in the heroic cycle. The Icelandic-Canadian and -American material acts as a corrective to such thinking: stories emanating from more or less the same cultural environment can vary widely and reflect different outlooks, depending, in this case, on the gender of the person who tells the stories, rather than an all-inclusive taste shared by every member of the cultural unit under investigation.

As might be expected, the material varies greatly in quality. Taken together, however, it provides a rich source on the religious outlook, folk customs, and attitudes of people to the past and present, as well as being a witness to what people in the settlement considered most noteworthy in their own lives and of those around them and most worth passing on to visitors who had made the long journey from faraway Iceland and Czechoslovakia.

NEW LAND—NEW IDENTITY

One thing that distinguishes Hallfreður and Olga's corpus from other material collected from Icelandic Canadians and Icelandic Americans is that the centre of interest is not on recounting memories carried over from Iceland and describing emigration to America. Rather, the interviewers were primarily looking for the stories and attitudes of people who saw their origins as lying in New Iceland, where they claimed to have "incredibly deep roots," as one of their informants, Eðvarð Gíslason (Eddi), so expressed it (Sigurðsson 2002a). Eddi's attitude relates to how settlement myths have sprung up in America in order to sanctify the land there and establish a formal origin for Icelandic Canadians and Icelandic Americans in the New World (Arnason and Arnason 1994).

A case in point illustrating this attitude is the account in Hallfreður and Olga's collection (69–70; EF 72/11) given by Guðjón Árnason of Espihóll, Gimli, of the land claim of the first party to arrive in New Iceland. This story has been cast in the image of the myth, and it is striking how Guðjón links himself with the event by claiming to have once worked with the first ever native-born Canadian Icelander. In the minds of the settlers, the land in a sense became theirs when the first child was born. There are parallels with the *Landnámabók* (Book of settlements) account of the medieval settlement of Iceland: Þórunn *hyrna* is said to have borne a girl child while claiming land in Eyjaförður with her husband, Helgi *magri,* and we are told that Þórdís, the daughter of Ingimundur the Old, "was born at Þórdísarholt" in the same passage as we are told about Ingimundur's settlement of Vatnsdalur. Several of the Icelandic-Canadian and -American stories tell of this first child being born in a blizzard under a rock on the foreshore of the lake shortly after the arrival of the settlers and of an Indigenous woman having assisted at the birth.

STORIES OF GHOSTS AND ODDBALL CHARACTERS

Whatever may be said of the human emigrants, Icelandic ghosts seem to have had trouble making themselves at home in the New World. Most returned home to the old country, some of them even abandoning the voyage on the way over to America, according to some of the tales. Hallfreður and Olga's collection contains several of what might be called supernatural tales, covering a wide range of occurrences experienced by informants and others: for example, about dreams foretelling major events, fetches, and omens foreboding death. The collection also includes many tales of Icelandic ghosts (*draugur, móri, skotta*) and the "hidden people" (*huldufólk* 'elves'), often with names known from native Icelandic folk tales: Leirár-Skotta, Rauðafells-/Rauðamels-Móri, Írafells-Móri, Rauðpilsa, and Þorgeirsboli. In their encounters with Icelandic ghosts and spirits, there are examples of Icelandic Canadians and Icelandic Americans in the new settlements using a silver button or the gilt buttons from a sea pilot's uniform from the east of the old country to shoot the so-called Öldudraugur (Wave Ghost, 458–60; EF 72/44). When questioned about ghosts and supernatural phenomena, Hallfreður and Olga's informants frequently issue disclaimers: they say that the old people from Iceland believed these things implicitly, but they themselves consider much of this ghost lore very suspect. However, there are many people who claim to have experienced and believe in things that "cannot be explained by any science," as Magnús Elíasson expresses it in one place (338; EF 72/2).

At several places in the collection, we find storytellers expressing reluctance to vouch unconditionally for the truth of the stories they tell, in some cases saying it was the old people who were more interested in preserving the memory of Icelandic ghosts and spirits. Others have fun with made-up ghosts, either stuffed dummies found on a forest path or voice projection from some hidden place at séances, deceiving the gullible and those claiming second sight, to the merriment of other compatriots. The beings that inspire real horror in Icelandic Canadians and Icelandic Americans are in fact not of

Icelandic origin but dead "Indians" who remain part of the land and appear to hunters and travellers in wild parts of the country. Some of them, so it seems, have learned the customs and practices of monsters known from the Old World like Glámur from *Grettis saga*, since they visit Icelandic strongmen at night and wrestle with them until the Icelander comes out on top (for example, 190–92; 72/34).

Although various ghosts and other supernatural beings were brought, with their names, by the settlers to North America, they never achieve the same kind of power as the ones that already existed there, and their weakness is apparent as early as on the journey over. Some of them ran into problems finding a passage to accompany the settlers to North America, and we even hear of them missing the boat. This was the case, for example, with Rauðpilsa (Redskirt), a female ghost who had haunted a carpenter at Undirfell. He managed to get away safely to Winnipeg, but Rauðpilsa got left behind and "then took someone else" (434–35; 72/15). Some ghosts set off across the ocean, but things go badly on the journey—they sink, or get seasick and turn back. Many ghosts reached the New World in the company of the first settlers, but once these pioneers had passed on, the ghosts started to get fed up and trickled back home again (437–38; 72/31 and 72/17).

For the most part the stories deal with life in New Iceland and on the shores of Lake Winnipeg. They tell of the settlement years, hazardous fishing trips on the lake in summer and winter, getting lost in the forest, moose hunts, dreams, supernatural phenomena, and occasional verses put together as much by people in the new country as from back in Iceland. A large group consists of stories about witty or eccentric characters, great liars, strongmen, and crack-shot marksmen.

Of the very extensive group of comic tales about oddball characters, among the most common are those concerning Kristján Geiteyingur (121–38). Kristján is a well-known figure, and there are several variants of some of the stories. Most tell of Kristján's glib mendacity and how pleased he was with everything Icelandic, which he blew up out of all proportion when telling English-speaking people about the land of his forefathers. He also told tales about his blacksmithing, and played innocent practical jokes on gullible fellow citizens. These tales of Kristján Geiteyingur, with their wide distribution and their setting in a New World environment, provide clear evidence for the existence of a stable and deeply entrenched storytelling tradition among the Manitobans of Icelandic descent.

There is a group of miscellaneous humorous anecdotes that centre on the linguistic problems faced by the first settlers, many of whom spoke little English and often mixed up Icelandic and English with comic results. Notwithstanding what was said above about the absence of official language policy in New Iceland, these stories clearly reveal a strong consciousness of the language. Often, they are told as illustrations of how poorly Icelanders spoke English at first and plugged the gaps with Icelandic words. A few stories play on ambiguities that arise when words get mixed between English and Icelandic—in most cases words that have now become fully integrated into North American Icelandic (NAIcelandic, or NAI) and whose ambiguity is thus first and foremost in the ears of Icelanders from Iceland.

FOLK TALES OR PERSONAL ART?

As one would expect, the size of the repertoires of Hallfreður and Olga's informants varies greatly. There are thirty individuals who provide just a single story each, and twenty-one who are listed for two to four stories. Twenty-three tell five to nine stories, and it is with this group that one may start to speak of storytellers who in some sense cultivate the art of recital. In general, the more stories people have to tell, the more conscious their attitude becomes. Eight informants provide ten to nineteen stories, and six informants (two women and four men) provide more than twenty stories. Of the women the most prolific is Guðrún Þórðarson (Gimli, EF 72/13–72/14), most of whose tales fall into the class of stories of dreams and mysterious phenomena, a class generally greatly favoured by women over other classes in the collection. However, with all due respect to the other storytellers in the collection, it is Eðvarð Gíslason, or Eddi (1901–1986), who stands out for his skill and range, and he provides a good example of a storyteller who has developed and polished his art over a long career.

Being so many and varied, Eddi's stories provide an excellent opportunity to consider the world view manifested in oral tales—to what extent they preserve a shared and "semi-official" view of the past, history, and the community, or whether they should rather be regarded as a personal interpretation revealing the attitudes of individual storytellers that may even run directly counter to the "official" view of history (see Sigurðsson 2002b).

From the tales of master storyteller Eddi Gíslason, it is clear that he cherishes and is fully conscious of the artistic value of oral tales and of different storytellers' varying personal command of their material. Over a long life Eddi collected tales, selected from them, and polished the material that fit with his view of the world and taste in stories. He uses the stories and the humour in them to convey particular conceptions of life values and human worth. Often it is possible to speak of working-class attitudes in the sense that some of the stories are directed against officially accepted norms. They stand up for the private individual defending his corner through the storms of life, and they side with those who carry out their work conscientiously and with human warmth. But Eddi is always ready to forgive people without anything useful to contribute in some area if they turn out to be able to discuss poetry and are nifty with a pen. The personal tone and the consistent thread that run through Eddi's otherwise varied stories mean that it makes more sense to see them as his personal contribution to world culture rather than the common property of the Icelandic-speaking community in North America. These stories present various ways of looking at the world that often require their listeners to question accepted values and that run strictly counter to the middle-class virtues of the silent majority for getting by in the world.

WOMEN'S PERSPECTIVES AND THE ANCIENT EDDA POEMS

Commentators have often remarked on how long it took for women with literary aspirations—those who wanted to engage in a field traditionally dominated by men—to develop enough self-confidence to be able to write on their own terms rather than on the terms of the received male-created written tradition (Jakobsdóttir 1980). From the earliest days of literacy, it is men who have been both the bearers and principal inheritors of book culture. At the same time women seem to have had easier access to the oral poetic and narrative traditions, as was also the case with folk tales and popular verse (ballads, et cetera). This conjecture is backed up by collections made in later centuries (Ólason 1979, 82). It can thus be illuminating to read or listen to Hallfreður and Olga's collection through "gender" glasses or headphones and to consider particularly the kinds of stories that women told and contrast them with those told by men. In short, the goal is to look for distinctions on the basis of gender within a tradition that we are more accustomed to lump together as a single homogeneous entity under the label of "Icelandic-Canadian and -American folk culture."[3]

The following breakdown of the material requires various caveats. First, the material collected owes much to the collectors themselves, both in regards to whom they talked to and the kinds of questions they asked. Second, we can assume that the respondents reacted to the collectors in some particular way and selected material from their repertoires that they felt suited the specific occasion, in this case the visit from Iceland of an Icelandic/Czech husband-and-wife team with tape recorder in hand in search of stories in Icelandic among Icelandic Canadians and Icelandic Americans. One may imagine that the material offered might have been different if, for instance, Hallfreður or Olga had been travelling alone. Third, the form in which the material appears in the collection is partly the product of the editor's decision to restrict the published collection to "finished" stories—stories that could be considered "whole" or "complete." We might well come to fundamentally different conclusions if the interviews were presented in full. The selection has been filtered first through Hallfreður's reading of the material and subsequently my own as editor, which without doubt introduces an element of masculine taste to the equation: someone else might have selected differently. Allowing for these qualifications, the following describes the picture that emerges.

The group that I label "Memories from the Old Country" comprises thirteen stories from six men and three women. The men relate things like the quantity of verse that people used to know, their resourcefulness in the face of danger and adversity, how hard life was in Iceland, how strong the Icelanders were, and how they were able to struggle on in savage weather, regardless of heavy drinking. One of them tells a remarkable story about a dog that foresaw its own death in a dream (59–60; 72/6). In contrast, the women—Sigríður Kristjánsson (one story) and Sigrún Jónsdóttir Thorgrímsson (four stories)—tell about Icelandic ghosts (Sigríður), and dreams (Sigrún) foretelling marriage, offspring, recovery from sickness, the professional success of her husband, and death. Indíana Sigurðsson offers a "true" story about an avalanche that engulfed some men who bore false witness before the minister that a stranded whale belonged to his church. Indíana knew of this story in print but claimed she was telling it as it had been told to her by word of mouth (483–84; 72/30).

Nine stories, told by eight men and one woman, centre on the early years of the New Iceland settlement. The men tell about the founding of the colony when the first settlers landed in their flatboats and about their first contacts with the Indigenous people, the origins of place names, farming problems, a plague of locusts, smallpox, religious disputes, droughts, and economic hardship, and how Icelandic culture gained a foothold in the new country. The only woman in this group, Anna Sveinsson, tells a story about a couple who got married even though they were on different sides of the quarantine line during the smallpox epidemic that ravaged the settlement in its early years (73–74; 72/50).

A further group of fourteen stories describes memories of life and farming in the new country. Nine male respondents provided recollections of the heavy rains of the summer of 1907, the abundance of food during the Great Depression (despite the crushing poverty), infestations of flies, a horse that fell into a well, the first dances and how people acquired alcohol, slaughtering animals in the home, children's fear of the forests, the *Íslendingadagurinn* (Icelanders' day) festival; and general accounts of the struggle to survive, working practices, and relations with the "big neighbour" to the south who refuses to let a cow across the international border, though its owner is seen as a welcome guest. Two of the stories in this group are from women: Hólmfríður Daníelsdóttir recounts how she and the other girls were scared of bears and tried, in vain, to get the boys to shoot them, and Guðrún Olgeirsson tells about some children who were saved after their mother perished in a terrible snowstorm near Mountain, North Dakota.

Sixteen stories collected from ten men and one woman deal with perilous journeys, mostly about people losing their way in bad weather in the northern wastelands or out on Lake Winnipeg. This group also includes one story told by a woman, Ólína Benson, who describes how her husband got into difficulties on the lake. He managed to save himself and his crew through his undaunted courage, driving his men on to keep bailing in the boat.

One hundred and eighty-eight stories are classified as "Tales of notable individuals and miscellaneous humorous anecdotes." A large proportion of them come from forty-four male interviewees (on the most prolific of these, Eddi Gíslason, see above and Sigurðsson 2002b), and their contributions provide us with general insights into storytelling as a form of entertainment. The favourite subjects are Kristján Geiteyingur, Tryggvi Halldórsson, Snæbjörn Johnson, Guðmundur the Strong, Elías the Strong, Bible-Sigurður, Óli Vigfússon, Guttormur Guttormsson, Hálfdan the Runner, Baldi Andersson, Björn Hjörleifsson, Doctor Hjaltason, and a certain Fúsi, plus various others, named and unnamed. There are stories about strongmen and the tellers of tall tales. Missionaries, eccentrics, and book learning are all mocked, while poetry, independence, feats of strength, and narrow escapes from tight corners, through brains or brawn, are held up for admiration.

The tellers of this large and colourful group of tales are mostly men. Of the women contributors, Anna Nordal tells or plays a part in two stories about Kristján Geiteyingur, and Sigríður Kristjánsdóttir tells another, but otherwise the Kristján stories are a strictly male preserve. Aðalbjörg Sigvaldason knows of a clever comeback attributed to the poet Guttormur J. Guttormsson, and Bergþóra Sigurðsson tells two stories about Bible-Sigurður in connection with her father. The situation is thus similar to that of a tale about Tryggvi told by Erla Gunnarsdóttir Simundson, occasioned by a tale told by one of the men. Guðrún Stefánsson refers to another story about Tryggvi that she had heard and considered "*óttalega lygileg*" 'a frightful pack of lies' (161; 72/23). Lóa Finnsson also mentions Tryggvi more or less in passing but makes more of a story about a woman who swallowed a diamond that she had happened to pick up at an auction and needed to hide from the police. She recovered the diamond a couple of days later and was able to sell it—unlike the man who swallowed a gold coin and got only silver—five cents and ten cents—in return. Þóra Árnason interrupts a stream of stories from her husband, Einar, with three of her own, all self-contained comic anecdotes: one about an Icelander who adopts a highly idiosyncratic approach to his shopping; another about an Icelander who hollered at his car in the same way as he had at his horses;

and the third about a Ukrainian who refused to settle his account at Sveinn Þorvaldsson's store in Riverton on the grounds that, according to the bill, he had bought lots of "ditto," a commodity of which he had no knowledge (257; 72/6). This storekeeper, Sveinn, plays a minor part, anonymously, elsewhere in Icelandic literary history for his rather extreme reaction to a reading given by Halldór Laxness of his story "Nýja Ísland" (New Iceland), as recalled by Laxness in his collection of essays *Skáldatími* (The time of the poets): "When I read my newly written story 'New Iceland' in the settlement where it takes place, the village of Riverton, present at the reading was the local grocer, considerably the worse for drink, and a great jingoist, as is often the case with rural grocers. He became so worked up at the story that as the reading progressed he had to be held back from climbing onto the platform and laying hands on this pale and gawky author from outside the district who had come there to disparage his own people."[4]

The six "Tales of other nationalities" come entirely from four male interviewees. These stories mostly concern the squalid drinking habits of the Finns, the home-brewing activities of the Ukrainians (known to the Icelandic immigrants as "Galls," that is, Galicians), and an Icelandic-speaking Indigenous person. Women are better represented among the contributors of the fifteen "Tales of translation errors and language mixing." Hólmfríður F. Daníelsson tells two stories, one about a woman with toothache who goes to a quack doctor complaining of being "sick in *tönn*" (279; EF 72/3), the other about a man who is showing people how to load their *gripir* 'cattle, livestock' onto a train: "If you go with the wagon *á undan*, the *grips* will come much better walking *á eftir*" (279; EF 72/3). Bergþóra Sigurðsson has a story about an Icelandic Canadian at a hotel in Iceland who asks the man at the desk to make sure his wife is "knocked up" at ten o'clock and his daughter at eleven.[5] There is a similar mild double entendre in Rannveig Guðmundsson's tale of some Icelanders who late one night ask for somewhere to stay and say to their host "to lady tonight" instead of "too late tonight" (283–84; EF 72/40). For whatever reason the men interviewed do not seem to go in for stories based on this kind of unintentional intralingual double meaning, except perhaps for the oft-repeated tale of the boy who tells some people who drop in that his father is down at the shop *að sjúa* 'shoeing' the mare. Here, *sjúa* is a loan word from English, homophonous with Icelandic *sjúga,* 'sucking' (283; EF 72/39).

Twenty-two men and eight women provided stories in which poetry constitutes a central theme. However, this category gives a somewhat misleading picture of the interviews as a whole, since the material as published contains only verse that was associated with a narrative piece. The interviews also elicited a fair amount of uncontextualized verse—rhymes, mnemonics, odd stanzas, whole poems, et cetera—often known to the informants from printed books or newspapers, which the collectors originally intended to cover in a second selection.

The most prolific of the women contributors to the poetry section was Margrét Sæmundsson, who had a sizable body of verse she had learned from her grandfather Baldvin Halldórsson (in a similar way to many of the male informants). Her repertoire also included one verse about disappointed childhood dreams that she had learned from her mother. The verses Margrét had had from her grandfather covered subjects as diverse as the morning frost patterns on a windowpane; the death song of an old mare; lampoons about the meanness of neighbours; rampant inflation; patter verses about smoking, drinking, and parenthood; and a satire on shallow consumerism (308–11; 72/20, 72/30). Aðalbjörg Sigvaldsson knew some verses by Lúðvík Kristjánsson and said he had often taught her new ones when they met; several of the men also knew verses of Lúðvík's. Ólína Benson recited two verses by Einar Guðnason about lost joys and a broken clothespeg, and Petrína Þórunn Soffía Árnason knew a verse about a filthy fish that was "both little and useless, like him who gave it me" (302; EF 72/11). Both she and Guðrún Pálsson recited a poem contrasting Iceland and Mikley (Hecla Island in Lake Winnipeg). Indíana Sigurðsson recited a well-known quatrain from Skagafjörður in the north of Iceland, and there are some verses from Sigríður Kristjánsson that she ascribed to her grandmother Sigurbjörg Gísladóttir, both concerning the status of women (325–26; EF 72/18):

> Ketil velgja konurnar
> og kaffið svelgja forhertar,
> ófriðhelgar alls staðar,

ítum fjölga skuldirnar.
'The women heat the kettle and shameless gulp the coffee;
nowhere are inviolate, for men they mount up debts'.

Heldur gerir hug minn þjá
hreinlæti fær rýrnað,
sokkaleistum sínum á
Sigríður mjólkar kýrnar.
'A sinking feeling fills my heart, cleanliness withers away; in
her stocking feet, Sigríður milks the cows'.

The second verse here was addressed by Sigurbjörg to Sigríður when, as a little girl, she went out in her socks to do the milking. These two verses and the poem by Margrét Sæmundsson's mother are the only ones in the group that are said to have been composed by women. This tallies with Magnús Elíasson's observation about women's verses not being generally well-known. Magnús cultivated poetry throughout his long life and knew large quantities by heart, but he remarks that "there were women who could turn out a good verse but I didn't actually know any, didn't know much about it. Of course, there were Icelandic women poets. Yes, but I'm just not familiar with it." However, a little later he recalls that there was "a man in the Árnes settlement called Hjörtur Goodman who was really pretty handy at making verses and many people said he must have got it from his mother, that she had had something to do with it." He then recites an election jingle that "some people were saying his mother Guðrún, now dead, maybe had had something to do with it." Magnús ends his reflections thus: "But I simply don't remember there having been any women in New Iceland that—you heard very very little about it. No, I just don't remember. Of course, there were lots of incredibly clever women but I don't actually recall any poetry by them. No" (293–94; EF 72/2).

Women are, however, conspicuously well represented among the tellers of the 104 tales of dreams and the supernatural: fourteen women informants compared with twenty men. Hólmfríður Daníelsson recounts a well-known story about John Ramsay, the Saulteaux man who appeared in a dream to an Icelandic immigrant and asked him to tend his wife's grave, repaying him with a gift of fish. Guðrún Þórðarson tells twenty-four stories—more or less in a single go, clearly indicating that they formed part of a well-practised repertoire—about the dead appearing in dreams; dreams foreboding death, cures, and assistance "from the other side"; telaesthesia; the "mark of death" and visitations from beyond the grave; visions; the power of prayer; hauntings; predictions; second sight; and fate. Many of these stories involve Guðrún herself or her family, in which there was a strong tradition of psychic faculties. Ólína Benson tells three tales about a child with second sight, about a dream predicting longevity, and other dreams foretelling the birth of children. Þuríður Þorsteinsdóttir tells five stories concerning premonitions of her mother's death, spiritual cures, and the deaths of her husbands. Valdheiður Sigurðsson tells two stories about omens presaging news of accidents and the death of a young girl. Salome Johnson knew of a dream that had saved the lives of some people out on the ice. Steinunn Guðmundsdóttir Daníelsson relates a vision she had of the Lutheran church at Árborg being carried up into the heavens, and Málfríður Einarsson tells of a dream in which she saw the mark of death on her brothers some time before the end of the First World War. Margrét Sæmundsson and her daughter Erla Gunnarsdóttir Sæmundsson provided a group of eleven stories, including a dream about a name for a newborn, a dying father who appears in a dream, signs and portents of recovery from sickness, a dead father who returns in a dream to interfere in Margrét's love life, child care from beyond the grave, predictions, telaesthesia, second sight, and paranormal goings-on among children. Magnúsína Helga Jónasson describes how God sent her father home one day when an unknown and suspicious visitor turned up at the house. Margrét Sigurðsson's father, mother, and sister all came to her in dreams at the time of their deaths to take their leave of her, and Sigrún Jónsdóttir Thorgrímsson includes an account of a mischievous female ghost that acts as a *doppelgänger* and turns up in advance of people to announce their arrival, as well as telling Sigrún about a haunting outside Lund. Lastly, Anna Sigfússon tells about her mother seeing her father's death prefigured in the clouds.

The men interviewed also told many stories about dreams and the supernatural, to some extent comparable with those told by the women. Common themes include telaesthesia, premonitions of death, and contact with the dead, often associated with family members but more usually concerning unrelated people and faraway events, in the forests or on Lake Winnipeg, sometimes involving Indigenous people.

In only three stories, all told by men, do we get any mention of ghost stories, and women are less in evidence with ghost stories per se than with stories concerning other kinds of supernatural phenomena. The collection contains forty-five stories that can be categorized as ghost stories, collected from seventeen men and eight women. Valdheiður Sigurðsson tells the story mentioned earlier of a girl called Rauðpilsa. Along with her husband, Lárus, Anna Nordal tells about a girl who was killed in a shooting accident and returned from the grave to haunt the man responsible. Hólmfríður Daníelsson and Lára Mýrdal Daníelsson both tell of a malevolent female ghost that plagued the people of Borgarfjörður. Margrét Sæmundsson describes a ghost woman seen by a little girl at a birthday party. Erla Gunnarsdóttir Sæmundsson, whose family remained particularly strongly attached to traditional Icelandic customs and beliefs, had had dealings with the "hidden people" in her childhood, and her brother Ómar had seen the fearsome ghostly "minotaur" Þorgeirsboli. The celebrated story of Þorgeirsboli dragging a pair of ghosts behind it on its hide was also known to Indíana Sigurðsson, who said she had got it from a certain woman storyteller. Bergljót Sigurðsson provided three ghost stories: about a haunted Indigenous burial plot, about a harmless Indigenous ghost once seen by Guttormur the Poet (Guttormur J. Guttormsson), and about the time when she and her sister fled from a ghost that jumped out at them but on closer inspection turned out to be "a man who was a bit tipsy" (462–65; EF 72/44). This jokey tone is rare among the women: it is much more often the men who poke fun at belief in ghosts and spirits in this way. The men, for instance, have all kinds of tales about tricks and pranks played by ghosts—a tone that, however, as mentioned above, largely disappears when it comes to ghosts out in the wilds, presumably reflecting their experience of dark nights spent alone in the great unknown.

The collection includes versions of three well-known traditional Icelandic folk tales, all collected from women interviewees: Ólína Benson tells the tale of the magical cow Búkolla; Margrét Sæmundsson, the story of Loðinlappi (Hairy Paw); and Indíana Sigurðsson is the only informant I know of to provide a version of the tale of the Hall of Glass at Glerhallarvík behind the mountain Tindastóll (Sigurðsson 2002a, 176–77).

CONCLUDING REMARKS

So, what lessons can we draw from this brief outline of a large body of material? How justified are we in focusing specifically on tales told by women when discussing the self-image and story repertoire of immigrants in a new society—in this case, Icelandic Canadians and Icelandic Americans whom Hallfreður and Olga interviewed in Manitoba, North Dakota, and on the west coast? From the analysis above there seems to be a clear difference between the kinds of stories that the women told and those that the men told. It seems reasonable to explain this difference on the basis of the gender roles that these people occupied in their society and the home. In their stories the men identify themselves much more strongly with events outside the family and the Icelandic community—for instance, in the interest they show in the Ukrainian settlers and Indigenous people. They tell about strangers and eccentrics, about hunting trips and dangerous ventures into the wilds, while the women's stories tend to revolve largely around people and situations associated with family life—marriage, child rearing, the comforts of religion, sickness, and the death of family members. On the rare occasions that women tell stories from the male domain, they tend to identify them as men's stories, specifying their sources by name and without making them "their own" in the way that men do; or they tell about men from their own families as a tribute to their excellence. Emotional subjects, loss and regret, and nostalgia for the beauty of the Old Country feature more strongly in the verses women introduce into their stories than what we find with men.

The traditional folk tales occupy a special position in "women's culture." Margrét and Indíana both mention having passed them on to their children. Ólína, to be sure, heard the tale of Búkolla from a fifteen-year-old boy in Iceland when she was herself seven, but Margrét learned the story of Loðinlappi from her mother, and Indíana learned the story of the Hall of Glass from "an old woman." The status of folk tale adventures as children's stuff is in all probability linked to the fact that men do not tell them and that child rearing was largely the responsibility of women.

The differences in story material, selection, and treatment can therefore, in part at least, be put down to gender, which to a considerable extent determines the status and roles of individuals in the society from which the stories arise. If we lacked the names for these stories' sources—as happens, for example, with the ancient Edda poems—scholars might be tempted to attribute the differences between the stories to differences of age. Explanations along these lines have enjoyed considerable currency in the field of Edda studies—an early dominant taste for stories celebrating the exploits of great warriors being later superseded by a taste for sentiment and family issues (Sigurðsson 1990, 1998). This corpus acts as a corrective to such thinking: stories emanating from more or less the same cultural environment can in reality vary widely and reflect different outlooks, depending, in this case, on the gender of the person who tells the stories, rather than some all-inclusive taste shared by every member of the cultural unit under investigation. The findings here tend, therefore, to support the view that the differences in the ancient poems are better explained through the gender of those who preserved, transmitted, and performed them than by the age of the poems.

The personal outlook and gender-specific treatment of material apparent in the stories collected from Eddi and the women informants demonstrate the importance of interpreting folk tales and oral lore in their proper context wherever we find them—of paying attention to who is relating and under what conditions. An approach of this kind allows us to understand better the nature and function of folk tales in their original environment—not as recorded learning set down in print but as stories that fulfill a personal and ever-changing role every time they are told. However, in the case of the stories we have been looking at here, we need to keep in mind that Hallfreður and Olga's collection, though good, does not in all respects give a true and undistorted picture of the oral tales that Icelandic Canadians and Icelandic Americans told one other; it is first and foremost a record of what people considered proper to tell to these collectors who had made the long journey from faraway Iceland—the picture people wanted to present of themselves, their community, and the way they lived.

Given the customary, and necessary, proviso regarding the effect of the measurement on the thing being measured, as it were, Hallfreður and Olga's collection of folk stories from the New World is by far the most extensive of its kind in Icelandic and the best collection we have of folk tales from the Icelandic cultural whole that are recorded directly from oral preservation, without any intrusion from the pen and writing style of the recorder. In addition the collection gives an insight into a completely different world from the one familiar to Icelanders in Iceland and shows how the immigrants were able to use and adapt their language to come to grips with a new life in a new environment. The land was claimed and settled every bit as much by the language as by the people, and the stories are thus coloured by conditions and ideas that were entirely alien to those who stayed at home. This settlement of Icelandic in the New World offers us much more in the way of innovation than the memories that people brought with them from the old country. Rather than keep asking Icelandic Canadians and Icelandic Americans what they can still say about Iceland, it is high time we Icelanders showed a greater interest in the life our kinsfolk lived once they got to North America—and a better window onto that world than Hallfreður and Olga's collection would be hard to find.

Translated by Nicholas Jones

NOTES

1 The project was supported by the Páll Guðmundsson Fund at the University of Manitoba through the offices of Haraldur Bessason, then professor of Icelandic at the university.

2 References in the text are to page numbers in *Sögur úr Vesturheimi* (Sigurðsson 2012) and catalogue numbers in the sound archive of the Árni Magnússon Institute for Icelandic Studies. The printed book contains transcriptions of Hallfreður and Olga's field recordings; the digitized recordings can be accessed at https://arnastofnun.is/is/sogur-ur-vesturheimi. References to individual stories are based on decisions made for that edition. For a general overview see Mullarky (1968–69). Names of informants are spelled as they entered Hallfreður and Olga's field books, using Icelandic orthography.

3 For a gender-based analysis of a large corpus of collected folklore material, see Tangherlini (1994, 145–62); see also Rósa Þorsteinsdóttir (2011).

4 Halldór Laxness (1963, 82–83; translation by NJ). About the reception of Halldór Laxness's readings in New Iceland, see Gísli Sigurðsson (1988).

5 The pun in the original is untranslatable. Literally, the man asks the receptionist to give his wife and daughter a *kall* 'call' (a semantic loan word from English), but the word is homophonous with *karl* 'man' (283; EF 72/44).

REFERENCES

Arnason, David, and Vincent Arnason, eds. 1994. *The New Icelanders: A North American Community*. Winnipeg: Turnstone Press.

Jakobsdóttir, Svava. 1980. "Reynsla og raunveruleiki. Nokkrir þankar kvenrithöfundar." In *Konur skrifa*, edited by Valborg Bensdóttir, Guðrún Gísladóttir, and Svanlaug Baldursdóttir, 221–30. Reykjavík: Sögufélag.

Laxness, Halldór. 1963. *Skáldatími*. Reykjavík: Helgafell.

Mullarky, Magnús Einarsson. 1968–69. "The Folklore of New Iceland." *Tímarit þjóðræknisfélags Íslendinga* 50: 67–73.

Ólason, Vésteinn. 1979. "Inngangur." In *Sagnadansar*, edited by Vésteinn Ólason, 7–88. Reykjavík: Rannsóknastofnun í bókmenntafræði: Menningarsjóður.

Sigurðsson, Gísli. 1988. "Halldór K. Laxness in Manitoba." *Lögberg-Heimskringla,* 8 April, 6. [Icel.: "Halldór Laxness í Manitóba." *Þjóðviljinn,* 17 apríl, 14–15.]

———. 1990. "On the Classification of Eddic Heroic Poetry in View of the Oral Theory." In *Poetry in the Scandinavian Middle Ages*, edited by Teresa Pàroli, 245–55. Spoleto: Centro Italiano di studi sull'alto medioevo.

———, ed. 1998. *Eddukvæði*. Reykjavík: Mál og menning.

———. 2002a. "Þjóðsögur Vestur-Íslendinga." In *Úr manna minnum: Greinar um íslenskar þjóðsögur*, edited by Baldur Hafstað and Haraldur Bessason, 169–90. Reykjavík: Heimskringla.

———. 2002b. "What Does a Story Tell? Eddi Gíslason's (1901–1986) Personal Use of Traditional Material." *Canadian Ethnic Studies* 34 (2): 79–89.

———, ed. 2012. *Sögur úr Vesturheimi: Úr söfnunarleiðangri Hallfreðar Arnar Eiríkssonar og Olgu Maríu Franzdóttur um Kanada og Bandaríkin veturinn 1972–1973*. Reykjavík: Stofnun Árna Magnússonar í íslenskum fræðum.

Tangherlini, Timothy R. 1994. *Interpreting Legend: Danish Storytellers and Their Repertoires*. New York and London: Garland.

Þorsteinsdóttir, Rósa. 2011. *Sagan upp á hvern mann: Átta íslenskir sagnamenn og ævintýrin þeirra*. Reykjavík: Stofnun Árna Magnússonar í íslenskum fræðum.

CHAPTER 10

Raven Tracks across the Prairies: Icelandic Immigration and Manuscript Culture in the Canadian West

KATELIN PARSONS

Skriftin mín er stafastór
stílað illa letur,
hún er eins og kattarklór
eg kann það ekki betur.

"My script is hulking and the letters poorly formed,
like a cat's scratches; I can't do any better."

COMPARISONS BETWEEN PENMANSHIP and animal tracks abound in pre-modern Icelandic manuscript culture. Twelve-year-old Kristín Bjóla of Leslie, Saskatchewan, included the well-known ditty above in a letter to the Icelandic-Canadian children's magazine *Sólskin*, published on 25 February 1916 (4).[1] It was accompanied by a short handwritten story in Icelandic by Kristín, describing how she fed breadcrumbs to the snow buntings in winter with the help of a bird feeder made by her father.

One not infrequently finds the verse copied by Kristín, and others like it, in Icelandic manuscript marginalia and scribal self-commentaries (Driscoll 2004). While the verse in question compares handwriting with *kattarklór* or the clawmarks of a cat, *hrafnaspark* 'raven tracks' has long described illegible scribbling in Icelandic. Invoking the image of an unruly bird strutting across the page, leaving behind an inky trail, an anonymous scribe copying the early modern poem "Hjónaspegill" (Mirror of matrimony) disparaged his—or possibly her—hand as *hrafnslegt pennafar* 'raven-like pen strokes' in the seventeenth-century miscellany JS 204 8vo (f. 109v).

The discontinuity between Kristín's poem and the print periodical in which it survives is striking: no one need apologize for penmanship in a mass-produced medium where words are represented in uniform lines of movable type. As discussed in this chapter, however, writing for print publication was only one motivation for immigrants to hand-copy and share their stories. The majority of Icelandic immigrants would rarely, if ever, see their writing in print.

Literacy can be broadly defined as a constellation of social practices: the uses of writing and reading in people's daily lives within their homes and local communities (Hamilton and Barton 1998). The specific focus of this chapter is on the manuscript circulation of literature in Icelandic-Canadian settlements. Although print culture plays an undeniably important role in the literary lives of Icelandic Canadians (Neijmann 1997), manuscript culture also thrived in Iceland when immigration to Canada began in the 1870s.

Practices of creating and exchanging manuscripts did not vanish on the transatlantic crossing, and manuscripts brought to North America by Icelandic immigrants continued to be read and used upon arrival. For the most part, however, immigrant participants in manuscript culture did not receive institutional recognition for their activities, occupying marginal roles in literary history. The objective of this chapter is therefore to examine the presence of Icelandic-language manuscripts in the Canadian West and their significance for the immigrant community.

MANUSCRIPT CULTURE ON A LITERARY ISLAND

Iceland's manuscript heritage is central to the nation's identity as a literary island. When used to describe a pre-modern handwritten book, the term *handrit* evokes an object both ancient and deeply precious: remnants of darkened, battered medieval parchment rendered near-illegible by time, pored over tirelessly by generation after generation of scholars. These manuscripts are a reminder of the long, unbroken history of Icelandic as a language of literary expression, even during the centuries when Iceland was under Norwegian and later Danish rule.

Iceland's pre-modern literary reputation rests on a narrower corpus, including the *Íslendingasögur*, describing the often stormy interactions between the island's early settlers; skaldic and eddic poetry; and legends of ancient Scandinavia and the Nordic gods. This legacy was a source of pride and literary inspiration for Icelandic immigrants to North America (Neijmann 1997). The central role of medieval literature in representing the Icelandic immigrant experience is well-known, particularly in the case of sagas of Norse settlement and discovery, such as the Vinland sagas (Wolf 2001, 1991). Often overlooked in the shadow of these masterpieces is the proliferation of vernacular writings that explore matters beyond the island's own culture, laws, and history.

Among the most popular genres through the centuries were *rímur* (epic poetry) and prose romances, which circulated mainly in manuscript form (Driscoll 1990). Many such literary manuscripts date only from the nineteenth or early twentieth centuries and were copied not in scriptoria but in rural farmhouses by non-professional scribes. These younger manuscripts contain a diverse selection of material but were until recently considered of marginal importance except as a relic of medieval practice (Helgason 1958, 9).

In Iceland, the concept of *handritamenning síðari alda* 'post-print manuscript culture' has risen rapidly to prominence over the last three decades (Ólafsson 2017). With the growth of material and artifactual approaches originally drawn from medieval philology, attention has shifted from manuscripts as textual witnesses to the complex interactions involved in their production and the traces left in them by producers, owners, and users (Driscoll 2010; Nichols 1990). Whereas philologist Stephen Nichols used "manuscript culture" to describe book production in Europe before movable type, there is now a recognition that literary manuscripts continued to co-exist with printed books for centuries (Ezell 1999; Love 1993; Ólafsson 2012). Manuscripts are cultural objects as much as they are bearers of written text (Stead 2018). Emerging from this has come a re-examination of the narrative of the saga-consuming peasant of the North, leading to a much broader understanding of the written literature produced and consumed by ordinary Icelanders (Driscoll 1997).

Manuscript production is an inherently social activity, relying on the exchange of knowledge, exemplars, and the materials of production. Many recent studies have focused on the activities of a single participant in manuscript culture, consistently demonstrating a close relationship between scribes and larger communities or networks (for example, Hufnagel 2013; Ólafsson 2008, 2013; Parsons 2019). In Iceland, post-print manuscript production frequently took place within the space of the *kvöldvaka*: the long, dark winter evenings when it was common to socialize within the household and read aloud or chant *rímur* as household members worked at indoor tasks (Gíslason 1977). There was an economic dimension to manuscript culture, as self-taught scribes worked during the winter to produce books on commission for neighbours (Ólafsson 2008).

Sigurður Gylfi Magnússon and Davíð Ólafsson (2017) suggest that manuscript production was the product of a participatory culture, whereby men from underprivileged backgrounds could gain social recognition for their scribal practices. Their writing activities were generally seen in a positive light in their local community, and they made beneficial connections through their scribal work. However, this was not equally true of lower-class women. While non-elite women certainly owned manuscripts (Ingólfsdóttir 2011), the act of writing itself was considered more appropriate for men (Gísladóttir 1999; Sigurðsson 1912).

Manuscript culture was characterized by a lack of top-down support or institutional patronage, with a close connection between manuscript culture and practices of self-education (Magnússon and Ólafsson 2017). Non-professional scribes were frequently men in rural areas who worked as farmers, fishermen, and labourers. In nineteenth-century Iceland, schooling took place in the home for all but a privileged few. While reading in post-Reformation Iceland was considered a necessary skill for full participation in society, only the ability to sound out familiar religious texts was expected (Guttormsson 1990). Given that instruction in writing and arithmetic remained an optional part of childhood education until 1880, scribes were often wholly self-taught writers (Guttormsson 2003).

The interaction between print and manuscript culture in pre-modern Iceland was two-way. Older manuscripts formed the basis for new print editions, but print editions also became the source of manuscript copies potentially more beautiful than their mass-printed counterparts (Óskarsdóttir and Parsons 2017). Surviving manuscripts demonstrate that elaborate floral designs—embroidery-like in their intricacy—were considered a sign of artistic mastery of penmanship, despite similar patterns being associated with femininity when displayed on textiles. Manuscript culture was an outlet for creativity as well as self-education.

One of the best-studied nineteenth-century Icelandic illustrator-scribes is Guðlaugur Magnússon, who immigrated to Canada with his younger brother Jóhannes in 1873, leaving some manuscripts in Iceland with another brother, Guðmundur (Surmeli 2018). The interaction between text and image had also originally been an important element in Kristín Bjóla's submission to *Sólskin*, which, according to an editor's note, had been accompanied by a drawing that was impossible to reproduce.

IMMIGRANTS AND MANUSCRIPT CULTURE

Writing from New Iceland, Jóhann Briem (1878, 1) advised prospective immigrants to Canada to bring as many Icelandic books with them as they owned. This advice was heeded, with the outcome that an unknown number of Icelandic manuscripts crossed the Atlantic as personal luggage (Hreinsson 1994; Pétursson 1993, 1995). Probably disproportionately affected were the regions of North and East Iceland, due to higher numbers of immigrants from these regions (Parsons 2012).

Contemporary Icelandic scholars were aware of the challenges posed by mass emigration for the preservation of Iceland's literary heritage. Learning that a historically significant Icelandic manuscript from East Iceland was in Winnipeg, Jón Þorkelsson (1906, xlvi) remarked: "This incident—that one must now get this information from America—is among the things that teaches one that we will never truly know how much Icelandic lore, tangible heritage and culture has been transported to the New World with the people who have moved there from Iceland over the last 30 years. Most galling of all is that this will all soon vanish entirely, and be lost in the open ocean of another nationality and never again be of help for Icelanders."[2]

The manuscript in question belonged to Sigmundur Matthíasson Long, an active scribe and manuscript collector who had settled in Winnipeg (Sveinsson 2001). Like Long, lay participants in Icelandic manuscript culture typically received minimal scholarly recognition for their efforts; Jón Helgason (1958, 9) characterized nineteenth-century scribes as "true medieval men" rather than serious medievalists. True medieval men did not live in urban settlements in the Canadian West, however, and the immigrant scribes did not even enjoy acceptance as relics of the literary past.

Jón Þorkelsson's fears that Icelandic-language manuscripts would vanish in America were not unfounded. Immigrants' manuscripts were not objects of great material value, and years of circulation and perusal left them in poor shape. The manuscripts of Bjarni Bjarnason of Höfn in Arnes, who drowned in Lake Winnipeg in November 1878, were the least valuable items in his meagre estate ("Skýrsla yfir dánarbú" 1928). Within his home community in Iceland, he had had a reputation as a book lover. He owned a large collection of handwritten saga-books that he had produced and would lend to others (Björg Hansen 1994, 182); their whereabouts after his estate was settled are unknown.

Water and paper do not mix well. Most older manuscripts in North America are in less-than-pristine condition after surviving an Atlantic crossing and harsh environmental conditions upon arrival. They are not particularly beautiful objects as home decor, with shrivelled homemade bindings, stained and dirty pages, and odd smells. They are mouldy. They fall apart at the touch.

Identifying and tracking down manuscripts before they are discarded or damaged beyond salvaging is a priority, not least in light of the diasporic nature of Icelandic immigration. Unlike the migratory snow buntings of Kristín Bjóla's story, Icelanders' westward journeys across the Atlantic Ocean were virtually always one-way; immigrants encountering adversity typically responded by moving elsewhere within North America (Benediktsson 2014). Icelandic-language publishing activities were concentrated in urban hubs such as Winnipeg, but no such hubs channelled the movement of manuscripts that accompanied their owners in their search for home, whether in Eyford or Elfros, Minneapolis or Markerville, Cavalier or California.

The Fragile Heritage Project (Í fótspor Árna Magnússonar í Vesturheimi) is an initiative at the Árni Magnússon Institute for Icelandic Studies to document Icelandic manuscript heritage in North America. Beyond its role in heritage preservation, it represents the creation of a shared digital space for the study of Icelandic manuscript heritage, involving extensive collaboration with families, communities, libraries, and archives.

What has clearly emerged from the project is that handwritten books, diaries, and letters in Icelandic were deeply treasured possessions for their immigrant owners, and they remain so for many families today. Not unlike family photographs, these writings had the potential to preserve the memory of distant or deceased loved ones; the words themselves may have been of secondary importance to the personal connection between writer and owner. Just as with historical photographs, the connection between a physical object and a person represented is fragile, making it just as critical to preserve the memory of owner-creator relationships as it is to ensure the survival of the manuscripts themselves.

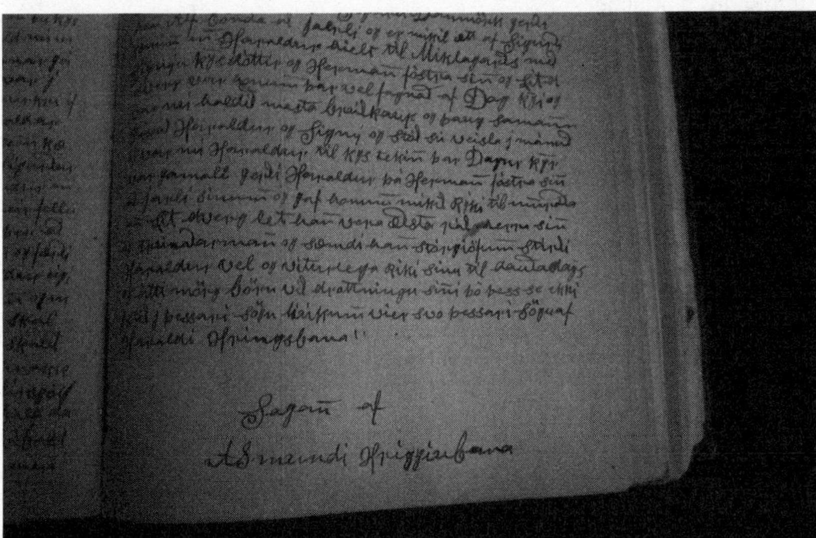

FIGURE 10.1. Numerous letters and diaries written by the Icelandic immigrants in Canada have been preserved. (Nelson Gerrard/Eyrarbakki Icelandic Heritage Centre)

A more unexpected finding has been the extent to which literary manuscripts were part of Icelandic immigrants' lives in the Canadian West and beyond. At least initially, Icelandic manuscript culture thrived in Icelandic immigrant communities in North America. Active participants in scribal culture travelled to Canada and the United States, taking their personal libraries with them but also the intangible heritage of scribal production knowledge. For these individuals, their travels within North America were a chance to make new connections and to access new material. Through informal circulation of manuscript collections, a surprisingly broad spectrum of literature was available within immigrant communities.

One example is *Ásmundar saga Hryggjubana*, a rare post-medieval romance. It survives in one Manitoba-produced manuscript in the New Iceland Heritage Museum in Gimli (NIHM 020012.3301) and a nineteenth-century manuscript in the National and University Library of Iceland (Lbs 2784 4to). The saga describes an evil king of Spain, Sigmundur, who decides to solve the problem of poverty in his kingdom by passing a law that allows *ómagar* 'paupers'—the elderly and the children of the poor—to be killed with impunity. Ásmundur, the protagonist, is a rebel who rises up against Sigmundur's injustice.

Ásmundar saga Hryggjubana is superficially set in Spain, but it is a thinly veiled critique of the treatment of paupers in rural nineteenth-century Iceland. Paupers too young, old, disabled, or infirm to support themselves could be farmed out to the lowest-bidding household in the parish, minimizing public expenses but leaving the destitute vulnerable to neglect, abuse, and outright starvation (Gunnlaugsson 1993; Magnússon 2010). Medieval Icelandic romances depict the poor negatively, or positively only as far as they loyally support high-born heroes (Glauser 1983; Hall, Richardson, and Þorgeirsson 2013). *Ásmundar saga Hryggjubana* inverts this dynamic, portraying the common people as the oppressed and the high-born as their oppressors.

The copy of *Ásmundar saga Hryggjubana* in the New Iceland Heritage Museum was completed on 28 April 1906, on Hecla Island, Manitoba. The scribe, Albert Jóhannesson (1847–1921), must have obtained his exemplar from one of his neighbours. There is limited evidence for Albert's participation in scribal activities prior to his immigrating in 1884, but many Icelandic immigrants on Hecla Island had been participants in scribal culture in Iceland (Parsons 2019).

Albert's early life was marked by extreme poverty; two of his siblings had lived in separate households as paupers from early childhood. Albert worked as a farm labourer from a young age and remained a farm labourer when he immigrated to North America in 1884. He was likely a human trafficking survivor, an aspect of the immigrant experience rarely discussed in contemporary histories of North American Icelandic immigrant communities (Jackson 1921, 120). A lone document survives in the National and University Library of Iceland (Lbs 4667 4to) that speaks to the traumatic nature of this experience (Parsons 2019).

Albert engaged extensively in scribal work during his later years, and his Canadian manuscripts—four in total—preserve a snapshot of the diverse non-print reading material circulating among first-generation Icelandic immigrants (Parsons 2019). His manuscripts also show that he rewrote narratives dealing with exploitation and child poverty in a manner that gave the victims an unambiguously happy ending.

Albert did not limit himself to copying manuscript exemplars. Some of his material derives from contemporary newspapers, including a translated short story by Anglo-Canadian author Charles G.D. Roberts, printed in *Heimskringla* in 1894. Most notably, Albert transformed Felicia Hemans's poem "Casabianca" (1826)—a classic of Anglo-Canadian school readers—from a tragic narrative about unquestioning obedience and bravery in war to the tale of a boy who did the sensible thing and jumped off a burning ship to save himself. The old immigrant fisherman's rejection of the glorification of a child soldier's death foreshadows the conflict within the Icelandic-Canadian community some years later over participation in the First World War (Kristjánsson 2017; Hreinsson 2012, 490–95; see also Úlfar Bragason, this volume).[3]

AT A LOSS FOR WORDS

While medieval and post-medieval romances have been derided as fantastical or unrealistic (Driscoll 1997), many of them deal with cross-cultural interactions from an outsider's perspective. Like immigrants, romance protagonists often find themselves in humiliating situations in bewilderingly cosmopolitan settings, experiencing betrayal and disappointment as they attempt to construct new social networks. Unlike the failed bridal quest of Einar H. Kvaran's "Vonir" (Hopes) (Guðsteinsdóttir 2018; see also Guðrún Guðsteinsdóttir, this volume), romances invariably end with the hero achieving social recognition and a high-status wife.

Language loss dominates a popular medieval Icelandic romance, *Konráðs saga keisarasonar* (Kalinke and Mitchell 1985). In this saga, the emperor's son Konráð is tricked by his foster-brother Róðbert into neglecting his language studies, which Róðbert claims are a waste of time for a great hero like Konráð; the menial task of interpretation can be safely left to Róðbert. When Róðbert gets Konráð's sister pregnant and must flee the empire, Konráð naïvely agrees to join him, only to discover that he is now entirely in Róðbert's power. Róðbert claims Konráð's identity as his own, and the roles of champion and minion are reversed. It is only with the help of the wise princess Matthildur of Greece, skilled in foreign languages, that Konráð regains his tongue and his stolen identity as the rightful heir of Saxony.

The saga of a hero rendered powerless, mute, and unknown through the act of migration must have resonated deeply; it was a popular saga in manuscript circulation within North America. Albert Jóhannesson produced a manuscript copy in the early 1900s, preserved in NIHM 020012.3301, and two others were donated to the library of the Jón Bjarnason Academy in Winnipeg (Hall and Parsons 2013). A fourth *Konráðs saga* manuscript in Manitoba was sold by Nikulás Ottenson (Össurarson) of Winnipeg to the Johns Hopkins University Library in Baltimore, now MS 9 4to of the Nikulás Ottenson Collection.

Ottenson participated actively in manuscript culture in Iceland, continuing to expand his library after immigrating to Canada in 1887. After finding permanent employment as a park warden in Winnipeg's River Park, he turned his efforts to the publication of manuscripts, starting with the *Rímur af Sörla hinum sterka* by his father, Össur Össurarson, in Gimli in 1910. The following year Ottenson published an edition of Snorri Björnsson's *Sagan af Starkaði Stórvirkssyni*, also based on a manuscript source. Other Icelandic-Canadian efforts to print literature brought to North America as manuscript copies include the 1889 editions of the late medieval romance *Nikulás saga leikara* and Gísli

Konráðsson's *Hellismannasaga*, a 1892 edition of *Faustus saga og Ermenu*, and Gísli Pétur Magnússon's 1910 edition of *Parmes saga loðinbjarnar*.

These publications are popular editions: the work of enthusiastic non-scholarly editors with minimal interest in documenting their manuscripts' provenance. They published material from manuscripts circulating in the community not because they believed these to be textually superior copies but because manuscripts often provided the sole medium of access for older literature.

THE END OF AN ERA

Evidence for the production, circulation, and use of Icelandic-language manuscripts in North America beyond the 1920s is limited. The Icelandic club Vestri in Ballard, Washington, had a long-standing tradition of producing a handwritten periodical, *Geysir*, which was read aloud during meetings, and surviving copies are preserved at the University of Washington. The last hand-copied issue of *Geysir* written in Icelandic dates from 1964. Another exception can be found in the handwritten volumes of *rímur* poetry created by Dagbjartur Guðbjartsson (1889–1970), who immigrated to Winnipeg in 1911 but later moved to Akra, North Dakota. His manuscripts date from the 1960s, including SÁM 176 from 1963, which was donated to the Árni Magnússon Institute for Icelandic Studies in 2018 by his granddaughter, Ann McKinley.

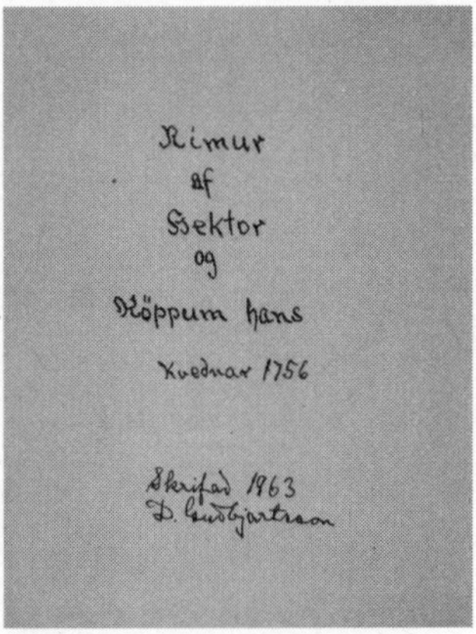

FIGURE 10.2. The title-page of *Rímur af Hektor og köppum hans* by the poet Ólafur Jónsson in SÁM 176 from 1963 (1r). The scribe, Dagbjartur Guðbjartsson (1889–1970), immigrated to Winnipeg as a young man in 1911. This manuscript was produced at his home in Akra, North Dakota. (Image: Sigurður Jónsson)

Dagbjartur's manuscripts belong to the tradition of scribal production in the home and are particularly remarkable for being copied entirely from memory. Dagbjartur, who was Nikulás Össurarson's nephew, had an exceptional memory for poetry and a particular interest in *rímur* (Haraldur Bessason 1999). In Winnipeg, he participated in the publication of a poorly preserved *rímur* in 1919, Sigurður Bjarnason's *Rímur af Án bogsveigi* from 1862.

Language loss is not the only explanation for the decline in the production and circulation of handwritten texts in Icelandic within North American immigrant communities. A similar trend can be seen in Iceland in the first decades of the twentieth century (Driscoll 2017). A combination of factors was involved, including the disappearance of the *kvöldvaka* (Gíslason 1977). Access to formal schooling improved for children of all socio-economic backgrounds, and a growing number of young men and women had the opportunity to pursue higher education. As a vehicle for self-education and creative expression, manuscript culture played a diminished role, and formerly popular genres such as romance and *rímur* fell into comparative obscurity (Driscoll 1997). In Iceland and in North America alike, traditional manuscript culture arguably ended with the last generation of self-taught writers.

Kristín Bjóla's father, Helgi Bjólan Dagbjartsson (1862–after 1926), belonged to that generation. Helgi, almost certainly a self-taught writer, was orphaned as a young boy and raised as a pauper, with extremely minimal opportunities for book learning. Kristín's mother, Oddný Aðalbjörg Kristjánsdóttir (1878–1962), represented the new generation for whom learning to write was now a basic right rather than a personal achievement. They departed for Canada on 12 June 1903, joining around 400 others on the emigrant ship *Vesta* ("Vesturfarar" 1903, 2).

The Bjóla family valued literacy in the modern sense, and their Canadian-born children learned to read and write Icelandic in the home. A short letter from Kristín's seven-year-old sister, Valgerður (K. Bjóla 1916, 4), was published in *Sólskin* immediately below a contribution from the young H. Guðjónsson from Laxnes in Iceland, the future author Halldór Kiljan Laxness. The Bjóla family were subscribers to at least one other weekly immigrant paper, *Voröld*, according to an enthusiastic letter from Helgi ("Úr bréfum til Voraldar" 1919, 6). For the Bjóla children, Icelandic was a language of creative expression, and they were encouraged to share their stories. Had she lived to adulthood, Kristín might have gone on to become an author like H. Guðjónsson. Sadly, Kristín died on 23 October 1919, only a few years after writing to *Sólskin*.

CONCLUSION

A hundred years on, searching for immigrants' manuscripts is like chasing ravens' trails across the Prairies. Manuscripts are inherently portable objects, but the very processes that enabled Icelandic manuscript culture to endure into the twentieth century, such as extensive sharing of exemplars, also put manuscripts at risk of being lost or discarded. From a researcher's perspective it is easy to represent manuscripts' movements as a narrative of loss, particularly as they crossed the Atlantic in immigrants' sea chests. Yet, hand-copied sagas were central to the literary practices of many Icelandic immigrants. Perhaps, in sagas set in distant lands, where protagonists became exiles, accidental migrants, and explorers, readers could find their own tracks.

NOTES

1 Established in 1916, *Sólskin* was printed at the bottom of the weekly Icelandic-Canadian newspaper *Lögberg* (Kristjánsdóttir 2014).

2 "Þetta atvik, að nú verður að sækja þessa fræðsluna til Ameríku, er eitt með öðru, sem kennir manni það, að seint verður séð út yfir það, hvað mikið af íslenzkum fróðleik, menjum og menningu hefir borizt til Vesturheims með fólki því, er fluzt hefir þangað frá Íslandi hin síðustu 30 árin. Sárast er að fyrir öllu slíku liggur innan skamms tíma að hverfa alveg og týnast í úthafi annars þjóðernis og koma Íslendingum aldrei framar að liði."

3 *Voröld*, to which the Bjóla family in Saskatchewan subscribed, published a short story by Hörður Höggvandi (a pseudonym) in the paper on 14 January 1919 (4) that encapsulates the response of many adult immigrants to the war: "Sorgir" (Sorrows) describes in a few scant paragraphs the perspective of an Icelandic immigrant widow whose husband sacrifices himself in the belief that he is securing the freedom and future of his unborn son, only for the Canadian government to arrive twenty-two years later to claim that son as cannon fodder in a distant bloodbath in Europe.

REFERENCES

Manuscripts

Árni Magnússon Institute for Icelandic Studies, Reykjavík

SÁM 176

Johns Hopkins University Library, Baltimore, Maryland

Nikulás Ottenson Collection, MS 9 4to

National and University Library of Iceland, Reykjavík

JS 204 8vo

Lbs 2784 4to

Lbs 4667 4to

New Iceland Heritage Museum, Gimli, Manitoba

NIHM 020012.3301

Published Sources

Benediktsson, Frímann. 2014. "'Þrengra útgöngu en inngöngu': Heimflutningur íslenskra vesturfara á árabilinu 1870–1916." Master's thesis, University of Iceland.

Bessason, Haraldur. 1999. *Bréf til Brands*. Seltjarnarnes: Ormstunga.

Bjarnason, Sigurður. 1919. *Rímur af Án bogsveigir*. Edited by Samson Bjarnason and Dagbjartur Guðbjartsson. Winnipeg: n.p.

Bjóla, Kristín. 1916. "Kæri ritstjóri Sólskins." *Sólskin: Barnablað Lögbergs,* 8 June, 4.

Bjóla, Valgerður. 1916. "Kæri ritstjóri Sólskins." *Sólskin: Barnablað Lögbergs,* 15 June, 4.

Björnsson, Snorri. 1911. *Sagan af Starkaði Stórvirkssyni: prentuð eftir gömlu handriti.* Winnipeg: N. Ottenson.

Briem, Jóhann. 1878. "Nokkrar leiðbeiningar fyrir vesturfara." *Framfari,* 4 January, 1–2.

Driscoll, Matthew James. 1990. "Þögnin mikla: Hugleiðingar um riddarasögur og stöðu þeirra í íslenskum bókmenntum." *Skáldskaparmál* 1: 157–68.

———. 1997. *The Unwashed Children of Eve: The Production, Dissemination and Reception of Popular Literature in Post-Reformation Iceland.* Enfield Lock: Hisarlik.

———. 2004. "Postcards from the Edge: An Overview of Marginalia in Icelandic Manuscripts." *Variants* 2–3: 21–36.

———. 2010. "The Words on the Page: Thoughts on Philology, Old and New." In *Creating the Medieval Saga: Versions, Variability and Editorial Interpretations of Old Norse Saga Literature*, edited by Judy Quinn and Emily Lethbridge, 87–104. Århus: University Press of Southern Denmark.

———. 2017. "Pleasure and Pastime: The Manuscripts of Guðbrandur á Hvítadal." In *Mirrors of Virtue: Manuscript and Print in Late Pre-Modern Iceland*, edited by Margrét Eggertsdóttir and Matthew James Driscoll, 225–76. Opuscula 15. Copenhagen: Museum Tusculanum Press.

Ezell, Margaret. 1999. *Social Authorship and the Advent of Print*. Baltimore: Johns Hopkins University Press.

Gísladóttir, Guðlaug. 1999. "'Það var vel artað barn og hafði fengið hreina sálu': Fyrsta þýdda barnabókin á íslensku." *Jón á Bægisá* 4: 29–36.

Gíslason, Magnús. 1977. "Kvällsvaka: En isländsk kulturtradition belyst genom studier i bondebefolkningens vardagsliv och miljö under senare hälften av 1800-talet och början av 1900-talet." PhD diss., University of Uppsala.

Glauser, Jürg. 1983. *Isländische Märchensagas: Studien zur Prosaliteratur im spätmittelalterlichen Island*. Basel: Helbing and Lichtenhahn.

Guðsteinsdóttir, Guðrún. 2018. "Margræðar 'Vonir' Einars H. Kvaran." In *Sigurtunga: vesturíslenskt mál og menning*, edited by Birna Arnbjörnsdóttir, Höskuldur Thráinsson, and Úlfar Bragason, 137–58. Reykjavík: Háskólaútgáfan.

Gunnlaugsson, Gísli Ágúst. 1993. "'Everyone's Been Good to Me, Especially the Dogs': Foster-Children and Young Paupers in Nineteenth-Century South Iceland." *Journal of Social History* 27 (2): 341–58.

Guttormsson, Loftur. 1990. "The Development of Popular Religious Literacy in the Seventeenth and Eighteenth Centuries." *Scandinavian Journal of History* 15 (1–2): 7–35.

———. 2003. "Lestrarhættir og bókmenning." In *Alþýðumenning á Íslandi 1830–1930*, edited by Ingi Sigurðsson and Loftur Guttormsson, 195–214. Reykjavík: Háskólaútgáfan.

Hall, Alaric, and Katelin Parsons. 2013. "Making Stemmas with Small Samples, and Digital Approaches to Publishing Them: Testing the Stemma of *Konráðs saga keisarasonar*." *Digital Medievalist* 9. DOI: https://doi.org/10.16995/dm.51.

Hall, Alaric, Steven D.P. Richardson, and Haukur Þorgeirsson. 2013. "*Sigrgarðs saga frækna*: A Normalised Text, Translation, and Introduction." *Scandinavian-Canadian Studies/Études scandinaves au Canada* 21: 80–155.

Hamilton, Mary, and David Barton. 1998. *Local Literacies: Reading and Writing in One Community*. London: Routledge.

Hansen, Björg. 1994. "Endurminningar 1861–1883." *Skagfirðingabók* 23: 170–200.

Helgason, Jón. 1958. *Handritaspjall*. Reykjavík: Mál og menning.

Höggvandi, Hörður. 1919. "Sorgir" [Sorrows]. *Voröld*, 14 January, 4.

Hreinsson, Viðar. 1994. "Icelandic Canadian Literature." In *The New Icelanders: A North American Community*, edited by David Arnason and Vincent Arnason, 87–90. Winnipeg: Turnstone Press.

———. 2012. *Wakeful Nights: Stephan G. Stephansson, Icelandic-Canadian Poet*. Calgary: Benson Ranch.

Hufnagel, Silvia. 2013. "The Farmer, Scribe and Lay Historian Gunnlaugur Jónsson from Skuggabjörg and his Scribal Network." *Gripla* 24: 235–68.

Ingólfsdóttir, Guðrún. 2011. *"Í hverri bók er mannsandi": Handritasyrpur—bókmenning, þekking og sjálfsmynd karla og kvenna á 18. öld*. Studia Islandica 62. Reykjavík: Bókmennta- og listfræðastofnun Háskóla Íslands.

Jackson, Thorleifur. 1921. *Frá austri til vesturs: Framhald af landnámssögu Nýja-Íslands*. Winnipeg: Columbia Press.

Kalinke, Marianne E., and P.M. Mitchell. 1985. *Bibliography of Old Norse-Icelandic Romances*. Islandica XLIV. Ithaca: Cornell University Press.

Konráðsson, Gísli. 1889. *Hellismannasaga*. Winnipeg: Heimskringla.

Kristjánsdóttir, Dagný. 2014. "'Við hérna í vestrinu': Um bernsku og barnaefni í íslenskum barnablöðum í Vesturheimi." *Ritið* 14 (1): 103–19.

Kristjánsson, Jakob Þór. 2017. *Mamma, ég er á lífi: Íslenskir piltar í víti heimstyrjaldar*. Reykjavík: Sögur.

Love, Harold. 1993. *Scribal Publication in Seventeenth-Century England*. Oxford: Clarendon Press.

Magnússon, Sigurður Gylfi. 2010. *Wasteland with Words: A Social History of Iceland*. London: Reaktion.

Magnússon, Sigurður Gylfi, and Davíð Ólafsson. 2017. *Minor Knowledge and Microhistory: Manuscript Culture in the Nineteenth Century*. New York: Routledge.

Neijmann, Daisy. 1997. *The Icelandic Voice in Canadian Letters*. Ottawa: Carleton University Press.

Nichols, Stephen G. 1990. "Introduction: Philology in a Manuscript Culture." *Speculum: A Journal of Medieval Studies* 65 (1): 1–10.

Ólafsson, Davíð. 2008. "Wordmongers: Post-medieval Scribal Culture and the Case of Sighvatur Grímsson." PhD diss., University of St. Andrews.

———. 2012. "Vernacular Literacy Practices in Nineteenth-Century Icelandic Scribal Culture." In *Att läsa och att skriva: Två vågor av vardaligt skriftbruk i Norden 1800–2000*, edited by Ann-Catrine Edlund, 65–85. Nordliga studier 3: Vardagligt skriftbruk 1. Umeå: Umeå universitet.

———. 2013. "Scribal Communities in Iceland: The Case of Sighvatur Grímsson." In *White Field, Black Seeds: Nordic Literacy Practices in the Long Nineteenth Century*, edited by Anna Kuismin and Matthew Driscoll, 40–49. Helsinki: Finnish Literature Society.

———. 2017. "Post-medieval Manuscript Culture and the Historiography of Texts." In *Mirrors of Virtue: Manuscript and Print in Late Pre-Modern Iceland*, edited by Margrét Eggertsdóttir and Matthew James Driscoll, 1–30. Opuscula 15. Copenhagen: Museum Tusculanum Press.

Óskarsdóttir, Svanhildur, and Katelin Parsons. 2017. "The Glacier's Long Shadow: Guðmundur Runólfsson and His Manuscripts." In *Mirrors of Virtue: Manuscript and Print in Late Pre-Modern Iceland*, edited by Margrét Eggertsdóttir and Matthew Driscoll, 87–125. Opuscula 15. Copenhagen: Museum Tusculanum Press.

Össurarson, Össur. 1910. *Rímur af Sörla hinum sterka*. Gimli: Nikulás Össursson.

Parmes loðinbjörn: skáldsaga. 1910. Gimli: G.P. Magnússon.

Parsons, Katelin Marit. 2012. "The Great Manuscript Exodus?" Paper presented at the 15th International Saga Conference, "Sagas and the Use of the Past," Aarhus University, Aarhus, Denmark, 5–11 August.

———. 2019. "Albert Jóhannesson and the Scribes of Hecla Island: Manuscript Culture and Scribal Production in an Icelandic-Canadian Settlement." *Gripla* 30: 7–46.

Pétursson, Einar G. 1993. "Ah, Very True: What Don't They Sleep on, Our Fine Old Ladies." *Icelandic Canadian* 51: 141–49.

———. 1995. "About Icelandic Books and Manuscripts in North America." *Lögberg-Heimskringla,* May 26, 1, 3–4.

Sagan af Faustusi og Ermenu. 1892. Gimli: G.M. Thompson.

Sagan af Nikulási konungi leikara. 1889. Winnipeg: Heimskringla.

Sigurðsson, Árni. 1912. "Í Breiðdal fyrir 60 árum" [In Breiðdalur 60 years ago]. *Lögberg*, 18 January, 3–4.

"Skýrsla yfir dánarbú." 1928. *Almanak Ólafs S. Thorgeirssonar* 34: 115–17.

Stead, Evanghelia. 2018. "Introduction." In *Reading Books and Prints as Cultural Objects*, edited by Evanghelia Stead, 1–30. Cham: Palgrave Macmillan.

Surmeli, Þorsteinn Árnason. 2018. "Creating in Color: Illustrations of Njáls Saga in a Nineteenth-Century Icelandic Paper Manuscript." In *New Studies in the Manuscript Tradition of Njáls Saga: The Historia Mutila of Njála*, edited by Svanhildur Óskarsdóttir and Emily Lethbridge, 257–81. Kalamazoo: Medieval Institute Publications.

Sveinsson, Gunnar. 2001. "Sigmundur Matthíasson Long, 1841–1924." *Ritmennt* 6: 27–66.

"Úr bréfum til Voraldar." 1919. *Voröld,* 14 January, 6.

"Vesturfarar." 1903. *Bjarki*, 19 June, 1–2.

Wolf, Kirsten. 1991. "Heroic Past, Heroic Present: Western Icelandic Literature." *Scandinavian Studies* 63 (4): 432–52.

———. 2001. "Emigration and Mythmaking: The Case of the Icelanders in Canada." *Canadian Ethnic Studies* 33 (2): 1–15.

Þorkelsson, Jón. 1906. *Tyrkjaránið á Íslandi 1627*. Reykjavík: Sögufélag.

CHAPTER 11

Word Meanings in North American Icelandic: More North American or More Icelandic?

MATTHEW WHELPTON

ONE OF THE things that fascinates people about language is the way that you can say things easily in one language that are much harder to express in another. Social media periodically lights up with examples of words for things that are "impossible" to express in another language, such as the German *Ohrwurm* for a piece of music that is stuck in your head. The irony of many such examples is that the intended meaning is instantly recognizable to the speakers of other languages, as if all that is lacking is a label for it: some English speakers have duly copied the German word by translating its parts and use the term *earworm* to refer to this phenomenon (and not the agricultural pest also known as a "corn earworm").

The fascination of such examples lies in the realization that the vocabulary of a language does not in fact simply involve labelling aspects of experience that jump out to every observer and demand attention. Rather, vocabulary is a selective classification, and there can be plenty of mismatches from one language to another. Any translator will be able to give many examples of such mismatches between source and target language. Many of these are far more problematic than the earworm example because they are clearly in no sense labels for "the same thing." For instance, Icelandic *hús* and *bygging* look very similar to English *house* and *building*, but the way that they group together actual human constructions is subtly different: English *house* is restricted to dwellings for people, but Icelandic *hús* is not. In cases like these the languages are not simply providing alternative labels; rather, each language is packaging experience in different ways.

When more than one language is spoken within a community, each has an opportunity to influence the other, for instance, by borrowing the words of one language into the other. Crucially, when a word is borrowed, it does not mean that the meaning of the original is borrowed whole. Usually, words are borrowed in a context of use and carry that contextualized meaning with them; once the word makes itself at home in the new language, it is free to develop and change within the new host language.

The direction and possibilities for borrowing will reflect the cultural and social status of the languages and the community in which they are spoken. Icelandic as spoken in Iceland is under the influence of a strong purist tradition that is a legacy of nineteenth-century nationalism and the twentieth-century independence movement (see Ásta Svavarsdóttir, this volume). Tore Kristiansen and Helge Sandøy (2010, 3) give a widely accepted ranking of seven Nordic speech communities in terms of purism where Iceland is on the top, and they show that popular perceptions of relative levels of purism match this hierarchy fairly closely. Ásta Svavarsdóttir, Ulla Paatola, and Helge Sandøy (2010) report a study on the degree of adaptation of English loan words in spoken language to native features of pronunciation and morphology and find, again, that Icelandic is one of the Nordic languages that adapts its loan words most towards the native system. Icelandic, as it developed in North America after the great emigrations from Iceland in the nineteenth century, was relatively free of such purist influences and was quick to adapt itself to a new environment, both physical and cultural, borrowing from the English, which was dominant in this new land of possibilities (Arnbjörnsdóttir 2006; Arnbjörnsdóttir and Thráinsson 2018; Svavarsdóttir 2018; Bragason 2018).

Implicit in this discussion is the question of how the meanings of words vary both within and between languages. Are there categories of objects "out there" waiting to be labelled, or is every category created by a culture on its own terms? Are there universal pressures on meaning that limit or direct variation in meaning? Or is variation an unrestrained kaleidoscope of possibilities? How can we get a handle on the relative influences of socio-cultural pressure and historical relatedness? Clearly, selecting random words, however fascinating, will not give a sense of how much variation there is or hint at what factors play a role, if any, in conditioning variation. In this chapter we look at the results of a study that followed on from a large-scale European research project on the nature of semantic variation and change in closely related languages. It provides a mathematically robust way of quantifying the degree to which languages vary in their classification of aspects of everyday experience and it studies whether different semantic categories (that is, different kinds of things that we talk about) vary to different extents.

The focus of interest here is the variation between European Icelandic and North American Icelandic. From an initially identical state, the two languages develop in very different cultural and linguistic environments. To provide context data are also provided from the North American English spoken in the same heritage communities as North American Icelandic, as well as British English (European context). To add an extra dimension to this consideration of cultural influence, we also include data in the category of colour naming for Icelandic Sign Language. Both Icelandic and Icelandic Sign Language are spoken in Iceland by Icelanders (Sverrisdóttir and Þorvaldsdóttir 2016; Guðmundsdóttir Beck and Whelpton 2019), but Icelandic Sign Language is quite different in formal and typological characteristics from Icelandic (though as there is no written standard for Icelandic Sign Language, many in the deaf community can read and write Icelandic). Any differences here would be likely related to typological differences in the linguistic systems.

‖ STUDYING SEMANTIC VARIATION BETWEEN LANGUAGES

A common approach to studying semantic variation between languages is to choose a number of unrelated languages and consider the similarities and differences between them. The data are often extracted from texts and consider the relation between words in use. By contrast the Evolution of Semantic Systems (EoSS) project (Majid, Jordan, and Dunn 2011) exploits developments in evolutionary biology and phylogenetic modelling, where computational techniques allow the classification of hierarchically related entities such as species and languages (Majid, Jordan, and Dunn 2015). Comparison in this case requires a set of fixed reference points to compare meanings. Building on work in experimental psychology, the EoSS project considers how speakers name fixed arrays of objects, such as particular hues or specific containers (Berlin and Kay 1999; Malt et al. 1999). Unlike the textual approach mentioned above, this is what is known as an "extensional approach." In formal semantics the extension of a word is the set of all the actual objects that a word can be used to refer to. EoSS experiments therefore collect data on the set of objects from a fixed array of options that a word can be used to name. Statistical techniques can then quantify the degree of similarity in how individual languages group certain objects together under the same name.

To see whether different aspects of our experience are more or less open to variation in the way that different languages classify them, we can choose different categories of phenomena to classify. The original EoSS categories were chosen in light of an ongoing controversy concerning the relative importance of external stimuli and internal cognitive constraints (Majid, Jordan, and Dunn 2015).

The psychologist Dedre Gentner argues that directly perceptible individuated entities vary less than abstract relational entities (Gentner 1981; Gentner and Boroditsky 2001), so physical objects that are readily separated from their surroundings will show less variation in naming than will abstract relations between objects. This suggests that our senses have a stronger role in classification than our internal cognitive systems.

By contrast the linguist Leonard Talmy argues that closed class grammatical terms vary less than open class substantive terms (Talmy 1983; Landau and Jackendoff 1993; Haspelmath 2003). Just as optical illusions work because our brain has a particular way of handling what we perceive with our eyes and can be tricked into interpreting that input in such a way that we see what is not there, so, in this view, the brain has developed ways of perceiving abstract relations in our environment that could not easily be learned directly from perception but that are repeatedly encountered and useful to perceive.

In this view our brain/mind inclines us to see abstract relations between objects in a particular way, whereas physical objects that we can manipulate can be classified more freely according to circumstance and culture.

FIGURE 11.1. A container stimulus (Ameel et al. 2005).

In light of such controversies, the EoSS project selected four contrasting semantic categories to investigate. To represent physical artifacts, EoSS selected kitchen containers (like cups, plates, and bowls). These are physical objects that are self-contained (individuated) and can be manipulated (picked up and moved around). They are also cultural artifacts, designed for a purpose. Another kind of physical object was selected to represent the whole-part relation: body parts. Arms and legs are physical entities and named as discrete parts, but in fact there is no definite point of transition between the part and the rest of the whole. There is therefore the possibility of slippage in how the parts are divided up. Further, these are natural parts of our own bodies. Moving in a more abstract direction, colours were chosen to represent the properties or qualities that we attribute to things. Last, at the most abstract, relations are represented by spatial location, such as a cup on a table, where a figure (the cup) is situated with respect to a ground (the table).

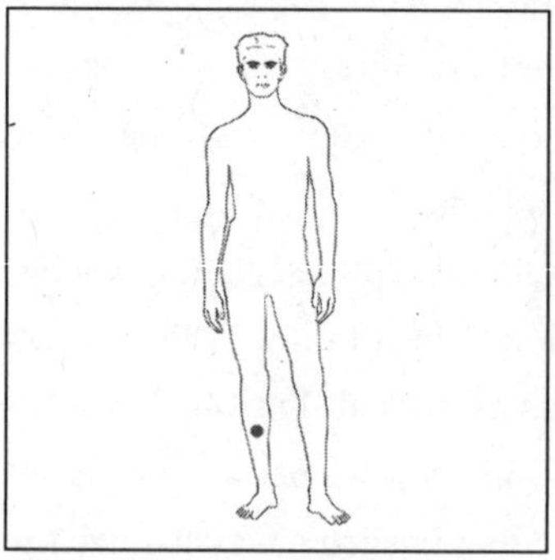

FIGURE 11.2. A body part stimulus (Jordan, Dunn, and Majid 2009).

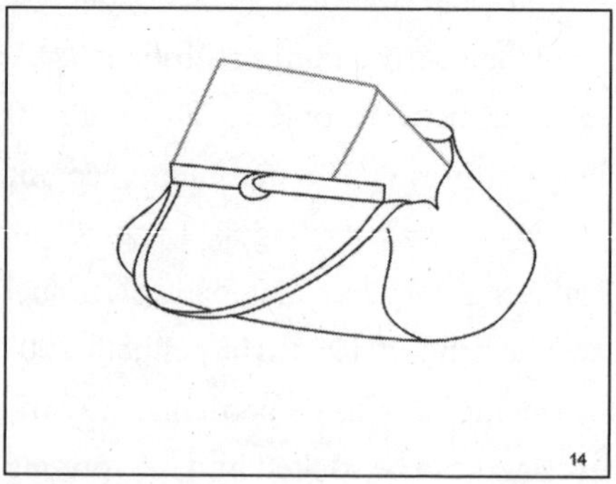

FIGURE 11.3. A spatial relation stimulus (Bowerman and Pederson 1992).

For each semantic category there is a fixed array of pictures representing a referential or extensional space. Data are collected concerning the way pictures are grouped together under a single name. It is then possible to see how much variation there is between languages in these groupings and to see whether there is a difference in the degree of variation between the different semantic categories; in particular, does the way we name containers like cups and bowls vary more or less than the way we name colours like red and orange?

THE LANGUAGES AND PARTICIPANTS

Icelandic (ICE)[1] was one of the fifty European languages for which data were elicited as part of the EoSS project, as was British English (BRE).[2] Data from North American Icelandic (NAI)[3] and North American English (NAE) were collected as part of the Heritage Language Project (2013 to 2015), led by principal investigators (PIs) Höskuldur Thráinsson and Birna Arnbjörnsdóttir and funded by the Icelandic Research Fund (see the introduction to this volume). Colour naming data for North American Icelandic and North American English were collected in 2014 in Manitoba, Saskatchewan, and North Dakota. Naming data in the other three EoSS categories were collected in 2013 in Manitoba. Data for Icelandic Sign Language (ISL) were collected as part of the project Colour in Context (2014 to 2016), led by PI Matthew Whelpton and funded by the University of Iceland Research Fund.[4]

Two points require immediate comment. Participants in the EoSS project were primarily undergraduates, and the mean age of participants was in the twenties. North American Icelandic, on the other hand, is a disappearing heritage language. The participants were therefore considerably older, with a mean age of seventy-eight. The English participants were selected from the same communities as the North American Icelandic speakers and were often the carers who brought them to the experimental site. Though younger than the North American Icelandic speakers, the North American English speakers are also considerably older than the EoSS participants, with a mean age of sixty-seven. Icelandic Sign Language is spoken by a very small community in Iceland, and it would not have been possible to find twenty volunteers if participation had been restricted by age; the mean age of participants was forty-eight. This means that age is a potentially confounding factor in interpreting differences between the languages. However, this will also make the similarities that are discovered all the more striking.

LANGUAGE (PROJECT)	PARTICIPANTS (F)	MEAN AGE	RESEARCHERS
Icelandic (EoSS)	21 (10)	29	Matthew Whelpton, Þórhalla Guðmundsdóttir Beck
British English (EoSS)	20 (9)	22	Linnaea Stockall, Euphemia Snell
North American English (Heritage Language Project)	51 (36)	67	Matthew Whelpton, Þórhalla Guðmundsdóttir Beck
North American Icelandic (Heritage Language Project)	30 (19)	78	Íris Edda Nowenstein, Kristín M. Jóhannsdóttir, Matthew Whelpton, Þórhalla Guðmundsdóttir Beck
Icelandic Sign Language (Colour in Context)	21 (14)	48	Kristín Lena Þorvaldsdóttir, Matthew Whelpton; Þórhalla Guðmundsdóttir Beck

TABLE 11.1. Participant information.

THE EXPERIMENTS

Following the EoSS protocol each participant was presented with a series of stimuli in a fixed random order. An experimenter[5] asked them to name each stimulus using the first word that came to mind, and participants were encouraged to use simple everyday language. Participants were also tested for colour-blindness, and the colour naming results for colour-blind participants were excluded.[6] Responses were audio-recorded (video-recorded in the case of sign language) and transcribed and coded by the researcher afterwards.

Experimental Stimuli

Body Parts

Stimuli in the body part task comprised ninety line drawings: seventy of the human body viewed from the front and back, and twenty of the head and face viewed from the front. A red dot on each line drawing identified the area to be named. The stimuli were developed for the EoSS project by the principal investigators (Jordan, Dunn, and Majid 2009). Participants were prompted: "Maðurinn er með punkt á . . . ?" (The man has a dot on his . . . ?).

Containers

Stimuli in the containers task comprised sixty-seven colour photographs of household containers, primarily kitchen containers, which were developed by and used in Ameel et al. (2005). Items were photographed from a fixed distance against a neutral background with a ruler in the foreground. Participants were asked: "Hvað heitir þetta?" (What is this called?).

Spatial Relations

Stimuli in the spatial relation task comprised seventy-one line drawings from the Topological Relations Picture Series (Bowerman and Pederson 1992). Each drawing shows a figure in orange set against a ground in black. Participants were asked: "Hvar er [X]?" (Where is the [X]?).

Colour Naming

Stimuli in the colour naming task comprised eighty-four Munsell colour chips. Four colours were achromatic (black-grey-white). The remaining eighty varied in hue, brightness, and saturation. There were twenty equally spaced hues at four degrees of brightness. Saturation varied so that colours were generally at the maximal possible chroma for that point in the colour space. Only Munsell-certified colour sheets were used. As light conditions critically affect perception, colours were presented under a daylight bulb simulating the full spectral range of daylight. On being presented with an individual colour chip, participants were asked: "Hvaða litur er þetta?" (What colour is this?).

Coding the Responses

Each participant's complete response to each stimulus was transcribed into a spreadsheet as the "full response," and the researcher then coded these full responses for the "main response." In most cases the coded main response is the transparent morphological and semantic head of the noun used to name the stimulus. If a participant responded "whisper pink, very light pink," then *pink* was the coded main response: whisper pink is a kind of pink. If the participant did not respond, gave an unintelligible response, or responded in a way unrelated to the stimulus, an error was coded. All other responses were coded. Three kinds of response were common in the NAI data: Icelandic terms like *skál*; English terms like *bowl* pronounced with English phonology, which were coded according to English spelling conventions, for example, *bowl*; and English terms like *bowl* pronounced with Icelandic phonology, which were then coded according to Icelandic spelling conventions, for example, *ból*.

In some cases the choice of a coded main response was problematic, because there was not a simple transparent semantic relation between the complex expression and the apparent head word. For instance, in Icelandic, the conventional translation of *orange* is *appelsínugulur*, which is literally *orange yellow*. However, most speakers no longer accept that *appelsínugulur* is a kind of *gulur* 'yellow', thus treating the compound as a distinct colour term. In this case *appelsínugulur* was coded as a main term in its own right.

THE RESULTS

Some Comments on the Data

Tables 11.2 to 11.5 provide some general information about the responses in each of the four semantic categories. The main term, as discussed above, is the transparent morphological and semantic head of the noun used to name the stimulus (for example, *pink* instead of *whisper pink*). The dominant term is then defined as the main term that is used more often than any other to describe a particular stimulus. Errors are responses that could not be coded because the participant did not respond, gave an unintelligible response, or responded in a way unrelated to the stimulus.

LANGUAGE	MAIN	DOMINANT	ERRORS
BRE	84	32	3
ICE	128	39	6
NAE	143	31	3
NAI	184	25	340

TABLE 11.2. Results for body parts.

LANGUAGE	MAIN	DOMINANT	ERRORS
BRE	33	11	3
ICE	36	13	3
NAE	50	10	6
NAI	57	6	154

TABLE 11.3. Results for containers.

LANGUAGE	MAIN	DOMINANT	ERRORS
BRE	31	12	38
ICE	46	16	40
NAE	125	15	30
NAI	123	9	21

TABLE 11.4. Results for spatial relations.

LANGUAGE	MAIN	DOMINANT	ERRORS
BRE	54	12	0
ICE	26	11	2
ISL	52	11	0
NAE	93	13	1
NAI	63	11	16

TABLE 11.5. Results for colour naming.

There are a number of interesting points here, especially with respect to North American Icelandic. As one would expect, there are far more main terms than dominant terms, because it takes only one participant to introduce an imaginative description for a stimulus, resulting in a new coded main term, but it requires a consensus for a dominant term to emerge. From this point of view it is intriguing to see how similar the numbers of dominant terms are overall, especially when compared with the huge range of main terms: in body parts, for instance (Table 11.2), there are between 84 and 184 main terms used but only twenty-five to thirty-nine dominant terms. This is particularly striking for colour naming (Table 11.5), where the range of main terms is twenty-six to ninety-three but the number of dominant terms is eleven to thirteen.

Another striking pattern is that North American Icelandic tends to use the most main terms but the fewest dominant terms: North American Icelandic has the most main terms for body parts and containers and is approximately the same as North American English for spatial relations; however, in all but colour terms, North American Icelandic is sharply below the general level for dominant terms. This reflects lexical attrition: the loss of stable vocabulary. Dominant terms are the core terms that most people use to describe the relevant semantic space. For heritage speakers this set of core terms is limited and must be made to do more work. Main terms, on the other hand, reflect the range of options available. The high numbers for North American Icelandic speakers reflect the fact they are drawing on both Icelandic and English to name stimuli, for instance, using English *bowl*, Icelandicized *ból*, or Icelandic *skál*. This contrasts with the North American English speakers, where the high numbers of main terms generally reflect a larger and more elaborate vocabulary in English.

Lexical attrition is also reflected in the high error rate for North American Icelandic, with body parts (340) and containers (154) proving to be particularly challenging for participants. Errors generally occurred when participants chose not to respond: if an English word was given, then it was coded as the NAI response and not as an error. Although we attempted to recognize the difference between an English loan word with Icelandic pronunciation (for example, *ból*) and the simple use of English with English pronunciation (for example, *bowl*), it was not possible to reflect every aspect of variation in the coding of main terms. There was in fact enormous variation in the forms of responses, including pronunciation and morphosyntactic class. For instance, North American English *eyebrow* and Icelandic *augabrún* might appear in North American Icelandic responses as *augabrún*, *augnbrún*, *eygabrúr*, *augabrýr*, or *eygabrár*. Similarly, North American English *arm* and Icelandic *handleggur* (masc.) might appear as *armur* (masc.), *armið* (neut.) or *armini* (fem.). It was decided to code such continua of variation by a single standard form as the main response (*augabrún* and *armur,* respectively).

The Statistical Analysis

As the previous section makes clear, the raw naming data, even when coded by main term, is extremely complex and the options for comparing across languages seemingly intractable. In this section we look at a statistical method for quantifying the variation between languages,[7] which the EoSS investigators (Majid, Jordan, and Dunn 2015) take from earlier work (Malt et al. 1999). It involves the use of similarity matrices for the languages, which are compared using Pearson correlations.

A similarity matrix is a way of coding the ways that items are grouped together or kept apart: in this case, when two items are given the same name versus when they are given different names. To take containers as an example: there are sixty-seven colour photographs of household containers. We want to know, for two containers, whether an individual gives them the same name or a different name. For instance, for stimulus 10 and stimulus 37, was the same name given or a different name? If the same main response was given to both stimuli, the value of 1 was assigned; otherwise, a value of 0 was assigned. For each individual participant, there will therefore be a 67 x 67 matrix representing which stimuli were grouped under the same name and which were not. For instance, row 10, column 37, will be 1 if stimulus 10 and stimulus 37 were given the same name, and 0 otherwise. This is the similarity matrix for that participant.

We can then take an average for all the participants in a particular language to see what proportion of them used the same name for a particular pair of stimuli: it might be the case that, for stimulus 10 and stimulus 37, 75 percent used the same main term and 25 percent used a different main term. Averaging the participant similarity matrices will therefore give us a language similarity matrix, where each cell has a value between 0 and 1, representing the proportion of participants in that language who assigned each pair of stimuli the same name.

A Pearson correlation is a standard statistical method for comparing two such similarity matrices. It gives a value between 1 (meaning the matrices are identical) and -1 (meaning that the matrices are the exact mirror opposite), with 0 indicating no correlation (randomly related). Every pair of languages in this study was compared. Table 11.6 shows the resulting Pearson correlation values: *Min* shows the pair of languages that were least related, *Max* shows the pair of languages that were most related, and *Mean* shows the average correlation of all language pairs.

CATEGORY	MEAN	MAX	MIN
Colour Naming	0.92	ICE~ISL 0.94	BRE~NAI 0.89
Body Parts	0.91	NAE~BRE 0.97	ICE~NAI 0.84
Containers	0.86	NAE~BRE 0.94	ICE~NAI 0.80
Spatial	0.86	NAE~BRE 0.90	BRE~ICE 0.83

TABLE 11.6. Pearson correlations for four semantic categories.

All four semantic categories are significantly positively correlated. In three of the four categories, North American English and British English are the most strongly correlated, as one might expect for two language varieties that are closely historically related and share strong cultural ties. In the category of colour, it is Icelandic and Icelandic Sign Language that are the most correlated, suggesting the importance of a shared cultural environment. In fact, the three language pairs most highly correlated for colour naming all have strong cultural ties: ICE~ISL (0.9421), BRE~NAE (0.9392), and NAE~NAI (0.9390). We return to this point in our discussion of Table 11.10.

From our point of view, an equally significant finding is that in three of the four categories, North American Icelandic defines one of the poles in the least related pair; even more striking is the fact that Icelandic and North American Icelandic contrast most strongly for body parts and containers. It is possible that this reflects the fragmentation of the naming patterns in North

American Icelandic caused by lexical attrition, which makes this heritage language more likely to have distinctive naming patterns when compared with the non-heritage languages.

If one considers just the relation between North American Icelandic and its two main competing influences, Icelandic and North American English, then one sees the relatively strong influence of North American English. Tables 11.7 to 11.10 show the correlation rankings for these three languages in each of the four semantic categories. For every category except spatial relations, the pair with North American English (NAE~NAI) has a stronger correlation with North American Icelandic than the pair with Icelandic (ICE~NAI).

LANGUAGE PAIR	PEARSON CORRELATION (BODY PARTS)
ICE~NAE	0.92
NAE~NAI	0.91
ICE~NAI	0.84

TABLE 11.7. Pearson correlations for body parts for NAI, NAE, ICE.

LANGUAGE PAIR	PEARSON CORRELATION (CONTAINERS)
ICE~NAE	0.86
NAE~NAI	0.84
ICE~NAI	0.80

TABLE 11.8. Pearson correlations for containers for NAI, NAE, ICE.

LANGUAGE PAIR	PEARSON CORRELATION (SPATIAL RELATIONS)
ICE~NAI	0.87
NAE~NAI	0.85
ICE~NAE	0.83

TABLE 11.9. Pearson correlations for spatial relations for NAI, NAE, ICE.

LANGUAGE PAIR	PEARSON CORRELATION (COLOUR NAMING)
NAE~NAI	0.94
ICE~NAE	0.91 (0.9149394)
ICE~NAI	0.91 (0.9144994)

TABLE 11.10. Pearson correlations for colour naming for NAI, NAE, ICE.

We already saw in our discussion of Table 11.6 that strong cultural ties have an influence on colour naming: NAE~NAI is one of the top correlated pairs in colour naming. As Table 11.10 shows, the historical relation to Icelandic does not offset this strong cultural influence.

This historical relationship does, however, appear to be significant in the category of spatial relations. As reported in Raphael Berthele et al. (2015, 87–88), Icelandic differs sharply from four other Germanic languages, including Norwegian, in how frequently it uses complex prepositional combinations. Even in simple static locational descriptions, complex prepositional elements are often used (Berthele et al. 2015, 88 ex. 13).

1. Kanína-n er inni í búri-nu
   rabbit-the is inside in hutch-the
   'The rabbit is in the hutch'.

North American Icelandic showed a similar delight in these complex prepositions, with a few examples shown in (2–4).

2. upp við 'on' (literally 'up against', used of an insect on wall)
3. út í 'on' (literally 'out in', used of raindrops on a windowpane)
4. fyrir innan 'inside' (literally 'for from inside', used of a house surrounded by a fence)

This grammatical similarity has a strong influence on the correlation between North American Icelandic and Icelandic with respect to how they describe spatial relations and overrides the otherwise dominant cultural influence of North American English.

This brings us to the more general point concerning the differences in degree of variation between semantic categories. As Table 11.6 showed, the categories fall into two pairs: colour naming and body parts have a score over 0.9, whereas spatial relations and containers have a score under 0.9. This is in line with the findings of the original EoSS study of twelve Germanic languages, shown in Table 11.11.

CATEGORY	MEAN
Body parts	0.94
Colour naming	0.93
Containers	0.82
Spatial	0.73

TABLE 11.11. Pearson corrections for the 12 EoSS Germanic languages. (See Majid, Jordan, and Dunn 2015, 8 Table 2)

As I argue in Whelpton (2018, 37–38), the top two categories, body parts and colour naming, are precisely those categories for which humans have specialized neurocognitive support: the proprioception and visual perception systems, respectively. Containers, on the other hand, are cultural artifacts, the general constraints on which are largely functional and sensitive to local cultural variations: convenient ways of eating, drinking, storing, cooking, and distributing consumables. The marking of spatial relations with prepositions is highly sensitive to the grammatical system, with important typological differences in how such information is formally coded even within the Germanic family.

There are two differences of interest between our results in Table 11.6 and the general Germanic results in Table 11.11. Spatial relations in our language group are not significantly different from containers; this is presumably related to less typological diversity in our language sample, which does not include the extensive use of verb particles in German or of dispositional verbs in Frisian (Berthele et al. 2015). Colour naming in our sample shows the highest correlation, not body parts. We have seen that colour naming is sensitive to cultural influence, on top of the neuropsychological factors contributed by the visual system. Once again our language sample includes tight cultural clusters. This may give colour naming the edge over body parts in our sample.

CONCLUSIONS

Applying phylogenetic statistical methods to experimental extensional semantics can provide insight into the ways that semantic categories vary, even between closely related languages. Our results show that the cultural influence of North American English has a stronger effect on North American Icelandic categories than those of historically related (European) Icelandic, with the exception of prepositional marking of spatial relations, where the shared grammatical system holds the heritage language closer to its parent language.

Taking a broader perspective, we see that categories grounded in specialized neuropsychological systems (proprioception for body parts and the visual system for colour naming) tend to vary less than the naming of cultural artifacts (like containers) or abstract relations grounded in the grammatical system (like spatial prepositions), which are subject to typological variation. However, there is no single simple conditioner for variation in these categories, and we also find a clear effect of cultural influence on colour naming, in addition to the neuropsychological factors.

NOTES

1 This work stems from the Evolution of Semantic Systems (EoSS) project, which received financial support from the Max Planck Gesellschaft. The EoSS data for Icelandic was collected by the author and Þórhalla Guðmundsdóttir Beck.

2 I would like to thank Linnaea Stockall for the use of the British English data.

3 "North American Icelandic" is abbreviated in different ways, depending on the writer. As many tables are drawn from the EoSS-derived data analysis, I will keep the code used there: NAI.

4 Icelandic Sign Language (ISL) data were collected in September 2014 by Kristín Lena Þorvaldsdóttir, a sign language specialist working on behalf of the Communication Centre for the Deaf and Hard of Hearing (SHH). I would like to thank Rannveig Sverrisdóttir for her input on data analysis for Icelandic Sign Language.

5 According to the EoSS protocol, the experimenter should be a native speaker of the target language. However, for practical and funding reasons, this was not possible for the heritage and sign language projects. The experimenter for North American Icelandic spoke European Icelandic; for North American English, the experimenter spoke British English; and for Icelandic Sign Language, the experimenter was a fluent non-native speaker.

6 Participants also took a focal colour test, but those results are not discussed here (see Guðmundsdóttir, Beck, and Whelpton 2019; Whelpton 2018).

7 The analysis presented here is based on a snapshot of the data from September 2017. The analysis is conducted in R version 3.3.2 (2016-10-31). I would like to thank Michael Dunn, Joe Jalbert, and Helgi Guðmundsson for their help with the R analysis. All errors and misunderstandings remain mine solely.

REFERENCES

Ameel, Eef, Gert Storms, Barbara C. Malt, and Steven A. Sloman. 2005. "How Bilinguals Solve the Naming Problem." *Journal of Memory and Language* 53 (1): 60–80. https://doi.org/10.1016/j.jml.2005.02.004.

Arnbjörnsdóttir, Birna. 2006. *North American Icelandic: The Life of a Language*. Winnipeg: University of Manitoba Press.

Arnbjörnsdóttir, Birna, and Höskuldur Thráinsson. 2018. "Hvað einkennir vesturíslensku? Yfirlit um fyrri rit og rannsóknir" [What defines North American Icelandic? An overview of previous scholarship and research]. In *Sigurtunga: Vesturíslenskt mál og menning*, edited by Birna Arnbjörnsdóttir, Höskuldur Thráinsson, and Úlfar Bragason, 211–55. Reykjavík: Háskólaútgáfan.

Berlin, Brent, and Paul Kay. 1999. *Basic Color Terms: Their Universality and Evolution.* The David Human Series (Philosophy and Cognitive Science Reissues). Stanford, CA: CSLI Publications.

Berthele, Raphael, Matthew Whelpton, Åshild Næss, and Pieter Duijff. 2015. "Static Spatial Descriptions in Five Germanic Languages." *Language Sciences* 49: 82–101. https://doi.org/10.1016/j.langsci.2014.07.006.

Bowerman, Melissa, and Eric Pederson. 1992. "Topological Relations Picture Series." In *Space Stimuli Kit 1.2: November 1992*, edited by Stephen C. Levinson, 51. Nijmegen: Max Planck Institute for Psycholinguistics.

Bragason, Úlfar. 2018. "Menning og saga—Yfirlit um fyrri rit og rannsóknir" [Culture and history—An overview of previous scholarship and research]. In *Sigurtunga: Vesturíslenskt mál og menning*, edited by Birna Arnbjörnsdóttir, Höskuldur Thráinsson, and Úlfar Bragason, 21–35. Reykjavík: Háskólaútgáfan.

Gentner, Dedre. 1981. "Some Interesting Differences between Verbs and Nouns." *Cognition and Brain Theory* 4 (2): 161–78.

Gentner, Dedre, and Lera Boroditsky. 2001. "Individuation, Relativity, and Early Word Learning." In *Language Acquisition and Conceptual Development*, edited by Melissa Bowerman and Stephen C. Levinson, 215–56. Language Culture and Cognition. Cambridge: Cambridge University Press. http://dx.doi.org/10.1017/CBO9780511620669.010.

Guðmundsdóttir Beck, Þórhalla, and Matthew Whelpton. 2019. "Universals and Variability of Color-Naming in Icelandic, Icelandic Sign Language and North American Icelandic." In *Lexicalization Patterns in Color Naming: A Cross-Linguistic Perspective*, edited by Ida Raffaelli, Daniela Katunar, and Barbara Kerovec, 333–58. Amsterdam: John Benjamins Publishing.

Haspelmath, Martin. 2003. "The Geometry of Grammatical Meaning: Semantic Maps and Cross-Linguistic Comparison." In *The New Psychology of Language: Cognitive and Functional Approaches to Language Structure*, edited by Michael Tomasello, 2: 211–42. Mahwah, NJ: Lawrence Erlbaum Associates.

Jordan, Fiona M., Michael Dunn, and Asifa Majid. 2009. *Body Part Naming Booklet. Developed for the EoSS Project.* Nijmegen: Max Planck Institute for Psycholinguistics.

Kristiansen, Tore, and Helge Sandøy. 2010. "Introduction. The Linguistic Consequences of Globalization: The Nordic Laboratory." *International Journal of the Sociology of Language* 2010 (204): 1–7. https://doi.org/10.1515/ijsl.2010.027.

Landau, Barbara, and Ray Jackendoff. 1993. "Whence and Whither in Spatial Language and Spatial Cognition?" *Behavioral and Brain Sciences* 16: 255–65. https://doi.org/10.1017/S0140525X00029927.

Majid, Asifa, Fiona Jordan, and Michael Dunn. 2011. *Evolution of Semantic Systems Procedures Manual.* Nijmegen: Max Planck Institute for Psycholinguistics.

———. 2015. "Semantic Systems in Closely Related Languages." In "Semantic Systems in Closely Related Languages," edited by Asifa Maijd, Fiona Jordan, and Michael Dunn, special issue, *Language Sciences* 49 (May): 1–18. https://doi.org/10.1016/j.langsci.2014.11.002.

Malt, Barbara C., Steven A. Sloman, Silvia Gennari, Meiyi Shi, and Yuan Wang. 1999. "Knowing versus Naming: Similarity and the Linguistic Categorization of Artifacts." *Journal of Memory and Language* 40 (2): 230–62. https://doi.org/10.1006/jmla.1998.2593.

Svavarsdóttir, Ásta. 2018. "Að flytja mál milli landa—Breytilegar málaðstæður heima og heiman" [Moving a language between countries—Differing language circumstances home and away]. In *Sigurtunga: Vesturíslenskt mál og menning*, edited by Birna Arnbjörnsdóttir, Höskuldur Thráinsson, and Úlfar Bragason, 257–78. Reykjavík: Háskólaútgáfan.

Svavarsdóttir, Ásta, Ulla Paatola, and Helge Sandøy. 2010. "English Influence on the Spoken Language—with a Special Focus on Its Social, Semantic and Functional Conditioning." *International Journal of the Sociology of Language* 204: 43–58. https://doi.org/10.1515/ijsl.2010.030.

Sverrisdóttir, Rannveig, and Kristín Lena Þorvaldsdóttir. 2016. "Why Is the SKY BLUE? On Colour Signs in Icelandic Sign Language." In *Semantic Fields in Sign Languages, Colour, Kinship and Quantification*, edited by Ulrike Zeshan and Keiko Sagara, 209–50. Berlin: De Gruyter Mouton. https://doi.org/10.1515/9781501503429.

Talmy, Leonard. 1983. "How Language Structures Space." In *Spatial Orientation: Theory, Research and Application*, edited by Herbert L. Pick Jr. and Linda P. Acredolo, 225–82. New York: Plenum Press. http://link.springer.com/chapter/10.1007/978-1-4615-9325-6_11.

Whelpton, Matthew. 2018. "The Variability of Semantic Categories: An Experiment in Extensional Semantics." *Nordiske Studier i Leksikografi* 14: 29–44.

CHAPTER 12

Understanding Complex Sentences in a Heritage Language

SIGRÍÐUR MAGNÚSDÓTTIR, IRIS EDDA NOWENSTEIN, AND HÖSKULDUR THRÁINSSON

IT IS NOT equally easy to understand all the sentences that we hear or read, even if we recognize all the words. Linguists want to understand why this is the case, as this phenomenon can teach us something about the nature of human language and the differences between languages and between groups of speakers.

But what makes some sentences more difficult to understand than others? Consider the set of pictures in Figure 12.1. Now suppose you were presented with one of the following sentences and asked to point to the picture that describes the relevant action:

1. **a.** The boy hits the girl.
   b. The girl is hit by the boy.
   c. It is the boy who hits the girl.
   d. It is the girl whom the boy hits.

The reader will probably find it easy to see that all the sentences in (1) describe the action depicted by picture *a* in Figure 12.1. Although these sentences may all seem relatively simple to the reader, there is evidence that healthy adult

FIGURE 12.1. A set of action pictures from a sentence-picture matching test (Magnúsdóttir and Þórðardóttir 2013).

native speakers of English are more likely to misinterpret sentences like (1b, d) than (1a, c) (see, for example, Ferreira 2003).

Figure 12.1 is taken from a sentence-picture matching test that was designed to compare comprehension of different types of Icelandic sentences by Icelandic-speaking children in Iceland, healthy adults, and aphasic patients (Magnúsdóttir and Þórðardóttir 2013; see also Magnúsdóttir 2000). This test was included in the test package used in the Icelandic Heritage Language Project to elicit data about the nature of North American Icelandic (NAI) and compare the results with those for two age groups of adult speakers of Icelandic in Iceland (IceIce). The results were compared with results that had already been obtained for Icelandic-speaking children and people with aphasia. The goal was to answer the following research questions:

2. **a.** Are Icelandic sentences that have been shown to be difficult to understand for children acquiring Icelandic and for Icelandic aphasic patients also difficult to understand for speakers of NAI?

   b. Are these sentences also difficult to understand for different age groups of adult speakers of IceIce?

   c. What do the results tell us about the nature of challenges involved in the comprehension of syntactically complex sentences?

SUBJECTS AND METHODOLOGY

Subjects

The new data elicited for this study come from the three groups of speakers described in Table 12.1.[1] The data for speakers of NAI were collected in the field trips to Canada and the United States in 2013–14 described in the introduction to this book. The data for the adult speakers of Icelandic in Iceland were collected in Reykjavík in 2015.

SPEAKER GROUP	MALE	FEMALE	TOTAL	MEAN AGE
Adult NAI	11	22	33	73.2
Older IceIce (> 70)	10	20	30	76.6
Younger IceIce (30–40)	10	20	30	34.4

TABLE 12.1. Three groups of speakers compared in the present study.

As described in the introduction to this volume, speakers of NAI are descendants of the Icelanders who emigrated to North America between 1870 and 1914. English was the dominant language in the areas of Canada and the U.S. where the immigrants settled, so they had to learn it to some extent. Later generations grew up in an environment where both Icelandic and English were used, and eventually the Icelandic they used developed into a typical heritage language and its use was for the most part limited to interaction with members of the family and friends (see, for example, Arnbjörnsdóttir 2006, especially ch. 2). In circumstances such as these, heritage languages tend to eventually die out, and this presumably will be the fate of NAI, although it has lasted longer than many languages in a similar situation (for possible reasons, see the discussion in the introduction to this volume, and Arnbjörnsdóttir 2006, ch. 2). The subjects interviewed in our Heritage Language Project spoke NAI to different degrees, some of them very fluently, others to a limited extent. As is to be expected, receptive use (understanding) was typically better than productive use (speaking). But even speakers who have good receptive command of languages may find some syntactic constructions more difficult than others.

Methodology

As briefly illustrated above, the stimulus material used in this study consisted of line drawings, arranged horizontally in a three-picture choice format. Each set of three consisted of a picture depicting the action described in the relevant sentence (for example, picture *a* in the set in Figure 12.1 above for the sentences in (1)), a reversible of the target sentence (for example, picture *c* in Figure 12.1 for the sentences in (1)), and a lexical foil, a picture showing some totally different action (cf. *b* in Figure 12.1). There was a total of sixty test sentences and sixty sets of pictures. The test sentences were read to the subjects, one at a time, and the subjects were asked to respond by pointing to the picture that best described the content of each sentence. All the sentences were grammatically well-formed (see, however, the comments on sentence (4b) below). Six transitive lexical verbs were used in the stimulus sentences, and all refer to actions that could easily be depicted in a simple drawing. The verbs used are listed in (3) and, as shown there, three of them take an accusative object and three a dative object (see also the example sentences in (4)):

3. **a.** lemja 'hit' (acc.)
   b. ýta 'push' (dat., for example, in a swing)
   c. klappa 'pat' (dat., for example, on the head)
   d. kitla 'tickle' (acc.)
   e. greiða 'comb' (dat., as in combing one's hair)
   f. mála 'paint' (acc., as in face painting)

Some of the pictures, however, depicted other actions (in the lexical foils), such as driving (cf. picture *b* in Figure 12.1), kissing, catching, chasing, et cetera. At the beginning of the testing session, the examiners made sure that the subjects were familiar with the six main verbs used in the stimulus sentences. The nouns *stelpan* 'the girl' and *strákurinn* 'the boy' were used alternatively as agents and patients (see the example sentences in (4) below), and the order of the stimulus sentences was randomized.

THE SENTENCE TYPES TESTED

To be able to point to the appropriate picture in the test described above, the participants had to identify the agent and the patient in the stimulus sentence. What this involves can be explained by using the English examples (1a, b), repeated here for convenience:

1. **a.** The boy hits the girl.
   b. The girl is hit by the boy.

In a simple active sentence like (1a), the subject *the boy* is the agent and the object *the girl* is the patient and the relevant activity is shown in picture *a* in Figure 12.1 above. In sentence (1a) the subject precedes the object, which is the default word order in English. In the passive variant (1b), the grammatical subject is *the girl*, and it comes in the initial position in the sentence but is still the patient of the action. The agent *the boy* follows it in the prepositional phrase *by the boy*. We see, then, that the agent does not always precede the patient in English sentences, although that is typically the case. A common description of the relationship between active-passive pairs like (1a, b) states that in the passive version, the phrase that would be the object in the active variant has been "moved" to the subject position but its semantic role (here that of a patient) remains unchanged.

The syntax of Icelandic is very similar to that of English in many respects. In both languages the default word order is SVO (subject-verb-object). Since the subject of a simple active sentence is very often the agent of the action, this means that agent-first sentences are very common in Icelandic. With this in mind, the test used was designed in a way that made it possible to investigate, among other things, whether the order of agent versus patient influenced the interpretation of the sentences. An annotated list of the ten stimulus sentence types is given in (4). The examples in (4) all involve the lexical verb *lemja* 'hit', but in the actual test all six main verbs listed in (3) were used in every sentence type, giving a total of sixty stimulus sentences:

4. a. **Active**. Agent subject precedes patient object.

Strákurinn	lemur	stelpuna.
boy-the (nom.)	hits	girl-the (acc.)

'The boy hits the girl.'

b. **New impersonal/passive**. Dummy subject *það* 'there', patient in object position, no agent mentioned.

Það	er	lamið	strákinn.
there	is	hit (n.sg.)	boy-the (acc.)

'The boy is hit.'

c. **Short passive**. Patient subject, no agent mentioned.

Strákurinn	er	laminn.
boy-the (nom.)	is	hit

'The boy is hit.'

d. **Long passive**. Patient subject precedes the agent, which is in a prepositional phrase.

Stelpan	er	lamin	af stráknum.
girl-the (nom.)	is	hit	by boy-the (dat.)

'The girl is hit by the boy.'

e. ***Wh*-subject question**. Asks about the agent—hence the agent precedes the patient.

Hvaða stelpa	lemur	strákinn?
which girl (nom.)	hits	boy-the (acc.)

'Which girl hits the boy?'

f. ***Wh*-object question**. Asks about the patient—hence the patient precedes the agent.

Hvaða stelpu	lemur	strákurinn?
which girl (acc.)	hits	boy-the (nom.)

'Which girl does the boy hit?'

g. **Subject cleft sentence** (that includes a relative clause). Focuses on the agent—hence the agent precedes the patient.

Það	er	stelpan	sem	lemur	strákinn.
it	is	girl-the (nom.)	that	hits	boy-the (acc.)

'It is the girl who hits the boy.'

h. **Object cleft sentence** (relative clause). Focuses on the patient—hence the patient precedes the agent.

Það	er	stelpan	sem	strákurinn	lemur.
it	is	girl-the (nom.)	that	boy-the	hits

'It is the girl whom the boy hits.'

i. **Topicalization** with an auxiliary verb. The patient precedes the agent.

Stelpuna	er	strákurinn	að lemja.
girl-the (acc.)	is	boy-the (nom.)	to hit (inf.)

'The girl, the boy is hitting.'

j. **Topicalization** with no auxiliary verb. The patient precedes the agent.

Stelpuna	lemur	strákurinn.
girl-the (acc.)	hits	boy-the (nom.)

'The girl, the boy hits.'

As the glosses and the idiomatic translations indicate, some of the syntactic structures tested have close parallels in English and should need no particular explanation. Some clarifications are in order, however:

5. **a.** The **New impersonal/passive** in (4b) has no counterpart in English. It is a relatively new construction in Icelandic (see, for example, Maling and Sigurjónsdóttir 2002), and it has the same auxiliary-main verb combination as a regular passive (the verb *vera* 'be' plus a past participle, for example, *er lamið* 'is hit'). But it is a hybrid construction because despite the passive auxiliary, the object patient stays in situ, following the main verb, as in the active sentence (4a), and keeps the relevant object case (here, accusative). Because of this hybrid nature (see most extensively Sigurðsson 2012), it goes by two different names in the linguistic literature. This construction is much more readily accepted by younger than older speakers.

b. Since Icelandic is a V2 (verb-second) language, the finite verb will immediately follow the first constituent in the sentence, even when this constituent is a fronted object as in (4f, i, j). Hence, we get the order OVS (object-verb-subject) in sentences of this type and not the default SVO. This is different from English, as the glosses and idiomatic translations show, because English is not a V2 language.

c. In Icelandic the arguments (the subject and object noun phrases, NPs) are case marked. This is an important cue for the correct interpretation of some of the structures, especially when the word order may be misleading. Note in particular that in (4f) the order of the arguments is patient-agent, namely the opposite of the usual order, and **the only cue** that tells the listener (reader) that this is so is the case marking of the arguments: the accusative on *hvaða stelpu* 'which girl' shows that it must be the object—and hence the patient—although it precedes the nominative subject *strákurinn* 'the boy'. Similarly, in (4j) **the only cue** for correctly interpreting the arguments is the case marking: the accusative on *stelpuna* and nominative on *strákurinn* show that the former must be the patient-object and the latter the agent-subject. Thus (4j) means the same thing as (4a), although the order of the noun phrases (the arguments) is reversed.

Previous research on Icelandic has shown that (some) Icelandic speakers with aphasia can make use of case marking as a morphological cue for argument interpretation (see Magnúsdóttir 2000), and so can young Icelandic children (four to seven years old) to some extent (see Hreggviðsdóttir 2018). But they still find sentences difficult to interpret when the interpretation solely depends on the case marking, as in (4f, i) (see Hreggviðsdóttir 2018; Sigurjónsdóttir 2015). In the next section we will see to what extent speakers of NAI can make use of case marking as an interpretation cue.

Picture selection tasks of various kinds are commonly used to assess the linguistic development of children (for an overview and evaluation, see Gerken and Shady 1996). The particular test under discussion here was originally designed for a study of the nature of agrammatism in Icelandic subjects (Magnúsdóttir 2000), and revised versions were later used to evaluate the linguistic development of Icelandic-speaking children (Þórðardóttir 2014; Sigurjónsdóttir 2015; Hreggviðsdóttir 2018). These studies indicated that the order of agent versus patient in the stimulus sentences was one of the characteristics that had an effect on the score of the subjects. That may be a part of the reason why these subjects found passive sentences containing two arguments more difficult to understand than corresponding actives, for instance. There is also some evidence that heritage language speakers tend to have problems understanding passives and sentences where the word order deviates from the default one. Thus Benmamoun, Montrul, and Polinsky (2013, 150) report on a study of Russian heritage speakers (Polinsky 2009) whose dominant language was English (the default word order in Russian is SVO as in English). Their conclusion was that "regardless of voice, heritage speakers have serious problems when the word order departs from SVO; they also have problems with the passive" (Benmamoun, Montrul, and Polinsky 2013, 150). They also report on a number of studies on heritage languages (2013, 151) that suggest that heritage speakers may have problems with *wh*-questions (see (4e–f) above) and object relative clauses (cf. the object cleft in (3h)). Anderssen and Westergaard (2016) also mention problems with non-canonical word order by speakers of heritage Norwegian.

Given this background it will be interesting to compare the results for the heritage speakers of NAI on the test under discussion with results obtained for different groups of speakers of Icelandic.

RESULTS AND DISCUSSION

The Heritage Language Results in the Light of Previous Research

In this section we will first answer research question (2a), repeated here for convenience:

2. **a.** Are Icelandic sentences that have been shown to be difficult to understand for children acquiring Icelandic and for Icelandic aphasic patients also difficult to understand for speakers of NAI?

This question is obviously interesting from a descriptive point of view since its answer will tell us something about the properties of NAI. But it is also important from a theoretical point of view. Recall that many of the syntactically complex sentences exemplified in (4) above include "displaced" arguments, that is, noun phrases (NPs) that refer to patients of the relevant action but precede the agent NP, which is not the "canonical" order of constituents, or occur in a position that is more commonly occupied by the agent. As pointed out above, this is often described in terms of "movement" of these constituents to particular structural positions. Linguists have argued that understanding sentences of this type requires the ability to make use of complex structures and computations in the mental grammar of the speakers. While the accounts of the problems that children and aphasic patients have in understanding certain syntactically complex sentence types vary in detail, they can be divided roughly into two main groups. Their main differences are summarized in a simplified fashion as hypotheses A and B:

6. **Hypothesis A:** The problems can be attributed to underdeveloped internal grammar (in the case of children) or to the loss of critical properties of syntactic knowledge and processes in general (in the case of speakers with aphasia).

   Hypothesis B: The reason why these sentence types are difficult to understand for children and people with aphasia is the fact that they are difficult to process for structural reasons, not because the relevant grammatical structures have not been acquired (by children) or because they have been lost (in speakers with aphasia).

It is not necessary for our purposes to go into the theoretical details behind these hypotheses.[2] It is enough in this context to realize that the two hypotheses (or two types of hypotheses) make different predictions:

7. a. Under **Hypothesis A** there is no particular reason to expect that healthy adult speakers of heritage languages will have similar problems as children and people with aphasia in understanding these syntactically complex sentences since their general capability to learn a language (their mental grammars) is clearly fully developed and normal, as seen in their linguistic competence in the dominant language.

   b. Under **Hypothesis B** we expect that heritage speakers might have similar problems as children and speakers with aphasia in understanding these syntactically complex sentences since they should be difficult to process for all speakers, albeit to different degrees.

To test these predictions, we will now compare the results for a group of NAI speakers with those previously obtained for two other groups:

8. a. Three Icelandic-speaking agrammatic patients, sixty-two, sixty-three, and sixty-eight years old (see Magnúsdóttir 2000, 56).

   b. One hundred and twenty Icelandic-speaking children between two and a half and six years old (more specifically aged two years and six months to five years and eleven months, see Þórðardóttir 2014, 32).

   c. Thirty-three speakers of NAI around seventy years of age (mean age 73.2 years).

The percentage of target answers (correct answers) by these three groups for the ten different sentence types can be seen in Figure 12.2.[3] As Figure 12.2 shows, the following holds for all three groups:

- Structures where the patient has been "displaced" from its regular position and comes first (and thus precedes the agent where there is one) are more likely to be wrongly interpreted than structures where the patient is "in situ" (in its default place). Thus, passives are more difficult than actives (see (4c,d) versus (4a)—and also (4b)), object *wh*-questions are more difficult than subject *wh*-questions (see (4f) versus (4e)), object clefts are more difficult than subject clefts (see (4h) versus (4g)), and both topicalization structures are relatively difficult (see (4i,j)).

- Note also that even for the difficult types, all three groups typically score over 50 percent (the exceptions will be discussed below). This is interesting from a theoretical point of view since some of the accounts proposed for the performance of aphasics and children on structures of this kind predict that they should perform at a chance level since they would basically be guessing who is the agent and who is the patient (see the overview in Grodzinsky 2000, for instance).[4]

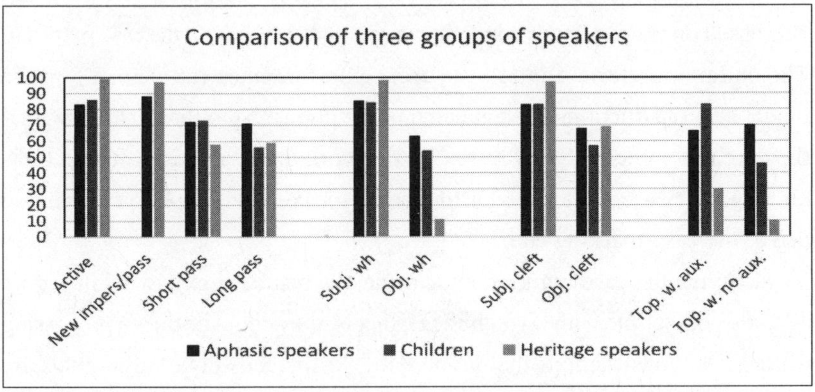

FIGURE 12.2. Scores on the sentence-picture matching test for three groups of speakers.

As Figure 12.2 shows, the New impersonal/passive patterns with the regular active. This is not surprising since the only argument in that construction is the patient in situ and thus it does not involve any "displacement" of arguments. It is also interesting to see that the short passive, where no agent is mentioned (see (4c)), seems slightly easier to interpret for the children than the longer version, where the agent is present in a final prepositional phrase (see (4d)). It is not entirely clear why this is the case.

The similarities just described arguably support Hypothesis B rather than Hypothesis A: the structures that are difficult for Icelandic children and speakers with aphasia are also difficult for the heritage speakers. Not surprisingly, the "easy" constructions are also easy for the heritage speakers. It is interesting to note that the heritage speakers typically perform perfectly on those, whereas the other speakers make a few mistakes.

There is one glaring exception to the similarities: the heritage speakers cannot really make any use of the case-marking cue, whereas the other groups can, to some extent, especially the aphasic patients.[5] As explained above, case marking is the only cue that distinguishes object *wh*-questions from subject *wh*-questions. In the topicalization without an auxiliary verb (see (4j)), case marking is the only cue that indicates that the first NP is actually the patient and the second one the agent, namely that the order is the reverse of the default one. As Figure 12.2 shows, the heritage speakers misinterpreted these structures about 90 percent of the time. This means that their interpretation was based on the expected order of the arguments and not on the case marking. The children perform a little over chance performance (50 percent) on the object *wh*-constructions and topicalization without an auxiliary, showing that they are not completely led astray by the word order in these constructions although they are not as good as the adult speakers with aphasia in making use of the case-marking cue.

Leaving the case-marking issue aside, the results summarized in Figure 12.2 are compatible with Hypothesis B; that is, they could be due to processing difficulties: constructions that involve the "displacement" of arguments are more difficult to process than those that do not, other things being equal. But why are they difficult for heritage speakers? Recall that the mean age of the heritage speakers tested was around seventy years. One possibility is thus that this relatively high age had some influence on their performance in the sentence-picture matching task.

Speakers of North American Icelandic and Icelandic Icelandic

One interesting aspect of heritage language research in small language communities is the speakers' demographics. As has been mentioned, NAI currently survives in older speakers of the North American Icelandic communities. This adds an interesting dimension to the research project: namely, whether characteristics of NAI speakers are shared by IceIce speakers of the same age. In the case of the understanding of complex sentences, we therefore wanted to investigate whether the difficulties experienced by NAI speakers were also present in two control groups of adult IceIce speakers. As shown in Table 12.1 above, the average age of the older control group was about the same as that of the heritage speakers (76.6 versus 73.2 years), whereas the other group was much younger (average age 34.4 years). By comparing these three groups of normal adult speakers, we hoped to be able to disentangle the effects of being a heritage speaker and the effects of simply being an older speaker.

It is important for researchers to learn more about possible age effects on language tasks to be better able to interpret results where age makes a difference. But why would we expect there to be an age effect when it comes to understanding complex sentences? While it is widely recognized that language production shows marked age-related decline, particularly word-finding difficulties, increased slips of the tongue, and pauses in speech, language comprehension is typically considered to be well-preserved in older adults (see Burke and Shafto 2008). But, relevant to Hypothesis B in the previous section, studies on the processing of complex sentences have shown that older speakers might make use of compensatory knowledge-based strategies where plausibility evaluation may play a role. In other words older speakers are able to compensate for difficulties in the processing of complex sentences by making use of their experience (Federmeier and Kutas 2005; Wingfield and Grossman 2006). One question is then whether this also holds true for heritage speakers, who by definition have not had the same exposure to the relevant language as the native speakers—their linguistic experience is less extensive.

Recall that in the previous section, it became clear that NAI speakers tended to interpret the sentences based on the argument order and that case cues in particular were not useful. In Figure 12.3 we compare their results to the IceIce control groups.

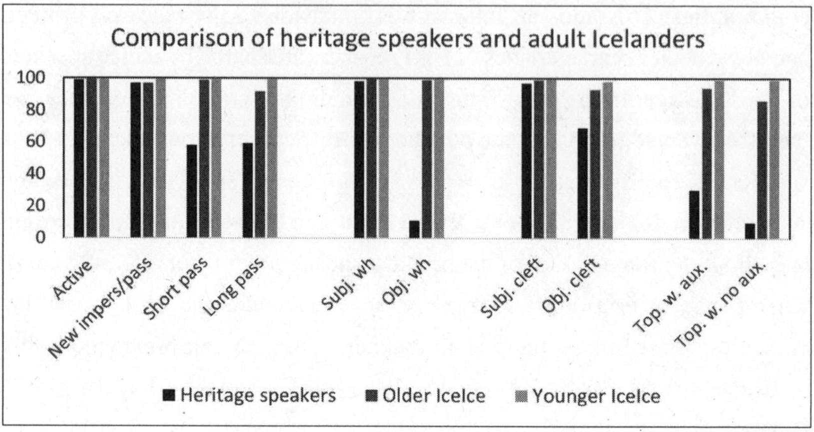

FIGURE 12.3. Scores on the sentence-picture matching test arranged by sentence types.

In Figure 12.3 the results for the different sentence types are presented in the same way as in Figure 12.2. One of the key results emerging in the patterns across sentence types, as has been mentioned already, is that the difficulties heritage speakers encounter are not general sentence comprehension difficulties but are linked to specific constructions. This is also true of the older IceIce speakers, who do have slightly more difficulties than the younger IceIce speakers but fewer than the heritage speakers. The reported effects are present only in certain contexts. As can be seen in Figure 12.3, this pattern (Younger IceIce speakers > Older IceIce speakers > NAI speakers) appears in the results for short and long passives, *wh*-object questions, object clefts, and both topicalization structures. A statistical analysis of the results further confirms the effects of sentence type, age, and heritage speaker status.[6] This leads us to the conclusion that sentences where there has been some "movement" are hard to understand but that argument reversal might prove even more difficult. This is particularly true for the NAI speakers, with their scores differing the most from the IceIce speakers, and in some cases dropping below chance, when the patient appears before the agent. The sentences that cause the most difficulties across groups are those where both movement and argument reversal are present and case is the only cue for the roles of the arguments and therefore the meaning of the sentence.

In Figure 12.4 the scores are arranged by speaker groups to show more clearly that the differences between the groups are both quantitative and qualitative. Figure 12.4 shows, for instance, together with Figure 12.3, that the heritage speakers find short and long passives equally difficult to interpret while the older IceIce speakers find long passives more difficult than the short ones. Conversely, the NAI results show a large contrast between *wh*-subject and *wh*-object questions while the difference is very small for the older IceIce speakers. However, the contrasts between the two types of clefts and between the two types of topicalization are similar. Therefore, we can say that an agent-patient argument order helps everyone, but heritage speakers depend on it. Additionally, case is a useful cue for the IceIce speakers, but many heritage speakers do not make any use of it. Lastly, we could argue that frequency/naturalness is important for older (but not younger) non-heritage speakers, since the long passives scores are significantly lower than the scores for the short passive (long passives are less common in Icelandic than in English, for instance). It is also interesting to note that the older IceIce speakers are the only group where the scores for the New impersonal/passive are lower than the scores of the active, despite the fact that this construction is not used in North America, to the best of our knowledge. As pointed out above, this is a construction that is hardly ever used by older speakers of IceIce, so familiarity will arguably not play a role for them.[7]

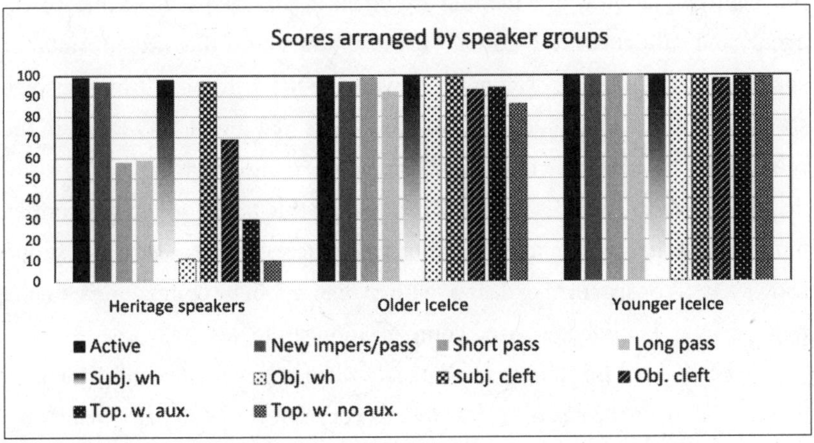

FIGURE 12.4. Scores on the sentence-picture matching test arranged by speaker groups.

Summing up, we can say that aging effects are present in the data but are much less extensive than the effects of being a heritage speaker. The aging effects are qualitatively different, allowing us to partly disentangle the different components of difficulties in the understanding of complex sentences. In general, the results underline the need for a broader interpretation of age correlations in heritage language studies and point to possible confounds in language comprehension/processing research. More specifically, the fact that the two groups of adult IceIce speakers show (minor) difficulties in the same sentence types that prove the hardest for heritage speakers, children, and people with aphasia provides further evidence for Hypothesis B. Certain sentences are difficult for all groups of speakers.

‖ CONCLUSION

Although the sentence-picture matching method has been used to some extent in previous research on heritage languages, our study involves a systematic comparison of more constructions and more groups of speakers than any studies of which we are aware. This allows us to reach the following conclusions.

Although certain sentence types prove to be difficult across all five groups of speakers we tested, more specific patterns are present. The heritage speakers show results similar to those found in language acquisition data: rigid word order interpretation where the first argument is analyzed as the subject (and agent) and case cues are ignored. This is contrary to some of the results for speakers with aphasia but consistent with previous findings from heritage speakers of other languages. One of the factors that might play a role in the NAI speakers' results is their age, since processing abilities are known to decline in healthy aging. Our results show that this factor would play only a minor role. When compared with the heritage speakers, the older IceIce group shows a less consistent and clear pattern, which might be compatible with the hypothesis of knowledge-based compensation strategies.

In general, we find that some sentences seem to be complex and difficult to understand for everyone, or at least for our very diverse set of participants. We hope that such a simple finding provides a useful reminder that the performance of speakers in a given task cannot easily be attributed to a specific aspect of their background, and neither can it justify certain assumptions about the speakers' general linguistic capabilities.

NOTES

1 In a previous article (Magnúsdóttir, Nowenstein, and Thráinsson 2018), we reported on the score by twenty-one of the thirty-three Icelandic heritage speakers included here. Hence, the figures in the present paper are slightly different but the conclusions are the same.

2 For a presentation of some of the arguments for Hypothesis A, see the overview paper by Grodzinsky (2000). For a critical discussion, partly supporting Hypothesis B, see the comments accompanying that paper. See also Grodzinsky's replies to these and the papers by Grodzinsky (2006) and Drai (2006) for further discussions along the same lines. Compare also Hirsch and Wexler (2006) on word order and passive, and Kemper and Sumner (2001) on working memory, sentence length, vocabulary, and complex grammar.

3 The New impersonal/passive construction was not a part of the test administered to the aphasic subjects.

4 For a discussion of how to account for intersubject variation in the performance of aphasics, see Drai (2006).

5 The children tested by Hólmfríður Hreggviðsdóttir (2018) were in general older than the ones reported on here and were able to make more use of the case-marking cue.

6 Nested comparison of mixed effects logistic regression models—first for the general dataset and then for each sentence type. The fit of the general model (Likelihood Ratio Test) improved significantly for each added fixed effect: age ($\chi 2$ (1) = 15.43, $p < 0.001$, ±heritage $\chi 2$ (1) = 70.43, $p < 0.001$, and sentence type $\chi 2$ (9) = 887.90, $p < 0.001$). The age and ±heritage variables both improved the model fit for long passives and topicalization sentences without an auxiliary but patterned differently otherwise.

7 Note also that one of the differences between regular passive and the New impersonal/passive is the case marking of the argument, cf. *Strákurinn er barinn* 'The boy (nom.) is hit' versus *Það er barið strákinn lit.* 'There is hit the boy (acc.).' For older speakers of IceIce, who do not use the New impersonal/passive, this may contribute to the strangeness of the construction, whereas case marking seems to be generally ignored by many speakers of NAI.

REFERENCES

Anderssen, Merete, and Marit Westergaard. 2016. "Word Order Variation in Norwegian Heritage Language. Complexity, Frequency or Crosslinguistic Influence." Paper presented at Georgetown University Round Table (GURT 2016), 10–12 March.

Arnbjörnsdóttir, Birna. 2006. *North American Icelandic: The Life of a Language*. Winnipeg: University of Manitoba Press.

Benmamoun, Elabbas, Silvina Montrul, and Maria Polinsky. 2013. "Heritage Languages and Their Speakers: Opportunities and Challenges for Linguistics." *Theoretical Linguistics* 39: 129–81.

Burke, Deborah, and Meredith Shafto. 2008. "Language and Aging." In *The Handbook of Aging and Cognition*, edited by Fergus I. M. Craik and Timothy A. Salthouse, 373–443. 3rd ed. New York: Psychology Press.

Drai, Dan. 2006. "Evaluating Deficit Patterns of Broca Aphasics in the Presence of High Intersubject Variability." In *Broca's Region*, edited by Yosef Grodzinsky and Katrin Amunts, 108–18. Oxford: Oxford University Press.

Federmeier, Kara, and Marta Kutas. 2005. "Aging in Context. Age Related Changes in Context Use during Language Comprehension." *Psychophysiology* 42 (2): 133–41.

Ferreira, Fernanda. 2003. "The Misinterpretation of Noncanonical Sentences." *Cognitive Psychology* 47: 164–203.

Gerken, LouAnn, and Michele E. Shady. 1996. "*The Picture Selection Task.*" In *Language, Speech, and Communication: Methods for Assessing Children's Syntax*, edited by Dana McDaniel, Cecile McKee, and Helen S. Cairns, 125–45. Cambridge: MIT Press.

Grodzinsky, Yosef. 2000. "The Neurology of Syntax: Language Use without Broca's Area." *Behavioral and Brain Sciences* 23: 1–71.

———. 2006. "A Blueprint for a Brain Map of Syntax." In *Broca's Region*, edited by Yosef Grodzinsky and Katrin Amunts, 83–107. Oxford: Oxford University Press.

Hirsch, Christopher, and Kenneth Wexler. 2006. "Acquiring Verbal Passives. Evidence for a Maturational Account." Paper presented at the Annual Meeting of the Linguistics Society of America, Albuquerque, New Mexico, 5–8 January.

Hreggviðsdóttir, Hólmfríður. 2018. "Skilningur íslenskra barna á mismunandi setningagerðum, með og án sýnilegrar fallmörkunar" [Icelandic children's comprehension of different syntactic structures with and without overt case marking]. Master's thesis, University of Iceland.

Kemper, Susan, and Aaron Sumner. 2001. "The Structure of Verbal Abilities in Young and Older Adults." *Psychology and Aging* 16 (2): 312–22.

Magnúsdóttir, Sigríður. 2000. "On Grammatical Knowledge in Agrammatism. Evidence from Icelandic." PhD diss., Boston University.

Magnúsdóttir, Sigríður, Iris Edda Nowenstein, and Höskuldur Thráinsson. 2018. "Að skilja skrýtnar setningar" [Understanding strange sentences]. In *Sigurtunga: Vesturíslenskt mál og menning*, edited by Birna Arnbjörnsdóttir, Höskuldur Thráinsson, and Úlfar Bragason, 303–22. Reykjavík: Háskólaútgáfan.

Magnúsdóttir, Sigríður, and Sigríður Arndís Þórðardóttir. 2013. *Setningafræðipróf. Skilningur barna á ólíkum setningagerðum* [A test of the understanding of different syntactic structures]. Reykjavík: The National University Hospital of Iceland.

Maling, Joan, and Sigríður Sigurjónsdóttir. 2002. "The 'New Impersonal' Construction in Icelandic." *Journal of Comparative Germanic Linguistics* 5: 97–142.

Polinsky, Maria. 2009. "What Breaks in A- and A-bar Chains under Incomplete Acquisition." Poster presented at CUNY Sentence Processing Conference, University of California, Davis, 26–29 March. https://scholar.harvard.edu/files/mpolinsky/files/CUNY2009-chains_poster.latest.pdf.

Sigurðsson, Einar Freyr. 2012. "Germynd en samt þolmynd. Um nýju þolmyndina í íslensku" [Active yet passive. On the new passive in Icelandic]. Master's thesis, University of Iceland.

Sigurjónsdóttir, Sigríður. 2015. "Acquisition of the New Impersonal Construction in Icelandic." *Proceedings of the 39th Annual Boston University Conference on Language Development*, 385–97. Somerville, MA: Cascadilla Press.

Wingfield, Arthur, and Murray Grossman. 2006. "Language and the Aging Brain: Patterns of Neural Compensation Revealed by Functional Brain Imaging." *Journal of Neurophysiology* 96 (6): 2830–39.

Þórðardóttir, Sigríður Arndís. 2014. "Skilningur barna á ólíkum setningagerðum. Þróun kynjamunar, tengsl við menntun foreldra og lestrarvenjur fjölskyldunnar" [Children's comprehension of different syntactic structures]. Master's thesis, University of Iceland.

CHAPTER 13

"And the Dog Is Sleeping Too": The Use of the Progressive in North American Icelandic

KRISTÍN M. JÓHANNSDÓTTIR

WHEN WE SPEAK we make all kinds of decisions regarding the structure of our narrative. One of the things we do unconsciously is to bind our narrative in time. Are we talking about something that has already happened or something that is going on right now? Does our narrative refer to something that has not yet happened? The words we choose and the sentence structure usually aim at giving our audience certain information about the time of events. In most cases we can choose various ways to deliver this information, and we can assume that someone with a strong sense of the language and an extensive vocabulary uses more expressive language and has more varied ways to describe relations in time than someone who speaks the language less fluently. It can also be assumed that someone who stops using the mother tongue at a young age, or who does not speak it very regularly during the adult years, uses fewer and in some ways less complicated structures than someone who is surrounded by their mother tongue throughout their life.

Most of the North American Icelanders who still speak Icelandic share in common that they spoke Icelandic for the first six years of their lives or so, but then English took over and Icelandic became the home language that they spoke with their parents, siblings, relatives, and friends but did not use in the community (see, for example, Neijmann 2018). Icelandic therefore became a heritage language and North American Icelanders became heritage language speakers. It is common to heritage languages that certain elements have the tendency to be simplified, particularly those that do not have a direct correlation in the majority language—for instance, morphological case in North American Icelandic (NAI). Certain modes of expression can thus be standardized to some extent, such as how the speaker expresses the relation between time and events. This is indeed the case in NAI as it is now spoken in Canada and the United States. The focus in this chapter is on one example of such simplification, the *progressive aspect.* The progressive aspect is particularly interesting as it is similar in the two languages, but there are nevertheless certain differences in the use of the progressive between them, particularly when it comes to certain verbs of posture (for example, *sit/sitja, lie/liggja*) or residence in a certain place (*live/búa*). We would therefore expect the progressive aspect to be used with a greater variety of verbs in NAI than in Home Icelandic.

PROGRESSIVE ASPECT IN ENGLISH

In narration all kinds of decisions have to be made regarding structure and presentation, such as how to bind the narration in time. If a past event is being described, the past tense is used and sometimes also an adverbial phrase that gives further information, such as *yesterday*:

1. John **biked** to school *yesterday.*

However, when the present tense of the verbs is used, the meaning differs based on the nature of the verbs. The present tense of verbs describing some kind of a state, such as *know* and *live,* indicates a situation:

2. Ben **knows** many poems.

Verbs that refer to events rather get the reading of repeated events or a habit:

3. Gertie **smokes** cigarettes.

This means that if the speaker intends to report on an event that is going on at the time of speaking, the so-called progressive aspect is used. In English this means using the present participle; that is, the verb *be* plus the affix *-ing* on the main verb:

4. John **is *eating***.

This construction is also frequently used when the idea is to describe what is going on at a particular time (5a) or even when some other event is taking place (5b).

5. **a.** John **was eating** *at 3:00 o'clock.*
   b. John **was eating** *when Adam entered the kitchen.*

The progressive shows the relation between two times: the **event time**, the time when John was eating; and the **reference time**, which in (5a) is at 3:00 and in (5b) the time that Adam entered the kitchen.

The progressive construction of English is in some ways simpler than the present or past tense as the main verb is always in the present participle *-ing* form and only the auxiliary *be* is inflected for person, number, and tense. Research has shown that those who speak English as a second language use the progressive considerably more than those who speak it as a first language (Ranta 2006), and one of the explanations given is that it is quite easy to learn the construction in English, compared with other sentence structures, as it involves only adding one affix to the main verb (Dulay and Burt 1973). In addition research indicates that the progressive is learned earlier in English than similar constructions in other languages (Giacalone Ramat 1997).

Let us now look at the progressive in Icelandic to compare the two languages.

PROGRESSIVE ASPECT IN ICELANDIC

Like English, Icelandic uses special inflections or auxiliaries to describe whether an event has taken place or is taking place:

6. a. Jón **át** melónu.
Jón ate (past) melon
'Jón ate a melon'.

b. Jón **étur** melónu.
Jón eats (present) melon
'Jón eats a melon'.

The sentence in (6a) describes an event that has already taken place. However, even though the verb in (6b) is in the present tense, it does not necessarily mean that John is eating melons at this very moment but instead that he is a melon-eater. To properly get the reading that an event is ongoing, Icelandic uses the progressive, just like English. The Icelandic progressive is formed with the auxiliary verb *vera* 'be', inflected appropriately (by person, number, and tense), as well as the main verb in the infinitive:

7. a. Jón **er** *að borða.*
Jón is to eat (inf.)
'Jón is eating'.

b. Börnin **eru** *að drekka.*
children the are to drink (inf.)
'The children are drinking'.

In many ways, using the progressive in Icelandic is easier than using the present or past tense as Icelandic verbs conjugate by person, number, tense, and mood and can be either regular or irregular. A learner of Icelandic, whether a child learning it as a first language or someone learning it as a foreign language, needs to learn the rules for verbal inflection, and these are slightly different for the various inflectional classes. These rules make it possible for the language learner to generate over twenty inflectional forms for each main verb. Here, we do not even count the past participle, which inflects by gender, number, and case, both weak and strong. As the progressive requires only conjugation of the copula, a learner of Icelandic can use any verb in the progressive, even if they know only its infinitive form, as long as they can conjugate the copula. The use of the progressive is therefore not only easier for someone learning the language but also for someone who does not use the language very much, and particularly if they have rarely used it since they were a child. This could influence the use of the progressive in NAI.

Even though the progressive in Icelandic is mostly used in the same way as in English, there are certain verbs that are common in the progressive in English whereas corresponding verbs are generally not possible in the progressive construction in Icelandic. These are verbs that indicate posture (8a), verbs of staying (8b), weather verbs (8c), the linking verb *be* (8d), and verbs like *sleep* where the division between states and events are not always very clear (8e):

8. **a.** The cat is sitting on the floor.
   b. John is living with his parents.
   c. It is raining.
   d. Adam is being a fool.
   e. He is sleeping.

In Icelandic corresponding verbs are typically ungrammatical in the progressive:[1]

9. **a.** Kötturinn **situr/*er að sitja** á gólfinu.
   cat.the sits/is to sit on floor.the
   'The cat sits/is sitting on the floor'.

   b. Jón **býr/*er að búa** hjá foreldrum sínum.
   Jón lives/is to live at parents his
   'John lives/is living with his parents'.

   c. Það **rignir/*er að rigna**.
   it rains/is to rain
   'It rains/is raining'.

   d. Adam **er** fífl/??**að vera** fífl.
   Adam is idiot/to be idiot
   'Adam is an idiot/being an idiot'.

e. Hann **sefur/??er að sofa**.
he sleeps/is to sleep
'He is sleeping'.

Even though the use of the progressive in Icelandic and English is in many ways comparable, there are obviously some differences between the languages in this respect, which makes it interesting to see how the progressive works in NAI.

PROGRESSIVE ASPECT IN NAI

Two main methods were used in this research: a) participants took a test where their use of tense and aspect was explored, and b) they told a story based on pictures in a book.

The test was divided into two parts, Test A and Test B. Test A showed three pictures on each page. The first picture showed a man who was about to do something, the second showed him performing that action, and in the third he had completed the action. In the first and third pictures we were looking for inchoative aspect and the perfective, but the middle picture focused on the progressive. The sentences in (10) are typical descriptions of the event shown in picture 1:[2]

FIGURE 13.1. Example of pictures from Test A.

10. a. Maðurinn **ætlar að fara að borða**...
Man.the intends to go to eat
'The man is about to eat'.

b. Maðurinn **er að borða**...
Man.the is to eat
'The man is eating'.

c. Maðurinn **er búinn að borða**... /
Man.the is finished to eat
'The man has finished eating'.

As this study focuses on the progressive, we will be looking only at the results of the b-sentences.

In Test B the participants were shown pictures of a man performing various actions, and they were asked questions such as "Can you describe this picture?" A possible response is given in (11a). In order to get the past tense, the participants were given questions such as: "If this had happened yesterday, how would you then describe it?" A possible response is given in (11b):

11. a. Maðurinn **borðar/er að borða**...
Man.the eats/is to eat
'The man **eats/is eating** ...'.

b. Maðurinn **borðaði/var að borða**...'
Man.the ate/was to eat
'The man **ate/was eating** ...'.

Then the participants were shown the picture book *Frog, Where Are You?* by Mercer Mayer (1969). There is no text in the book, but the pictures tell the story of a boy and his dog where they end up in all kinds of adventures looking for the boy's pet frog that had escaped during the night. The participants turned the pages of the book and told the story as they saw it unfold in the pictures. This form of linguistic research is open, and the speakers can choose what to describe. This means that if they are not sure of a particular word or grammatical item, they can simply skip it. They are, however, bound by the events taking place in the story. What makes this story particularly useful for this kind of study are the relations between various events, so the speaker has to describe the timeline of the story.

The interviews were recorded and transcribed. Descriptive statistics were used for calculations where the number of answers was given as well as their proportion.

The Participants

The data used in this study were collected in Canada and the United States in 2013 and 2014. Fourteen speakers took the verb tests, seven men and seven women, all from Manitoba. Their average age was seventy-eight years. Thirty-nine speakers told the *Frog* story, twelve men and twenty-seven women. Of these, twenty-one live in Manitoba, two in Saskatchewan, five in Alberta, three in British Columbia, five in North Dakota, and three in Washington State. The average age was 76.2 years.

In order to compare NAI with Home Icelandic, the same tests were given to Icelandic participants. In 2013 ten Home Icelanders took the verb test (six men and four women), and in 2015 nine Home Icelanders told the *Frog* story (five men and four women). The speakers chosen were a similar age as the speakers in North America. The average age of those who took the verb test was 70.2 years and those who told the *Frog* story, 73.1 years.

In addition sixteen speakers (eleven women and five men) told the *Frog* story in English. All of them also told the story in Icelandic. All were from Manitoba, and their average age was 75.6.

RESULTS OF THE STUDY

When the results of the study are examined, we see a considerable difference between the North American Icelanders and the Home Icelanders in the comparison group, particularly with regard to the use of the progressive.

Test A

As we see in Table 13.1, the North American Icelanders use the progressive considerably more than the Home Icelanders.[3] The North American Icelanders used the progressive 71.3 percent of the time, as in the following examples:[4]

12. *Progressive aspect*
    a. Hérna **er** hann **að klæða** krakkann. (R84)
    Here is he to dress kid.the
    'Here he is dressing the kid'.

    b. Hann **er að saga**. (R83)
    He is to saw
    'He is sawing'.

Instead of the progressive, the Home Icelanders were more likely to use simple present (thirteen), some kind of an inchoative (fourteen), and even describe the status of the event (fifteen):

13. Hann **opnar** pakkann og **snýr** sér við. (Í8)
    He opens package.the and turns self around
    'He opens the package and turns around'.

14. Og 8b hann **er byrjaður að saga**. (Í2)
    And 8b he is started to saw
    'And in 8b he has started sawing'.

15. Og ...hérna **er** hann **búinn að koma** því í peysuna . . . . (Í5)
    And here is he finished to come it in sweater.the
    'And he has managed to put the sweater on [the child]'.

TEST A	HOME ICELANDIC		NAI	
	REAL NUMBERS	PERCENTAGES	REAL NUMBERS	PERCENTAGES
Progressive	29	38.2%	72	71.3%
Simple present	21	27.6%	7	6.9%
Other	26	34.2%	22	21.8%

TABLE 13.1. Use of the progressive and simple present in Test A.

Test B

The results from Test B do not show as clear a difference as the results from Test A. As Table 13.2 shows, the Home Icelanders use the progressive 73 percent of the time, but the North American Icelanders, 89 percent. However, the speakers of North American Icelandic never used the simple present in this context, whereas the Home Icelanders used it 25 percent of the time. The progressive was thus by far the most common sentence structure of the North American Icelanders, just as in Test A. However, the Home Icelanders used the progressive much more in this part of the test than in Test A. The reason for this might be that when the picture is shown on its own, the focus is completely on what is ongoing at the time, in which case the progressive is the most natural structure. In Test A, however, the focus was no longer on the event itself but on how it evolved, which means that the speakers sometimes reported on the event having now started.

TEST B PRESENT TENSE	HOME ICELANDIC		NAI	
	REAL NUMBERS	PERCENTAGES	REAL NUMBERS	PERCENTAGES
Progressive	111	73%	85	89.5%
Simple present	38	25%	0	0%
Other	3	2%	10	10.5%

TABLE 13.2. Results from the present tense part of Test B.

Let us also explore the difference in the use of the simple present. Home Icelanders use it 25 percent of the time but speakers of NAI not at all. As mentioned above, the simple present of both languages usually has the meaning that a certain event is general, some kind of a habit or situation, but not necessarily that it is ongoing at a certain time—the progressive is used for that. And yet, the Home Icelanders use the simple present 25 percent of the time for events that are ongoing! This might indicate a slight difference between the meaning of the simple present in the two languages, but we cannot explain exactly what it is. But what about the past tense?

TEST B PAST TENSE	HOME ICELANDIC		NAI	
	REAL NUMBERS	PERCENTAGES	REAL NUMBERS	PERCENTAGES
Progressive	40	26.7%	67	56.8%
Simple present	109	72.7%	32	27.1%
Other	1	0.7%	19	16.1%

TABLE 13.3. Results from the past tense part of Test B.

Again the progressive is much more common in NAI, even though the numbers are somewhat lower than in Test A. The progressive in the past tense is almost always used when describing that a certain event took place at a certain particular time or during events, as in the examples from (5) when John was eating at 3:00 and when Adam entered the kitchen. In both sentences (5a, b), the reference time is a particular time that falls within the event time. When the reference time is considerably long, such as *yesterday*, it is difficult to place it within the event time, and the progressive is generally not used in such a situation.[5] Instead, the simple present is used. However, as the question was simply how the participants would describe the event had it taken place yesterday, *í gær* 'yesterday' does not have to refer to the whole day but might simply mean that the event took place at some point yesterday.

16. Í gær var þessi maður að klæða barn. (G29)
In yesterday was this man to dress child
'Yesterday, this man was dressing a child'.

As can be seen in Table 13.3, 26.7 percent of the Icelandic sentences in this part of the test are in the progressive, but in those cases they seem to refer to events that can take a longer time, as in (17), or adverbs such as *þarna* 'there' give the reference time, as in (18):

17. Í gær var hann að sauma . . . treyju. (Í7)
In yesterday was he to sew shirt
'Yesterday, he was sewing a shirt'.

18. Þarna var hann að borða spaghettí. (Í2)
There was he to eat spaghetti
'There he was eating spaghetti'.

As there are several examples of Home Icelanders using the progressive with the reference time *yesterday* in a similar way as the North American Icelanders, such sentences are obviously not completely ungrammatical in Icelandic.

The *Frog* Story

When we analyze events in the *Frog* story by sentence structures, we see a similar difference: the speakers of NAI use the progressive in 40.7 percent of the cases but the Home Icelanders only in 6.1 percent of the cases. Instead, the Home Icelanders use the simple present in 77.5 percent of all sentences. The NAI speakers who never used the simple present in Test B use it in 28.1 percent of the cases in the *Frog* story. These results are in accordance with the results from the tests: North American Icelanders use the progressive much more than Home Icelanders do—both when speaking English and Icelandic—whereas the Home Icelanders are more likely to use the simple present. However, the North American Icelanders use the simple present much more in the *Frog* story than in the tests, and at this point it is not clear why that is.[6]

This is the only data we have from the NAI speakers speaking English, and the results are quite clear. Even though they do not use the progressive as much as in their Icelandic, the difference is substantive, and it is obvious that they use it a lot more than the Icelanders do. So, the difference is not just between the two Icelandic dialects but also between North American English and Home Icelandic.

	HOME ICELANDIC	
	REAL NUMBERS	PERCENTAGES
Progressive	30	5.8%
Simple present	378	73.3%
Simple past	32	6.2%
Other	76	14.7%

	NAI	
	REAL NUMBERS	PERCENTAGES
Progressive	521	41.7%
Simple present	350	28%
Simple past	122	9.8%
Other	211	20.5%

	ENGLISH	
	REAL NUMBERS	PERCENTAGES
Progressive	374	36.9%
Simple present	480	47.3%
Simple past	129	12.7%
Other	31	3.1%

TABLE 13.4. Aspect and tense in the *Frog* story.

WHERE ICELANDIC AND ENGLISH DIFFER

As mentioned before, the use of the progressive in English and Icelandic differs in certain aspects, particularly as certain verbs occur freely in the progressive in English but not in Icelandic. Unfortunately, none of these verbs were a part of the tests, so we need to look at the results from the *Frog* story to see how these verbs behave in NAI. Two such verbs appeared there, the verbs *sofa* 'sleep' and *standa* 'stand'. Both appeared in the progressive and in the simple present:[7]

19. a. Og hundurinn e- **er að standa** á honum...(G70)
And dog.the is to stand on him
'An the dog is standing on him'.

b. Og hann **er að sofa**. Og hundurinn **er að sofa** líka. (A57)
And he is to sleep. And dog.the is to sleep too
'And he's sleeping. And the dog is sleeping too'.

20. a. Og hundurinn **stendur** upp á loggnum. (A52)
And dog.the stands up on log.the
'And the dog is standing on the log'.

b. Og hundurinn **sefur** til fóta í rúminu með honum. (R81)
And dog.the sleeps to feet in bed.the with him
'And the dog is sleeping at his feet in the bed with him'.

When looking through the data from Hallfreður Örn Eiríksson and Olga María Franzdóttir (Sigurðsson 2012), we see that sentences like the ones in (19) are rare but can nevertheless be found, as seen in the following example:

21. Þá kalla ég á fósturforeldra mína, sem mér fannst að **vera að standa**
Then call I at foster.parents mine that I found to be to stand
í eldhúsinu.
in kitchen.the
'Then I call to my foster parents, who I felt were standing in the kitchen'.

The fact that posture verbs can be found in the progressive in these examples from 1972 can indicate influence from English, as comparable sentences would be in the progressive in English (for example, *people* ***were sitting*** *together*) but not in Home Icelandic of that time. Sentences as these are nevertheless becoming more common in Icelandic now, even though they can still be seen as rare (Jóhannsdóttir 2011, 2015).

Possible Reasons for the Increased Use of the Progressive in NAI

The results discussed here indicate that NAI speakers use the progressive considerably more than do Home Icelanders, who are more likely to use the simple present or past. It is possible that this heavy use of the progressive has to do with its simple form, given that it does not require as much knowledge of the complicated morphological system of the language as the simple present or past. It is therefore natural to expect that the progressive is commonly used more by those who have a weaker grip on the grammar of the language. That is clearly seen in Alexander Andrason's study (2008) of the syntactic construction BÚNA, which is common in the Icelandic of some immigrants and consists of the construction *vera búin(n) að* 'have finished doing'. The construction has been simplified, with the inflected copula deleted (as in *Ég* ***búna*** *kaupa bíl* for *Ég* ***er búin(n) að*** *kaupa bíl*), and the construction is likewise used in a much wider context than the corresponding structure among native speakers of Home Icelandic. Even though we do not have any clear examples of such simplification in our North American data, as the copula is generally not deleted and there are no other clear indications of a change in the construction itself, it is clear that the use of the progressive has also expanded in North American Icelandic.

As previously mentioned, heritage speakers have the tendency to somewhat standardize how they express certain information, such as the relations between time and events, and in that way the variability of the language is limited. Such overstandardization is very common in the morphology of heritage speakers (see, for example, Polinsky and Kagan 2007), and the increase of the progressive fits with such theories. Birna Arnbjörnsdóttir (2006) has also mentioned such standardization in NAI, such as irregular verbs being inflected as regular ones, changes in the inflectional category of verbs, and simplification of the inflectional paradigm of irregular verbs (see also Arnbjörnsdóttir and Thráinsson 2018). This is particularly common in the past tense of verbs, where the difference between regular and irregular verbs is clearest. Birna Arnbjörnsdóttir's results are in accordance with the results of researchers Hrafnhildur Ragnarsdóttir, Hanne Gram Simonsen, and Kim Plunkett (1999), who showed that the complicated morphological system of Icelandic influences the past tense use by children during their acquisition period, as they have the tendency to generalize the past tense ending of regular verbs during their first years. The difference between Home Icelandic and NAI when it comes to the progressive is particularly clear in the past tense: the Home Icelanders barely use it, but North American Icelanders use it considerably. Here it is worth keeping in mind that most of the North American Icelanders of the study learned English no later than at around six years of age, so it is likely that many of them had not fully mastered Icelandic verbal morphology before English took over.

However, we should not forget that even though the North American Icelanders use the progressive more in their Icelandic than their English, they also use it much more in their English than the Home Icelanders in their Icelandic. That, and the fact that the progressive in English is used with a greater variety of verbs than the Icelandic progressive, shows that the two progressives do not behave exactly the same, even though they are quite comparable. So the NAI progressive might be somewhat influenced by English. Therefore, this high frequency of the progressive in NAI could be due to the synergistic effect of the progressive being morphologically simple and as a result of influence from English.

CLOSING REMARKS

The North American Icelanders in this study used the progressive considerably more than did the Home Icelanders in the comparison group. It is not possible to claim that this goes for all North American Icelanders, but as the difference is extensive in this sample, we must find it likely that we would see similar tendencies if the data pool was larger.

A possible explanation for the difference could be that we have here synergetic effects of two factors. First, Home Icelanders, who not only have Icelandic as their mother tongue but many of whom have it as their only language, have a stronger language awareness of Icelandic and a bigger vocabulary, and speak it more fluently than those who have barely used the language since they started school, except in discussions with a few particular individuals within the family or possibly friends. The North American Icelanders therefore have to rely on simpler constructions and have the tendency of using the same ones over and over. By this overuse of certain construction, the language becomes more standardized, something that is well-known among heritage language speakers, and comes from the position they are in, that is, to have as a mother tongue a language that is little or barely used in the society. Second, as the North American Icelanders also used the progressive more in their English than the Icelanders in their Icelandic, this frequent use of the progressive in NAI might be to some extent reflecting the use of the progressive in English.

As has been pointed out in many articles, research into NAI does not only give us information on this particular dialect spoken in North America, it is also an important addition to research into heritage language in general and how heritage languages develop.

NOTES

1 Note that * means that the construction is unacceptable in Icelandic. There are nevertheless some cases where it may be used in certain contexts, such as in the response Ég er þá ekkert að búa hér lengur fyrst þú . . . 'Then I'm not living here anymore, since you . . .'. Two question marks indicate that the variant is rejected by most speakers but not all.

2 The pictures are from a test created by Sigríður Magnúsdóttir and Höskuldur Thráinsson for another purpose.

3 Behind these numbers are fourteen North American Icelanders but only ten Home Icelanders. It should also be kept in mind that the speakers didn't necessarily use the same number of sentences.

4 The letter-number combination in parentheses after each sentence refers to the speaker. The letter refers to the place where the speakers live (R for Riverton, Í for Iceland, et cetera), and the number refers to the (random) number they were given.

5 It is worth mentioning that when the event time is long, this can work:

John was playing football yesterday.

Gerry was writing his book all year last year.

6 This goes, of course, only for the *Frog* story, as the North American Icelanders did not take the verb test in English.

7 It is not clear that the speakers thought of the sentences in (19) as the progressive, even though they use that construction. The fact that English uses the progressive with such verbs does, however, somewhat support the hypothesis that this is in fact a progressive reading.

REFERENCES

Andrason, Alexander. 2008. "The BÚNA-construction in Pidgin Icelandic." *Íslenskt mál* 30: 121–40.

Arnbjörnsdóttir, Birna. 2006. *North American Icelandic: The Life of a Language*. Winnipeg: University of Manitoba Press.

Arnbjörnsdóttir, Birna, and Höskuldur Thráinsson. 2018. "Hvað einkennir vesturíslensku? Yfirlit um fyrri rit og rannsóknir" [What characterizes Western Icelandic? An overview of previous publications and research]. In *Sigurtunga: Vesturíslenskt mál og menning*, edited by Birna Arnbjörnsdóttir, Höskuldur Thráinsson, and Úlfar Bragason, 211–55. Reykjavík: Háskólaútgáfan.

Dulay, Heidi C., and Marina K. Burt. 1973. "Should We Teach Children Syntax?" *Language Learning* 23: 245–58.

Giacalone Ramat, Anna. 1997. "Progressive Periphrases, Markedness, and Second-Language Data." In *Language and Its Ecology*, edited by Stig Eliasson and Ernst Håkon Jahr, 261–85. Berlin: Mouton de Gruyter.

Jóhannsdóttir, Kristín M. 2011. "Aspects of the Progressive in English and Icelandic." PhD diss., University of British Columbia.

———. 2015. "'Nafnháttarsýki.' Um eðli og þróun orðasambandsins *vera að* + nafnháttur" [Infinitive sickness: On the nature and development of the phrase *vera að* + infinitive]. *Íslenskt mál og almenn málfræði* 37: 9–68.

Mayer, Mercer. 1969. *Frog, Where Are You?* New York: Dial Press.

Neijmann, Daisy. 2018."Mál til samskipta eða tengsla? Gildi íslenskunnar í Vesturheimi" [Communicative and symbolic functions of North American Icelandic]. In *Sigurtunga: Vesturíslenskt mál og menning*, edited by Birna Arnbjörnsdóttir, Höskuldur Thráinsson, and Úlfar Bragason, 279–302. Reykjavík: Háskólaútgáfan.

Polinsky, Maria, and Olga Kagan. 2007. "Heritage Languages: In the 'Wild' and in the Classroom." *Language and Linguistics Compass* 1 (5): 368–95.

Ragnarsdóttir, Hrafnhildur, Hanne Gram Simonsen, and Kim Plunkett. 1999. "The Acquisition of Past Tense Morphology in Icelandic and Norwegian Children: An Experimental Study." *Journal of Child Language* 26 (3): 577–618.

Ranta, Elina. 2006. "The 'Attractive' Progressive: Why use the *-ing* Form in English as a Lingua Franca?" *Nordic Journal of English Studies* 1 (2): 95–116.

Sigurðsson, Gísli, ed. 2012. *Sögur úr Vesturheimi.* Reykjavík: Stofnun Árna Magnússonar í íslenskum fræðum.

CHAPTER 14

Language and Identity: The Case of North American Icelandic

LAURA MOQUIN AND KIRSTEN WOLF

EXAMINATIONS OF NORTH American Icelandic (NAI) have largely focused on phonological, morphological, syntactic, or lexicographic aspects; sociolinguistic topics have received limited attention, though Birna Arnbjörnsdóttir (2006) has addressed different social contexts and their effects on the two varieties of Icelandic, and in more recent articles, Ásta Svavarsdóttir (2018) includes an account of historical sociolinguistic circumstances (see also Ásta Svavarsdóttir, this volume), and Daisy Neijmann (2018) discusses the symbolic role of language as it relates to feelings of identity. The aim of our chapter is to contribute to this growing field of work by investigating notions of identity in heritage communities as reflected in participant responses to a series of questions about their own associations of language with heritage identity.[1] Our survey seeks to get a sense of how important knowledge of Icelandic is as a component of heritage identity. More broadly, we wanted to learn more about the heritage language experience and language attitudes within this heritage language community. We take a descriptive approach and connect our findings to a variety of relevant theoretical perspectives.

Even though there are now few speakers of North American Icelandic, there are still lively, connected, and engaged heritage communities throughout

North America. Many heritage language communities are largely made up of individuals who feel strong ties to their heritage, yet do not use the heritage language as an everyday means of communication. It is important to include them in our efforts to understand the relationship between language, culture, and identity within heritage language communities. These individuals still have meaningful connections to the language of their communities and ancestors, but the language has taken on new roles and meanings.

BACKGROUND

Icelandic immigrants were no different from other immigrants in terms of wanting to keep their native language alive. Some of the most fervent efforts were in the establishment of a North American Icelandic press; the early immigrants published numerous books, newspapers, and periodicals in Icelandic. A variety of organizations, heritage societies, and interest groups were formed, which facilitated many opportunities for the immigrants to converse in Icelandic. There was also instruction in Icelandic—first at Wesley College (1901 to 1927) and later at the Jon Bjarnason Academy (1913 to 1940)—in Winnipeg. This was, of course, in addition to local elementary schools in the various Icelandic communities in North America (see the discussion in the introduction to this volume). However, one of the most significant testimonies to the desire of the Icelandic immigrants to preserve and promote the Icelandic language in North America is without doubt the establishment of the Chair of Icelandic at the University of Manitoba. Following years of campaigning and fundraising, the foundation of the Chair of Icelandic Language and Literature was formally announced by the president of the university in 1951, and classes commenced in the same year. This established an important institutional legacy for Icelandic language, literature, history, and culture to stand alongside the prolific grassroots efforts of the heritage communities themselves.

THEORETICAL CONSIDERATIONS

Our topic and some of our findings (especially those discussed in the analysis section below) run parallel with Daisy Neijmann's 2018 article. Therefore, we looked first to her selected theoretical points of departure, which proved helpful in aligning our own theoretical perspectives. She cites John Edwards (2009), who maintains that all languages serve similar symbolic and communicative purposes but that these purposes are separable, and further that a language can have a symbolic purpose without necessarily being used for communication. Neijmann's article also includes Fredrik Barth's (1969) description of societal demarcation and cultural division where divisions are flexible and changed by necessity, as well as Hubert Gans's (1979) concept of "symbolic ethnicity," where third and later generations hold on firmly to symbolic elements of ethnic identity.

We drew primarily on three points of theory as we compiled our survey and examined the results. The first echoes Edwards's emphasis on the separability of the symbolic and functional roles of language and comes from the field of linguistic anthropology, where the topic of language and identity has been thoroughly covered, and which, according to Mary Bucholtz and Kira Hall (2004), has become a central focus of the field: "Among the many symbolic resources available for the cultural production of identity, language is the most flexible and pervasive. The fact that so much scholarship on identity in sociocultural anthropology draws on linguistic evidence . . . attests to the crucial if often unacknowledged role language plays in the formation of cultural subjectivities" (Bucholtz and Hall 2004, 369).

Detailed study of language and identity is only beginning to emerge in heritage language work, and there is much to learn from these and other linguistic anthropologists (see also the work of Jonathan Rosa, for example, 2019). The characterization of language as a symbolic resource for identity production is especially relevant, as heritage language communities find much value in the heritage language even outside of its communicative purposes. Bucholtz and Hall also distinguish between social meaning and referential meaning: "It is precisely this duality of language—its ability to convey meaning at two levels, one semantic or referential and one pragmatic or contextual—that make it such a rich resource for semiotic production within human societies" (Bucholtz and Hall 2004, 377). The "semantic or referential" level refers to language's purpose as a tool for communication, and the "pragmatic or contextual" level refers to language's social and symbolic purposes. This information is helpful in delineating types of meaning and purpose, but it is important to make more sense of the unique and somewhat imbalanced purpose and meaning conditions found in heritage languages. For example, what does it mean for heritage identity when a heritage language has more social meaning and less referential meaning?

Our second theoretical point of reference complements and helps answer the question raised within the first: postvernacularity. The term, coined by Jeffrey Shandler (2005) in the context of Yiddish as a heritage language, describes when a language's symbolic value and social meaning take precedence over referential meaning and everyday communication. Shandler shines a positive light on this alternative experience of language: "Postvernacularity can be a liberating concept, prompting possibilities of language use other than the vernacular model of full fluency in an indigenous mother tongue. Thus, postvernacularity has important implications for the interrelation of language, culture, and identity—indeed, for the notion of what might constitute a 'speech community'" (Shandler 2005, 23). Postvernacularity can be found wherever language is being used or valued for what it conveys as a cultural symbol. It can be seen within the linguistic landscape of a heritage language community; it can be spoken, written, performed, remembered, and felt. How elements of the heritage language are used or experienced and what they mean to those who use and/or experience them are central to learning about the relationship between language and heritage identity, especially among a group often overlooked in the field of heritage linguistics in North America: monolingual speakers of English. We look to these individuals in particular to see if and how they challenge the notion of who constitutes the North American Icelandic "speech community."

The third theoretical perspective, "Hansen's Law," was a useful and relevant theory to check our own data against, considering the strong representation among our respondents (about 70 percent) from the third and later generations with North American Icelandic heritage. Sometimes called "the principle of third generation interest," this theory offers one account of intergenerational differences when it comes to interest in heritage language, culture, or history, and has been mentioned in other studies of heritage language communities in the United States (Wilkerson and Salmons 2019; Arvio 2019; Daniels 1988). We save further discussion of Hansen's Law for the section describing the participants, where it can be examined in closer proximity to our data.

METHODOLOGY

Like other examinations of language attitudes and identity within North American Icelandic communities (Arnbjörnsdóttir 1990;[2] Neijmann 2018), our results rely on the data and personal experiences shared by willing participants. Our survey-based examination is different, however, in regard to the sheer number of responses we received, which provided ample quantitative *and* qualitative data to consider. Moreover, we rely on additional theoretical frameworks and pay special attention to the third and later generations. We wrote twenty-five questions,[3] many of which are open-ended to allow respondents to be as detailed about their thoughts and experiences as they wished. Any question could be skipped, which meant that not every respondent answered every question in the survey. Surveys with less than 40 percent completion were not counted in our final tally.

We relied on the Department of Icelandic at the University of Manitoba, North American-Icelandic organizations, individuals, and social media (Facebook) for the distribution of the survey. The survey was launched on 8 April 2020, and within the first week, we had received 100 responses. When, on 20 June 2020, we ended the collection of data, we had received 349 responses from six Canadian provinces and more than thirty states in the United States. We provided the survey in two formats: one online through the survey software Qualtrics and another that could be filled out by hand and mailed to us. We recognize, of course, that there is a caveat to a survey of this kind and—by extension—our study and conclusions. Although we reached out to as many people as we possibly could via organizations and word of mouth, we were probably able to contact mainly those North Americans of

Icelandic descent who are connected to and active within Icelandic heritage groups and organizations.

Participant Overview

More than half (55 percent) of our survey respondents live in Canada, with most residing in Manitoba (21 percent). Respondents from Alberta (11 percent) and British Columbia (10 percent) made up the second-largest groups, while Ontario represented 5 percent and Saskatchewan 2 percent. Respondents from the U.S. contributed 45 percent of our survey responses but had much smaller regional concentrations. Utah led with 8 percent, while California (5 percent), North Dakota (4 percent), and Minnesota (3 percent) had slightly smaller groups. The remainder of respondents were widely dispersed throughout other U.S. states.

Sixty percent of all respondents identified themselves as being between the ages of fifty-five and eighty-four, with those age categories making up 79 percent of all third-generation respondents. We see significantly fewer survey responses from each of the other age groups. There are not many living speakers of North American Icelandic (see, for example, Arnbjörnsdóttir 2006, 2015), and Figure 14.1 reflects this already known fact. More than 75 percent of respondents report that their level of Icelandic is either limited or non-existent. Conversely, this means that almost a quarter of respondents feel fairly or very confident in their Icelandic language abilities. With so many of our respondents reporting their Icelandic language level as "non-existent" or "limited," our body of data that pertains to the non-speakers is ideal for investigating the ways in which identity can be connected to heritage language, even in the absence of active command of the language. That is to say, this is an excellent collection of data to explore postvernacular relationships within Icelandic heritage communities.

AGE RANGE	18–24	25–34	35–44	45–54	55–64	65–74	75–84	85+
%	4%	6%	9%	11%	24%	25%	17%	4%

TABLE 14.1. Ages of all respondents.

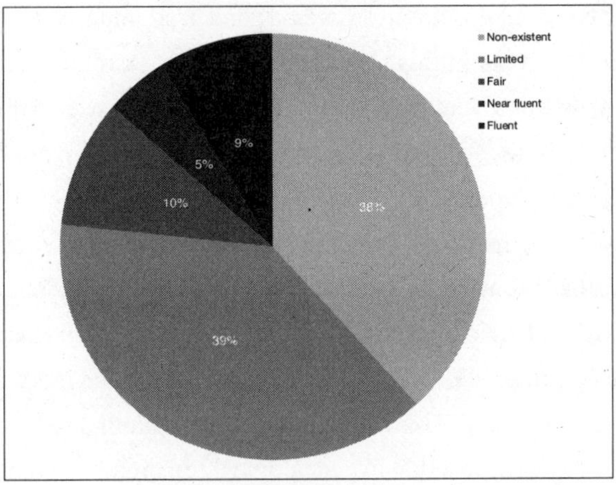

FIGURE 14.1. Self-reported language ability.

ANALYSIS

Respondents Reporting "Non-existent" Icelandic Language Level

Narrowing in further to the respondents who described their Icelandic language level to be "non-existent" (38 percent of all respondents), we see, overwhelmingly, that these individuals still value some kind of relationship with the Icelandic language. More than 90 percent of respondents in this group give some indication that they have reverence for or feel in some way connected to the Icelandic language. This sentiment was indicated in a variety of responses on the survey, but one such place was in the responses to the question "How important to you is it that Icelandic be maintained as a heritage language in North America?" See Table 14.2 for more details.

ANSWER	%	COUNT
Extremely important	19%	23
Very important	23%	29
Moderately important	26%	32
Slightly important	25%	31
Not at all important	7%	9
Total	100%	124

TABLE 14.2. Importance of maintaining Icelandic as a heritage language in North America among respondents reporting Icelandic language level as "non-existent".

Only 7 percent of this group answered, "not at all important." Thirty-seven percent of respondents in this same group provided explanations as to why and/or how they value Icelandic in the responses to a variety of the survey's open-ended questions. We placed these explanations into two non-hierarchical groups/categories depending on the manner in which respondents reported interacting with the heritage language, that is, externalized attachments and internalized attachments to the language, neither occurring more often than the other. Externalized attachments to the heritage language are characterized by actual use of language elements and by efforts made by the individual to learn or maintain the language. This includes taking or planning to take a language course, learning words to assist in genealogical research or an Iceland-themed hobby or interest (1), using Icelandic familial titles (2), choosing to give or to keep Icelandic names (3), using Icelandic phrases in speech or ceremony (4), and singing in Icelandic.

1. Doing genealogical work for the last 5 years has exposed me to written Icelandic. I still use Google Translate a lot but am about to get the "gist" of an obituary. There are about 100 words that I recognize.

2. My children called mom "Amma" and continuing the tradition, I am also "Amma" to my grandkids.

3. Our granddaughter (5th generation) married this past October and has kept her Icelandic surname.[4]

4. [I] incorporate certain words/phrases into everyday use: (i.e., calling to dinner table is always [ph] "garath savell").[5]

Internalized attachments to the heritage language are characterized by desires, feelings, and general appreciation. Examples include expressing a desire to learn the language, feeling connected to one's heritage by one's Icelandic name (5), enjoying the sound of Icelandic (6), encouragement and admiration of those studying Icelandic (7), and cherishing inherited artifacts containing Icelandic language (8); and genealogies, books, and writings.

5. I love being Icelandic, I love having the uniqueness of my Icelandic first name most of all and I have always been proud of that, I have an Icelandic named dog too.

6. I have some Icelandic songs—small choral pieces, and I enjoy the sound of the language.

7. [Icelandic language] classes are held on a regular basis at the Scandinavian Cultural Center—My full moral support.

8. My sons know of the family dictionary and grandfather's dissertation. (Written in Icelandic and translated into English.)

The importance of knowing cultural vocabulary, which can range from expletives to greetings to traditional foods, depending on the individual, was often emphasized and could be in either of these categories, depending on whether the individual used them or was simply familiar with them. Personal names were another theme that could be grouped into either category depending on whether the explanation was based in action or sentiment. In addition to seeing similar themes in both the externalized and internalized attachment categories, the individuals who provided details often offered a blended account including both kinds of attachments. These categories of heritage language attachments might tell us something about the different ways heritage language interacts with heritage identity; we suspect that externalized attachments parallel the expression of identity, as it is outwardly signalled to others, and that internalized attachments correspond with the inner elements of identity, reflecting the personal associations and feelings that help to construct identity.

Analysis: How Important Is Communicating in Icelandic?

Looking at the answers to what we considered to be our "big" question ("How important is communicating in Icelandic to your identity as someone of Icelandic heritage?"), we see that they are more or less evenly distributed (Table 14.3). Looking at this information in isolation does not tell us much, but when we take into consideration how important communicating in Icelandic is to a respondent's sense of identity as someone of Icelandic heritage compared with the level of self-described language ability (Table 14.4), there is a notable correlation.

ANSWER	%	COUNT
Extremely important	17%	54
Very important	14%	47
Moderately important	21%	69
Slightly important	27%	89
Not at all important	21%	68
Total	100%	327

TABLE 14.3. "How important is communicating in Icelandic to your identity as someone of Icelandic heritage?" (all respondents).

ANSWER	FLUENT	NEAR FLUENT	FAIR	LIMITED	NONE
Extremely important	23	8	10	10	3
Very important	1	6	10	23	7
Moderately important	2	2	10	36	19
Slightly important	0	0	3	48	38
Not at all important	1	0	1	13	53

TABLE 14.4. Degree of importance of the language broken down by self-described language ability of respondents (all respondents).

It appears that the less proficient a respondent is in Icelandic, the less important communicating in Icelandic is as a marker of identity for someone of Icelandic heritage. Several respondents at both ends of the scale qualified their own feelings with messages of understanding for differently balanced relationships with language and identity: see (9) and (10). This is not surprising, but it is a clear indication that the relationship between the importance of communicating in Icelandic and feelings of Icelandic identity is highly individualized, and that this is recognized and accepted within the community itself.

9. Language is a very important part of one's identity and I would like nothing more than to be able to learn to listen/speak/read/write more fluently. I don't feel that not being able to communicate fluently has diminished my sense of identity as someone of Icelandic descent, but I do acknowledge that if I had a better command of the language, my sense of identity would shift.
10. For me personally it is very important as it has given me greater access and understanding of Icelandic culture, history, traditions etc. I know that those Icelanders without language skills still have a very strong identity of being Icelandic and I am sure I would have too even without the opportunity to learn the language but in fact it is based more on emotion and based on a limited glimpse of Icelandic culture.

At the start of this project, we believed that the question "How important is communicating in Icelandic to your identity as someone of Icelandic heritage?" would be a leading feature of our collected data. This turned out not to be the case, even though the quantity and richness of the data we collected surpassed our expectations. With more than 75 percent of our respondents reporting limited to no Icelandic proficiency, we realize that it might have been better to formulate the question without emphasis on communication. We know now that the majority of respondents in this community are more likely to engage in and find value in postvernacular relationships with language. While evidence for this can be found in several areas of the survey, it would have been prudent to include questions that target this reality directly. Ideas for questions on future language and identity surveys include "What about the language is important or special to you?" or, more directly, "What symbolic significance, if any, does Icelandic hold for you?"

Analysis: The Third and Later Generations

We conclude this analysis of our survey with observations on notable findings within the third and later generations. Not only do the later generations make up the majority of our respondents (Figure 14.2), but their responses tend to differ from those of the first two generations, though certainly there is a thematic overlap. Within these later generational groups, there are distinct experiential themes and interpretations of terms that illustrate the relationship between heritage identity and elements or memories of the Icelandic language. Feelings of nostalgia, loss, or exclusion and deeply personal connections rooted in family and childhood memory are a common thread running through all heritage language communities that have undergone language shift. It makes sense that these connections can be especially strong among the generations and individuals who can remember the heritage language being spoken more abundantly by loved ones and neighbours who have since passed away.

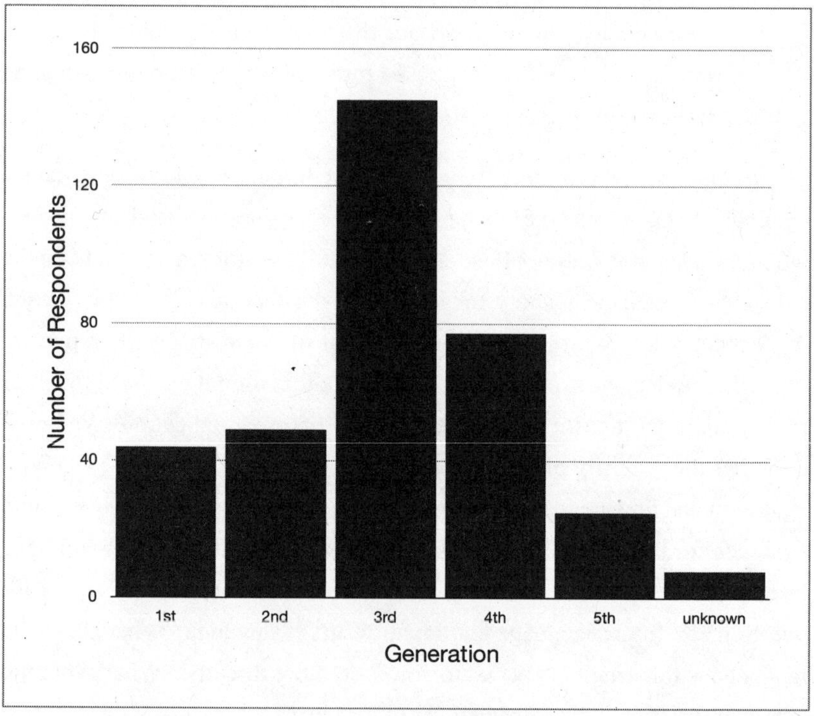

FIGURE 14.2. Immigrant generations of all respondents.

There are also theoretical reasons to spotlight the third generation, such as Hansen's Law. Immigration historian Marcus Hansen describes the historical experience of the second-generation American immigrant as one of conflict and rebellion: "Whereas in the schoolroom they were too foreign, at home they were too American" (Hansen 1938, 204). The third generation, however, with its footing more grounded in "Americanness," felt safer to then reach back to explore and embrace the story of their past: "The theory is derived from the almost universal phenomenon that what the son wishes to forget the grandson wishes to remember" (206). This perspective lends itself to the consideration of our third-generation respondents who are descendants of the earliest immigrants from Iceland to North America but has little to say about how future third-generation immigrants might feel, or how our current first- and second-generation respondents feel—especially considering the fact that a general interest in matters of heritage was an important factor in respondent participation.

Challenges to the universality of Hansen's theory include immigrant groups whose religion supersedes other ethnic ties or where group trauma is a factor (Bender and Kagiwada 1968), and cases where immigrant groups are not white ethnic Europeans (Levitt and Waters 2006). At least in Canada, there may be political reasons for third- and later-generation immigrants to look inward and to self-identify with their ethnic roots. In contrast to the U.S., which has long advocated for integration, Canada has pursued the policy of multiculturalism in recent decades. Canada's federal multiculturalism policy was adopted in 1971 by Prime Minister Pierre Trudeau's Liberal government. It was intended as a policy solution to manage both rising francophone nationalism and increasing cultural and ethnic diversity across Canada.

Some experiential themes appear to be almost entirely exclusive to the third generation. For example, 26 percent of third-generation respondents reported lack of encouragement or direct discouragement from learning Icelandic. Some shared their personal experiences on this topic (11) and (12), and others relayed the experiences of family members (13) and (14).

11. Parents were interested in speaking only English to their children. Possibly because of the embarrassment in school of having to learn English as a second language.

12. Sadly, my mother did not think we would ever need to know the language so discouraged us from learning it.

13. When we were young, we were told we had to be Canadian not Icelandic. Our parents were told it was important to assimilate and speak only English. I feel like my heritage was taken away from us.

14. My grandmother and her family spoke Icelandic. She never spoke Icelandic with her children because she was afraid of being targeted as a foreigner during World War I. She called herself Canadian.

In response to more than one open-ended question, many of the respondents described that they were discouraged or even prevented from learning Icelandic. Examples (11) through (14) represent each of the four most common explanations for discouragement: difficulties in school, lack of utility, emphasis on assimilation, and fear during times of war and xenophobia.

A second theme specific to the third generation is that of Icelandic being used as a secret language between parents or other family members. Eight percent of all third-generation respondents described this as a feature of their heritage language experience:

15. It really was a strange language and seemed to be used often by the speakers as a "secret language"—was not encouraged to learn.

16. My grandparents and parents spoke it when I was small so I had to know this special language so I understood the hidden good stuff. They used it as a secret code so there was a lot of incentive to learn the language.

17. Icelandic was a secret language between my mother and grandmother when they did not want the kids to know what they were talking about.
18. When Mother and Aunt were discussing the neighborhood gossip in my presence, when they got to the "juicy" part, they switched into Icelandic!

Exclusion, principally implemented by older Icelandic-speaking family members, is key to understanding both sets of these examples. Hansen does not account for this known aspect of language shift in his theory, that is, that language or heritage access is often blocked by the ideologies and actions of the earlier generations, as well-intentioned as they may have been. Although Hansen addresses the difficulty of dualism endured by the second generation (from which they would have understandably wanted to protect their children), he tends to overgeneralize this same group's utter dedication to "their policy of forgetting" (1938, 207). He also does not mention the nuances and causal relationships between the second and third (or later) generations that might have ultimately strengthened his theory. Without delving too much into psychological matters, we consider that it is possible that being excluded from linguistic exchanges led to, for example, a sense of determination in some cases, like (16), a resurgence of interest in more reflective periods of life, or even a sense of resignation that language and/or heritage was forever out of reach.

Immediately after the question "How important is communicating in Icelandic to your identity as someone of Icelandic heritage?" there was an open-ended follow-up question: "Have your views on this changed over time?" The third and later generations reported more change (by 10 percent) than the first and second generations. More than half of third- to fifth-generation respondents reported some change in importance, with 92 percent indicating an increase in importance. Whether or not they reported a change in importance, 23 percent of respondents from these later generations expressed some degree of regret or loss in their response to this question, the greatest collective expression of this sentiment compared with any other question in the survey. Most of the examples, like (19), (20), and (21), describe missed opportunities in youth, while others expressed an impending sense of loss, as in (22) and (23).

19. As a child I did not appreciate the language as my exposure to it was minimal at best. Now as an adult I aspire to gain that skill, but those individuals who might be able to teach me are no longer accessible to me. I fear it won't be something I ever obtain, and this upsets me.

20. Only got connected and started learning when all my grandmother's generation had passed away. . . . Also don't do well with language so haven't tried to learn—regrettably. I am very sad about it though if that counts for anything.

21. Yes, I wish like heck I would have kept up with it. As a teenager, it didn't seem like a cool thing. It is far more important to me now.

22. I fear the Icelandic language will be soon totally gone from our small Icelandic community and with that, our special identity!

23. The older I have become the less Icelandic I hear at social gatherings, family events, etc., and the less I feel able to start to learn how to speak Icelandic. I am a part of the first generation who do not speak Icelandic in our area, it will not be long before western Icelanders will not be able to speak Icelandic.

Shandler (2005, 18) remarks that Yiddish "gained new value as a signifier of loss," even calling the absence of the language "a compelling metonym for the tragic loss of its speakers." The loss felt by North American Icelanders is not to be compared with the catastrophic loss of life and trauma brought on by the Holocaust, but the idea is applicable in that feelings of loss associated with a heritage language, or with its speakers, can contribute to that language's evolution into a symbol. Herein are two important takeaways: (1) the relationship of language to heritage identity is variable, not only between individuals but fluctuating over a single individual's lifetime; and (2) the relationship of language to heritage identity can be characterized by deeply emotional personal experiences, which can have profound effects on how language is valued as a symbol of heritage identity.

The previous themes are sentimental ones that make language a symbol of connection with family and inner self, but the present is a theme of unexpected interpretation, in which respondents expressed the symbolism of Icelandic indirectly. In the two questions "Do you feel you have taken an active role in maintaining Icelandic within your family or community?" and "What efforts do you know of that are currently being made to preserve Icelandic in your community and how do you feel about them?" our intention was to focus on the Icelandic language. However, many interpreted the questions to be about Icelandic *culture* or *heritage*. In fact, 60 of 134 respondents (45 percent) who answered "yes" to having taken a role in maintaining Icelandic within family or community answered as if the question were specific to Icelandic culture or heritage, with no mention of language. In response to the question #17 ("Do you feel you have taken an active role in maintaining Icelandic within your family or community?"), 34 of 154 (22 percent) who listed efforts being made answered in this way:

24. A small role. In the kitchen making vineterta and pannekokur. We attend the Icelandic festival almost every year.

25. To some degree, I believe that as the family historian I have been able to help instill a sense of pride in my children and some of my nieces and nephews in their Icelandic heritage.

26. I am proud of my Icelandic heritage. I attend annual Icelandic events when possible. I have been to Iceland twice with relatives.

Question #25 asked: "What efforts do you know of that are currently being made to preserve Icelandic in your community and how do you feel about them?" Below are some responses:

27. We celebrate our Icelandic heritage and culture annually and I feel very strongly about continuing that tradition!

28. Cultural clubs provide opportunities for interested people; they are helpful. Cultural festivals to share with the broader community are good.

Posing these questions more directly would have meant missing out on this interesting pattern. This theme of interpretation might be an indication that for many of the respondents, the word *Icelandic* is first and foremost a representation of culture, history, and/or heritage, and has moved away from its usage in reference to the language itself. While not exactly an example of postvernacularity in its own right, this reflects what is seen elsewhere—a shift of focus away from the Icelandic language to Icelandic cultural heritage.

CONCLUDING REMARKS

At the outset of this project, we were uncertain about the level of interest and participation this survey-based study would inspire. Also unknown was the effectiveness of an online survey in eliciting the kind of information for which we were looking. Our results indicate that this method of data collection, though less personal than one-on-one interviews, can generate large-scale interest and response as well as contribute to our understanding of the relationship between heritage language and identity.

Even without its referential or conversational applications, North American Icelandic is providing useful symbolic tools to maintain a connection to one's self, family, and history—thus maintaining a sense of heritage identity. The extent to which language functions as a symbolic marker of heritage identity varies greatly between individuals, and often changes over the course of a lifetime.

Postvernacularity proved to be a helpful lens through which to view the perspectives and experiences generously shared with us. Shandler (2005, 24) claims that in order to understand postvernacular language, we must "investigate into the desires of those who choose to pursue it" and find out what "draws people in." Much of the draw, according to our respondents, comes from strong personal and familial connections and a need for having some grasp on an individual's place in history and in the world. It appears that the North American Icelandic "speech community" includes individuals who engage with this heritage language only in the postvernacular ways; they are aware of and able to participate in the exchange of its symbols. Two categories of postvernacular phenomena, internalized and externalized attachments, were identified, but further work is needed to relate them to the processes of heritage identity expression and construction. This study serves as an example of one way to incorporate language and identity survey data into heritage language research, but it leaves plenty of room for us, and for others, to build upon in future projects.

NOTES

1 We are deeply grateful to the Department of Icelandic at the University of Manitoba, the many organizations, and numerous individuals who participated in and shared our survey on which this article is based. We especially want to thank Linda Sigurdson for her efforts. We realize that it took time and effort to fill out the survey, and we greatly appreciate the fact that so many people were willing to share with us their personal thoughts and experiences. We also want to acknowledge the help of Hayden Godfrey, who participated in the earlier stages of this project, and Professor Joe Salmons at the University of Wisconsin–Madison for his sage advice. This research was carried out under the auspices of the University of Wisconsin ED/SBS IRB board, protocol number 2020–0234.

2 Birna Arnbjörnsdóttir (2015) references her own unpublished study (1990) and informal survey of language attitudes that she distributed in an Icelandic-American community in North Dakota in 1986. Fifty people were surveyed, but the 2015 article was concerned exclusively with language use.

3 The project began as a course ("Topics in Scandinavian Linguistics") at the University of Wisconsin–Madison in the spring of 2020, during which we worked mostly on the survey and decided on questions.The survey can be viewed in its entirety in the "Sociolinguistic Surveys" section under the "Research" tab at http://www.lmoquin.com.

4 This was part of the respondent's answer to the question "Do you feel you have taken an active role in maintaining Icelandic within your family or community?" The remainder of the answer goes on to list the ways other family members have taken an active role. While it is possible that the granddaughter had other reasons

for keeping the surname, it is interpreted by the respondent as a choice to maintain Icelandic within the family.

5 Icelandic gjörið/gerið svo vel 'here you go' or, in the context of eating together, 'enjoy your meal'.

REFERENCES

Arnbjörnsdóttir, Birna. 1990. "Use of Icelandic Among Bilinguals in North Dakota." Unpublished surveys.

———. 2006. *North American Icelandic: The Life of a Language*. Winnipeg: University of Manitoba Press.

———. 2015. "Re-examining Icelandic as a Heritage Language in North America." In *Germanic Heritage Languages in North America: Acquisition, Attrition and Change*, edited by Janne Bondi Johannessen and Joseph C. Salmons, 72–93. Amsterdam: John Benjamins Publishing.

Arvio, Anni. 2019. "Thinking about Finnish heritage, Living the American life." MA thesis, University of Oulu.

Barth, Fredrik. 1969. *Ethnic Groups and Boundaries: The Social Organization of Cultural Difference*. London: Allen and Unwin.

Bender, Eugene, and George Kagiwada. 1968. "Hansen's Law of 'Third-Generation Return' and the Study of American Religio-Ethnic Groups." *Phylon* 29 (4): 360–70.

Bucholtz, Mary, and Kira Hall. 2004. "Language and Identity." In *A Companion to Linguistic Anthropology*, edited by Alessandro Duranti, 369–94. Malden, MA: Blackwell Publishing.

Clausing, Stephan. 1984. "Dialect Preservation in American-Icelandic: A Methodological Study." *Word* 35 (1): 77–87.

Daniels, Roger. 1988. *Asian America: Chinese and Japanese in the United States Since 1850.* Seattle: University of Washington Press.

Edwards, John. 2009. *Language and Identity.* Cambridge: Cambridge University Press.

Gans, Herbert. 1979. "Symbolic Ethnicity: The Future of Ethnic Groups and Cultures in America." *Ethnic and Racial Studies* 2 (1): 1–20.

Hansen, Marcus Lee. 1938. *The Problem of the Third Generation Immigrant*. Rock Island, IL: Augustana Historical Society.

Kristjanson, Wilhelm. (1965) 1990. *The Icelandic People in Manitoba: A Manitoba Saga.* Winnipeg: R.W. Kristjanson.

Levitt, Peggy, and Mary C. Waters, eds. 2006. *The Changing Face of Home: The Transnational Lives of the Second Generation.* New York: Russell Sage Foundation.

Neijmann, Daisy. 2018. "Mál til samskipta eða tengsla? Gildi íslenskunnar í Vesturheimi." In *Sigurtunga: Vesturíslenskt mál og menning*, edited by Birna Arnbjörnsdóttir, Höskuldur Thrainsson, and Úlfar Bragason, 279–302. Reykjavík: Háskólaútgáfan.

Rosa, Jonathan. 2019. *Looking like a Language, Sounding like a Race: Raciolinguistic Ideologies and the Learning of Latinidad.* New York: Oxford University Press.

Salus, Peter H. 1971. "Icelandic in Canada: A Survey of Immigration and Language Loyalty." In *Linguistic Diversity in Canadian Society*, edited by Regna Darnell, 231–43. Edmonton: Linguistic Research.

Shandler, Jeffrey. 2005. *Adventures in Yiddishland. Postvernacular Language and Culture.* Berkeley: University of California Press.

Svavarsdóttir, Ásta. 2018. "Að flytja mál milli landa: Breytilegar málaðstæður heima og Heiman." In *Sigurtunga: Vesturíslenskt mál og menning*, edited by Birna Arnbjörnsdóttir, Höskuldur Thráinsson, and Úlfar Bragason, 257–77. Reykjavík: Háskólaútgáfan.

Wilkerson, Miranda E., and Joseph Salmons. 2019. "English in German-Speaking Wisconsin and the Aftermath." In *English in the German-Speaking World*, edited by Raymond Hickey, 361–83. Studies in English Language. Cambridge: Cambridge University Press.

CHAPTER 15

The Heritage Language Project: Impact and Implications

BIRNA ARNBJÖRNSDÓTTIR

IN THIS FINAL chapter some of the major findings of the Icelandic Heritage Language Project that served as the impetus for this volume are placed in their theoretical context and their practical implications described. The project's contribution to sociolinguistics, language ideology, and literacy practices at the community and family levels includes how home language practices affect identity construction, educational trajectories, and social participation in heritage communities. North American Icelandic (NAI) has been thoroughly documented almost from the first days of settlement in North America. The uniqueness of these findings lies in the multiple data sources it has generated that allow examination of the development of the language over time, as well as its variance across communities, families, and individuals, and which illustrate the variation and complexity of heritage languages.

LANGUAGE IDEOLOGY AND SOCIAL PARTICIPATION IN ICELANDIC HERITAGE COMMUNITIES

The early emphasis on plurilingualism and the written word, in the home and in the community, seems to have served the Icelandic heritage speakers well and still lingers, four generations after the first immigrations. These findings are highly relevant to the social and educational consequences of the enormous demographic changes and increasingly multilingual and multicultural societies of today.

Language policy, according to linguistics scholar Bernard Spolsky (2004, 2012), comprises three components: language management, language ideology, and language practices. Each can be implemented officially or unofficially by governments, in linguistic communities by influential individuals, and in homes and families where conscious or unconscious decisions are made about language and literacy practices. Sociolinguist Jan Blommaert (2007) suggests that decisions about language use follow layered scales from the strictly global macro-level management of social structure that includes government policies, such as that Icelandic is the official language of Iceland (*Íslensk málstefna*), to the other end of the scales, where unofficial language policies govern community ideologies at the local or the micro level of communications, within families and between individuals. This corresponds with his notion of *superdiversity* (Blommaert 2007), or the idea that multilingual communities are not made up of only discrete ethnic groups who speak separate and discrete languages, but that communities are rather more than the sum of their ethnolinguistic backgrounds. Language use varies by age, sex, education, status within the community, topic and intent, and relationships among its speakers, and is therefore more complex than most language policies allow for and can have wide implications for social participation. Shirley Brice-Heath's seminal anthropological linguistic work from the 1980s demonstrated this variety of language use within different groups of speakers of English in the American South and their consequences for educational achievement (1986).

Recently, there has been increased interest in exploring the effects of these micro-level community and family language policies on heritage language speakers' linguistic practices and subsequent social inclusion. Heritage speakers bring with them ideologies, beliefs, and behaviours ingrained in their home language use. These language-based behaviours transcend languages and take longer to change than the actual shift from heritage language to the host language (Connor 2002). Ideologies shape language practices within families, which have a profound impact on children's cognitive development, identity construction, and academic trajectories (De Houwer 1999). An example from plurilingual homes would be when parents who speak different languages natively decide to use only one of the languages in the home or use a one-parent–one-language approach with their children. These are termed *language acquisition policies*—when parents decide what languages children will learn and use and how they will use them, consciously or not (see also Siiner, Hult, and Kupisch 2018; Pennycook 2006).

The reality of language use at the micro level is usually not as clear-cut and more akin to plurilingualism and translanguaging,[1] as speakers use the range of their linguistic repertoire to communicate and create meaning, regardless of how the languages they use are delineated or managed officially (Peskova 2021; Arnbjörnsdóttir 2010; Garcia and Wei 2014; Blommaert 2007).

Language and heritage culture ideologies affect individual identity construction and the heritage groups' identity construction vis-à-vis the host culture. Linguists Aneta Pavlenko and Bonny Norton (2007) introduced the notion of *imagined communities* to better understand the relationship between second-language learning and identity in heritage communities. They argue that heritage language learners' actual and desired memberships in imagined communities affect their learning trajectories, and influence their agency, motivation, investment, and resistance in adopting the host language. Language ideology also affects and directs language practices at home and thus affects educational achievement. All these factors influence participation in the new culture. When addressing social participation of heritage speakers, especially in education, official policies tend to promote a form of monolingualism, or even multiple monolingualism, and often reflect a deficit model where multilingualism/bilingualism is seen as detrimental to academic achievement (Baker 2011). Virginia Collier and Wayne Thomas's (2017) landmark studies showed that multilingualism, in and of itself, is not detrimental to educational achievement. The reality is more complex and is more often tied to the dissonance that is frequently present between literacy practices in the home and at school (Brice Heath 1983). The debate about the connection between home language and school/host language, and about which educational policies and practices are most beneficial to heritage speakers, has been ongoing for decades. Acceptance of both the old and new community, imagined or otherwise, rather than resistance to one or the other, is seen as a positive force in social inclusion.

The importance of literacy and multilingualism in Icelandic heritage communities in North America, and especially within families, is a recurrent theme in all the chapters in this book and repeated regularly in our interviews with Icelandic heritage language speakers. The authors were not directed to focus specifically on literacy or literary practices, but rather on the shifting identities as the Icelandic heritage speakers transitioned to a new culture. The chapters and other publications on the findings of the Heritage Language Project depict the beliefs and behaviours the Icelandic emigrants brought with them from Iceland that prevailed, regardless of when they shifted to English. The findings of this project convey the importance of language ideology, expressed from the outset of emigration, in the decisions made about language and cultural upbringing and maintenance, namely, literary activities and literacy as central to Icelandic identity.

The findings of this project allow us to examine the consequences of a particular ideology held by the first generation of immigrants for the lives of heritage speakers up to four generations later, and demonstrate that an emphasis on literacy in heritage speakers' homes and families can promote positive social and educational trajectories. This ideology permeates the content of this volume in the form of views expressed by influential community figures, rich social debates in widely circulated periodicals and newsletters in many NAI communities, and home-based literacy practices (see Ásta Svavarsdóttir, this volume, and Guðrún Björk Guðsteinsdóttir, this volume).

Traditionally, governments are seen as the dispensers of the policies that govern language and education. Nonetheless, community leaders, poets, and writers can also serve as agents and purveyors of unofficial language policies (Spolsky 2012). The chapters by Guðrún Björk Guðsteinsdóttir, Dagný Kristjánsdóttir, and Birna Bjarnadóttir each depict the views of important public figures in the Icelandic heritage community who advocated plurilingualism and multiculturalism. Einar Hjörleifsson Kvaran, editor and writer, advocated "full participation in Canadian life, politics and education but without sacrificing Icelandic identity and culture" (quoted by Matthías Viðar Sæmundsson, cited in Guðrún Björk Guðmundsdóttir, this volume). Einar also wrote, "Icelanders need not have an inferiority complex, but should consider themselves equals to local Anglo-Canadians . . . who have no interest in science, poetry, and the fine arts, there are no books of merit, no drama of quality" (see Guðrún Björk Guðsteinsdóttir, this volume). Perhaps this reflects the dual nature of the way Icelanders saw themselves vis-à-vis how others saw them. This is reflected in Einar's short story "Hopes," which describes the newly arrived immigrants from two different viewpoints: the insider who is full of hope, and the outsiders who see only downtrodden aliens coming off the immigrant train (see Guðrún Björk Guðsteinsdóttir, this volume). Scholar Haraldur Bessason discusses this duality and the comfort with membership in two communities of some of the NAI immigrants in his writings (1967, 134).

One of the most revered leaders in the NAI community was the poet and "social prophet" Stephan G. Stephansson. While Stephan G. wrote all his poetry in Icelandic (see Birna Bjarnadóttir, this volume), he was a lifelong advocate of bilingualism (Hreinsson 2012). Duality and bilingualism/biculturalism are also seen in Dagný Kristjánsdóttir's depiction of the writer and educator Jóhann Magnús Bjarnason, and how he saw his "nationality as a source of strength," (this volume) bolstering his self-confidence and cultural capital (Bordieu 1992). But Jóhann Magnús was also a public-school teacher in the Icelandic settlements and served as a liaison to the larger English-speaking community as an interpreter. His being fluent in English thus served as a reminder that knowing and using both languages was not a barrier to participation in Canadian society.

These leaders found a voice very early on in the multiple debating societies and literary organizations that were formed in the Icelandic enclaves, many with their own publications supported through subscription. The debates about the merits of emigration continued from Iceland and participation in debating societies proved essential for Icelanders to take their place in social discourse and social equality in Winnipeg, including pioneering roles in women's rights issues in Canada led by Margaret Benedictsson (see Vilhelm Vilhelmsson, this volume, and Ólafur Arnar Sveinsson, this volume). Even children had their own periodicals (see Dagný Kristjánsdóttir, this volume). The Icelandic publishing scene was astonishingly prolific in a community that comprised a little over the 15,000 Icelandic speakers and their descendants.

Not all Icelandic immigrants settled in the Icelandic enclaves and not all first- and second-generation children were brought up to be bilingual. It became clear in early studies of NAI that even though not everyone agreed on the value of maintaining Icelandic as a heritage language, the use of Icelandic seemed to follow familial lines, often developing into family dialects where certain families seemed to have developed ways of speaking Icelandic that were particular to their family (Arnbjörnsdóttir 2006). This author was informed many times by different interviewees in her study from 1986 and again for the Heritage Language Project that in earlier times, speakers were able to tell their interlocutor's place of origin by their Icelandic speech. Yet, even among those immigrants who chose to seek their fortunes away from their countrymen, literacy practices such as reading and letter writing led to social engagement (see Alda Möller, this volume, and Úlfar Bragason, this volume). It is telling that Úlfar Bragason's protagonist, Jón Halldórsson, named his son Hrólfur (later Ralph Emerson), and by all indications Jón's offspring spoke Icelandic as young children even though they later adopted English. But more importantly, Jón's children grew up with books and reading and rich letter-writing traditions, which seem to have served them well, as those of his children who survived into adulthood became inventors, industry owners, and well-established citizens of Chicago (Bragason 2017). Home literacy practices in and of themselves, regardless of language, are important in promoting education. It is not the language itself but the ways with languages that encourage social participation. Gísli Sigurðsson's and Katelin Parsons's contributions to this book portray the literary traditions the Icelandic immigrants brought with them from the old country that found a new context in North America. They include a rich storytelling tradition at *kvöldvökur* 'evening reading' and the circulation of handwritten manuscripts for reading in the heritage communities. They also suggest that Icelandic literary rituals lived a century after immigrations began and sixty years after immigration ceased during the First World War.

The number of Icelandic heritage speakers who are of the third and fourth generations from the original settlers allow us to examine the consequences of the ideologies held by their ancestors about their language and culture. The findings have important implications today with massive migrations and subsequent educational challenges (Siiner, Hult, and Kupisch 2018). They are also important to an increasingly plurilingual world, as they tell us about successful ways to interact across languages and cultures and demonstrate the value of literacy to academic achievement and the social benefits of education.

One of the more distinct manifestations of community and literacy practices in the Icelandic heritage enclaves can be seen in the maintenance of Icelandic in North America into the third and fourth generations. The result is a remarkably well-documented heritage language.

NORTH AMERICAN ICELANDIC AND HERITAGE LINGUISTICS

The massive and multiple data sources available on North American Icelandic allow for deep engagement with the language and demonstrate how a heritage language may evolve in different social contexts, and even in individuals, over time. North American Icelandic is not a discrete heritage language system. The language consultants who participated in the Heritage Language Project span the whole proficiency scale from those who speak very little to speakers who are fluent. Data also span the development of Icelandic as a heritage language in individuals through extensive letter writing throughout a person's lifetime (Björnsdóttir 2018), and the documentation of speech available from the same consultants in different studies, at discrete intervals, over a span of decades. Icelandic as a heritage language cannot be described with reference to a single grammatical system. The data show evidence of "tendencies" towards change in syntax, morphology, phonology, semantics, and the lexicon that reflect a changing reality and intense language contact, not change that has completed its course (see the Introduction, this volume). The data set also reflects the speech of "all kinds of people" and not just those who were most educated, best at telling stories, or most fluent in Icelandic. The data are based on multiple instruments using ethnographic approaches such as interviews and natural speech, Labovian interview methods (1972), elicited speech through picture description, and different types of grammatical and semantic tests. Most of all the data speak of the enormous variability found in Icelandic as a heritage language, an often-underestimated feature of heritage linguistics (Benmamoun, Montrul, and Polinsky 2010).

FIGURE 15.1. A participant in the Heritage Language Project in Manitoba filling out a form for Birna Arnbjörnsdóttir. (Courtesy of Höskuldur Thráinsson)

The findings on NAI address the most challenging questions in modern linguistics, for instance, how grammatical knowledge is stored in the brain and how it evolves from one acquisition stage to the next. Other questions include how first and subsequent languages are learned, how they influence each other, and, in the case of many heritage speakers, how they attrite. Heritage languages allow us to examine the results of the type and amount of input on grammatical structures across generations (Polinsky and Scontras 2020). They can show us which structures are vulnerable to change based on when and if acquisition was interrupted, where grammar and the lexicon are likely to change depending on context, and what effect literacy and language ideology have on linguistic structure (Page and Putnam 2015). Icelandic as a heritage language is in many ways unique in this field as we have available for examination the evolution of the language as a heritage language in North America across several generations without the interference of renewal from newcomers to the community.

Four chapters in the book describe the findings of studies of NAI collected under the umbrella of the Icelandic Heritage Language Project in 2013 and 2014. The participants are third-, fourth-, and fifth-generation Icelandic Canadians and Icelandic Americans with an average age of seventy-seven.

Different linguistic and cultural contexts have different cognitive manifestations. Matthew Whelpton (this volume) describes how perceptions of the heritage speakers change under intense language contact conditions as they transition from one language and culture to another. Cultural influence of English has a stronger effect on North American Icelandic semantic categories for body parts, colours, containers, and spatial relations than Icelandic, with the exception of the use of prepositions to mark spatial relations, as prepositions and the cases they govern seem to be held together by the grammar.

Ásta Svavarsdóttir (this volume) addresses lexical changes, given the new the social and geographical context of the speakers (see also Bessason 1967; Arnbjörnsdóttir 2006). Not surprisingly, the changes reflect the changed context in North America as speakers found new words to describe their new existence and new meaning and different words through convergence (Johannessen and Salmon 2015). Previous studies have examined the potential loss of long-distance binding in the pronominal system of NAI (Putnam and Arnbjörnsdóttir 2015), changes in word order (Arnbjörnsdóttir, Thráinsson, and Nowenstein 2016), object shift (Jónsson 2018), and the evolution of an individual's grammatical system over a lifespan from a learnability perspective (Björnsdóttir 2018).

Sigríður Magnúsdóttir, Irís Edda Nowenstein, and Höskuldur Thráinsson (this volume) found minimal difference between heritage speakers' judgments and those of Icelanders of a similar age and even Icelanders in general, with one exception, where relations depended on grammatical cues marked by case. The finding suggests that heritage speakers depend on subject/predicate agent/ patient argument order (typical of English) more than non-heritage speakers do, who utilize case markings to determine functional relations. Kristín M. Jóhannsdóttir (this volume) describes how the use of present progressive, a characteristic of learner language and of English as a lingua franca (Ranta 2006), is also prevalent in the language of Icelandic heritage speakers, even more so than in native English speech, again suggesting that this feature of language may be less complex for heritage (and second language) speakers than the simple present. Kristín suggests that because it is a relatively simple and frequently used grammatical form, it is a well-known linguistic strategy to overuse the same (simple) and already acquired construction in speech. Both studies seem to suggest a difficulty hierarchy dominated by the grammatical structure of the dominant language, or even a universal hierarchy of difficulty in maintaining syntactic relations.

CONCLUDING WORDS: THE FUTURE OF NORTH AMERICAN ICELANDIC RESEARCH

It is clear that the evolution of Icelandic as a heritage language is relevant to heritage language studies and to linguistic theory in general. The editors of this book hope that the research presented in this volume can serve as an impetus for further studies of Icelandic heritage language and culture in North America.

The limitations of the Heritage Language Project, from a methodological perspective, is that participants were, in a sense, self-selected. A random selection of participants was not possible as there is no comprehensive census of the population on Icelandic speakers. It is quite possible that only those with special interest or pride in their heritage agreed to take part in the study.

Clearly, the findings call for further research. There is a great deal of still unanalyzed data amassed from the Icelandic Heritage Language Project, along with several corpora that include letters, diaries, interviews, and older data collections. These are corpora preserved at the University of Iceland and at the Árni Magnússon Institute for Icelandic that await further study. But there is also material in the Icelandic heritage enclaves in North America and especially in the Icelandic Collection at the Dafoe Library at the University of Manitoba. The Árni Magnússon Institute for Icelandic has launched an initiative to identify and document manuscripts that may still be in private collections in North America. The project, *Fragile Heritage: In the Footsteps of Árni Magnússon*, is directed by Katelin Parsons.[2] As Katelin says in her contribution to this volume: "A hundred years on, searching for immigrants' manuscripts is like chasing ravens' trails across the Prairies. Manuscripts are inherently portable objects, but the very processes that enabled Icelandic manuscript culture to endure into the twentieth century, such as extensive sharing of exemplars, also put manuscripts at risk of being lost or discarded. From a researcher's perspective, it is easy to represent manuscripts' movements as a narrative of loss, particularly as they crossed the Atlantic in immigrants' sea chests. Yet, hand-copied sagas were central to the literary practices of many Icelandic immigrants."

These collections, both in Iceland and in North America, not only bear witness to the linguistic evolution of Icelandic as a heritage language but are also a valuable source for historical, cultural, ethnographic, and literary research. Many areas need further study. This includes the study of underexplored contact and relations with Indigenous peoples begun by Ryan Eyford (2019) and Laurie Bertram (2020), the larger context of immigrant stories worldwide, the effect of the rise of external manifestations of Icelandic heritage organizations, with the famed rise of the Falcons hockey team, to name only a few examples. Additionally, a prolific artistic scene with writers and cinematographers depicts or is influenced by Icelandic heritage themes. These include authors such as Laura Goodman Salverson, Betty Jane Wylie, W.D. Valgardson, Bill Holm, David Arnason, Kristjana Gunnars, Christina Sunley, Guy Maddin, and Sturla Gunnarsson, to name but a few. Their works bear witness to the continued storytelling legacy of the Icelandic diaspora in North America and their engagement with its distinct cultural and historical traces. Lastly, the developments in Icelandic as a heritage language speak to possible but as yet unexplored changes in Icelandic in Iceland today due to intensive contact with English. This includes, for example, lexical transfer of English words into Icelandic, and structural changes in the use of subjunctive and in meaning and use of pronoun and prepositions.

In conclusion, it is the hope of the editors of this book that its content may inspire young scholars to study Icelandic heritage culture in North America. Although many researchers, especially linguists, have delved into Icelandic as a heritage language, there is still more to examine about the history, culture, and literature of the Icelandic diaspora in North America. Therefore, it is especially important to identify and preserve documents and memorabilia that reflect the life of the settlements as well as of those who lived away from the Icelandic enclaves, especially those areas we were unable to visit. The enduring impression left as a result of working on this project is the pride expressed by the Canadian and American participants in their Icelandic heritage, and their generosity in sharing their knowledge for the purpose of this research. We hope the book reflects their invaluable contribution.

NOTES

1 Translanguaging is used when speakers use more than one language to create meaning within the same utterance.

2 See http://www.arnastofnun.is/page/fragile_heritage_arni_magnusson.

REFERENCES

Arnbjörnsdóttir, Birna. 2006. *North American Icelandic: The Life of a Language*. Winnipeg: University of Manitoba Press.

———. 2010. Skólar og fjölskyldur sem málsamfélög [Schools and families as linguistic communities]. In *Fjölmenning og skólastarf*, edited by Hanna Ragnarsdóttir and Elsa S. Jónsdóttir, 313–36. Reykjavík: Háskólaútgáfan.

Arnbjörnsdóttir, Birna, and Hafdís Ingvarsdóttir. 2018. *Language Development across the Life Span: The Impact of English on Education and Work in Iceland*. Berlin: Springer.

Baker, Colin. 2011. *Foundations of Bilingual Education and Bilingualism*. 5th ed. Bristol: Multilingual Matters.

Benmamoun, Elabbas, Silvina Montrul, and Maria Polinsky. 2010. "Prolegomena to Heritage Linguistics." White Paper. Cambridge, MA: Harvard University.

Bertram, Laurie. 2020. *The Viking Immigrants: Icelandic North Americans*. Toronto: University of Toronto Press.

Bessaon, Haraldur. 1967. "A Few Specimens of North American Icelandic." *Scandinavian Studies* 39 (2): 115–46.

Björnsdóttir, Sigríður Mjöll. 2018. "Hún er svo montin af að vera íslenskt. Málbreytingar í sendibréfum Vestur-Íslendings" [She is so proud to be Icelandic (n.): Linguistic change in letters from a North American Icelander]. In *Sigurtunga: Vesturíslenskt mál og menning*, edited by Birna Arnbjörnsdóttir, Höskuldur Thráinsson, and Úlfar Bragason, 341–59. Reykjavík: Háskólaútgáfan.

Blommaert, Jan. 2007. "Sociolinguistic Scales." *Intercultural Pragmatics* 4 (1): 1–19.

Bourdieu, Pierre. 1992. *Language and Symbolic Power*. Cambridge, MA: Polity Press.

Bragason, Úlfar. 2017. *Frelsi, menning, framför: Um bréf og greinar Jóns Halldórssonar* [Freedom, culture, progress: On letters and articles by Jón Halldórsson]. Reykjavík: Háskólaútgáfan.

Brice Heath, Shirley. 1983. *Ways with Words: Language, Life and Work in Communities and Classrooms*. Cambridge: Cambridge University Press.

Collier, Virginia P., and Wayne P. Thomas. 2017. "Validating the Power of Bilingual Schooling: Thirty-Two Years of Large-Scale, Longitudinal Research." *Annual Review of Applied Linguistics* 37: 203–17. doi:10.1017/S0267190517000034.

Connor, Ulla. 2002. *Contrastive Rhetoric: Cross-Cultural Aspects of Second Language Writing*. Cambridge: Cambridge University Press.

De Houwer, Annick. 1999. "Environmental Factors in Early Bilingual Development: The Role of Parental Beliefs and Attitudes." In *Bilingualism and Migration*, edited by Guus Extra and Ludo Verhoeven, 75–95. Berlin: Mouton de Gruyter. doi:10.1515/9783110807820.75.

Eyford, Ryan. 2019. *White Settler Reserve: New Iceland and the Colonization of the Canadian West*. Vancouver: University of British Columbia Press.

García, Ofelia, and Li Wei. 2014. *Translanguaging: Language, Bilingualism and Education*. Houndmills: Palgrave Macmillan.

Hreinsson, Viðar. 2012. *Wakeful Nights: Stephan G. Stephansson, Icelandic-Canadian Poet*. Calgary: Benson Ranch.

Johannessen, Janne Bondi, and Joseph C. Salmons, eds. 2015. *Germanic Heritage Languages in North America: Acquisition, Attrition and Change*. Amsterdam: John Benjamins.

Jónsson, Jóhannes Gísli. 2018. "'Þú skilur ekki þetta.' Andlagsstökk í vestur-íslensku" [You don′t understand this. Object Shift in N American Icelandic]. In *Sigurtunga: Vesturíslenskt mál og menning*, edited by Birna Arnbjörnsdóttir, Höskuldur Thráinsson, and Úlfar Bragason, 361–74. Reykjavík: Háskólaútgáfan.

Labov, William, 1972. *Sociolinguistic Patterns*. Philadelphia: University of Pennsylvania Press.

Page, B. Richard, and Michael T. Putnam, eds. 2015. *Moribund Germanic Heritage Languages in North America: Theoretical Perspectives and Empirical Findings*. Empirical Approaches to Linguistic Theory 8. Leiden: Brill.

Pavlenko, Aneta, and Bonny Norton. 2007. "Imagined Communities, Identity, and English Language Learning." In *International Handbook of English Language Teaching*, edited by Jim Cummings and Chris Davidson, 669–80. Springer International Handbooks of Education, vol 15. Dordrecht: Springer. https://doi.org/10.1007/978-0-387-46301-8_43.

Pennycook, Alastair. 2006. *Global Englishes and Transcultural Flows*. London: Routledge.

Peskova, Renata Emilson. 2021. "School Experience of Plurilingual Students: A Multiple Case Study from Iceland." PhD diss., University of Iceland.

Polinsky, Maria, and Gregory Scontras. 2020. "Understanding Heritage Languages." *Bilingualism: Language and Cognition* 23 (1): 4–20. doi:10.1017/S1366728919000245.

Putnam, Michael T., and Birna Arnbjörnsdóttir. 2015. "Minimizing (Interface) Domains: The Loss of Long-Distance Binding in North American Icelandic." In *Moribund Germanic Heritage Languages in North America: Theoretical Perspectives and Empirical Findings*, edited by B. Richard Page and Michael T. Putnam, 203–23. Leiden: Brill.

Ranta, Elina. 2006. "The 'Attractive' Progressive—Why Use the *-ing* Form in English as a Lingua Franca?" *Nordic Journal of English Studies* 5 (2): 95–116. doi: http://doi.org/10.35360/njes.13.

Siiner, Maarja, Francis M. Hult, and Tanja Kupisch. 2018. *Language Policy and Language Acquisition Planning.* Dordrecht: Springer.

Spolsky, Bernard. 2004. *Language Policy*. Cambridge: Cambridge University Press.

———. 2012. "Family Language Policy—The Critical Domain." *Journal of Multilingual and Multicultural Development* 33 (1): 1–9. doi:10.1080/01434632.2011.638072.

Acknowledgements

A LARGE UNDERTAKING like the Icelandic Heritage Language Project is not possible without the help of a great number of people and institutions. We would like to acknowledge their contribution and express our profound gratitude for their participation and support of the project and this volume.

Funding for the research described here was provided by RANNÍS, the Icelandic Research Fund. We want to thank them, as without their support there would not have been a project at all. We would also like to thank the research team, especially Daisy Neijmann, Iris Edda Nowenstein, Kristín M. Jóhannsdóttir, Matthew Whelpton, Nicole Dehé, Sigríður Mjöll Björnsdóttir, and Sigríður Magnúsdóttir, who travelled across Canada and the United States with the editors to collect the data that provided most of the sources for this book. We are grateful to the authors who contributed their work and to this edited volume, and to the Páll Guðmundsson from Rjúpnafell Fund at the University of Iceland, and the Department of Icelandic at the University of Manitoba for supporting its publication. To Jill McConkey, Pat Sanders, Glenn Bergen, David Carr, and David Larsen at the University of Manitoba Press, we express our gratitude for a wonderful collaboration during the publication process, and to three anonymous reviewers whose comments enhanced the quality of the text. We thank Katelin Parsons and Jay Darcy for making sure the English of the non-native English writers was legible, and thank Sarah Wood for the design of the book.

We would like to acknowledge the contributions of Nelson Gerrard, who lent us photographs from his wonderful collection. Contacting and engaging the help of the almost 300 participants in this study would not have been possible without the assistance of the faculty and staff of the Department of Icelandic at the University of Manitoba, especially Birna Bjarnadóttir and John Paul Buchan, and also Gunnar Ólafur Hansson at the University of British Columbia. We owe a debt of gratitude to them for connecting us with liaisons in the various communities. This proved to be the most important facet of the project and a significant stroke of luck. We want to especially thank our liaisons: Gunnvör Danielsdóttir, Elva Simundsson, Svava Simundsson, Signy McGinnis, Keith Eliasson, Joan Eyolfson Cadham, Susan Sigurdson Powers, Loretta Bernhoft, Jón Örn Jónsson, Audrey Shepherd, Dennis Oleson, Ásta Smart, Judy Gleich, Joedy Englesby, Gerri McDonald, Rob Olason, Leona Olason, Pauline de Haan, David Johnson, Emily Kristjanson, Linda Bjarnason, and Elin Ross. These individuals connected us to the most wonderful and engaging participants any researcher could hope for. We are eternally grateful for their enthusiasm, insight, and willingness to share their language and culture with us. We hope that this book reflects their invaluable contributions.

Reykjavík
31 May 2022

Birna Arnbjörnsdóttir
Höskuldur Thráinsson
Úlfar Bragason

Contributors

GUÐNI TH. JÓHANNESSON

President of Iceland

ELIZA REID

First Lady of Iceland

BIRNA ARNBJÖRNSDÓTTIR

birnaarn@hi.is

Professor emeritus of Second Language Studies at the University of Iceland. PhD in Linguistics from the University of Texas, Austin. Her research interests include multilingualism and language contact. She is the project director of Icelandic Online and she has studied North American Icelandic as a heritage language for over thirty years.

ÚLFAR BRAGASON

ulfar.bragason@arnastofnun.is

Professor Emeritus, Árni Magnússon Institute for Icelandic Studies. PhD in Scandinavian Languages and Literature from the Unversity of California, Berkeley. His area of specialization includes Icelandic medieval literature, the emigration of Icelanders to North America, and the studies of the Icelandic language and culture abroad.

‖ BIRNA BJARNADÓTTIR

birna@hi.is

Stephan G. Stephansson researcher at the Vigdís Finnbogadóttir Institute of Foreign Languages. PhD in Icelandic Literature from the University of Iceland. She is former Chair of Icelandic at the University of Manitoba. Her research interests include Icelandic-Canadian literature, Icelandic-American literature, and immigration in modern literature.

‖ GUÐRÚN BJÖRK GUÐSTEINSDÓTTIR

gsteins@hi.is

Professor of English Literature at the University of Iceland. PhD in English Literature at the University of Alberta. Her main topic of research is the literary tradition of Icelandic immigrants and their descendants in North America. This includes a book on the short story in Canada which contains Icelandic translations of work by W.D. Valgardson, David Arnason, and Kristjana Gunnars.

‖ KRISTÍN M. JÓHANNSDÓTTIR

kristinj@unak.is

Assisstant Professor of Icelandic Linguistics at the University of Akureyri. PhD in Linguistics from the University of British Columbia. Former Instructor of Icelandic at the University of Manitoba. Research interests include semantics, aspect, foreign language teaching, and North American Icelandic as a heritage language.

‖ DAGNÝ KRISTJÁNSDÓTTIR

dagny@hi.is

Professor emeritus of Modern Icelandic Literature at the University of Iceland. PhD in Icelandic Literature from the University of Iceland. Former Associate Professor (*førsteamanuensis*) of Icelandic language and literature at the University of Oslo, Norway. Her main research interests include feminist literature, literature and medical humanities, and children's literature and culture.

SIGRÍÐUR MAGNÚSDÓTTIR

siggatal@gmail.com

Associate Professor emeritus of Speech Pathology at the University of Iceland and former faculty member of the National University Hospital of Iceland. ScD in Speech Pathology from Boston University. Her main research area is speech pathology, where she has developed diagnostic tests of various kinds but mainly does research on aphasia.

ALDA MÖLLER

AldaM@outlook.com

Graduate student of Icelandic Studies at the University of Iceland, former Head of Department at Icelandic Group (an international seafood company). PhD in Food Science from the University of Reading, England. Her recent research includes work on the development of Icelandic in the nineteenth century and the emigration of Icelanders to North America.

LAURA MOQUIN

laura.moquin@wisc.edu

PhD candidate in Scandinavian Studies and Linguistics at the University of Wisconsin-Madison. Her main areas of study include language contact and change, and language and identity. She is currently researching Norwegian-influenced contact phenomena in regional English and the relationship of those features to regional and heritage identity.

IRIS EDDA NOWENSTEIN

irisen@hi.is

PhD candidate in Icelandic Linguistics at the University of Iceland, has a Master's degree in Speech Pathology and works part time as a Speech Pathologist at the National University Hospital of Iceland. In linguistics she has mainly done research on language acquisition and linguistic variation.

KATELIN PARSONS

katelin@hi.is

Postdoctoral Researcher at the Árni Magnússon Institute for Icelandic Studies. PhD in Icelandic Literature from the University of Iceland. Her research focuses on manuscript culture in early modern Iceland and the handwritten books brought to North America by Icelandic immigrants. She has been project manager of the Fragile Heritage Project from 2015.

GÍSLI SIGURÐSSON

gisli.sigurdsson@arnastofnun.is

Research Professor at the Árni Magnússon Institute for Icelandic Studies, former visiting associate professor at the University of Manitoba. PhD in Icelandic literature from the University of Iceland. His research includes work on Icelandic medieval literature and manuscripts, Gaelic influence in Iceland, oral tradition, and folklore.

ÁSTA SVAVARSDÓTTIR

asta.svavarsdottir@arnastofnun.is

Research Associate Professor and Department Head at the Árni Magnússon Institute for Icelandic Studies, former assistant professor of Icelandic as a second language at the University of Iceland. MA in Icelandic linguistics from the University of Iceland. Her research includes work on lexicology, language variation, and the development and standardization of Icelandic in the nineteenth century.

ÓLAFUR ARNAR SVEINSSON

olafusv@hi.is

PhD candidate in History at the University of Iceland. In his research he concentrates on the concept of identity, especially concerning the Icelandic immigrants in North America, including the interaction between national and cultural identity.

HÖSKULDUR THRÁINSSON

Professor emeritus of Icelandic Linguistics at the University of Iceland. PhD in Linguistics from Harvard University. His main research area has been Icelandic syntax and linguistic variation, but he has also worked on Faroese, aphasia, and North American Icelandic as a heritage language.

VILHELM VILHELMSSON

vilhelmv@hi.is

Director of the University of Iceland Research Centre North-West. PhD in History from the University of Iceland. His research focuses on power relations in everyday life in pre-industrial Iceland as well as the cultural and social history of Icelandic immigrants in North America.

MATTHEW WHELPTON

whelpton@hi.is

Professor of English Linguistics at the University of Iceland. DPhil in English Linguistics from the University of Oxford. He has done research on the syntax-semantics interface in Icelandic, the evolution of semantic systems, neurolinguistics, and language technology.

KIRSTEN WOLF

kirstenwolf@wisc.edu

Professor in the Department of German, Nordic, and Slavic and Chair of the Department of Art History at the University of Wisconsin-Madison. She is a former Professor and Chair of Icelandic Language and Literature at the University of Manitoba. Her research includes work on Old Norse-Icelandic language and literature.